도서
출판 **밀알서원** 〔Wheat Berry Books〕은 CLC가 공동으로 운영하는 복음주의 출판사로서 신앙생활과 기독교문화를 위한 설교, 시, 수필, 간증, 선교·경건서적 등을 출판하고 있습니다.

아홉 켤레의 신발로 남은
영문법

English Grammar Left over by Nine Pairs of Shoes
Written by Chulwhan Bae
All rights reserved.
Korean Edition Copyright ⓒ 2024 by Wheat Berry Books , Seoul, Korea.

아홉 켤레의 신발로 남은 영문법

2024년 5월 20일 초판 발행

지 은 이 | 배철환

편　　집 | 전희정
디 자 인 | 이보래, 서민정
펴 낸 곳 | 도서출판 밀알서원
등　　록 | 제21-44호(1988. 8. 12.)
주　　소 | 서울특별시 동대문구 천호대로71길 39
전　　화 | 02-586-8761~3(본사) 031-942-8761(영업부)
팩　　스 | 02-523-0131(본사) 031-942-8763(영업부)
이 메 일 | clckor@gmail.com
홈페이지 | www.clcbook.com
송금계좌 | 기업은행 073-085404-01-017 예금주: 밀알서원
일련번호 | 2024-58

ISBN 978-89-7135-156-7 (03740)

이 책의 출판권은 도서출판 밀알서원이 소유합니다.
신저작권법에 의하여 한국 내에서 보호를 받는 저작물이므로 무단 전재와 무단 복제를 금합니다.

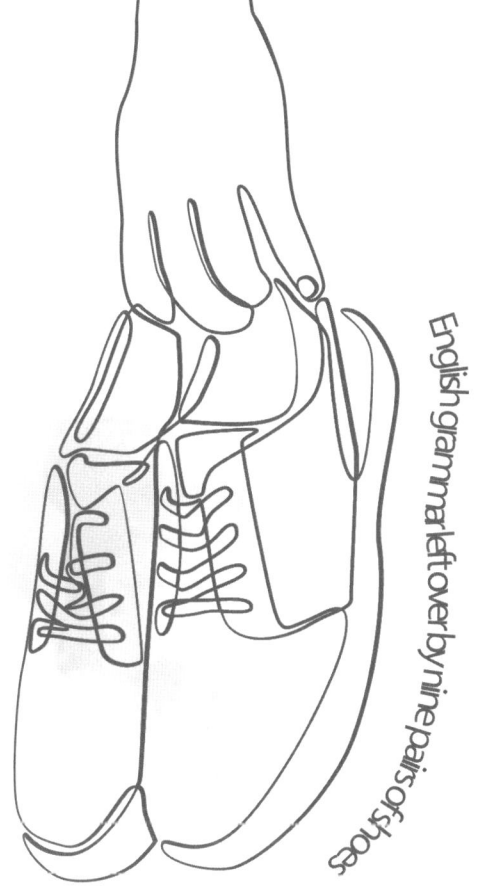

아홉 켤레의 신발로 남은
영문법

English grammar left over by nine pairs of shoes

배철환 지음

도서출판 밀알서원

CONTENTS

머리말 ▪ 6

1 명사(名詞) Noun ▪ 7
연습 문제 ▪ 18 / 숙어 ▪ 25

2 명사의 數, 性, 格 ▪ 28
연습 문제 ▪ 42 / 숙어 ▪ 43

3 관사(冠詞) Article ▪ 46
연습 문제 ▪ 61 / 숙어 ▪ 64

4 대명사(代名詞) Pronoun ▪ 67
연습 문제 ▪ 94 / 숙어 ▪ 100

5 대명사(代名詞) Pronoun ▪ 103
연습 문제 ▪ 114 / 숙어 ▪ 117

6 형용사(形容詞) Adjective ▪ 120
연습 문제 ▪ 133 / 숙어 ▪ 140

7 형용사 비교(形容詞 比較) ▪ 142
연습 문제 ▪ 149 / 숙어 ▪ 152

8 동사(動詞) Verb ▪ 155
연습 문제 ▪ 168 / 숙어 ▪ 179

9 시제(時制) Tense ▪ 182
연습 문제 ▪ 201 / 숙어 ▪ 203

10 조동사(助動詞) Auxiliary verb ▪ 206
연습 문제 ▪ 228 / 숙어 ▪ 231

11	태(態) Voice ▪ 234
	연습 문제 ▪ 238 / 숙어 ▪ 242

12	법(法) Mood ▪ 245
	연습 문제 ▪ 256 / 숙어 ▪ 259

13	부정사(不定詞) Infinitive ▪ 262
	연습 문제 ▪ 277 / 숙어 ▪ 281

14	동명사(動名詞) Gerund ▪ 284
	연습 문제 ▪ 294 / 숙어 ▪ 296

15	분사(分詞) Participle ▪ 298
	연습 문제 ▪ 308 / 숙어 ▪ 312

16	일치와 화법(一致와 話法) ▪ 315
	연습 문제 ▪ 322 / 숙어 ▪ 324

17	부사(副詞) Adverb ▪ 327
	연습 문제 ▪ 349 / 숙어 ▪ 355

18	전치사(前置詞) Preposition ▪ 358
	연습 문제 ▪ 381 / 숙어 ▪ 389

19	접속사(接續詞) Conjunction ▪ 391
	연습 문제 ▪ 405 / 숙어 ▪ 412

20	도치, 강조, 생략, 공통관계, 삽입, 동격 ▪ 414
	연습 문제 ▪ 425 / 숙어 ▪ 427

독해 연습 ▪ 429
종합 문제 ▪ 509

머리말

배 철 환 장로
한국기독교장로회 행화정교회, 건축시공기술사

    시중의 영어 교육 시장에서 자웅을 겨루는 책들이 헤아릴 수도 없이 많은데다 책의 종류만큼이나 영어 학습 방법이 가지각색이다. 이 책은 취미 학습을 통한 영어 공부가 가장 효과적이라는 확신을 갖고 쓰게 되었다.

    이 책을 읽다 보면 영어 공부를 하는 건지 성경 공부를 하는 건지 본말이 전도된 느낌을 가질 수도 있다. 또 이 책에는 단시간 내에 높은 점수에 이르게 하는 비밀이 있는 것도 아니기 때문에 영어에 한이 맺혀 오로지 영어 정복이 목표인 분들에게는 그다지 권할 만한 책은 아니다. 그러나 어디서도 큰 만족을 느끼지 못했다면 이 교재에서 색다른 맛을 느낄 수는 있을 것이다.

    가장 효과적인 영어 학습 방법은 재미있게 공부하는 것이다. 그래서 좋아하는 취미 생활을 즐기듯이 영어를 학습한다면 영어 학습이 지루하지 않을 것이다. 마치 운동을 하면 건강해지는 원리와 같이 꾸준히 취미를 즐기다 보면 영어 실력은 저절로 따라와서 일석이조의 효과가 나는 것이다.

    이 책은 그런 방편의 하나로, 영어 공부를 하면서 성경 지식도 곁들여 얻을 수 있도록 되어 있다. 8품사 중심의 기존 영문법 체계를 본떴으나, 예문은 거의 NIV(New International Version by International Bible Society, 1978) 영어 성경에서 따왔고, 예문마다 성경전서 개역한글판(대한성서공회, 1956)을 함께 적어 바로 해석을 볼 수 있다.

    또한, 각각의 문법에 여러 개의 성경 문구를 인용하여 문법이 활용되는 형식들을 경험적으로 터득할 수 있도록 했고, 각 단원마다 역시 NIV 성경에서 인용된 예문의 문제를 실었다. 예문이 장문(長文)인 경우도 있어서 함께 인용된 한글 성경을 보면 저절로 독해 연습이 될 수 있을 것이다. 이 책이 영어 학습자들에게 좋은 책으로 남길 바란다.

1. 명사(名詞)
Noun

A. 名詞의 정의: 명사는 사람, 장소, 물건의 이름이다

The **Israelites** ate manna forty years, until they came to a land that was settled; they ate manna until they reached the border of **Canaan**.
이스라엘 자손이 사람 사는 땅에 이르기까지 사십년 동안 만나를 먹되 곧 가나안 지경에 이르기까지 그들이 만나를 먹었더라(출 16:35).

B. 名詞의 기능: 명사는 주어, 목적어 및 보어의 기능을 한다

The **waters** continued to recede until the tenth month.(waters = 동사continue의 주어)
A man planted a **vineyard**.(vineyard= planted의 목적어)
He put a wall around it, dug a pit for the **winepress** and built a watchtower.(winepress = 전치사 for의 목적어)
You are the **light** of the world. (light = 동사 are의 주격 보어)

C. 名詞의 종류

명사의 종류를 분류하는 방법에는 다음 세 가지가 주로 쓰인다.

- 보통명사와 고유명사
- 물질명사와 추상명사
- 가산명사, 불가산명사, 집합명사

한 개의 명사는 여러 종류의 명사로 구분할 수 있다.
Mary has known five **Georges** in his life. (Georges = 고유, 가산명사)

또한, 보통명사이던 것이 고유명사로 되거나 물질명사가 보통명사로 쓰이기도 하기 때문에 명사는 문장 안에서의 쓰임새에 따라 종류가 결정된다.
A **boy** and his **friend** dined at a pizza **restaurant**. (보통명사)
George and **Mary** dined at **Papa John's**. (고유명사)

He will baptize you with the **Holy Spirit** and with fire. (고유명사)
그는 성령과 불로 너희에게 세례를 주실 것이요 (눅 3:16).

1. 보통명사와 고유명사 (common noun & proper noun)

1) 보통명사 (common noun)
일반적인 이름으로 문장의 첫 글자가 아닌 이상 대문자로 시작할 수 없다. (고유명사는 특정한 것을 지칭하며 항상 대문자로 시작한다.)

(1) 눈에 보이는 것
refrigerator, stove, microwave, window, curtain, coffee maker, wallpaper, spatula, sink, faucet, plate

(2) 장소
mall, restaurant, school, post office, backyard, beach, supermarket, gas station

(3) 사람
teenager, grandmother, salesclerk, police officer, toddler, mother, father, manager, janitor, shoplifter

(4) 보통명사의 비교

① **play와 game**
play; 희곡 (문학)
Julius Caesar is one of Shakespeare's early **plays**.
My daughter is acting in her school **play**.

Game; chess, football, basketball과 같은 경기
Chess is a very slow **game**.
Have you ever **played rugby football**?

② **Street와 road**
Street; 양쪽에 집이 늘어서 있는 도시의 도로를 가리킨다.

Cars can park on both sides of our **street**.
Road; 도시와 시골 모두에 쓸 수 있다.
Cars can park on both sides of our **road**.
There's a narrow winding **road** from our village to the next one.

(5) a, the + 단수 보통명사 = 대표 단수
A student is not above his teacher.
제자가 그 선생보다 높지 못하나(눅 6:40).

The ax is already at the root of the trees.
이미 도끼가 나무 뿌리에 놓였으니(눅 3:9).

A man ought not to cover his head, since he is the image and glory of God; but **the woman** is the glory of man.
남자는 하나님의 형상과 영광이니 그 머리에 마땅히 쓰지 않거니와 여자는 남자의 영광이니라(고전 11:7).

A son honors his father, and **a servant** his master.
아들은 그 아비를, 종은 그 주인을 공경하나니(말 1:6).

(6) 복수 보통명사 = 대표 복수
Foxes have holes and **birds** of the air have nests.
여우도 굴이 있고 공중의 새도 집이 있으되(눅 9:58).

Do not give **dogs** what is sacred; do not throw your pearls to **pigs**.
거룩한 것을 개에게 주지 말며 너희 진주를 돼지 앞에 던지지 말라(마 7:6).

(7) the + 단수 보통명사 = 추상명사
I will bring you out from under **the yoke** of the Egyptians.
내가 애굽 사람의 무거운 짐 밑에서 너희를 빼어 내며(출 6:6).

2) 고유명사
특정한 사물의 이름으로 항상 대문자로 쓴다.

The **Marroons** were transported from **Jamaica** and forced to build the fortifications in **Halifax**.

Many people dread **Monday** mornings.
Beltane is celebrated on the first of **May**.
Abraham appears in the **Talmud** and in the **Koran**.
Last year, I had a **Baptist**, a **Buddhist**, and a **Gardnerian Witch** as roommates.

A man from **Bethlehem** in **Judah**, together with his wife and two sons, went to live for a while in the country of **Moab**.
유다 베들레헴에 한 사람이 그 아내와 두 아들을 데리고 모압 지방에 가서 우거하였는데(룻 1:1).

둘 다 불가산명사로 관사를 못 붙이고 복수가 없는 것이 원칙이다. 일정한 형태가 없는 물질의 이름은 물질명사이며, 사람의 5감(시각, 청각, 후각, 미각, 촉각) 중 어느 하나로도 경험할 수 없으면 추상명사이다.

2. 물질명사와 추상명사(mass noun & abstract noun)

1) 물질명사

water, ash, sand, heat, snow, frost, wine, tea, fruit, dust, ivory, bronze, hair, seed, curl 등

Cakes of **bread** made without **yeast** and mixed with **oil**.
기름 섞은 무교병(레 7:12).

But if it is cooked in a bronze pot, the pot is to be scoured and rinsed with **water**.
유기에 삶았으면 그 그릇을 닦고 물에 씻을 것이며(레 6:28).

When Moses stretched out his staff toward the sky, the LORD sent **thunder** and **hail**, and **lightning** flashed down to the ground.
모세가 하늘을 향하여 지팡이를 들매 여호와께서 뇌성과 우박을 보내시고 불을 내려 땅에 달리게 하시니라 (출 9:23).

Anything living in **the** water that does not have fins and scales is to be detestable to you. (the water; 水中)
수중 생물에 지느러미와 비늘 없는 것은 너희에게 가증하니라(레 11:12).

2) 추상명사

ability, frailty, weakness, strength, writing, liberty, disease, filing, kindness, happiness

She never tips the delivery boy from the laundry; **politeness** is not one of her strong points.
Tillie is amused by people who are nostalgic about **childhood**.
Justice often seems to slip out of our grasp.
Some scientists believe that **schizophrenia** is transmitted genetically.
Buying the fire extinguisher was **an afterthought**.

Do not take revenge, my friends, but leave **room** for God's wrath.
내 사랑하는 자들아 너희가 친히 원수를 갚지 말고 진노하심에 맡기라(롬 12:19).

Their tongues practice **deceit**.
그 혀로는 속임을 베풀며(롬 3:13).

They turn their backs and run because they have been made liable to **destruction**.
그 앞에서 돌아섰나니 이는 자기도 바친 것이 됨이라(수 7:12).

(1) 집합적 물질명사

furniture, clothing, machinery, produce, game, baggage, merchandise 등은 물건의 집합체이지만 양(量)으로 다루므로 부정관사가 안 붙고, 항상 단수 취급을 한다. 이들은 a piece of, an article of, much, little 등으로 양을 표시한다.

(2) 물질명사의 수량 표시 a cup of, a piece of, a pound of

Now a man named Ananias, together with his wife Sapphira, also sold **a piece of** property.
아나니아라 하는 사람이 그 아내 삽비라로 더불어 소유를 팔아(행 5:1).

And if anyone gives even **a cup of** cold water to one of these little ones because he is my disciple.
또 누구든지 제자의 이름으로 이 소자 중 하나에게 냉수 한 그릇이라도 주는 자는(마 10:42).

We have here only five **loaves of bread** and two fish.
여기 우리에게 있는 것은 떡 다섯 개와 물고기 두 마리 뿐이니이다(마 14:17).

Does not the potter have the right to make out of the same **lump of** clay some pottery for noble purposes and some for common use?
토기장이가 진흙 한 덩이로 하나는 귀히 쓸 그릇을 하나는 천히 쓸 그릇을 만드는 권이 없느냐(롬 9:21).

The priest shall take **a handful of** the fine flour and oil, together with all the incense,
제사장은 그 고운 기름 가루 한 줌과 그 모든 유향을 취하여(레 2:2).

From the throne came **flashes of** lightning, **rumblings and peals of** thunder.
보좌로부터 번개와 음성과 뇌성이 나고(계 4:5).

His clothes became as bright as **a flash of** lightning.
그 옷이 희어져 광채가 나더라(눅 9:29).

You have profaned me among my people for a few **handfuls of** barley and **scraps of** bread.
너희가 두어 움큼 보리와 두어 조각 떡을 위하여 나를 내 백성 가운데서 욕되게 하여(겔 13:19).

3. 가산명사, 불가산명사, 집합명사(count, noncount, & collective noun)

1) 가산명사

별개의 사물, 사람, 개념 등 셀 수 있는 이름으로서 숫자와 a/an을 쓸 수 있고, 단수 혹은 복수로 만들 수 있는 명사, A cat, three cats, a newspaper, two newspapers

We painted the **table** red and the **chairs** blue.
Since he inherited his **aunt's library**, Jerome spends every **weekend** indexing his **books**.
Miriam found six silver **dollars** in the **toe** of a **sock**.
The oak **tree** lost three **branches** in the **hurricane**.
Over the **course** of twenty-seven **years**, Martha Ballad delivered just over eight hundred **babies**.

2) 불가산명사

별개의 대상으로 인식할 수 없는 재료, 액체 등의 이름으로서 숫자와 a/an을 쓸 수 없고, 단수만 있는 명사로 보통 숫자로 세지 않는다.

Water, wool, weather, health, English

Mary got severe **indigestion**.
(Indigestion = 불가산명사); "Mary got eleven indigestions"라고 쓸 수 없음.

Joseph Priestly discovered **oxygen**.
Oxygen is essential to human life.
We decided to sell the **furniture** rather than take it with use when we moved.
The **furniture** is heaped in the middle of the room.
The crew spread the **gravel** over the roadbed.
Gravel is more expensive than I thought.

3) 집합명사

(1) 단체를 지칭하는 것으로 단체가 한 개의 단위라도 구성원은 둘 이상이다

army, audience, board, cabinet, cattle, class, committee, company, corporation, council, department, faculty, family, firm, group, jury, majority, minority, navy, people, police, public, school, society, team, troupe

집합명사는 동사나 대명사와 일치시킬 때 혼동되는데, 그 이유는 집합명사 구성원의 행동에 따라 단수도 되고 복수로도 되기 때문이다. 예를 들어, 구성원들이 한 단위로서 움직이며, 모든 구성원이 동시에 똑같은 일을 하면 단수 취급을 한다.

(2) 단수 취급

Despite the danger to **its** new van, the **team pursues** the pizza-eating monster through the streets of Miami.
The **jury is** dining on take-out chicken tonight.
The steering **committee meets** every Wednesday afternoon.
The **class was** startled by the bursting light bulb.
The **audience was** a large one.(청중은 많았다.)

(3) 복수 취급

The **police are** searching for a tall dark man with a beard.

People are funny.
Cattle are selling for very low prices this year.
My family have decided to move to the country.
My family are wonderful. They do all they can do for me.

How are the team? They are very confident. They are the only team who have ever won all their matches right through the season.

The people are building it with large stones and placing the timbers in the walls.
(사람들이). 전을 큰 돌로 세우며 벽에 나무를 얹고(스 5:8).

What am I to do with these people?
내가 이 백성에게 어떻게 하리이까(출 17:4).

부분을 나타내는 말; part, portion, half, the rest, the majority, most, the bulk 등은 뒤에 오는 말에 따라 그 수가 결정된다.

The rest of the grain offering belongs to Aaron and his sons
그 소제물의 남은 것은 아론과 그 자손에게 돌릴지니(레 2:3).

D. 명사의 전용

1. 명사는 문장 안에서의 쓰임새에 따라 종류가 결정된다

2. 물질명사도 한정되면 관사를 붙인다

The sons of Aaron the priest are to put fire on the altar and arrange wood on the fire.
제사장 아론의 자손들은 단 위에 불을 두고 불 위에 나무를 벌여 놓고(레 1:7).

3. 물질명사라도 바로 앞에 나온 것을 가리킬 때는 관사를 붙인다

This is the meaning of the vision of the rock cut out of a mountain, but not by human hands--a rock that broke **the iron, the bronze, the clay, the silver** and **the gold** to pieces.
왕이 사람의 손으로 아니하고 산에서 뜨인 돌이 철과 놋과 진흙과 은과 금을 부숴뜨린 것을 보신 것은(단 2:45).

4. 많은 명사는 물질명사(불가산)/보통명사(가산) 양쪽 모두 쓸 수 있다

I'd like some white **paper**. (불가산)
I'm going out to buy **a paper**. (= a newspaper, 가산)
The window is made of unbreakable **glass**. (불가산)
Would you like **a glass** of water? (가산)
Could I have some **coffee**? (불가산)
Could we have **two coffees**, please? (= cups of coffee, 가산)
She has red **hair**. (불가산)
He has two white **hairs**. (가산)
Angola is a hot **country**. (가산, nation/land)
How many **countries** are there in Asia? (가산)
My parents live in **the country** near Jinju. (불가산, open land without many buildings, 이런 의미로는 a country, countries를 쓸 수 없다.)
Would you rather live in the town or **the country**? (불가산)

A fire will spread from there to the whole house of Israel.
그 속에서 불이 이스라엘 온 족속에게로 나오리라(겔 5:4).

Which of you, if his son asks for bread, will give him **a stone**?
너희 중에 누가 아들이 떡을 달라 하면 돌을 주며(마 7:9).

Their father had given them many gifts of silver and gold and articles **of value**, as well as fortified cities in Judah.
그 부친이 저희에게는 은 금과 보물과 유다 견고한 성읍들을 선물로 후히 주었고(대하 21:3).

Physical training is of some **value**.
육체의 연습은 약간의 유익이 있으나(딤전 4:8).

Ill-gotten treasures are **of no value**, but righteousness delivers from death.
불의의 재물은 무익하여도 의리는 죽음에서 건지느니라(잠 10:2).

The tongue of the righteous is choice silver, but the heart of the wicked is **of little value**.
의인의 혀는 천은과 같거니와 악인의 마음은 가치가 적으니라(잠 10:20).

The man **of integrity** walks securely, but he who takes crooked paths will be found out.
바른 길로 행하는 자는 걸음이 평안하려니와 굽은 길로 행하는 자는 드러나리라(잠 10:9).

They worship me **in vain**; their teachings are but rules taught by men.
사람의 계명으로 교훈을 삼아 가르치니 나를 **헛되이** 경배하는도다(마 15:9).

I will spare them, just as **in compassion** a man spares his son who serves him.
사람이 자기를 섬기는 아들을 아낌 같이 내가 그들을 아끼리니(말 3:17).

Daniel spoke to him **with wisdom and tact**.
다니엘이 **명철하고 슬기로운** 말로(단 2:14).

The work is being carried on **with diligence** and is making rapid progress under their direction.
부지런히 하므로 역사가 그 손에서 형통하옵기로(스 5:8).

Even though my illness was a trial to you, you did not treat me **with contempt** or **scorn**.
너희를 시험하는 것이 내 육체에 있으되 이것을 너희가 업신여기지도 아니하며 버리지도 아니하고(갈 4:14).

He will be called **a Nazarene**.
나사렛 사람이라 칭하리라(마 2:23).

You are **a Jew**, yet you live like **a Gentile** and not like **a Jew**.
네가 유대인으로서 이방을 좇고 유대인답게 살지 아니하면서(갈 2:14).

The woman was **a Greek**, born in Syrian Phoenicia.
그 여자는 헬라인이요 수로보니게 족속이라(막 7:26).

연습 문제

1. We saw his star _____ and have come to worship him.
   1) in the east   2) in east   3) at the east   4) at east

2. Man does not live _____ alone, but on every word that comes from the mouth of God.
   1) by bread   2) by the bread   3) on bread   4) on the bread

*물질명사

They will turn to **blood**.

Pray to the LORD, for we have had enough **thunder** and **hail**.

Blood will be everywhere in Egypt, even in the wooden buckets and stone jars.
애굽 온 땅에와 나무 그릇에와 돌 그릇에 모두 피가 있으리라 (출 7:19).

3. The people living in darkness _____ seen a great light.
   1) have   2) has   3) was   4) were

People **curse** the man who hoards grain, but blessing crowns him who is willing to sell.
곡식을 내지 아니하는 자는 백성에게 저주를 받을 것이나 파는 자는 그 머리에 복이 임하리라 (잠 11:26).

4. You are the salt _____. But if the salt loses its saltiness, how can it be made salty again?
   1) in the sky   2) in earth   3) of earth   4) of the earth

These are the two who are anointed to serve the Lord of all **the earth**.

He will march in the storms of **the south**.

Lift up your eyes from where you are and look **north** and **south**, **east** and **west**.

The Mount of Olives will be split in two from **east** to **west**.

His rule will extend from **sea** to **sea**.

As long as the earth endures, seedtime and harvest, cold and heat, summer and winter, day and night will never cease.

5. _____ people pick grapes from thornbushes, or figs from thistles?
   1) Does   2) When   3) Do   4) Are

6. When he saw the crowds, he had compassion on them, because they were harassed and helpless, like _____ without a shepherd.
   1) a sheep   2) sheep   3) sheeps   4) the sheeps

Every living thing that moved on the earth perished--birds, **livestock**, wild animals, all the creatures that swarm over the earth, and all mankind.
Abram acquired **sheep** and **cattle**, male and female donkeys, menservants and maidservants, and camels.
The herds mill about because they have no pasture; even the flocks of **sheep** are suffering.

The hand of the LORD will bring a terrible plague on your **livestock** in the field--on your horses and donkeys and camels and on your **cattle** and **sheep** and goats.
여호와의 손이 들에 있는 네 생축 곧 말과 나귀와 약대와 우양에게 더하리니 심한 악질이 있을 것이며(출 9:3).

7. We played the flute for you, and you did not dance; we sang _____, and you did not mourn.
   1) a dirge   2) dirge   3) a song   4) song

8. His disciples were hungry and began to pick some _____ of grain and eat them.
   1) piece   2) pieces   3) head   4) heads

Then Moses cried out to the LORD, and the LORD showed him **a piece of** wood. He threw it into the water, and the water became sweet. There the LORD made a decree and a law for them, and there he tested them.
모세가 여호와께 부르짖었더니 여호와께서 그에게 한 나무를 지시하시니 그가 물에 던지매 물이 달아졌더라. 거기서 여호와께서 그들을 위하여 법도와 율례를 정하시고 그들을 시험하실쌔(출 15:25).

That evening quail came and covered the camp, and in the morning there was **a layer of** dew around the camp.

저녁에는 메추라기가 와서 진에 덮이고, 아침에는 이슬이 진 사면에 있더니 (출 16:13).

9. The kingdom of heaven is like _____ that a woman took and mixed into a large amount of flour until it worked all through the dough.
   1) honey   2) a honey   3) yeast   4) a yeast

10. Once again, the kingdom of _____ is like a net that was let down into the lake and caught all kinds of fish.
    1) heaven   2) the heaven   3) sky   4) the sky

11. We have here only five _____ of bread and two fish.
    1) lumps   2) lump   3) loaves   4) loaf

12. "The _____ has come," he said. "The kingdom of God is near. Repent and believe the good news!"
    1) times   2) time   3) hours   4) hour

13. Without _____ he called them, and they left their father Zebedee in the boat with the hired men and followed him.
    1) delay   2) a delay   3) delaying   4) a delaying

14. Jesus healed many who had various _____.
    1) decease   2) deceases   3) disease   4) diseases

15. A crowd _____ sitting around him.
    1) was   2) were   3) has   4) have

A large population is a king's glory, but without subjects a prince is ruined.
백성이 많은 것은 왕의 영광이요, 백성이 적은 것은 주권자의 패망이니라 (잠 14:28).

16. _____ went out to sow his seed.
    1) Farmer   2) A farmer   3) Farmers   4) The farmers

Men do not despise a thief if he steals to satisfy his hunger when he is starving.

도적이 만일 주릴 때에 배를 채우려고 도적질하면 사람이 그를 멸시치는 아니하려니와 (잠 6:30).

17. With many similar _____ Jesus spoke the word to them, as much as they could understand.
    1) story   2) stories   3) parable   4) parables

18. Afterward the disciples picked up seven _____ of broken pieces that were left over.
    1) basketfuls   2) basketful   3) basket   4) lump

19. This kind can come out only by _____.
    1) a prayer   2) prayer   3) prayers   4) the prayers

20. This is _____. Come, let's kill him, and the inheritance will be ours.
    1) a heir   2) the heir   3) heirs   4) heir

21. The Son of Man came eating and drinking, and you say, 'Here is _____ and a drunkard, a friend of tax collectors and "sinners."'
    1) a wizard   2) wizard   3) a glutton   4) glutton

22. These women were helping to support them out of their own _____.
    1) height   2) heights   3) mean   4) means

23. As he was praying, the appearance of his face changed, and his clothes became as bright as _____ of lightning.
    1) flash   2) a flash   3) ray   4) a ray

The priest shall take a **handful** of the fine flour and oil.
The voice of the LORD strikes with **flashes** of lightning.

24. Everyone brings out the choice wine first and then the cheaper wine after the guests have had too _____ to drink.
    1) much   2) many   3) little   4) few

25. But here is _____ that comes down from heaven, which a man may eat and not die.
   1) the bread   2) bread   3) a bread   4) the breads

26. Where shall we buy _____ for these people to eat?
   1) the bread   2) bread   3) a bread   4) the breads

27. _____ cannot be established through wickedness, but the righteous cannot be uprooted.
   1) The Men   2) Women   3) A man   4) Man

28. The watchman opens the gate for him, and the sheep _____ to his voice.
   1) listens   2) listen   3) hears   4) hear

29. How long will you keep us in _____? If you are the Christ, tell us plainly.
   1) suspense   2) a suspense   3) suspenses   4) the suspense

Why do the nations conspire and the peoples plot **in vain**?
I will lie down and sleep **in peace**, for you alone, O LORD, make me dwell **in safety**.
O LORD, heal me, for my bones are **in agony**. My soul is **in anguish**.
He lies **in wait** near the villages; from ambush he murders the innocent, watching **in secret** for his victims.
Everyone lies to his neighbor; their flattering lips speak **with deception**.
They close up their callous hearts, and their mouths speak **with arrogance**.
They will be put to shame who are treacherous **without excuse**.
He will spend his days **in prosperity**, and his descendants will inherit the land.
I will take vengeance **in anger and wrath** upon the nations that have not obeyed me.
Your hand will be lifted up **in triumph** over your enemies.

Whoever listens to me will live **in safety** and be **at ease**, without fear of harm."
나를 듣는 자는 안연히 살며 재앙의 두려움이 없이 평안하리라 (잠 1:33).

30. Selling their possessions and goods, they gave to anyone as he had _____.
   1) the need   2) needs   3) a need   4) need

31. He was led like a sheep to the slaughter, and as _____ before the shearer is silent, so he did not open his mouth.
   1) lamb   2) a lamb   3) lambs   4) the lamb

32. If she marries another man while her husband is still alive, she is called _____.
   1) an adulteress   2) adulteress   3) an adulterer   4) adulterer

33. Now if I do what I do not want to do, it is no longer I who do it, but it is ___ living in me that does it.
   1) sinful   2) a sin   3) sin   4) sins

34. Share with God's people who are in _____.
   1) a deed   2) deed   3) a need   4) need

35. So let us put aside the deeds of _____ and put on the armor of light.
   1) dark   2) darks   3) darkness   4) a darkness

36. The people sat down to eat and drink and got up to indulge in pagan _____.
   1) revelry   2) revel   3) house   4) meal

37. We were under great pressure, far beyond our _____ to endure, so that we despaired even of life.
   1) ability   2) capability   3) facility   4) criticality

38. If anyone is in Christ, he is a new _____ ; the old has gone, the new has come!
   1) creator   2) create   3) creation   4) creations

39. Now is the _____ of God's favor, now is the day of salvation.
   1) hour   2) time   3) month   4) second

40. The law was put into _____ through angels by a mediator.
   1) effect   2) an effect   3) effectual   4) effective

41. Whoever finds his life will lose it, and whoever loses his life for my _____ will find it.
   1) side   2) right   3) return   4) sake

42. First collect _____ and tie them in bundles to be burned; then gather the wheat and bring it into my barn.
   1) the weeds   2) the weed   3) weed   4) weeds

43. _____ the builders rejected has become the capstone.
   1) Stones   2) The stones   3) The stone   4) Stone

44. It throws him into convulsions so that he foams at _____.
   1) the mouth   2) mouth   3) the eye   4) eye

정답

1) 1, 2) 3, 3) 1, 4) 4, 5) 3, 6) 2, 7) 1, 8) 4, 9) 3, 10) 1
11) 3, 12) 2, 13) 1, 14) 4, 15) 1, 16) 2, 17) 4, 18) 1, 19) 2, 20) 2
21) 3, 22) 4, 23) 2, 24) 1, 25) 1, 26) 2, 27) 3, 28) 2, 29) 1, 30) 4
31) 2, 32) 1, 33) 3, 34) 4, 35) 3, 36) 1, 37) 1, 38) 3, 39) 2, 40) 1
41) 4, 42) 1, 43) 3, 44) 1

숙어

Above all; 특히, 더욱이, 무엇보다도 (more than anything else)
Above all, my brothers, do not swear--not by heaven or by earth or by anything else.
내 형제들아 무엇보다도 맹세하지 말지니 하늘로나 땅으로나 아무 다른 것으로도 맹세하지 말고(약 5:12).

ability at (ability in이 아님); ~을 할 수 있는 능력
She shows great ability at mathematics.

abstain from; 삼가다, 절제하다, 끊다
Dear friends, I urge you, as aliens and strangers in the world, to abstain from sinful desires, which war against your soul.
사랑하는 자들아, 나그네와 행인 같은 너희를 권하노니 영혼을 거스려 싸우는 육체의 정욕을 제어하라(벧전 2:11).

according to; ~에 따라, (~에 의하면)
And we know that in all things God works for the good of those who love him, who have been called according to his purpose.
우리가 알거니와 하나님을 사랑하는 자 곧 그 뜻대로 부르심을 입은 자들에게는 모든 것이 합력하여 선을 이루느니라(롬 8:28).

I will repay each of you according to your deeds.
내가 너희 각 사람의 행위대로 갚아 주리라(계 2:23).

afraid of (afraid by가 아님); ~을 두려워하여
Are you afraid of spiders?

after all; 그럼에도 불구하고 (보통 문미에), 더구나 (보통 문두에)
I am sorry. I thought I could come and see you this evening, but I am not free after all.
I expected to fail the exam, but I passed after all.
It's not surprising you're hungry. After all you didn't have breakfast.

1. 명사(名詞) Noun 25

again and again; 몇 번이고, 재삼
And he begged Jesus **again and again** not to send them out of the area.
자기를 이 지방에서 내어보내지 마시기를 간절히 구하더니 (막 5:10).

agree about (a subject of discussion)
We **agree about** most things.

agree with (a person); 동의하다, 적합하다 (be of the same mind, suit)
I entirely **agree with** you.

agree on (a matter for decision); 합의에 도달하다
Let's try to **agree on** a date.

agree to (a suggestion); ~에 동의하다 (consent to)
I'll **agree to** your suggestion if you lower the price.

angry with (혹은 at) a person for doing something; 성내다
I'm **angry with** her for not telling me.

angry about (혹은 at) something; 성내다
What are you so **angry about**?

apologize for; 사과하다, 해명하다, 변명하다
I must **apologize for** disturbing you.

apply to; 적용되다 (concern, fit)
The same law **applies to** the native-born and to the alien living among you.
본토인에게나 너희 중에 우거한 이방인에게나 이 법이 동일하니라 (출 12:49).

apply for; 지원하다 (ask to be given)
He **applied for** a special position.

arrive at (in) (arrive to가 아님); 도착하다

What time do we **arrive at** London?

When did you **arrive in** England?

at a distance; 거리를 두고, 좀 떨어져서

His sister stood **at a distance** to see what would happen to him.

그 누이가 어떻게 되는 것을 알려고 멀리 섰더니(출 1:12).

at a distance of 5 meters; 5미터 떨어져서

2. 명사의 數, 性, 格

A. 명사의 복수

영어의 수(數)에는 단수(singular)와 복수(plural)가 있으며, 복수를 만들 때는 규칙변화와 불규칙변화가 있다.

1. 규칙변화; 어미에 -s, -es를 붙임

1) 무성음 [p,t,k,f,θ] 등 다음에서는 어미 s가 s로 발음
books,

2) 유성음 다음에서는 z로 발음
pens, pigs, fathers, trees

3) 어미가 s, x, sh, ch로 끝나면 -es를 붙이고, iz로 발음
churches, foxes, wishes, buses, glasses, boxes, dishes, benches
* monarchs[-ks]

4) 자음 + y는 y를 i로 고치고 -es를 붙임
duty – duties
army – armies
lady – ladies
city – cities
baby – babies

5) 모음 + y는 그대로 -s만 붙임
day – days
play – plays
key – keys
boy – boys

6) 자음 + o는 -es를 붙임
potatoes, heroes, cargoes, mottoes

*bamboos

(예외) pianos, photos, solos, autos / folios, Hindoos, cameos

7) 어미가 f, fe로 끝나면 –ves

calf – calves
wife – wives
leaf – leaves

(예외) chiefs, roofs, cliffs, dwarfs, safes, griefs, proofs, strifes

8) 문자, 숫자, 약어는 보통 's를 붙임

T's, 7's, M.P.'s(혹은 MP's)

2. 불규칙 변화

1) 모음을 변화시킴

foot – feet
goose – geese
louse – lice
man – men
woman – women
mouse – mice
tooth – teeth

2) –en형 변화

ox – oxen
brother – brethren
child – children

3) 라틴어(Latin) 변화

addendum – addenda
datum – data
alumnus – alumni

fungus – fungi
radius – radii larva - larvae

4) 희랍어(Greek) 변화
criterion – criteria
phenomenon – phenomena
stigma – stigmata

5) 뜻에 따라 두 개의 복수형이 있다
genius – geniuses(천재), genii(수호신)
penny – pennies(수), pence(가치)
brother – brothers(형제), brethren(교우, 동업자)
cloth – cloths(천), clothes(의복)
index – indexes(색인), indices(지수)

6) 단수와 복수가 같은 형
동물, 수량, 집합성을 뜻하는 낱말에 많다.
sheep, deer, swine, fish, salmon, trout, buffalo, giraffe, million, people, cattle

7) 복합어는 그 중요한 것을 복수로
brothers-in-law, commanders-in-chief, goings on, men-of-war, passers-by, knights-errant, courts-martial, hangers-on

Naomi and her **daughters-in-law** prepared to return home from there.
두 자부와 함께 일어나 모압 지방에서 돌아오려 하여(룻 1:6).

The slaughter was very great; Israel lost thirty thousand foot **soldiers**.
살육이 심히 커서 이스라엘 보병의 엎드러진 자가 삼만이었으며(삼상 4:10).

8) 명사를 포함하지 않는 복합어는 –s를 어미에 붙인다
go-betweens, also-rans, drive-ins, turn-outs

B. 복수형의 용법

분리할 수 없는 두 개의 요소로 구성되어 있는 물건의 이름은 항상 복수형으로 쓴다.

1. 짝을 이루는 것은 복수형

1) 의복

trousers, drawers, breeches, knickerbockers, pantaloons, braces, gloves

2) 도구

scissors, spectacles, shears, pincers, tongs, compasses

Its rider was holding **a pair of scales** in his hand.
그 탄 자가 손에 저울을 가졌더라(계 6:5).

2. 건물, 장소

archives, barracks, shambles, outskirts, straits, eaves

3. 학과 이름

athletics, economics, ethics, gymnastics, linguistics, phonetics, politics, physics, statistics

4. 신체 각 부분

bowels, brains, gums, whiskers, entrails, intestines

5. 복수형(단수 취급)

brains(두뇌), billiards(당구), measles(홍역), suburbs(교외), works(공장), means(수단), belongings(소유물)

6. 복수가 되면 뜻이 달라지는 예

arm(팔) – arms(무기)
advice(충고) – advices(information)
air(공기) – airs(젠 체함)
color(색깔) – colors(깃발)
force(힘) – forces(army)
quarter(4분의 1) – quarters(막사)
trouble(고통) – troubles(탈 분쟁)

Nine o'clock. Here **is** the news.

He has performed mighty deeds with his **arm**.
그의 팔로 힘을 보이사(눅 1:51).

Every man, young and old, who could bear **arms** was called up and stationed on the border.
갑옷 입을 만한 자로부터 그 이상이 다 모여 그 경계에 섰더라(왕하 3:21).

Vision(sight, imagination[시각, 상상력], 추상명사) / Visions(허깨비들, 환상들, 보통명사)

For you this whole **vision** is nothing but words scaled in a scroll.
그러므로 모든 묵시가 너희에게는 마치 봉한 책의 말이라(사 29:11).

Your sons and daughters will prophesy, your young men will see **visions**.
너희의 자녀들은 예언할 것이요 너희의 젊은이들은 환상을 보고(행 2:17).

interest(관심, 이자, 중요성) / interests(이익)

I have no one else like him, who takes a genuine **interest** in your welfare. (관심)
이는 뜻을 같이하여 너희 사정을 진실히 생각할 자가 이밖에 내게 없음이라(빌 2:20).

You must not lend him money at **interest** or sell him food at a profit.
너는 그에게 이식을 위하여 돈을 꾸이지 말고 이익을 위하여 식물을 꾸이지 말라(레 25:37).

Why let this threat grow, to the detriment of the royal **interests**? (이익)
어찌하여 화를 더하여 왕들에게 손해가 되게 하랴 하였더라(스 4:22).

7. 가산명사로 쓰일 때

Nation, army, people(민족),
party - 단수로도 되고 복수로도 된다.

From these the **nations** spread out over the earth after the flood.
이들에게서 땅의 열국 백성이 나뉘었더라(창 10:32).

I will make you into a great **nation** and I will bless you.
내가 너로 큰 민족을 이루고 네게 복을 주어(창 12:2).

The peoples around them set out to discourage the people of Judah and make them afraid to go on building.
이로부터 그 땅 백성이 유다 백성의 손을 약하게 하여 그 건축을 방해하되(스 4:4).

C. 복수형의 단수 취급

1. Hundred, thousand, dozen, score 등이 수사 다음에 올 때

단수형으로 한다. 단 막연히 단독으로 "많음"을 나타낼 때는 복수로 한다.

Noah was six **hundred** years old when the floodwaters came on the earth.
홍수가 땅에 있을 때에 노아가 육백 세라(창 7:6).

So they sat down in groups of **hundreds** and fifties.
떼로 혹 백 씩 혹 오십 씩 앉은 지라(막 6:40).

He gave them permission, and the evil spirits came out and went into the pigs. The herd,

about two thousand in number, rushed down the steep bank into the lake and were drowned.
허락하신 대 더러운 귀신들이 나와서 돼지에게로 들어가니 거의 이천 마리 되는 떼가 바다를 향하여 비탈로 내리 달아 바다에서 몰사하거늘(막 5:13).

2. pair, couple, yoke 등이 짝을 나타낼 때

단수로도, 복수로도 쓸 수 있다.

He had fourteen thousand sheep, six thousand camels, a thousand **yoke** of oxen and a thousand donkeys.
그가 양 일만 사천과 약대 육천과 소 일천 겨리와 암 나귀 일천을 두었고(욥 42:12).

3. 꼴은 복수지만 단수 취급을 한다

The **mathematics** that I did at school **has** not been very useful to me.
Billiards is an easier game than chess.
Measles was widespread in Europe.

A cheerful look brings joy to the heart, and good **news gives** health to the bones.
눈의 밝은 것은 마음을 기쁘게 하고 좋은 기별은 뼈를 윤택하게 하느니라(잠 15:30).

4. 한 개의 단위로 생각하여 단수 취급을 한다

Where **is** that **five dollars** I lent you?
Twenty miles is a long way to walk.

5. more than one + 단수명사; 단수 취급

More than one person is going to lose his job.

6. anybody, anyone, somebody, someone, nobody, no-one, everybody, everyone

Is everybody here?

*** 비교;**

구어체에서 대명사로 지칭할 때는 복수로 받는다. 문어체에서는 단수로 받는다.

If **anybody** calls, tell **them** I'm out, but take **their** name and address.
Nobody phoned, did **they**?
Somebody left **their** umbrella behind yesterday.
Everybody thinks **they** are different from everybody else.
When **somebody** does not want to live, **he** can be very difficult to help. (단수)

D. 성(性)

1. 성의 표시법

1) 다른 말을 사용

man – woman
bachelor – spinster
son – daughter
uncle – aunt
nephew – niece
lad – lass
widower – widow
cock – hen
drake – duck
drone – bee

2) 어미를 변경

master – mistress
Jew – Jewess
duke – duchess
waiter – waitress
fox – vixen
bride – bridegroom

3) 성을 나타내는 접두어를 붙임

he-goat – she-goat
man-servant – woman-servant
bull-calf – cow-calf
boy-friend – girl-friend

He must bring to the LORD a **female lamb** or goat from the flock as a sin offering.
(여호와께), 양 떼의 암컷 어린 양이나 염소를 끌어 다가 속죄제를 드릴 것이요(레 5:6).

2. 무생물의 성

1) 남성; 남성적이고 웅대한 물건

sun, anger, fear, day, ocean, war, winter, death

2) 여성; 여성적이고 부드러운 것, 도시, 선박, 강, 국가 이름

moon, mercy, liberty, ship, country, peace, spring, ocean, boat

Wisdom has built her house: **she** has hewn out its seven pillars.
지혜가 그 집을 짓고 일곱 기둥을 다듬고(잠 9:1).

3) 중성; 감정을 배제하고 객관적으로 기술할 때, 국토를 지칭할 때

He then presented the bull for the sin offering, and Aaron and his sons laid their hands on **its** head.
모세가 또 속죄제의 수송아지를 끌어오니 아론과 그 아들들이 그 속죄제 수송아지 머리에 안수하매(레 8:14).

E. 격(格)

1. 소유격의 형성

1) 생물인 명사 어미에 's를 첨가

my father's car, my parents' house, the children's room

When he had called together all the **people**'s chief priests and teachers of the law
왕이 모든 대제사장과 백성의 서기관들을 모아(마 2:4).

Have seven priests carry trumpets of **rams**' horns in front of the ark.
제사장 일곱은 일곱 양각나팔을 잡고 언약궤 앞에서 행할 것이요(수 6:4).

Their hair was like **women**'s hair, and their teeth were like **lions**' teeth.
또 여자의 머리털 같은 머리털이 있고 그 이는 사자의 이 같으며(계 9:8).

They devoted themselves to the **apostles**' teaching and to the fellowship, to the breaking of bread and to prayer.
저희가 사도의 가르침을 받아 서로 교제하며 떡을 떼며 기도하기를 전혀 힘쓰니라(행 2:42).

As their lives ebb away in their **mothers**' arms.
그 어미의 품에서 혼이 떠날 때에(아 2:12).

I took the little scroll from the **angel**'s hand and ate it.
내가 천사의 손에서 작은 책을 갖다 먹어버리니(계 10:10).

2) 고유명사는 s로 끝나도 's를 붙이지만 예외 있음

Jesus' mother and brothers arrived.
예수의 모친과 동생들이 와서(막 3:31).

If the Gentiles have shared in the **Jews**' spiritual blessings
만일 이방인들이 그들의 신령한 것을 나눠 가졌으면(롬 15:27).

3) 복합명사는 마지막에 's를 붙임

fountain pens, blackbirds, family names, spoonfuls

2. 소유격의 의미

1) 소유

He recovered all the goods and brought back **his** relative Lot and **his** possessions.

The lips **of** the wise spread knowledge: not so the hearts **of** fools.
지혜로운 자의 입술은 지식을 전파하여도 미련한 자의 마음은 정함이 없느니라 (잠 15:7).

The good seed stands for the sons **of** the kingdom.
좋은 씨는 천국의 아들들이요 (마 13:38).

The weeds are the sons **of** the evil one.
가라지는 악한 자의 아들들이요 (마 13:38).

The desire **of** the righteous ends only in good, but the hope **of** the wicked only in wrath.
의의의 소원은 오직 선하나 악인의 소망은 진노를 이루느니라 (잠 11:23).

The words **of** the wicked lie in wait for blood, but the speech **of** the upright rescues them.
악인의 말은 사람을 엿보아 피를 흘리자 하는 것 이어니 와 정직한 자의 입은 사람을 구원하느니라 (잠 12:6).

2) 주격 관계

His failure (He failed)

3) 목적 관계

You know that the testing **of** your faith develops perseverance.
너희 믿음의 시련이 인내를 만들어 내는 줄 너희가 앎이라 (약 1:3).

The fear **of** the LORD is the beginning of knowledge, but fools despise wisdom and discipline.
여호와를 경외하는 것이 지식의 근본 이어 늘 미련한 자는 지혜와 훈계를 멸시 하느니라 (잠 1:7).

3. 소유격의 용법

1) 생물은 's 소유격으로 표시, 다른 한정사와 함께 쓰이지 않음

My **father's** house (Not; the house of my father)
The **plan's** importance 또는 the importance **of** the plan

The car that is John's is **John's** car, not the John's car.
Have you met **Jack's** new girl-friend?

The slave **woman's** son will never share in the inheritance with the free **woman's** son.
계집종의 아들이 자유하는 여자의 아들로 더불어 유업을 얻지 못하리라(갈 4:30).

The chains fell off **Peter's** wrists.
쇠사슬이 그(베드로의). 손에서 벗어지더라(행 12:7).

2) 무생물은 of + 명사로 표시

When I saw that they were not acting in line with the truth **of the gospel**
나는 저희가 복음의 진리를 따라 바로 행하지 아니함을 보고(갈 2:14).

3) 시간, 거리, 가격, 무게는 's 소유격으로 표시

four **days'** journey, a **week's** holiday, **today's** paper, a **pound's** weight
this **evening's** performance, last **Sunday's** paper, next **week's** TV programmes, this **year's** profits, ten **minutes'** walk, two **weeks'** holiday

단, 시간이 일반적인 의미를 가질 때는 소유격을 쓰지 않는다.
The nine o'clock news, a Sunday newspaper

또한, 복합 명사의 형태로 쓸 수도 있다.
A table leg, a Sunday newspaper

4) sake 앞과 관용구

Moses told his father-in-law about everything the LORD had done to Pharaoh and the Egyptians **for Israel's sake** and about all the hardships they had met along the way and how the

LORD had saved them.
모세가 여호와께서 이스라엘을 위하여 바로와 애굽 사람에게 행하신 모든 일과 길에서 그들의 당한 모든 고난과 여호와께서 그들을 구원하신 일을 다 그 장인에게 고하매(출 18:8).

5) 명사의 중복을 피하기 위한 용법
Whose computer is that? Peter's.

보통 건물, 집, 상점 등을 생략한다.
This house is **my sister's**.
Alice is at the **hairdresser's**.
We had a nice time at **John and Susan's** last night.

6) 이중소유격; 한정사 + 명사 + of + 소유격
관사, this, that, some, any, no등과 같이 쓸 때 소유격은 of 뒤에

a friend of mine, this book of hers
That policeman is **a friend of mine**.
Here's **that friend of yours**.
I met **another boyfriend of Lucy's** yesterday.
He's **a cousin of the Queen's**.
Have you heard **this new idea of the boss's**?

This bread of ours was warm when we packed it at home on the day we left to come to you.
우리의 이 떡은 우리가 당신들에게 오려고 떠나던 날에 우리들의 집에서 오히려 뜨거운 것을 양식으로 취하였더니(수 9:2).

Everyone who hears **these words of mine** and puts them into practice
누구든지 나의 이 말을 듣고 행하는 자(마 7:24).

For when we came into Macedonia, **this body of ours** had no rest
우리가 마게도나에 이르렀을 때에도 우리 육체가 편치 못하고(고후 7:5).

연습 . 문제

1. Then _____ mother and brothers arrived. Standing outside, they sent someone in to call him.
   1) Jesus'   2) Jesus   3) Jesus's   4) Jesus of

   You yourselves have seen what I did to Egypt, and how I carried you on **eagles' wings** and brought you to myself.
   나의 애굽 사람에게 어떻게 행하였음과 내가 어떻게 독수리 날개로 너희를 업어 내게로 인도하였음을 너희가 보았느니라 (출 19:4).

2. A large herd of pigs _____ feeding on the nearby hillside.
   1) have   2) has   3) was   4) were

3. The herd, about two _____ in number, rushed down the steep bank into the lake and were drowned.
   1) thousands   2) thousand   3) hundreds   4) herds

   Noah was six hundred years old when the floodwaters came on the earth.

4. As far as the gospel is concerned, they _____ on your account.
   1) is enemies   2) is enemy   3) are enemies   4) are enemy

5. People were bringing little _____ to Jesus to have him touch them, but the disciples rebuked them.
   1) children   2) child   3) childs   4) childrens

정답
1) 1, 2) 3, 3) 2, 4) 3, 5) 1

숙어

at every turn; 가는 곳마다, 항상
but we were harassed **at every turn**--conflicts on the outside, fears within.
사방으로 환난을 당하여 밖으로는 다툼이요 안으로는 두려움이라(고후 7:5).

at first; 처음에는, 최초는
Remember the height from which you have fallen! Repent and do the things you did **at first**. If you do not repent, I will come to you and remove your lampstand from its place.
그러므로 어디서 떨어진 것을 생각하고 회개하여 처음 행위를 가지라 만일 그리하지 아니하고 회개치 아니하면 내가 네게 임하여 네 촛대를 그 자리에서 옮기리라(계 2:5).

at once; 동시에, 당장, 즉시
At once the girl hurried in to the king with the request.
저가 곧 왕에게 급히 들어가 구하여 가로되(막 6:25).

The one who received the seed that fell on rocky places is the man who hears the word and **at once** receives it with joy.
돌 밭에 뿌리웠다는 것은 말씀을 듣고 즉시 기쁨으로 받되(마 13:20).

A fool shows his annoyance **at once**, but a prudent man overlooks an insult.
미련한 자는 분노를 당장에 나타내거니와 슬기로운 자는 수욕을 참느니라(잠 12:16).

avenged oneself on; ~에게 복수하다
So the sun stood still, and the moon stopped, till the nation **avenged itself on** its enemies, as it is written in the Book of Jashar. The sun stopped in the middle of the sky and delayed going down about a full day.
태양이 머물고 달이 그치기를 백성이 그 대적에게 원수를 갚도록 하였느니라 야살의 책에 기록되기를 태양이 중천에 머물러서 거의 종일토록 속히 내려가지 아니하였다 하지 아니하였느냐(수 10:13).

bad at (bad in이 아님); 서투른, 익숙하지 못한
I'm not **bad at** tennis.

be about to; 막 ~ 하려고 하다 (be just going to)
Do not be afraid of what you **are about to** suffer
네가 장차 받을 고난을 두려워 말라 볼지어다(계 2:10).

be amazed at; ~에 몹시 놀라다
And he **was amazed at** their lack of faith. Then Jesus went around teaching from village to village.
저희의 믿지 않음을 이상히 여기셨더라. 이에 모든 촌에 두루 다니시며 가르치시더라(막 6:6).

be ashamed of; ~을 부끄러워하다
If anyone **is ashamed of** me and my words, the Son of Man will **be ashamed of** him when he comes in his glory and in the glory of the Father and of the holy angels.
누구든지 나와 내 말을 부끄러워하면 인자도 자기와 아버지와 거룩한 천사들의 영광으로 올 때에 그 사람을 부끄러워하리라(눅 9:26).

be ashamed to; 부끄러워 ~ 하지 못하다
I **was ashamed to** ask the king for soldiers and horsemen to protect us from enemies on the road, because we had told the king, "The gracious hand of our God is on everyone who looks to him, but his great anger is against all who forsake him."
이는 우리가 전에 왕에게 고하기를 우리 하나님의 손은 자기를 찾는 모든 자에게 선을 베푸시고 자기를 배반하는 모든 자에게는 권능과 진노를 베푸신다 하였으므로 길에서 적군을 막고 우리를 도울 보병과 마병을 왕에게 구하기를 부끄러워하였음이라(스 8:22).

be aware of; ~을 알고 있다 (know)
When our enemies heard that we **were aware of** their plot and that God had frustrated it, we all returned to the wall, each to his own work.
그 밤에 시내를 좇아 올라가서 성벽을 살펴본 후에 돌이켜 골짜기 문으로 들어와서 돌아 왔으나(느 2:15).

be concerned about; ~에 관심을 가지다, ~을 걱정하다
An unmarried man **is concerned about** the Lord's affairs--how he can please the Lord.
장가 가지 않은 자는 주의 일을 염려하여 어찌하여야 주를 기쁘시게 할고 하되(고전 7:32).

be credited to; (공로, 명예를) ~에게 돌리다

Is this blessedness only for the circumcised, or also for the uncircumcised? We have been saying that Abraham's faith **was credited to** him as righteousness.
그런즉 이 행복이 할례자에게뇨 혹 무할례자에게도뇨 대저 우리가 말하기를 아브라함에게는 그 믿음을 의로 여기셨다 하노라 (롬 4:9).

And the scripture was fulfilled that says, "Abraham believed God, and it **was credited to** him as righteousness," and he was called God's friend.
이에 경에 이른 바 아브라함이 하나님을 믿으니 이것을 의로 여기셨다는 말씀이 응하였고 그는 하나님의 벗이라 칭함을 받았나니 (약 2:23).

3. 관사(冠詞)
Article

관사의 기능은 여러 사람이나 물건 중에서 하나를 지적하는 것이다. 따라서 주로 보통명사에 붙이며 특별히 지적할 필요가 없는 고유명사나 호격명사에는 관사를 붙이지 않고 추상명사에도 관사를 붙이지 않는 것이 원칙이다. 그러나 섬세한 어감을 표현하기 위해 원칙과 다르게 쓰이는 경우가 많다.

간단하게 말하면,
a(an)는 one of a class의 의미로 쓰이고,
the는 you know exactly which one의 의미로 쓰인다.

I live in a small flat at the top of an old house near the town hall.

모음 앞에서는 an이 쓰인다.

So he immediately sent an executioner with orders to bring John's head. The man went, beheaded John in the prison,
왕이 곧 시위 병 하나를 보내어 요한의 머리를 가져오라 명하니 그 사람이 나가 옥에서 요한을 목 베어 (막 6:27).

A. 부정관사

부정관사인 a, an도 정관사 the와 같이 여러 사람이나 물건 중에서 하나를 지적하는 기능을 가지며, 이야기 중에 처음 나오는 보통명사에 a를 붙여 이야기를 전개하며 그 외에도 다음의 여러 가지 의미로 쓰인다.

No one lights a lamp and hides it in a jar or puts it under a bed.
누구든지 등불을 켜서 그릇으로 덮거나 평상 아래 두지 아니하고(눅 8:16).

1. 종족 대표(a = any)

An unmarried man is concerned about the Lord's affairs--how he can please the Lord.
장가 가지 않은 자는 주의 일을 염려하여 어찌하여야 주를 기쁘시게 할꼬 하되(고전 7:32).

A fool finds pleasure in evil conduct, but a man of understanding delights in wisdom.
미련한 자는 행악으로 낙을 삼는 것 같이 명철한 자는 지혜로 낙을 삼느니라 (잠 10:23).

이 경우는 정관사 the를 사용할 수도 있기 때문에 a와 the 사이에 구별이 없다.

A(The) dog is a faithful animal.

2. a = one

Do not give a war cry, do not raise your voices, do not say **a** word until the day I tell you to shout. Then shout!
너희는 외치지 말며 너희 음성을 들레지 말며 너희 입에서 아무 말도 내지 말라 그리하다가 내가 너희에게 명하여 외치라 하는 날에 외칠지니라 (수 6:10).

3. a = the same

Birds of **a** feather flock together.

4. a = a certain

Then **a** teacher of the law came to him and said.
한 서기관이 나아와 예수께 말씀하되 (마 8:19).

If **a** man sells his daughter as a servant, she is not to go free as menservants do.
사람이 그 딸을 여종으로 팔았으면 그는 남종같이 나오지 못할지며 (출 21:7).

5. a = per

Three times **a** year you are to celebrate a festival to me.
너는 매년 삼 차 내게 절기를 지킬지니라 (출 23:14).

Three times **a** day he got down on his knees and prayed, giving thanks to his God, just as he had done before.
전에 행하던 대로 하루 세 번씩 무릎을 꿇고 기도하며 그 하나님께 감사하였더라 (단 6:10).

6. a = some

The waters rose and covered the mountains to **a** depth of more than twenty feet.
물이 불어서 십오 규빗이 오르매 산들이 덮인지라(창 7:20).

Abram went down to Egypt to live there for **a** while.
아브람이 애굽에 우거하려 하여 그리로 내려갔으니(창 12:10).

You are to worship at **a** distance
여호와에게 올라와 멀리서 경배하고(출 24:1).

7. 감탄문에서 what + a + 단수 가산명사

What a lovely dress! (Not; What lovely dress!)

B. 정관사

명사가 특수화 또는 개별화되면 정관사 the를 붙인다.

1. 앞에 나온 명사를 반복할 때

And God said, "Let there be light," and there was light. God saw that **the** light was good, and he separated **the** light from the darkness.
하나님이 가라사대 빛이 있으라 하시매 빛이 있었고, 그 빛이 하나님의 보시기에 좋았더라. 하나님이 빛과 어두움을 나누사(창 1:3-4).

2. 수식어구로 한정될 때

Besides, she really is my sister, **the** daughter of my father though not of my mother; and she became my wife.
또 그는 실로 나의 이복 누이로서 내 처가 되었음이니라(창 20:12).

3. 전후 관계로 누구나 알 수 있을 때

Now return **the** man's wife, for he is a prophet, and he will pray for you and you will live.
이제 그 사람의 아내를 돌려보내라 그는 선지자라 그가 너를 위하여 기도하리니 네가 살려니와(창 20:7).

4. 종족 대표

As the deer pants for streams of water, so my soul pants for you, O God.
하나님이여 사슴이 시냇물을 찾기에 갈급 함같이 내 영혼이 주를 찾기에 갈급 하니이다(시 42:1).

5. 시간, 수량의 단위를 나타낼 때

Sugar is sold by **the** pound.
I hired a boat by **the** hour.
They sell it by **the** yard.

6. 소유격 대신 관용적으로 쓰이는 the: 신체의 부분을 나타냄

But he took her by **the** hand and said, "My child, get up!"
예수께서 아이의 손을 잡고 불러 가라사대 아이야 일어나라 하시니(눅 8:54).

So they led him by **the** hand into Damascus.
사람의 손에 끌려 다메섹으로 들어가서(행 9:8).

Suddenly an angel of the Lord appeared and a light shone in the cell. He struck Peter on **the** side and woke him up.
홀연히 주의 사자가 곁에 서매 옥중에 광채가 조요하며 또 베드로의 옆구리를 쳐 깨워 가로되(행 12:7).

He stretched out what looked like a hand and took me by **the** hair of my head.
그가 손 같은 것을 펴서 내 머리털 한 모숨을 잡으며(겔 8:3).

They struck this man on **the** head and treated him shamefully.
그의 머리에 상처를 내고 능욕하였거늘(막 12:4).

7. 관용구

In **the** beginning God created the heavens and the earth.
태초에 하나님이 천지를 창조하시니라(창 1:1).

The great God has shown the king what will take place in **the** future.
크신 하나님이 장래 일을 왕께 알게 하신 것이라(단 2:45).

This is the message you heard from **the** beginning
이는 너희가 처음부터 들은 소식이라(요일 3:11).

8. 유일한 것에는 the를 붙인다

Look at the birds of the air.
공중의 새를 보라(마 6:26).

Many will come from **the** east and **the** west
동서로부터 많은 사람이 이르러(마 8:11).

The birds of **the** air come and perch in its branches.
공중의 새들이 와서 그 가지에 깃들이느니라(마 13:32).

The field is **the** world
밭은 세상이요(마 13:38).

Saul got up from **the** ground.
사울이 땅에서 일어나(행 9:8).

Do you not know that the saints will judge **the** world?
성도가 세상을 판단할 것을 너희가 알지 못하느냐(고전 6:2).

In the same way, let your light shine before men, that they may see your good deeds and praise your Father **in heaven**. (in heaven; 천국에 가서, 죽어서)
저희로 너희 착한 행실을 보고 하늘에 계신 너희 아버지께 영광을 돌리게 하라(마 5:16).

9. 악기

I would like to learn **the** piano.
그러나 jazz나 pop music에서는 the를 쓰지 않는다.
This recording was made with Miles Davis on trumpet.

10. last와 the last

last week, last month; 지난 주, 지난 달
the last week, the last month; 말하는 시점에서 지난 일주일간(7일), 한 달간(30일)
I had a cold last week. (지난 주)
Were you at the meeting last Tuesday?
We bought this house last year.

I've had a cold for the last week. (= for the seven days up to today)
We've lived here for the last year.

11. next와 the next

next week, next month; 다음 주, 다음 달
the next week, the next month; 말하는 시점에서 다음 일주일간(7일), 한 달간(30일)

Goodbye! See you **next week**!
I'm spending **next Christmas** with my family.
Next year will be difficult (= the year starting next January)

I'm going to be very busy **the next week**. (= the seven days starting today)
The next year will be difficult. (= the twelve months starting now.)

C. 정관사와 고유명사

1. 강, 바다의 이름

the Han River, the Atlantic, the Thames, the Pacific

As Jesus was walking beside **the** Sea of Galilee
갈릴리 해변에 다니시다가 (마 4:18).

2. 반도, 군도, 해협, 산맥 등의 이름

the Korean Peninsula, the Malay Peninsula, the Philippines, the English Channel, the Alps, the West Indies, the Magellan Strait, the Rocky Mountains

The whole Israelite community set out from **the** Desert of Sin, traveling from place to place as the LORD commanded.
이스라엘 자손의 온 회중이 여호와의 명령대로 신 광야에서 떠나 그 노정대로 행하여 (출 17:1).

3. 어떤 나라의 이름이나 지명

the United States of America, the Sahara, the U.S.S.R., the Netherlands, the Hague, the Riviera

4. 관공서, 공공 건물

the White House, the London Zoo, the British Museum

역, 항구, 호수, 다리, 공항, 공원에는 일반적으로 the를 안 붙인다.
Pusan Harbor, Lake Como, Waterloo Bridge, Kimpo Airport

5. 배, 열차, 항공기, 철로의 이름

the Mayflower, the Pullman, the Comet, the Queen Mary, the Jet Arrow

6. 학회, 협회, 연구소의 이름

the Royal Society, the British Broadcasting Corporation, the Royal Academy

7. 신문의 이름

the New York Times, the Washington Post

그러나 잡지는 the를 붙이지 않는다.
Time, Newsweek, Punch, New Scientist

8. 성질을 나타내는 형용사가 인명에 붙을 때는 the를 붙인다

The ambitious Caesar

그러나 old, young, dear, great, good등 흔한 형용사가 올 때는 the를 붙이지 않는다.
Honest Dick

9. 국어 이름과 특정한 말을 나타낼 때

the English language
What is the German for the English flower?

D. 관사의 위치

1. so, as, too, how, however + 형용사 + a + 명사

He is **as kind a boy** as you are.

When they had done so, they caught such a large number of fish that their nets began to break.
그리한 즉 고기를 에운 것이 심히 많아 그물이 찢어지는지라(눅 5:6).

2. quite, rather 다음에는 부정 관사

He is **quite a** good fisherman.
She is **rather a** beautiful woman.

3. all, both, double + the + 명사

I will give you honor and praise among **all the peoples** of the earth.
너희로 천하 만민 중에서 명성과 칭찬을 얻게 하리라(습 3:20).

Of **all the creatures** living in the water
물에 있는 모든 것 중(레 11:9).

But a Pharisee named Gamaliel, a teacher of the law, who was honored by **all the people**, stood up in the Sanhedrin
바리새인 가말리엘은 교법사로 모든 백성에게 존경을 받는 자라 공회 중에 일어나(행 5:34).

But the LORD is in his holy temple; let **all the earth** be silent before him.
오직 여호와는 그 성전에 계시니 온 천하는 그 앞에서 잠잠할지니라(합 2:20).

I will give you **all their authority** and splendor, for it has been given to me.
이 모든 권세와 그 영광을 내가 네게 주리라 이것은 내게 넘겨준 것이므로(눅 4:6).

Take double the amount of silver with you, for you must return the silver that was put back into the mouths of your sacks.
너희 손에 돈을 배나 가지고 너희 자루 아구에 도로 넣어 온 그 돈을 다시 가지고 가라 (창 43:12).

E. 관사의 생략

1. 호격

Teacher, I will follow you wherever you go.
선생님이여 어디로 가시든지 저는 좇으리이다 (마 8:19).

Father, if you are willing, take this cup from me;
가라사대 아버지여 만일 아버지의 뜻이어 든 이 잔을 내게서 옮기시옵소서 (눅 22:42).

Away from me, **Satan**!
사단아 물러가라 (마 4:10).

2. 가족 관계

Without **father** or **mother**, without genealogy, without beginning of days or end of life, like the Son of God he remains a priest forever.
아비도 없고 어미도 없고 족보도 없고 시작한 날도 없고 생명의 끝도 없어 하나님 아들과 방불하여 항상 제사장으로 있느니라 (히 7:3).

3. 고유명사 앞에 붙는 관직, 칭호, 신분을 나타내는 말

President Bush

4. 식사, 질병, 운동의 이름

He is suffering from **fever**.
Plague went before him; **pestilence** followed his steps.
온역이 그 앞에서 행하며 불덩이가 그 발 밑에서 나오도다(합 3:5).

5. man(인간, 남성), woman(여성)

Man does not live on bread alone, but on every word that comes from the mouth of God.
사람이 떡으로만 살 것이 아니요 하나님의 입으로 나오는 모든 말씀으로 살 것이라(마 4:4).

6. 관직 혹은 신분을 나타내는 말이 보어로 쓰였을 때: 이런 경우는 명사가 보어로써 형용사처럼 쓰인 것임

This Melchizedek was **king** of Salem and **priest** of God Most High.
이 멜기세덱은 살렘 왕이요 지극히 높으신 하나님의 제사장이라(히 7:1).

Where is the one who has been born **king** of the Jews?
유대인의 왕으로 나신 이가 어디 계시뇨(마 2:2).

A man named Sheshbazzar, whom he had appointed **governor**.
그 세운 총독 세스바살이라 이름한 자(스 5:14).

7. a kind of, a sort of 다음에는 일반적으로 관사가 없음

There is a kind of **man** who curses his father, and does not bless his mother.
아비를 저주하며 어미를 축복하지 아니하는 무리가 있느니라(잠 30:11).

8. 짝을 이루는 두 개의 명사가 전치사 혹은 접속사로 밀접하게 연결될 때

Morning by **morning** he dispenses his justice.
아침마다 간단없이 자기의 공의를 나타내시거늘(습 3:5).

Sun and moon stood still in the heavens.
해와 달이 그 처소에 멈추었나이다(합 3:11).

We are the servants of the God of **heaven and earth**
우리는 천지의 하나님의 종이라(스 5:11).

Where is **bread and wine**?
곡식과 포도주가 어디 있느뇨(아 2:12).

For he had often been chained **hand and foot**, but he tore the chains apart and broke the irons on his feet.
이는 여러 번 고랑과 쇠사슬에 매였어도 쇠사슬을 끊고 고랑을 깨뜨렸음이러라(막 5:4).

9. 공공 건물 等이 본래의 목적으로 쓰일 때

Woe, woe, the great city, in which all who had ships **at sea** became rich by her wealth, for in one hour she has been laid waste!
화 있도다 화 있도다 이 큰 성이여, 바다에서 배 부리는 모든 자들이 너의 보배로운 상품을 인하여 치부하였더니 일시간에 망하였도다(계 18:19).

10. 관용구

1) 전치사 + 명사

to/at/from school/university/college/work
to/at/in/into/from church
to/in/into/out of bed/prison/hospital
to/at sea
to/in/from town
at/from home
for/at/to breakfast/lunch/dinner/supper
at night
by car/bus/bicycle/plane/train/tube/boat

on foot, go to sleep, watch television(TV), on TV

At daybreak Jesus went out to a solitary place.
날이 밝으매 예수께서 나오사 한적한 곳에 가시니(눅 4:42).

I have seen slaves **on horseback**, while princes go **on foot** like slaves.
또 보았노니 종들은 말을 타고 방백들은 종처럼 땅에 걸어 다니는도다(전 10:7).

If anyone eats a sacred offering **by mistake**, he must make restitution to the priest for the offering and add a fifth of the value to it.
사람이 부지 중 성물을 먹으면 그 성물에 그 오분 일을 더하여 제사장에게 줄지니라(레 22:14).

Darkness comes upon them in the daytime; **at noon** they grope as in the night.
그들은 낮에도 캄캄함을 만나고, 대낮에도 더듬기를 밤과 같이 하느니라(욥 5:14).

He knows the day of darkness is at hand.
흑암한 날이 가까운 줄을 스스로 아느니라(욥 15:23).

2) 동사 + 명사

take place; 일어나다

This will **take place** on the day when God will judge men's secrets through Jesus Christ, as my gospel declares.
곧 내 복음에 이른 바와 같이 하나님이 예수 그리스도로 말미암아 사람들의 은밀한 것을 심판하시는 그 날이라 (롬 2:16).

I will climb the palm tree; I will **take hold** of its fruit.
종려나무에 올라가서 그 가지를 잡으리라(아 7:8).

Take part in ~; ~에 참가하다
Catch cold; 감기들다
Lose sight of; 시야에서 놓치다
Keep house; 살림을 하다
Take hold of; 잡다, 쥐다

11. 신문의 헤드라인

Man killed on mountain

12. 안내문, 포스터

Super Cinema, Ritz Hotel, Open packet at other end

13. 메모

I think company needs new office.

F. 관사의 생략과 반복

But everything should be done in **a** fitting and orderly way.
모든 것을 적당하게 하고 질서대로 하라 (고전 14:40).

See, I lay a stone in Zion, **a** chosen and precious cornerstone
보라 내가 택한 보배롭고 요긴한 모퉁이 돌을 시온에 두노니 (벧전 2:6).

연습 문제

1. Jesus went through _____ towns and villages, teaching in their synagogues, preaching the good news of the kingdom and healing every disease and sickness.
   1) all the   2) all   3) all of   4) every

   All her idols will be broken to pieces; all her temple gifts will be burned with fire; I will destroy all her images.
   I will pour out my Spirit on all people.
   Heal the sick, raise the dead, cleanse those who have leprosy, drive out demons.

2. The blind receive sight, _____ walk, those who have leprosy are cured.
   1) the lamed   2) the lame   3) the weak   4) the old

   My shield is God Most High, who saves **the upright** in heart.
   The LORD is known by his justice; **the wicked** are ensnared by the work of their hands.

   The poor are shunned even by their neighbors, but **the rich** have many friends.
   가난한 자는 그 이웃에게도 미움을 받게 되나, 부요한 자는 친구가 많으니라(잠 14:20).

   Now I know that the LORD saves **his anointed.**

3. Though it is the smallest of all your seeds, yet when it grows, it is the largest of garden plants and becomes a tree, so that the birds of _____ come and perch in its branches.
   1) air   2) airs   3) the airs   4) the air

4. Then the righteous will shine like _____ in the kingdom of their Father.
   1) the sun   2) a sun   3) sun   4) suns

   The LORD said, "Throw it on **the** ground." Moses threw it on **the** ground and it became a snake, and he ran from it.

여호와께서 가라사대 그것을 땅에 던지라 곧 땅에 던지니 그것이 뱀이 된지라 모세가 뱀 앞에서 피하매 (출 4:3).

5. He had often been chained _____ and foot.
   1) the hand   2) hand   3) hands   4) the hands

6. _____ among the tombs and in the hills he would cry out and cut himself with stones.
   1) The night and day   2) The night and the day   3) night and the day   4) Night and day

Men will stagger from sea to sea and wander from north to east.

7. When he saw Jesus from _____ , he ran and fell on his knees in front of him.
   1) distance   2) a distance   3) the distance   4) distances

8. He took the blind man by _____ and led him outside the village.
   1) the hand   2) his hand   3) hand   4) a hand

Strike all my enemies on the jaw; break the teeth of the wicked.

9. As soon as _____ saw Jesus, they were overwhelmed with wonder and ran to greet him.
   1) all the people   2) all people   3) all peoples   4) all of people

The wealth of all the surrounding nations will be collected.
He makes all the rivers run dry
New wine will drip from the mountains and flow from all the hills.

10. He has sent me to proclaim freedom for the prisoners and recovery of _____ for the blind, to release the oppressed.
    1) sights   2) sight   3) a sight   4) seeing

11. God chose the foolish things of _____ to shame the wise; God chose the weak things of the world to shame the strong.

1) a world   2) worlds   3) the world   4) world

12. All the brothers here send you _____.
    1) greetings   2) greeting   3) a greeting   4) the greetings

13. I have not found anyone in Israel with _____ great faith.
    1) as   2) so a   3) such   4) such a

14. What goes into _____'s mouth does not make him unclean, but what comes out of his mouth, that is what makes him unclean.
    1) men   2) the men   3) a man   4) man

15. There ____ centurion's servant, whom his master valued highly, was sick and about to die.
    1) is a   2) is   3) was a   4) a

정답
1) 1, 2) 2, 3) 4, 4) 1, 5) 2, 6) 4, 7) 2, 8) 1, 9) 1, 10) 2
11) 3, 12) 1, 13) 3, 14) 3, 15) 4

숙어

be determined to; 굳게 결심한, 단호한
When the king heard this, he was greatly distressed; he **was determined to** rescue Daniel and made every effort until sundown to save him.
왕이 이 말을 듣고 그로 인하여 심히 근심하여 다니엘을 구원하려고 마음을 쓰며 그를 건져 내려고 힘을 다하여 해가 질 때까지 이르매(단 6:14).

be devoted to; 헌신적인, 열렬히 사랑하는, 애정이 깊은
Be devoted to one another in brotherly love. Honor one another above yourselves.
형제를 사랑하여 서로 우애하고 존경하기를 서로 먼저 하며(롬 12:10).

The city and all that is in it are to **be devoted to** the LORD. Only Rahab the prostitute and all who are with her in her house shall be spared, because she hid the spies we sent.
이 성과 그 가운데 모든 물건은 여호와께 바치니 기생 라합과 무릇 그 집에 동거하는 자는 살리라 이는 그가 우리의 보낸 사자를 숨겼음이니라(수 6:17).

be filled with; 차다, ~으로 충만하다
Everyone **was filled with** awe, and many wonders and miraculous signs were done by the apostles.
사람마다 두려워하는데 사도들로 인하여 기사와 표적이 많이 나타나니(행 2:43).

be guilty of; ~의 죄를 범하다
But whoever blasphemes against the Holy Spirit will never be forgiven; he **is guilty of** an eternal sin.
누구든지 성령을 훼방하는 자는 사하심을 영원히 얻지 못하고 영원한 죄에 처하느니라(막 3:29).

be out of one's mind; 제정신이 아니다, 미치다
So if the whole church comes together and everyone speaks in tongues, and some who do not understand or some unbelievers come in, will they not say that you **are out of your mind**?
그러므로 온 교회가 함께 모여 다 방언으로 말하면 무식한 자들이나 믿지 아니하는 자들이 들어와서 너희를 미쳤다 하지 아니하겠느냐(고전 14:23).

be possessed by; (귀신에게) 홀리다
When they came to Jesus, they saw the man who had **been possessed by** the legion of demons, sitting there, dressed and in his right mind; and they were afraid.
예수께 이르러 그 귀신 들렸던 자 곧 군대 지폈던 자가 옷을 입고 정신이 온전하여 앉은 것을 보고 두려워하더라(막 5:15).

be proud of; 자랑하다
They **were proud of** their beautiful jewelry and used it to make their detestable idols and vile images. Therefore I will turn these into an unclean thing for them.
그들이 그 화려한 장식으로 인하여 교만을 품었고 또 그것으로 가증한 우상과 미운 물건을 지었은 즉 내가 그것으로 그들에게 오예물이 되게 하여(겔 7:20).

I will give them praise and honor in every land where they **were put to shame**.
온 세상에서 수욕 받는 자로 청찬과 명성을 얻게 하리라(습 3:19).

be subject to; 지배를 받는, (피해 등을) 받기 쉬운, ~ 되기 쉬운, 조건으로서 ~을 필요로 하는
He **is subject to** guardians and trustees until the time set by his father.
그 아버지의 정한 때까지 후견인과 청지기 아래 있나니(갈 4:1-2).

I tell you that anyone who is angry with his brother will **be subject to** judgment.
나는 너희에게 이르노니 형제에게 노하는 자마다 심판을 받게 되고(마 5:22).

And a woman was there who had **been subject to** bleeding for twelve years.
열 두 해를 혈루증으로 앓는 한 여자가 있어(막 5:25).

But he himself **is not subject to** any man's judgment.
자기는 아무에게도 판단을 받지 아니하느니라(고전 2:15).

be worth ~ing; ~할 가치가 있다
Our present sufferings **are not worth comparing** with the glory that will be revealed in us.
생각건대 현재의 고난은 장차 우리에게 나타날 영광과 족히 비교할 수 없도다(롬 8:18).

be worthy of; ~하기에 족한, ~에 알맞은

Anyone who loves his father or mother more than me **is not worthy of** me; anyone who loves his son or daughter more than me is not worthy of me;
아비나 어미를 나보다 더 사랑하는 자는 내게 합당치 아니하고, 아들이나 딸을 나보다 더 사랑하는 자도 내게 합당치 아니하고 (마 10:37).

And anyone who does not take his cross and follow me **is not worthy of** me.
또 자기 십자가를 지고 나를 좇지 않는 자도 내게 합당치 아니하니라 (마 10:38).

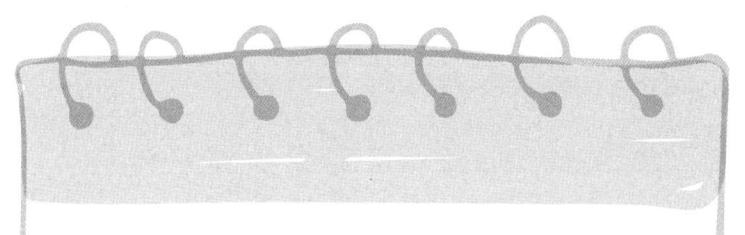

4. 대명사(代名詞)
Pronoun

대명사에는 인칭, 지시, 부정, 의문 및 관계대명사가 있으나, 용법에 따라 하나의 대명사가 여러 가지 대명사로 분류될 수 있다.

A. 인칭대명사

인칭대명사는 명사와 같이 수(number), 성(gender), 격(case) 및 인격(person)의 구별이 있다.

1. 일반인을 지칭; we, you, they

Yet **you** have a few people in Sardis who have not soiled their clothes.
그러나 사데에 그 옷을 더럽히지 아니한 자 몇 명이 네게 있어 (계 3:4).

2. It의 용법

1) 시간, 날씨, 거리, 현재 상태

(1) 시간
It is ten o'clock.
It is Monday again.
It took me months to get to know her.
How long does **it** take to get to Pusan from here?

Let me go, for **it** is daybreak.
날이 새려 하니 나로 가게 하라 (창 32:26).

By this time **it** was late in the day, so his disciples came to him. "This is a remote place," they said, "and **it**'s already very late.
때가 저물어 가매 제자들이 예수께 나아와 여짜오되 이곳은 빈 들이요 때도 저물어가니 (막 6:35).

(2) 날씨
It rained for three days.

It's thirty degree.

But there are many people here and *it* is the rainy season; so we cannot stand outside.
그러나 백성이 많고 또 큰 비가 내리는 때니 능히 밖에 서지 못할 것이요(스 10:13).

(3) 거리
It's ten miles to the nearest petrol station.

(4) 현재 상태
It's terrible. Everybody has colds, and the central heating isn't working.
Isn't it lovely here?

2) it의 기타 용법
문장의 주어가 to부정사이거나 절일 경우에는 문장의 첫머리에 잘 두지 않고 대신 it를 첫머리에 놓는다.

(1) 가주어

① **It + be + 형용사 + to 부정사**
It's nice to be with you.(To be with you is nice도 가능하지만 잘 쓰이지 않는다.)
It's probable that we'll be a little late.

It is lawful **to do** good on the Sabbath.
안식일에 선을 행하는 것이 옳으니라(마 12:12).

It is mine **to avenge**: I will repay.
원수 갚는 것이 내게 있으니 내가 갚으리라(롬 12:19).

It is good **for** us **to be** here.
우리가 여기 있는 것이 좋사오니(눅 9:33).

② **It + be + 형용사 + 절**
It's possible that I'll be here again next week.
It's surprising how many unhappy people there are.

It wasn't clear **what** she meant.
Is **it** true **that** your father's ill?

How is **it**, then, **that** you force Gentiles to follow Jewish customs?
어찌하여 억지로 이방인을 유대인답게 살게 하려느냐(갈 2:14).

Why then is **it** written **that** the Son of Man must suffer much and be rejected?
어찌 인자에 대하여 기록하기를 많은 고난을 받고 멸시를 당하리라(막 9:12).

Is **it** true, Shadrach, Meshach and Abednego, **that** you do not serve my gods or worship the image of gold I have set up?
사드락, 메삭, 아벳느고야 너희가 내 신을 섬기지 아니하며 내가 세운 그 신상에게 절하지 아니하니 짐짓 그리 하였느냐(단 3:14).

③ 기타
It's worth going to Seoul if you have the time.
It's no use trying to explain. I'm not interested.
It was nice seeing you.

(2) 가목적어
make it clear that, find it easy/difficult to, make it easy/difficult to에서 자주 쓰임

He made it clear that he wasn't interested.
I found it easy to talk to her.
You make it difficult to refuse.

Make **it** your ambition **to lead** a quiet life, **to mind** your own business and **to work** with your hands
종용하여 자기 일을 하고 너희 손으로 일하기를 힘쓰라(살전 4:11).

Furthermore, since they did not think **it** worthwhile **to retain** the knowledge of God,
또한 저희가 마음에 하나님 두기를 싫어하매(롬 1:28).

They owe it to the Jews to share with them their material blessings.
육신의 것으로 그들을 섬기는 것이 마땅하니라(롬 15:27).

So I thought it necessary to urge the brothers to visit you in advance and finish the arrangements for the generous gift you had promised.
이러므로 내가 이 형제들로 먼저 너희에게 가서 너희의 전에 약속한 연보를 미리 준비케 하도록 권면 하는 것이 필요한 줄 생각하였노니(고후 9:5).

They think it strange that you do not plunge with them into the same flood of dissipation, and they heap abuse on you.
이러므로 너희가 저희와 함께 그런 극한 방탕에 달음질하지 아니하는 것을 저희가 이상히 여겨 비방하나(벧전 4:4).

3) it ~ that의 강조 구문

If the spots are dull white, it is a harmless rash that has broken out on the skin;
그 피부의 색점이 부유스름하면 이는 피부에 발한 어루러기라(레 13:39).

It is by the prince of demons that he drives out demons.
지가 귀신의 왕을 빙자하여 귀신을 쫓아낸다(마 9:34).

It is not the healthy who need a doctor, but the sick.
건강한 자에게는 의원이 쓸데 없고 병든 자에게라야 쓸데 있느니라(마 9:12).

As you know, it was because of an illness that I first preached the gospel to you.
내가 처음에 육체의 약함을 인하여 너희에게 복음을 전한 것을 너희가 아는 바라(갈 4:13).

3. 소유대명사

mine, yours, his, hers, ours, theirs
소유대명사는 독립적으로 쓰인다.

In the days of her affliction and wandering Jerusalem remembers all the treasures that were hers in days of old.
예루살렘이 환난과 군박을 당하는 날에 옛날의 모든 즐거움을 생각함이여(애 1:7).

They said to him, "John's disciples often fast and pray, and so do the disciples of the Pharisees, but **yours** go on eating and drinking."
저희가 예수께 말하되 요한의 제자는 자주 금식하며 기도하고 바리새인의 제자들도 또한 그리하되 당신의 제자들은 먹고 마시나이다(눅 5:33).

명사의 소유격과 마찬가지로 a, some, any, no, this, that 따위와 같이 인칭대명사의 소유격을 쓸 때는 a friend of mine형이 된다(이중소유격).

Therefore everyone who hears **these words of mine** and puts them into practice is like a wise man who built his house on the rock.
그러므로 누구든지 나의 이 말을 듣고 행하는 자는 그 집을 반석위에 지은 지혜로운 사람 같으리니(마 7:24).

For when we came into Macedonia, **this body of ours** had no rest, but we were harassed at every turn--conflicts on the outside, fears within.
우리가 마게도냐에 이르렀을때에도 우리 육체가 편치 못하고 사방으로 환난을 당하여 밖으로는 다툼이요 안으로는 두려움이라(고후 7:5).

4. 재귀대명사

myself, yourself, himself, herself, itself, oneself, oneself, yourselves, ourselves, themselves

1) 목적어가 주어와 같을 때

We got out of the river and dried **ourselves**.
Why's she talking to **herself**?

단, 전치사 뒤에서는 인칭대명사를 쓴다.
She took her dog **with her**.

At this, some of the teachers of the law said to **themselves**, "This fellow is blaspheming!"
어떤 서기관들이 속으로 이르되 이 사람이 참람하도다(마 9:3).

The officers posted **themselves** behind all the people of Judah.
민장은 유다 온 족속의 뒤에 있었으며(느 4:16).

Guard **yourself** in your spirit, and do not break faith with the wife of your youth.
그러므로 네 심령을 삼가 지켜 어려서 취한 아내에게 궤사를 행치 말지니라(말 2:15).

wash, dress, shave 다음에는 재귀대명사를 쓰지 않는다.
Do you shave on Sundays?

2) "혼자, 단 하나"의 의미

It's quicker if you do it **yourself**.
The manager spoke to me **himself**.
The house **itself** is nice, but the garden's very small.

I **myself** will drive them out before the Israelites.
　내가 그들을 이스라엘 자손 앞에서 쫓아 내리니(수 13:6).

3) 강조

For I **myself** am a man under authority, with soldiers under me.
나도 남의 수하에 있는 사람이요 내 아래도 군사가 있으니(마 8:9).

4) By myself, by yourself 등은 두 가지 뜻으로 쓰인다

(1) Alone (혼자서)
I often like to spend time **by myself**.

In the same way, faith **by itself**, if it is not accompanied by action, is dead.
이와 같이 행함이 없는 믿음은 그 자체가 죽은 것이라(약 2:17).

I tell you the truth, the Son can do nothing **by himself**; he can do only what he sees his Father doing
내가 진실로 진실로 너희에게 이르노니 아들이 아버지의 하시는 일을 보지 않고는 아무것도 스스로 할 수 없나니(요 5:19).

(2) **Without help**(혼자 힘으로)
Can I help you? No, thanks. I can do it **by myself**.

I cannot carry all these people **by myself**; the burden is too heavy for me.
책임이 심히 중하여 나 혼자는 이 모든 백성을 질 수 없나이다(민 11:14).

5) for oneself; 스스로

Judge **for yourselves**.
너희는 스스로 판단하라(고전 11:13).

6) in itself; 스스로, 본질적으로

As one who is in the Lord Jesus, I am fully convinced that no food is unclean **in itself**.
내가 주 예수 안에서 알고 확신하는 것은 무엇이든지 스스로 속된 것이 없으되(롬 14:14).

B. 지시대명사

지시대명사는 일정한 사람이나 물건을 지시하는 기능을 가지며 this, that, these, those의 네 단어가 있다.

1. this, that

I tell **this** one, 'Go,' and he goes; and **that** one, 'Come,' and he comes. I say to my servant, 'Do **this**,' and he does it."
이더러 가라 하면 가고 저더러 오라 하면 오고 내 종더러 이것을 하라 하면 하나이다(마 8:9).
(앞의 this와 that는 형용사, 뒤의 this는 대명사)

For I tell you that unless your righteousness surpasses **that** of the Pharisees and the teachers of the law, you will certainly not enter the kingdom of heaven. (that = righteousness)
내가 너희에게 이르노니 너희 의가 서기관과 바리새인보다 더 낫지 못하면 결단코 천국에 들어가지 못하리라 (마 5:20).

The beast I saw resembled a leopard, but had feet like **those** of a bear and a mouth like **that** of a lion. (Those = feet, that = a mouth)
내가 본 짐승은 표범과 비슷하고, 그 발은 곰의 발 같고, 그 입은 사자의 입 같은데(계 13:2).

1) 전자, 후자

The latter do so in love, knowing that I am put here for the defense of the gospel. **The former** preach Christ out of selfish ambition, not sincerely, supposing that they can stir up trouble for me while I am in chains.

이들은 내가 복음을 변명하기 위하여 세우심을 받은 줄 알고 사랑으로 하나 저들은 나의 매임에 괴로움을 더하게 할 줄로 생각하여 순전치 못하게 다툼으로 그리스도를 전파하느니라(빌1:16~17).

(the latter; 후자, the former; 전자)

2) this는 앞 문장 전체를 받는다

If your enemy is hungry, feed him; if he is thirsty, give him something to drink. In doing **this**, you will heap burning coals on his head.

네 원수가 주리거든 먹이고 목마르거든 마시우라. 그리함으로 네가 숯불을 그 머리에 쌓아 놓으리라(롬 12:20).

3) those who; ~하는 사람들

Blessed are **those who** hunger and thirst for righteousness, for they will be filled.

의에 주리고 목마른 자는 복이 있나니 저희가 배부를 것임이요(마 5:6).

From now on **those who** have wives should live as if they had none;

이 후부터 아내 있는 자들은 없는 사같이 하여(고진 7:29).

His mercy extends to **those who** fear him, from generation to generation.

긍휼하심이 두려워하는 자에게 대대로 이르는도다(눅 1:50).

Those who survived the exile and are back in the province are in great trouble and disgrace.

사로잡힘을 면하고 남은 자가 그 도에서 큰 환난을 만나고 능욕을 받으며(느 1:3).

O LORD, God of heaven, the great and awesome God, who keeps his covenant of love with **those who** love him and obey his commands

하늘의 하나님 여호와 크고 두려우신 하나님이여, 주를 사랑하고 주의 계명을 지키는 자에게 언약을 지키시며 긍휼을 베푸시는 주여(느 1:5).

he has scattered **those who** are proud in their inmost thoughts.

마음의 생각이 교만한 자들을 흩으셨고(눅 1:51).

Watch out for those dogs, **those men who** do evil, those mutilators of the flesh.
개들을 삼가고 행악하는 자들을 삼가고 손할례 당을 삼가라(빌 3:2).

Those whom I love I rebuke and discipline. So be earnest, and repent.
무릇 내가 사랑하는 자를 책망하여 징계하노니 그러므로 네가 열심을 내라 회개하라(계 3:19).

How much more will your Father in heaven give good gifts to **those who** ask him!
하물며 하늘에 계신 너희 아버지께서 구하는 자에게 좋은 것으로 주시지 않겠느냐(마 7:11).

4) he who; ~하는 사람

Then all the churches will know that I am **he who** searches hearts and minds
모든 교회가 나는 사람의 뜻과 마음을 살피는 자인 줄 알지라(계 2:23).

This is **he who** was spoken of through the prophet Isaiah
저는 선지자 이사야로 말씀하신 자라(마 3:3).

These are the words of **him who** is holy and true, who holds the key of David.
거룩하고 진실하사 다윗의 열쇠를 가지신 이(계 3:7).

Him who overcomes I will make a pillar in the temple of my God.
이기는 자는 내 하나님 성전에 기둥이 되게 하리니(계 3:12).

Blessed is the **one who** reads the words of this prophecy, and blessed are **those who** hear it and take to heart what is written in it, because the time is near.
이 예언의 말씀을 읽는 자와 듣는 자들과 그 가운데 기록한 것을 지키는 자들이 복이 있나니 때가 가까움이라 (계 1:3).

2. such

1) 대명사로 쓰일 때

And **such** was his practice as long as he lived in Philistine territory.
(다윗이). 블레셋 사람의 지방에 거하는 동안에 이같이 행하는 습관이 있(었).다(삼상 27:11).

Your beauty should not come from outward adornment, **such** as braided hair and the wearing of gold jewelry and fine clothes.
너희 단장은 머리를 꾸미고 금을 차고 아름다운 옷을 입는 외모로 하지 말고(벧전 3:3).

Let the little children come to me, and do not hinder them, for the kingdom of heaven belongs to **such** as these.
어린아이들을 용납하고 내게 오는 것을 금하지 말라. 천국이 이런 자의 것이니라(마 19:14).

2) 형용사로 쓰일 때

such + a + 형용사 + 명사
단 명사가 단수 보통 명사일 경우에만 a를 쓸 수 있음

He is **such** a wicked man that no one can talk to him.
주인은 불량한 사람이라 더불어 말할 수 없나이다(삼상 25:17).

And I am not writing this in the hope that you will do **such** things for me.
또 이 말을 쓰는 것은 내게 이같이 하여 달라는 것이 아니라(고전 9:15).

Today they sacrificed their sin offering and their burnt offering before the LORD, but **such** things as this have happened to me.
오늘 그들이 그 속죄제와 번제를 여호와께 드렸어도 이런 일이 내게 임하였거늘(레 10:19).

Avoid **such** men as these.
이 같은 자들에게서 네가 돌아서라(딤후 3:5).

All Israel raised **such** a great shout that the ground shook.
온 이스라엘이 큰 소리로 외치매 땅이 울린지라(삼상 4:5).

Who is he? Where is the man who has dared to do **such** a thing?
감히 이런 일을 심중에 품은 자가 누구며 그가 어디 있느뇨(에 7:5).

I have not found anyone in Israel with **such** great faith.
이스라엘 중 아무에게서도 이만한 믿음을 만나보지 못하였노라(마 8:10).

3. the same; same에는 항상 the를 붙인다

1) 명사로 쓰일 때

Give me the same again. Please.

The man with two tunics should share with him who has none, and the one who has food should do the same. (do의 목적어)
옷 두 벌 있는 자는 옷 없는 자에게 나눠 줄 것이요, 먹을 것이 있는 자도 그렇게 할 것이니라(눅 3:11).

Do the same with your cattle and your sheep.
너의 소와 양도 그 일례로 하되(출 22:30).

2) 형용사로 쓰일 때

I want the same shirt as my friends.

In the same way, the Spirit helps us in our weakness.
이와 같이 성령도 우리 연약함을 도우시나니(롬 8:26).

They think it strange that you do not plunge with them into the same flood of dissipation.
너희가 저희와 함께 그런 극한 방탕에 달음질하지 아니하는 것을 저희가 이상히 여겨(벧전 4:4).

the same as와 the same that
the same as + (대)명사
Her hair's the same color as her mother's
The same that + 절
That's the same man that asked me for money yesterday.

3) 부사로 쓰일 때

Join five of the curtains together, and do the same with the other five.
그 앙장 다섯 폭을 서로 연하며, 다른 다섯 폭도 서로 연하고(출 26:3).

C. 부정대명사

1. One

1) 일반인 (one = anybody, speaker를 포함)

One usually knocks at a door before going into somebody's house.
Somebody's knocking at the door. (Not; One is knocking ---)
One can usually find people who speak English in Sweden.
One has to believe in something.
In the sixteenth century people believed in witches. (Not; --- one believed ---)

The one who trusts in him will never be put to shame.
저를 믿는 자는 부끄러움을 당치 아니 하리라 (롬 9:33).

The one who is least in the kingdom of God is greater than he.
하나님의 나라에서는 극히 작은 자라도 저보다 크니라 (눅 7:28).

No one sews a patch of unshrunk cloth on an old garment
생베 조각을 낡은 옷에 붙이는 자가 없나니 (막 2:21).

2) 명사의 반복을 회피

I'm looking for a flat. I'd like one with a garden. (= --- a flat with a garden)
Can you lend me a pen? Sorry, I haven't got one.
Which is your chair? The one in the blue coat.

Then it will be ready as a generous gift, not as one grudgingly given.
이렇게 준비하여야 참 연보답고 억지가 아니니라 (고후 9:5).

We are rebuilding the temple that was built many years ago, one that a great king of Israel built and finished.
오랜 옛적에 건축되었던 전을 우리가 다시 건축하노라 이는 본래 이스라엘의 큰 왕이 완전히 건축한 것이더니 (스 5:11).

(1) a + 형용사 + one

I'd like **a big one** with cream on.
I'd like **one** with cream on.

(2) **The 및 형용사 다음에는 복수형이 올 수 있다; ones**

Which showed do you want? The **ones** at the front of the window.
How much are the red **ones**?
I have five green **ones**.
I have **five**. (Not; five ones)

Of all the animals that live on land, these are the **ones** you may eat:
육지 모든 짐승 중 너희의 먹을만한 생물은 이러하니 (레 11:2).

They served as judges for the people at all times. The difficult cases they brought to Moses, but the simple **ones** they decided themselves.
그들이 때를 따라 백성을 재판하되 어려운 일은 모세에게 베풀고 쉬운 일은 자단하더라 (출 18:26).

(3) one을 쓸 수 없는 경우

① 불가산 명사 앞에서

If you have not fresh **milk** I'll take **tinned**. (Not; tinned one)
If you have not a fresh **chicken** I'll take a frozen **one**.

② 수사 다음

She has three cars and I have two.

2. other, another

1) another + 단수 가산명사

Would you like **another** potato?
Would you like **some more** meat?
Would you like **some more** peas?

2) another + few / number + 복수 명사

I am staying for **another** few weeks.
We need **another** three chairs.

If someone strikes you on the right cheek, turn to him **the other** also.
누구든지 네 오른편 뺨을 치거든 왼편도 돌려 대며 (마 5:39).

one for a sin offering and **the other** for a burnt offering.
하나는 속죄제물을 삼고, 하나는 번제물을 삼아 (레 5:7).

It was completely restored, just as sound as **the other**.
다른 손과 같이 회복되어 성하더라 (마 12:13).

From that day on, **half** of my men did the work, while **the other half** were equipped with spears, shields, bows and armor.
그때로부터 내 종자의 절반은 역사하고 절반은 갑옷을 입고 창과 방패와 활을 가졌고 (느 4:16).

The splendor of the heavenly bodies is **one** kind, and the splendor of the earthly bodies is **another**.

One has this gift, **another** has that.
하나는 이러하고 하나는 저러하니라 (고전 7:7).

Let us put up three shelters--**one** for you, **one** for Moses and **one** for Elijah.
우리가 초막 셋을 짓되 하나는 주를 위하여, 하나는 모세를 위하여, 하나는 엘리야를 위하여 하사이다 (눅 9:33).

3) each other = one another

Mary and I write to **each other/one another** every day.
They sat without looking at **each other/one another**.
Administer true justice; show mercy and compassion to **one another**.

When the Israelites saw it, they said to **each other**, "What is it?" For they did not know what it was. Moses said to them, "It is the bread the LORD has given you to eat.
이스라엘 자손이 보고 그것이 무엇인지 알지 못하여 서로 이르되, 이것이 무엇이냐 하니 모세가 그들에게 이르되, 이는 여호와께서 너희에게 주어 먹게 하신 양식이라(출 16:15).

We should love **one another**.
우리가 서로 사랑할지니(요일 3:11).

Why do we profane the covenant of our fathers by breaking faith with **one another**?
어찌하여 우리 각 사람이 자기 형제에게 궤사를 행하여 우리 열조의 언약을 욕되게 하느냐(말 2:10).

3. some, any

1) 용례
의문문, 부정문, 조건문에서는 any, 긍정문에서는 some. 긍정의 답을 예상하거나 권유할 때는 의문문에도 some을 쓸 수 있다.
any = it does not matter which, whichever you like
Would you like some ice-cream?

She also gave **some** to her husband, who was with her, and he ate it
자기와 함께한 남편에게도 주매 그도 먹은지라(창 3:6).

When shall I come? **Any** time.
Could you pass me a knife? Which one? It does not matter. **Any** one.

I have not used **any** of these rights.
내가 이것을 하나도 쓰지 아니하였고(고전 9:15).

If **anyone** is ashamed of me and my words, the Son of Man will be ashamed of him when he comes in his glory and in the glory of the Father and of the holy angels.
누구든지 나와 내 말을 부끄러워하면 인자도 자기와 아버지와 거룩한 천사들의 영광으로 올 때에 그 사람을 부끄러워하리라(눅 9:26).

2) 긍정문의 any; 어떤 ~ 이라도

You may eat **any** that have fins and scales.
지느러미와 비늘 있는 것은 너희가 먹되(레 11:9).

3) some = a certain

There must be some job I could do.
She's living in some village in China.

others, all, enough와 함께
Some people like the sea, **others** prefer the mountains.
Some of us were late, but we were **all** there by ten o'clock.
I've **some** money, but not **enough**.

4) 무관심을 나타낼 때

Mary's gone to Australia to marry **some** sheep farmer or other.
I don't want to spend my life doing **some** boring job.

4. none, no

1) none

(1) no one의 뜻으로 단독으로 쓰이는 부정대명사

How many of the books have you read? – **None**.

I will destroy you, and **none** will be left.
내가 너를 멸하여 거민이 없게 하리라(습 2:5).

(2) 한정사(the, my, this 등) 및 인칭대명사 앞에서 none of의 형태로 쓰임

None of the students passed the exam.
None of the keys would open the door.

(3) 두 사람(물건)에 관하여 말할 때는 none이 아니라 neither가 쓰임

Neither of my parents could be there.

2) no

(1) 명사 바로 앞에서 형용사로 쓰임. Not a, not any의 뜻

No airplane is 100% safe.
There is no time to talk about it now.
No Japanese people work in our office.

I have ~ , There is ~ 문형에서 not any 대신에 쓰여 "조금도 ~ 아닌"의 뜻을 나타낸다.

The fig tree does not bud and there are **no** grapes on the vines.
무화과나무가 무성치 못하며 포도나무에 열매가 없으며(합 3:17).

Among those born of women there is **no** one greater than John
여자가 낳은 자 중에 요한보다 큰 이가 없도다(눅 7:28).

They had **no** children
저희가 무자하고(눅 1:7).

I will accept **no** offering from your hands.
너희 손으로 드리는 것을 받지도 아니하리라(말 1:10).

5. each, every, all

1) each; 각자,

But **each** man has his own gift from God.
그러나 각각 하나님께 받은 자기의 은사가 있으니(고전 7:7).

2) every; 누구나 다, every + 단수

Please switch off every light.
I have written to every friend.

Every tree that does not produce good fruit will be cut down and thrown into the fire.
좋은 열매 맺지 아니하는 나무마다 찍혀 불에 던지우리라(눅 3:9).

Each day one ox, six choice sheep and some poultry were prepared for me, and **every ten days** an abundant supply of wine of all kinds.
매일 나를 위하여 소 하나와 살진 양 여섯을 준비하며 닭도 많이 준비하고 열흘에 한 번씩은 각종 포도주를 갖추었나니(느 5:18).
(Every ten days = every tenth day, 열흘마다)

3) 부분 부정; every, both, all등이 부정어와 같이 쓰이면 부분 부정이 됨

Everything is permissible for me--but **not everything** is beneficial.
모든 것이 내게 가하나 다 유익한 것이 아니오(고전 6:12).

4) all

(1) all + 복수
All children need love. (**Every** child needs love.)
All cities are noisy. (**Every** city is noisy.)

(2) 한정사(the, my, this 등) 앞에서는 every를 쓰지 않고 all을 쓴다
Please switch off **all** the lights. (Please switch off **every** light.)
I have written to **all** my friends. (Not; I have written to **every** my friend.)

(3) 불가산 명사 앞에서는 every가 아니라 all을 사용
I like **all** music.

(4) 단수 가산명사 앞에 all을 쓸 경우에는 every part of, the whole of의 의미
She was here **all** day. (= from morning to night)
She was here **every** day. (= Monday, Tuesday, Wednesday -----)

(5) all이 복수로 쓰일 때
all who were appointed for eternal life believed.
영생을 주시기로 작정된 자는 다 믿더라(행 13:48).

All who rely on observing the law are under a curse
무릇 율법 행위에 속한 자들은 저주 아래 있나니 기록된 바(갈 3:10).

(6) all이 단수로 쓰일 때

All this took place to fulfill what the Lord had said through the prophet:
이 모든 일의 된 것은 주께서 선지자로 하신 말씀을 이루려 하심이니(마 1:22).

By all this we are encouraged.
이로 인하여 우리가 위로를 받았고(고후 7:13).

(7) all (of) + 한정사(the, my, this등) + 명사; of를 안 쓸 수도 있음

All (of) my friends like reading.
She has eaten all (of) the cake.
그러나 한정사 없이 명사 앞에 쓰일 경우에는 of를 쓰지 않는다.
All children can be naughty sometimes. (Not; All of children ------.)

(8) 인칭대명사 앞에서는 all of를 사용

All of them can come tomorrow. (Not; All they)
Mary sends her love to all of us. (Not; all we)

(9) 목적격 인칭대명사 뒤에 all을 쓸 수 있음

I have invited them all.
Mary sends her love to us all.
I have made you all something to eat.

(10) all의 위치

① Be 동사, 조동사 + all
We can all swim.
They have all finished.
We are all tired.

② all + 일반 동사
My family all like traveling.

You all look tired.

(11) all 단독으로는 everybody의 의미로 쓰지 않음

Everybody stood up. (Not; All stood up.)
All the people stood up.

(12) all은 보통 "all + 관계절"의 구조에서만 everything의 의미로 쓰임

All (that) I have is yours. (혹은 Everything (that) I have is yours.)
Everything is yours. (Not; All is yours.)
She lost all she owned. (혹은 She lost everything she owned.)
She lost everything. (Not; She lost all.)

이 구조는 주로 부정적 의미를 갖는다. (nothing more 혹은 the only thing)
This is all I have got.
All I want is a place to sleep.

every, both, all등이 부정어와 함께 쓰이면 부분 부정이 된다.
-> 이 내용은 앞에 나온 내용 3)번과 중복입니다. 생략할까요?

(13) At all; 조금도, 조금이라도

Go and get your own straw wherever you can find it, but your work will not be reduced at all.
너희는 짚을 얻을 곳으로 가서 주우라 너희 일은 조금도 감하지 아니하리라(출 5:11).

On the first day hold a sacred assembly, and another one on the seventh day. Do no work at all on these days.
너희에게 첫날에도 성회요 제 칠일에도 성회가 되니니, 이 두 날에는 아무 일도 하지 말고(출 12:16).

Son of man, these men have set up idols in their hearts and put wicked stumbling blocks before their faces. Should I let them inquire of me at all?
인자야 이 사람들이 자기 우상을 마음에 들이며 죄악의 거치는 것을 자기 앞에 두었으니 그들이 내게 묻기를 내가 조금인들 용납하랴(겔 14:3).

Their cities are destroyed; no one will be left--no one **at all**.
그 모든 성읍이 황폐되며, 사람이 없으며 거할 자가 없게 되었느니라(습 3:6).

6. ~ thing, ~body; any와 some의 용법에 준한다

1) 의문문, 부정문 및 조건문에서는 any, 긍정문에서는 some

That man should not think he will receive **anything** from the Lord
이런 사람은 무엇이든지 주께 얻기를 생각하지 말라(약 1:7).

2) ~ thing의 대명사를 수식하는 형용사는 대개 그 뒤에 위치함

True instruction was in his mouth and **nothing** false was found on his lips.
그 입에는 진리의 법이 있었고, 그 입술에는 불의함이 없었으며(말 2:6).

Cursed is everyone who does not continue to do **everything** written in the Book of the Law.
누구든지 율법 책에 기록된 대로 온갖 일을 항상 행하지 아니하는 자는 저주 아래 있는 자라 하였음이라 (갈 3:10).

I have never eaten **anything** impure or unclean.
속되고 깨끗(하)지 아니한 물건을 내가 언제든지 먹지 아니하였삽나이다(행 10:14).

You give them **something to eat**.
너희가 먹을 것을 주라(마 14:16).

If your enemy is hungry, feed him: if he is thirsty, give him **something** to drink.
네 원수가 주리거든 먹이고 목마르거든 마시우라(롬 12:20).

3) 비교

These are the regulations concerning animals, birds, **every living thing** that moves in the water and every creature that moves about on the ground.
이는 짐승과 새와 물에서 움직이는 모든 생물과 땅에 기는 모든 기어 다니는 것에 대한 규례니(레 11:46).

7. either; (둘 중의) 어느 한 쪽, 어느 쪽도

1) 대명사

Either causes a loss to the company.
Take either of the chairs.

2) 형용사

(1) (둘 중) 어느 하나의
Put the lamp at either end.
Is there a desk in either room?

(2) (둘 중) 어느 쪽의 ~도
Twelve lions stood on the six steps, one at either end of each step.
또 열 두 사자가 있어 그 여섯 층계 좌우편에 섰으니(대하 9:19).

3) 부사; (부정적 표현 뒤에서) ~도 또한 아니다

The LORD has not chosen this one either.
이도 여호와께서 택하지 아니하셨느니라(삼상 16:8).

4) 접속사; (either ~ or ~ 의 형태로) ~ 이든가 또는 ~

Then God came to Laban the Aramean in a dream at night and said to him, "Be careful not to say anything to Jacob, either good or bad."
밤에 하나님이 아람 사람 라반에게 현몽하여 가라사대 너는 삼가 야곱에게 선악간 말하지 말라 하셨더라 (창 31:24).

8. neither

1) 대명사

(양자 중) 어느 쪽도 ~ 않다.
(셋 중) 어느 것도 ~ 않다.

In this meaningless life of mine I have seen both of these: a righteous man perishing in his righteousness, and a wicked man living long in his wickedness. Do not be overrighteous, **neither** be overwise-- why destroy yourself?
내가 내 헛된 날에 이 모든 일을 본즉 자기의 의로운 중에서 멸망하는 의인이 있고 자기의 악행 중에서 장수하는 악인이 있으니, 지나치게 의인이 되지 말며 지나치게 지혜자도 되지 말라. 어찌하여 스스로 패망케 하겠느냐(전 7:15, 16).

2) 형용사

Neither statement is true.

3) 부사

(부정문에 이어서) ~도 또한 아니다 (= Nor)
Neither/nor + 조동사 + 주어

I can't swim. **Neither** can I. = I can't either. (Not; I also can't.)
I don't like opera. **Neither** do I. = I don't either. (Not; I don't too.)

Death and Destruction are never satisfied, and **neither** are the eyes of man.
음부와 유명은 만족함이 없고, 사람의 눈도 만족함이 없느니라(잠 27:20).

No branch can bear fruit by itself; it must remain in the vine. **Neither** can you bear fruit unless you remain in me.
가지기 포도나무에 붙어 있지 아니하면 설로 과실을 맺을 수 없음 같이, 너희도 내 안에 있지 아니하면 그러하리라(요 15:4).

4) 접속사

(neither ~ nor ~ 의 형태로) ~ 도 아니고 ~ 아니다: both ~ and ~의 반대

Neither James **nor** Virginia was at home.
I **neither** smoke **nor** drink.
The film was **neither** well made **nor** well acted.

Neither he **nor** any of his men will be left alive.
저와 그 함께 있는 모든 사람을 하나도 남겨 두지 아니할 것이요(삼하 17:12).

Keep falsehood and lies far from me; give me **neither** poverty **nor** riches, but give me only my daily bread.
곧 허탄과 거짓말을 내게서 멀리 하옵시며 나로 가난하게도 마옵시고 부하게도 마옵시고 오직 필요한 양식으로 내게 먹이시옵소서 (잠 30:8).

9. both

1) both (of) + 한정사(the, my, these ---) + 명사

both (of) my parents like riding.
She's eaten both (of) the chops.

2) Both of + 대명사

Both of them can come tomorrow.
Mary sends her love to both of us.

3) 목적격 인칭대명사 + both

I've invited them both. Mary sends us both her love.
I've made you both something to eat.

10. 한정사(determiners)

1) 종류

a, the, my, this, some, any, either, every, enough, several 등

(1) Group A
A/an, the
My, your, hi, her, its, our, your, their, one's, whose
This, these, that, those

(2) Group B
Some, any, no

Each, every, either, neither
Much, many, more, most, little, less, least
Few, fewer, fewest, enough, several
What, whatever, which, whichever
All, both, half

2) 명사(구) 앞에 위치하여 명사(구)를 수식하며 형용사와 구별된다

The moon, a nice day, **my** fat old cat, **this** house, **every** week, **several** young students

3) 2개의 한정사를 함께 쓸 수 없다

The my house, the this house, this my house (x)

만약 Group B의 한정사를 Group B의 한정사 앞에 놓을 때는 of를 사용해야 한다.
Some of the people
Would you like **some of** this ice-cream?
I can't find **any** pencils.
I can't find **any of** my pencils.

Each of my children
Neither of these doors
Most of the time
Which of your records
Enough of those remarks

Can I have some **more of** the red wine, please?
Do you have any **more of** that smoked fish?
I don't think any **more of** them want to come.

I've eaten **most of** the salad.
You've read **most of** my books.
Most of us feel the same way.

How **much of** the house do you want to paint this year?
I don't think I'll pass the exam; I've missed too **many of** my lessons.

You didn't eat **much of** it.
How **many of** you are there?

Neither of my brothers can sing.
Neither of us saw it happen.

All, both, half 뒤에는 of 생략 가능
All (of) his ideas, **both (of)** my parents, **half (of)** the time

4) No(= not a, not any) + 명사

None of + 한정사 + 명사, none of + 대명사
No airplane is 100% safe.
There is **no time** to talk about it now.
None of my friends, **every one of** these books
None of the keys would open the door.
None of my brothers remembered my birthday.
None of us speaks French.

연습 문제

1. _____ tree that does not produce good fruit will be cut down and thrown into the fire.
   1) All   2) Every   3) All the   4) Most

2. Blessed are the poor in spirit, for _____ is the kingdom of heaven.
   1) their's   2) there   3) theirs   4) their

3. Blessed are _____ who mourn, for they will be comforted.
   1) those   2) they   3) these   4) he

   I will bless those who bless you.

   Understanding is a fountain of life to **those who** have it, but folly brings punishment to fools.
   명철한 자에게는 그 명철이 생명의 샘이 되거니와 미련한 자에게는 그 미련한 것이 징계가 되느니라 (잠 16:22).

4. For I tell you that unless your righteousness surpasses _____ of the Pharisees and the teachers of the law, you will certainly not enter the kingdom of heaven.
   1) this   2) those   3) it   4) that

   Has your counselor perished, that pain seizes you like **that** of a woman in labor?
   They had wings like **those** of a stork.

   But the LORD will make a distinction between the livestock of Israel and **that** of Egypt, so that no animal belonging to the Israelites will die.
   여호와가 이스라엘의 생축과 애굽의 생축을 구별하리니 이스라엘 자손에 속한 것은 하나도 죽지 아니하리라 (출 9:4).

5. If someone strikes you on the right cheek, turn to him _____ also.
   1) the other   2) other   3) others   4) another

   It rises at **one** end of the heavens and makes its circuit to **the other**; nothing is hidden from its heat.

   When **Moses**' hands grew tired, they took a stone and put it under him and he sat on it. Aaron and Hur held his hands up--one on **one** side, one on **the other**--so that his hands **remained steady** till sunset.
   모세의 팔이 피곤하매 그들이 돌을 가져다가 모세의 아래에 놓아 그로 그 위에 앉게 하고 아론과 훌이 하나는 이편에서 하나는 저편에서 모세의 손을 붙들어 올렸더니 그 손이 해가 지도록 내려 오지 아니한지라 (출 17:12).

6. Love your enemies and pray for _____ who persecute you.
   1) they   2) these   3) he   4) those

7. But small is the gate and narrow the road that leads to life, and only _____ find it.
   1) a few   2) few   3) a little   4) little

8. Therefore everyone who hears these words of _____ and puts them into practice is like a wise man who built his house on the rock.
   1) me   2) mine   3) my   4) I

   Then the LORD said to Moses, "Go to Pharaoh, for I have hardened his heart and the hearts of his officials so that I may perform these miraculous signs of **mine** among them
   여호와께서 모세에게 이르시되 바로에게로 들어가라. 내가 그의 마음과 그 신하들의 마음을 완강케 함은 나의 표징을 그들 중에 보이기 위함이며(출 10:1).

   All these officials of **yours** will come to me, bowing down before me and saying, 'Go, you and all the people who follow you!' After that I will leave." Then Moses, hot with anger, left Pharaoh.
   왕이 이 모든 신하가 내게 내려와서 내게 절하며 이르기를 너와 너를 좇는 온 백성은 나가라 한 후에야 내가 나가리라 하고 심히 노하여 바로에게서 나오니라(출 11:8).

9. The harvest is plentiful but the workers are _____.
   1) a little   2) small   3) few   4) little

10. Whatever town or village you enter, search for some worthy person there and stay at _____ house until you leave. 4
    1) their   2) its   3) your   4) his

11. Do not be afraid of _____ who kill the body but cannot kill the soul.
    1) they   2) those   3) these   4) he

12. _____ will be the members of his own household.
    1) A man's enemies   2) A man's enemy   3) Man's enemies   4) Man's enemy

13. Anyone who loves his father or mother more than _____ is not worthy of me.
    1) me   2) I   3) myself   4) mine

14. Everything is possible for _____ who believes.
    1) him   2) he   3) those   4) them

15. Whoever welcomes _____ of these little children in my name welcomes me.
    1) it   2) a child   3) such   4) one

16. _____ who does a miracle in my name can in the next moment say anything bad about me.
    1) No one   2) Some one   3) Everyone   4) One

Now Sarai was barren; she had no children.
Let's not have any quarreling between you and me.

17. It was because your hearts were hard _____ Moses wrote you this law.
    1) that   2) this   3) which   4) why

18. Whatever you ask for in prayer, believe that you have received it, and it will be _____.
    1) your   2) yours   3) your's   4) you

Now John's disciples and the Pharisees were fasting. Some people came and asked Jesus, "How is it that John's disciples and the disciples of the Pharisees are fasting, but **yours** are not?"

요한의 제자들과 바리새인들이 금식하고 있는지라. 혹이 예수께 와서 말하되 요한의 제자들과 바리새인의 제자들은 금식하는데 어찌하여 당신의 제자들은 금식하지 아니하나이까 (막 2:18).

19. He sent many others; some of them they beat, _____ they killed.
    1) others   2) other   3) another   4) the other

20. When they had done so, they caught _____ large number of fish that their nets began to break.
    1) such a   2) such   3) so   4) so a

Such a violent storm arose that the ship threatened to break up.

21. _____ tried to touch him, because power was coming from him and healing them all.
    1) The all people   2) All people   3) All of people   4) The people all

22. Love your enemies, do good to _____ who hate you.
    1) him   2) he   3) those   4) them

23. Jesus cured _____ who had diseases, sicknesses and evil spirits, and gave sight to many who were blind.
    1) many person   2) many   3) much   4) a lot

24. You have planted _____, but have harvested little.
    1) small   2) a few   3)   3) much   4) many

And when they measured it by the omer, he who gathered **much** did not have too much, and he who gathered **little** did not have too little. Each one gathered as much as he needed.

오멜로 되어 본즉 많이 거둔 자도 남음이 없고 적게 거둔 자도 부족함이 없이 각기 식량대로 거두었더라 (출 16:18).

25. I sent for you immediately, and _____ was good of you to come.
   1) that   2) it   3) this   4) I

It is God who arms me with strength and makes my way perfect.
Sing joyfully to the LORD, you righteous; it is fitting for the upright to praise him.

It is not lawful **for** you **to** have your brother's wife.
동생의 아내를 취한 것이 옳지 않다(막 6:18).

26. _____ food is clean, but it is wrong for a man to eat anything that causes someone else to stumble.
   1) All   2) All the   3) Of all   4) The all

All the people were astonished and said, "Could this be the Son of David?"
All the people in the synagogue were furious when they heard this.
A great number of people were brought to the Lord.
A large crowd of his disciples was there.
The crowd that gathered around him was so large that he got into a boat
The number of those who ate was about five thousand men, besides women and children.

27. It is better not to eat meat or drink _____ or to do anything else that will cause your brother to fall.
   1) wine   2) wines   3) a wine   4) the wine

28. The Lord has commanded that _____ who preach the gospel should receive their living from the gospel.
   1) him   2) he   3) those   4) them

29. So we make it our goal to please him, whether we are at home in the body or away from _____.
   1) it   2) one   3) home   4) there

30. Tour enthusiasm has stirred _____ them to action.
   1) the most of   2) most of   3) most   4) almost

31. If anyone thinks he is something when he is nothing, he deceives _____.
   1) he   2) his own   3) himself   4) him

32. Have _____ to do with the fruitless deeds of darkness, but rather expose them.
   1) nothing   2) something   3) anything   4) everything

33. _____ is better for you to lose one part of your body than for your whole body to go into hell.
   1) That   2) It   3) One   4) This

34. The man with two tunics should share with who has none, and the one who has food should do _____.
   1) same   2) the same   3) as same   4) a same

Pharaoh then summoned wise men and sorcerers, and the Egyptian magicians also did the same things by their secret arts:
바로도 박사와 박수를 부르매 그 애굽 술객들도 그 술법으로 그와 같이 행하되 (출 7:11).

정답

1) 2, 2) 3, 3) 1, 4) 4, 5) 1, 6) 4, 7) 1, 8) 2, 9) 3, 10) 4
11) 2, 12) 1, 13) 1, 14) 1, 15) 4, 16) 1 17) 1, 18) 2, 19) 1, 20) 1
21) 4, 22) 3, 23) 2, 24) 3, 25) 2, 26) 1, 27) 1, 28) 3, 29) 1, 30) 2
31) 3, 32) 1, 33) 2, 34) 2

숙어

be worthy to; 가치 있는, 적당한, 상당한
John answered them all, "I baptize you with water. But one more powerful than I will come, the thongs of whose sandals I **am** not **worthy to** untie.
요한이 모든 사람에게 대답하여 가로되 나는 물로 너희에게 세례를 주거니와 나보다 능력이 많으신 이가 오시나니 나는 그 신들메를 풀기도 감당치 못하겠노라(눅 3:16).

And this was his message: "After me will come one more powerful than I, the thongs of whose sandals I **am** not **worthy to** stoop down and untie.
그가 전파하여 가로되 나보다 능력 많으신 이가 내 뒤에 오시나니 나는 그의 신들메를 풀기도 감당치 못하겠노라(막 1:7).

beg for; 구걸하다, 청하다
the children **beg for** bread, but no one gives it to them.
어린 아이가 떡을 구하나 떼어 줄 사람이 없도다(애 4:4).

belong to; ~의 것이다 (be the property of ~)
In the time of Herod king of Judea there was a priest named Zechariah, who **belonged to** the priestly division of Abijah: his wife Elizabeth was also a descendant of Aaron.
유대 왕 헤롯 때에 아비야 반열에 제사장 하나가 있으니 이름은 사가랴요 그 아내는 아론의 자손이니 이름은 엘리사벳이라(눅 1:5).

beyond all question; 문제 될 것 없이, 물론
Beyond all question, the mystery of godliness is great: He appeared in a body, was vindicated by the Spirit, was seen by angels, was preached among the nations, was believed on in the world, was taken up in glory.
크도다 경건의 비밀이여 그렇지 않다 하는 이 없도다 그는 육신으로 나타난 바 되시고 영으로 의롭다 하심을 입으시고 천사들에게 보이시고 만국에서 전파되시고 세상에서 믿은 바 되시고 영광가운데서 올리우셨음이니라 (딤전 3:16).

be zealous for; 열광적인, 골똘한
For I can testify about them that they **are zealous for** God, but their zeal is not based on knowledge.
내가 증거하노니 저희가 하나님께 열심이 있으나 지식을 좇은 것이 아니라(롬 10:2).

believe in (God); ~의 존재를 믿다
I half **believe in** life after death.
believe (a person or something that is said) (= accept as true); 믿다, 신뢰하다
Don't **believe** her. I don't **believe** a word she says.

blot out; 지우다, 감춰 보이지 않게 하다, 죽이다
He who overcomes will, like them, be dressed in white. I will never **blot out** his name from the book of life, but will acknowledge his name before my Father and his angels.
이기는 자는 이와 같이 흰 옷을 입을 것이요 내가 그 이름을 생명책에서 반드시 흐리지 아니하고 그 이름을 내 아버지 앞과 그 천사들 앞에서 시인하리라(계 3:5).

break out; 갑자기 발생하다 (occur suddenly)
It will become fine dust over the whole land of Egypt, and festering boils will **break out** on men and animals throughout the land."
그 재가 애굽 온 땅의 티끌이 되어 애굽 온 땅의 사람과 짐승에게 붙어서 독종이 발하리라(출 9:9).

bring about; 발생시키다, 야기하다 (cause to happen)
for man's anger does not **bring about** the righteous life that God desires.
사람의 성내는 것이 하나님의 의를 이루지 못함이니라(약 1:20).

by any means; 어떤 일이 있어도
I tell you the truth, until heaven and earth disappear, not the smallest letter, not the least stroke of a pen, will **by any means** disappear from the Law until everything is accomplished.
진실로 너희에게 이르노니 천지가 없어지기 전에는 율법의 일점 일획이라도 반드시 없어지지 아니하고 다 이루리라(마 5:18).

by means of; ~에 의하여 (with the help of, by dint of)
Do not defile yourselves by any of these creatures. Do not make yourselves unclean **by means of** them or be made unclean by them.

너희는 기는바 기어다니는 것을 인하여 자기로 가증하게 되게 말며, 또한 그것을 인하여 스스로 더럽혀 부정하게 되게 말라(레 11:43).

To one there is given through the Spirit the message of wisdom, to another the message of knowledge by means of the same Spirit,
어떤 이에게는 성령으로 말미암아 지혜의 말씀을, 어떤 이에게는 같은 성령을 따라 지식의 말씀을 [주시나니] (고전 12:8).

5. 대명사(代名詞)
Pronoun

A. 의문대명사

1. 종류

who, what, which 등이 의문문에서 쓰일 때 의문대명사라고 하며, who는 whom(목적격) 및 whose(소유격)로 활용할 수 있다.

1) who; 사람의 성명, 혈족 관계

"**Who** is that man in the field coming to meet us?" "He is my master," the servant answered.
들에서 배회하다가 우리에게로 마주 오는 자가 누구뇨. 종이 가로되 이는 내 주인이니이다(창 24:65).

"**Who** is he, sir?" the man asked. "Tell me so that I may believe in him."
대답하여 가로되 주여 그가 누구시오니이까 내가 믿고자 하나이다(요 9:36).

2) what; 사람의 직업, 신분 및 물건

What is she? She is a violinist.

2. 의문문이 다른 문장의 종속절(명사절, 형용사절, 부사절)이 될 때

평서문의 어순이 된다.

1) 명사적 용법; 목적어

He did not know **what he was** saying.
자기의 하는 말을 자기도 알지 못하더라(눅 9:33).

Many followed him, and he healed all their sick, warning them not to tell **who he was**.
사람이 많이 좇는지라, 예수께서 저희 병을 다 고치시고 자기를 나타내지 말라 경계하셨으니(마 12:15, 16).

We don't know **who** put our silver in our sacks.
우리의 돈을 우리 자루에 넣은 자는 누구인지 우리가 알지 못하나이다(창 43:22).

2) 명사적 용법; 보어

God said to Moses, "I Am **Who** I Am. This is what you are to say to the Israelites: 'I Am has sent me to you.'"
하나님이 모세에게 이르시되 나는 스스로 있는 자니라. 또 이르시되 너는 이스라엘 자손에게 이같이 이르기를 스스로 있는 자가 나를 너희에게 보내셨다 하라 (출 3:14).

3. 의문사절이 전치사의 목적어가 될 때

전치사가 생략되는 경우가 많다.

They are ignorant (**of**) what they are after.

B. 관계대명사

관계대명사는 접속사처럼 두 개의 절을 연결한다.
There is the girl **who** works with my sister.

이어서 오는 동사의 주어 혹은 목적어이다.
What's the name of the tall man? He just came in.
What's the name of the tall man **who** just came in. (주격)
This is Ms Rogers. You met her last year.
This is Ms Rogers **whom** you met last year. (목적격)

관계대명사에는 who, whom, whose, which, that, what이 있다.
as나 but 등도 관계대명사로 쓰일 수 있다.
who, what에 ever나 soever가 붙으면 복합 또는 부정관계대명사가 된다.

용법은 제한적 용법과 계속적 용법이 있다.

제한적 용법
어떤 사람/사물을 말하는 것인지 설명한다.
Whose is the car **that** is parked outside?

But I tell you **who** hear me: Love your enemies, do good to those who hate you,
그러나 너희 듣는 자에게 내가 이르노니 너희 원수를 사랑하며 너희를 미워하는 자를 선대하며(눅 6:27).

Coming up to them at that very moment, she gave thanks to God and spoke about the child to all **who** were looking forward to the redemption of Jerusalem.
마침 이 때에 나아와서 하나님께 감사하고 예루살렘의 구속됨을 바라는 모든 사람에게 이 아기에 대하여 말하니라(눅 2:38).

계속적 용법
앞에 나온 명사에 대하여 더 설명한다. 관계대명사 앞에 쉼표(comma)를 쓴다.
This is Ms. Rogers, **whom** you met last year.
Have you seen my new car, **which** I bought last week?

Dear friends, I urge you, as aliens and strangers in the world, to abstain from sinful desires, **which** war against your soul.
사랑하는 자들아 나그네와 행인 같은 너희를 권하노니 영혼을 거슬러 싸우는 육체의 정욕을 제어하라(벧전 2:11).

Therefore, get rid of all moral filth and the evil that is so prevalent and humbly accept the word planted in you, **which** can save you.
그러므로 모든 더러운 것과 넘치는 악을 내어 버리고 능히 너희 영혼을 구원할 바 마음에 심긴 도를 온유함으로 받으라(약 1:21).

There was a priest named Zechariah, **who** belonged to the priestly division of Abijah:
아비야 반열에 제사장 하나가 있으니 이름은 사가랴요(눅 1:5).

He should ask God, **who** gives generously to all without finding fault, and it will be given to him
모든 사람에게 후히 주시고 꾸짖지 아니하시는 하나님께 구하라, 그리하면 주시리라(약 1:5).

I will send my messenger ahead of you, **who** will prepare your way before you.
내가 내 사자를 네 앞에 보내노니 저가 네 길을 네 앞에 예비하리라(마 11:10).

Let's go to Bethlehem and see this thing that has happened, **which** the Lord has told us about.
이제 베들레헴까지 가서 주께서 우리에게 알리신 바 이 이루어진 일을 보자(눅 2:15).

I am not that one. No, but he is coming after me, **whose** sandals I am not worthy to untie.
나는 그리스도가 아니라 내 뒤에 오시는 이가 있으니 나는 그 발의 신 풀기도 감당치 못하리라(행 13:25).

1. who

선행사가 사람인 경우에 쓰인다.

1) 주격

a wise man **who** built his house on the rock.
그 집을 반석위에 지은 지혜로운 사람(마 7:24).

2) 목적격

How can I curse those **whom** God has not cursed?
하나님이 저주치 않으신 자를 내 어찌 저주하며(민 23:8).

Give me my wives and children, for **whom** I have served you, and I will be on my way.
내가 외삼촌에게서 일하고 얻은 처자를 내게 주어 나로 가게 하소서(창 30:26).

3) 소유격; 명사를 수식하는 한정사로서의 역할도 한다

I saw a girl **whose** hair came down to her waist.
This is Filicity, **whose** sister you met last year.
Our friend John, at **whose** farmhouse we spent the summer, is moving to Germany.

Blessed is the man **whose** sin the Lord will never count against him.
주께서 그 죄를 인정치 아니하실 사람은 복이 있도다(롬 4:8).

But one more powerful than I will come, the thongs of **whose** sandals I am not worthy to untie.
나보다 능력이 많으신 이가 오시나니 나는 그 신들메를 풀기도 감당치 못하겠노라(눅 3:16).

At the resurrection **whose** wife will she be, since the seven were married to her?
일곱사람이 다 그를 아내로 취하였으니 부활을 당하여 저희가 살아날 때에 그 중에 뉘 아내가 되리이까 (막 12:23).

4) 선행사를 포함하는 관계대명사
Who steals my purse steals trash.

2. which

선행사가 사물인 경우에 쓰인다.

1) 주격
That **which** is devoted is among you, O Israel.
이스라엘아 너의 중에 바친 물건이 있나니 (수 7:13).

2) 목적격
This kindness is greater than that **which** you showed earlier.
너의 베푼 인애가 처음보다 나중이 더하도다 (룻 3:10).

Remember the height from **which** you have fallen! Repent and do the things you did at first.
어디서 떨어진 것을 생각하고 회개하여 처음 행위를 가지라 (계 2:5).
(전치사 from의 목적어)

3. that

제한적 용법에서 which, who, whom 대신에 쓴다.
I have a book **that** might interest you.
Do you have a map **that** shows all the motorways?
There's the woman **that** works in the photographer's
You remember the boy **that** I was talking about?

The only thing **that** counts is faith expressing itself through love.
그리스도 예수 안에서는 할례나 무할례가 효력이 없되 사랑으로써 역사하는 믿음뿐이니라 (갈 5:6).

The very fact **that** you have lawsuits among you means you have been completely defeated already.
너희가 피차 송사함으로 너희 가운데 이미 완연한 허물이 있나니(고전 6:7).

God saw all **that** he had made.
하나님이 그 지으신 모든 것을 보시니(창 1:31).

Since the first day **that** you set your mind to gain understanding and to humble yourself before your God, your words were heard.
네가 깨달으려 하여 네 하나님 앞에 스스로 겸비케 하기로 결심하던 첫날부터 네 말이 들으신 바 되었으므로(단 10:12).

4. what

what은 그 자체에 선행사가 포함된 관계대명사로, that(those) which, the thing which, all that의 뜻이다.

1) 주어

What I am saying is that as long as the heir is a child, he is no different from a slave, although he owns the whole estate.
내가 또 말하노니 유업을 이을 자가 모든 것의 주인이나 어렸을 동안에는 종과 다름이 없어서(갈 4:1-2).

What I mean, brothers, is that the time is short.
형제들아 내가 이 말을 하노니 때가 단축하여진고로(고전 7:29).

2) 목적어

If you had known **what** these words mean, 'I desire mercy, not sacrifice,' you would not have condemned the innocent.
나는 자비를 원하고 제사를 원치 아니하노라 하신 뜻을 너희가 알았더면 무죄한 자를 죄로 정치 아니하였으리라(마 12:7).

He did not know **what** he was saying.
자기의 하는 말을 자기도 알지 못하더라(눅 9:33).

For **what** I received I passed on to you as of first importance.
내가 받은 것을 먼저 너희에게 전하였노니(고전 15:3).

These are the words of him who is holy and true, who holds the key of David. **What he opens** no one can shut, and **what he shuts** no one can open.
거룩하고 진실하사 다윗의 열쇠를 가지신 이 곧 열면 닫을 사람이 없고 닫으면 열 사람이 없는 그이가 가라사대(계 3:7).

But go and learn **what** this means: 'I desire mercy, not sacrifice.
너희는 가서 내가 긍휼을 원하고 제사를 원치 아니하노라 하신 뜻이 무엇인지 배우라(마 9:13).

3) 전치사의 목적어

Love must be sincere. Hate **what** is evil: cling to **what** is good.
사랑엔 거짓이 없나니 악을 미워하고 선에 속하라(롬 12:9).

4) 보어

This is **what** is done to the man who will not build up his brother's family line.
그 형제의 집 세우기를 즐겨 아니하는 자에게는 이같이 할 것이라(신 25:9).

5) what의 관용구

What is more, he was chosen by the churches to accompany us as we carry the offering, which we administer in order to honor the Lord himself and to show our eagerness to help.
이뿐 아니라 저는 동일한 주의 영광과 우리의 원(願)을 나타내기 위하여 여러 교회의 택함을 입어 우리의 맡은 은혜의 일로 우리와 동행하는 자라(고후 8:19).

Brothers, think of **what you were** when you were called
형제들아 너희를 부르심을 보라(고전 1:26).

what you call; 소위
Is it only for bowing one's head like a reed and for lying on sackcloth and ashes? Is that **what you call** a fast, a day acceptable to the LORD?
그 머리를 갈대같이 숙이고 굵은 베와 재를 펴는 것을 어찌 금식이라 하겠으며 여호와께 열납될 날이라 하겠느냐(사 58:5).

5. 관계대명사의 생략

제한적 용법에서 목적격 관계대명사는 생략할 수 있다.

1) 동사나 전치사의 목적어가 될 때

(1) 동사의 목적어
he is a double-minded man, unstable in all (that) he does.
두 마음을 품어 모든 일에 정함이 없는 자로다(약 1:8).

First let the children eat all (that) they want.
자녀로 먼저 배불리 먹게 할지니(막 7:27).

because he almost died for the work of Christ, risking his life to make up for the help (which) you could not give me.
저가 그리스도의 일을 위하여 죽기에 이르러도 자기 목숨을 돌아보지 아니한 것은 나를 섬기는 너희의 일에 부족함을 채우려 함이니라(빌 2:30).

(2) 전치사의 목적어
You remember the boy (that) I was talking about?
I have found the paper (that) you were looking for.

The weapons (which) we fight with are not the weapons of the world.
우리의 싸우는 병기는 육체에 속한 것이 아니요(고후 10:4).

2) 관계대명사를 생략할 때, 관계대명사 앞에 있는 전치사는 뒤에 온다.
The clay pot (which) the meat is cooked in must be broken;
그 고기를 토기에 삶았으면 그 그릇을 깨뜨릴 것이요(레 6:28).

Since they could not get him to Jesus because of the crowd, they made an opening in the roof above Jesus and, after digging through it, lowered the mat (which) the paralyzed man was lying on.
무리를 인하여 예수께 데려갈 수 없으므로 그 계신 곳의 지붕을 뜯어 구멍을 내고 중풍병자의 누운 상을 달아내리니(막 2:4).

6. 복합관계대명사; ~ever

1) 명사적 용법

(1) 주어
Whoever finds his life will lose it, and **whoever** loses his life for my sake will find it.
자기 목숨을 얻는 자는 잃을 것이요 나를 위하여 자기 목숨을 잃는 자는 얻으리라 (마 10:39).

Whoever claims to live in him must walk as Jesus did.
저 안에 거한다 하는 자는 그의 행하시는 대로 자기도 행할지니라 (요일 2:6).

Whoever wants to be first must be slave of all.
누구든지 으뜸이 되고자 하는 자는 모든 사람의 종이 되어야 하리라 (막 8:44).

whoever = anyone who

For **whatever** is hidden is meant to be disclosed, and **whatever** is concealed is meant to be brought out into the open.
드러내려 하지 않고는 숨긴 것이 없고 나타내려 하지 않고는 감추인 것이 없느니라 (막 4:22).

(2) 목적어
I will not be with you anymore unless you destroy **whatever** among you is devoted to destruction.
그 바친 것을 너희 중에서 멸하지 아니하면 내가 다시는 너희와 함께 있지 아니하리라 (수 7:12).

Let me supply **whatever** you need.
그대의 모든 쓸 것은 나의 담책이니 (삿 19:20).

2) 형용사적 용법

Whatever value the priest then sets, that is what it will be.
제사장은 그 우열간에 정가할지니 그 값이 제사장의 정한 대로 될 것이며 (레 27:12).

If you come with us, we will share with you **whatever** good things the LORD gives us.
우리와 동행하면 여호와께서 우리에게 복을 내리시는 대로 우리도 당신에게 행하리이다(민 10:32).

3) 부사적 용법: 양보의 부사절을 유도

On the seventh day he is to examine it, and if the mildew has spread in the clothing, or the woven or knitted material, or the leather, **whatever** its use, it is a destructive mildew; the article is unclean.
칠일만에 그 색점을 살필지니 그 색점이 그 의복의 날에나, 씨에나, 가죽에나, 가죽으로 만든 것에 퍼졌으면 이는 악성 문둥병이라 그것이 부정하니(레 13:51).

7. 의사관계대명사

1) 관계대명사로서 as

선행사에 such, the same, as가 있을 때, 뒤의 as는 관계대명사로 본다.
But now you must rid yourselves of all **such** things **as** these: anger, rage, malice, slander, and filthy language from your lips.
이제는 너희가 이 모든 것을 벗어버리라. 곧 분과 악의와 훼방과 너희 입의 부끄러운 말이라(골 3:8).

2) 관계형용사

Now if you will show kindness and faithfulness to my master, tell me; and if not, tell me, so I may know **which** way to turn.
이제 당신들이 인자와 진실로 나의 주인을 대접하려거든 내게 고하시고 그렇지 않을지라도 내게 고하여 나로 좌우간 행하게 하소서(창 24:49).

연습 문제

1. _____ is conceived in her is from the Holy Spirit.
   1) This   2) Which   3) What   4) That

   He said, "If you listen carefully to the voice of the LORD your God and do **what** is right in his eyes, if you pay attention to his commands and keep all his decrees, I will not bring on you any of the diseases I brought on the Egyptians, for I am the LORD, who heals you."
   가라사대 너희가 너희 하나님 나 여호와의 말을 청종하고 나의 보기에 의를 행하며 내 계명에 귀를 기울이며 내 모든 규례를 지키면 내가 애굽 사람에게 내린 모든 질병의 하나도 너희에게 내리지 아니하리니 나는 너희를 치료하는 여호와임이니라(출 15:26).

2. All this took place to fulfill _____ the Lord had said through the prophet.
   1) this   2) which   3) what   4) that

3. When Joseph woke up, he did _____ the angel of the Lord had commanded him.
   1) something   2) which   3) that   4) what

4. So was fulfilled _____ the Lord had said through the prophet.
   1) something   2) which   3) that   4) what

5. This is he _____ was spoken of through the prophet Isaiah.
   1) who   2) that   3) which   4) what

6. But after me will come one who is more powerful than I, _____ sandals I am not fit to carry.
   1) who   2) his   3) who's   4) whose

7. And a voice from heaven said, "This is my Son, _____ I love; with him I am well pleased."
   1) whom   2) who   3) whose   4) that

Moreover, I have heard the groaning of the Israelites, **whom** the Egyptians are enslaving, and I have remembered my covenant.
이제 애굽 사람이 종을 삼은 이스라엘 자손의 신음을 듣고 나의 언약을 기억하노라(출 6:5).

8. Here is my servant whom I have chosen, the one I love, in _____ I delight.
   1) who   2) whom   3) him   4) he

9. The kingdom of heaven is like a mustard seed, _____ a man took and planted in his field.
   1) which   2) who   3) what   4) then

10. After me will come one more powerful than I, the thongs of _____ sandals I am not worthy to stoop down and untie.
    1) who   2) his   3) which   4) whose

11. Have you come to destroy us? I know _____ you are.
    1) that   2) which   3) who   4) that

12. On the way he asked them, "_____ do people say I am?"
    1) That   2) Who   3) whose   4) Whom

13. But they kept quiet because on the way they had argued about _____ was the greatest.
    1) who   2) whom   3) that   4) one

14. You aren't swayed by men, because you pay no attention to _____ they are.
    1) who   2) whom   3) which   4) where

15. On another Sabbath he went into the synagogue and was teaching, and a man was there _____ right hand was shriveled.
    1) whose   2) which   3) what   4) that

No one whose hope is in you will ever be put to shame.

16. Now Herod the tetrarch heard about all _____ was going on.
    1) what   2) whose   3) who   4) that

17. He came to that _____ was his own, but his own did not receive him.
   1) which   2) what   3) where   4) it

18. _____ loses his life for me and for the gospel will save it.
   1) Whichever   2) One   3) Whoever   4) Whomever

19. See, I will send my messenger, _____ will prepare the way before me.
   1) which   2) he   3) who   4) that

20. what의 용법이 다른 것 하나를 고르시오.
   1) Do not give dogs what is sacred; do not throw your pearls to pigs.
   2) What did you go out into the desert to see?
   3) What comes out of a man is what makes him unclean.
   4) The world cannot hate you, but it hates me because I testify that what it does is evil.

정답
1) 3, 2) 3, 3) 4, 4) 4, 5) 1, 6) 4, 7) 1, 8) 2, 9) 1, 10) 4
11) 3, 12) 2, 13) 1, 14) 1, 15) 1, 16) 4, 17) 1, 18) 3, 19) 3, 20) 2

숙어

by no means; 결코 ~ 아니다 (않다)
By no means! We died to sin; how can we live in it any longer?
그럴 수 없느니라 죄에 대하여 죽은 우리가 어찌 그 가운데 더 살리요 (롬 6:2).

But you, Bethlehem, in the land of Judah, are **by no means** least among the rulers of Judah; for out of you will come a ruler who will be the shepherd of my people Israel.
또 유대땅 베들레헴아 너는 유대 고을 중에 가장 작지 아니하도다. 네게서 한 다스리는 자가 나와서 내 백성 이스라엘의 목자가 되리라 (마 2:6).

by the name of; ~이라는 이름으로(의)
After this, Jesus went out and saw a tax collector **by the name of** Levi sitting at his tax booth. "Follow me," Jesus said to him,
그 후에 나가사 레위라 하는 세리가 세관에 앉은 것을 보시고 나를 좇으라 하시니 (눅 5:27).

be willing to; 기꺼이 ~ 하는
be willing to associate with people of low position. Do not be conceited.
도리어 낮은 데 처하며 스스로 지혜 있는 체 말라 (롬 12:16).

call after; (누구를) 따라 이름 짓다
We **called** him Thomas, **after** his grandfather.

call on; (사람을) 방문하다, ~에게 청하다, 요구하다, 부탁하다
And everyone who **calls on** the name of the Lord will be saved.
누구든지 주의 이름을 부르는 자는 구원을 얻으리라 (행 2:21).

cannot help ~ing; ~하지 않을 수 없다
For we **cannot help speaking** about what we have seen and heard.
우리는 보고 들은 것을 말하지 아니할 수 없다 하니 (행 4:20).

carry out; 수행하다 (accomplish, execute)

We assume the responsibility for **carrying out** the commands to give a third of a shekel each year for the service of the house of our God:
우리가 또 스스로 규례를 정하기를 해마다 각기 세겔의 삼분 일을 수납하여 하나님의 전을 위하여 쓰게 하되 (느 10:32).

clever at (clever in이 아님); 솜씨 좋은, 익숙한

I'm not very **clever at** cooking.

come true; 실현되다 (really happen, become fact)

And now you will be silent and not able to speak until the day this happens, because you did not believe my words, which will **come true** at their proper time.
보라 이 일의 되는 날까지 네가 벙어리가 되어 능히 말을 못하리니 이는 내 말을 네가 믿지 아니함이어니와 때가 이르면 내 말이 이루리라 (눅 1:20).

compare A with B; 비교하다

Then **compare** our appearance **with** that of the young men who eat the royal food, and treat your servants in accordance with what you see.
당신 앞에서 우리의 얼굴과 왕의 진미를 먹는 소년들의 얼굴을 비교하여 보아서 보이는 대로 종들에게 처분하소서 (단 1:13).

When they measure themselves by themselves and **compare** themselves **with** themselves, they are not wise.
그러나 저희가 자기로서 자기를 헤아리고 자기로서 자기를 비교하니 지혜가 없도다 (고후 10:12).

congratulate / congratulations on (Not; for); 축하하다

I must **congratulate** you **on** your exam results.
Congratulations on your new job!

crash into (Not; against); 무섭게 충돌하다

I wasn't looking where I was going, and **crashed into** the car in front.

day by day; 매일매일, 날마다 (daily)

Therefore we do not lose heart. Though outwardly we are wasting away, yet inwardly we are

being renewed **day by day**.
그러므로 우리가 낙심하지 아니하노니 겉 사람은 후패하나 우리의 속은 날로 새롭도다(고후 4:16).

depend on; 의존하다, 신뢰하다 dependent on (cf; independent of)

We may play football. It **depends on** the weather.
He doesn't want to be **dependent on** his parents.

It does not, therefore, **depend on** man's desire or effort, but on God's mercy.
그런즉 원하는 자로 말미암음도 아니요 달음박질하는 자로 말미암음도 아니요 오직 긍휼히 여기시는 하나님으로 말미암음이니라(롬 9:16).

6. 형용사(形容詞)
Adjective

A. 형용사의 용법

명사의 앞 또는 뒤에 붙어 직접 수식하는 한정(限定)용법과 be동사에 붙어 보어로써 명사를 수식하는 서술(敍述)용법이 있다.

1. 한정 용법과 서술 용법

1) 한정 용법

A **sleeping** baby
She is a very **healthy** woman.
He is a **sick** man.

2) 서술 용법

He is **asleep**.
He looks **ill**.
Your mother is very **well**.

2. 용법상의 주의

1) 한정 용법에만 쓰이는 형용사

drunken, elder, former, latter, only, inner, outer, sick, healthy, frightened, living, sleeping, lone, mere, sheer, upper, utmost, utter, very, wooden, sole, this, that 등

I am like a **drunken** man, like a man overcome by wine, because of the LORD and his holy words.
내가 취한 사람 같으며 포도주에 잡힌 사람 같으니 이는 여호와와 그 거룩한 말씀을 인함이라 (렘 23:9).

Then Rebekah took the best garments of Esau her **elder** son, which were with her in the house, and put them on Jacob her younger son.
리브가가 집안 자기 처소에 있는 맏아들 에서의 좋은 의복을 취하여 작은 아들 야곱에게 입히고 (창 27:15).

Ask now about the **former** days, long before your time, from the day God created man on the earth.
네가 있기 전 하나님이 사람을 세상에 창조하신 날부터 지금까지 지나간 날을 상고하여 보라(신 4:32).

As they faint like **wounded** men in the streets of the city,
저희가 성읍 길거리에서 상한 자처럼 혼미하여(아 2:12).

Watch out for **false** prophets.
거짓 선지자들을 삼가라(마 7:15).

2) 서술 용법에만 쓰이는 형용사

ill, well, afraid, alike, alive, alone, asleep, ashamed, awake, aware, content, fain, unable, wont, worth 등

I heard you in the garden, and I was **afraid** because I was naked; so I hid.
내가 동산에서 하나님의 소리를 듣고 내가 벗었으므로 두려워하여 숨었나이다(창 3:10).

A constant dripping on a day of steady rain And a contentious woman are **alike**.
다투는 부녀는 비 오는 날에 이어 떨어지는 물방울이라(잠 27:15).

My son is **alive** and your son is dead.
산 것은 내 아들이요 죽은 것은 네 아들이라(왕상 3:23).

We were **alone**; there was no one in the house but the two of us.
우리가 함께 있었고 우리 둘 외에는 집에 다른 사람이 없었나이다(왕상 3:18).

Go away. The girl is not dead but **asleep**.
물러가라. 이 소녀가 죽은 것이 아니라 잔다(마 9:24).

For I am poor and needy, and my heart is **wounded** within me.
나는 가난하고 궁핍하여 중심이 상함이니이다(시 109:22).

The righteous hate what is **false**, but the wicked bring shame and disgrace.
의인은 거짓말을 미워하나 악인은 행위가 흉악하여 부끄러운 데 이르느니라(잠 13:5).

They stripped him of his clothes, beat him and went away, leaving him half **dead**.
강도들이 그 옷을 벗기고 때려 거반 죽은 것을 버리고 갔더라(눅 10:30).

He died for us so that, whether we are **awake** or **asleep**, we may live together with him.
예수께서 우리를 위하여 죽으사 우리로 하여금 깨든지 자든지 자기와 함께 살게 하려 하셨느니라(살전 5:10).

3) 같은 말이 한정 용법, 서술 용법에 따라 뜻이 달라지는 단어가 있다.

(1) Present; 참석한
Those **present** were Peter, John, James and Andrew; Philip and Thomas, Bartholomew and Matthew; James son of Alphaeus and Simon the Zealot, and Judas son of James.
베드로, 요한, 야고보, 안드레와 빌립, 도마와 바돌로매, 마태와 및 알패오의 아들 야고보, 셀롯인 시몬, 야고보의 아들 유다가 다 거기 있어(행 1:13).

(2) Present; 현재의
our **present** sufferings are not worth comparing with the glory that will be revealed in us.
현재의 고난은 장차 우리에게 나타날 영광과 족히 비교할 수 없도다(롬 8:18).

3. 목적어를 취하는 형용사; worth, like

Take no bag for the journey, or extra tunic, or sandals or a staff; for the worker is **worth** his keep.
여행을 위하여 주머니나 두 벌 옷이나 신이나 지팡이를 가지지 말라. 이는 일군이 저 먹을 것 받는 것이 마땅함이니라(마 10:10).

He who doubts is **like** a wave of the sea, blown and tossed by the wind.
의심하는 자는 마치 바람에 밀려 요동하는 바다 물결 같으니(약 1:6).

his eyes were **like** blazing fire.
그의 눈은 불꽃 같고(계 1:14).

Our present sufferings are not **worth** comparing with the glory that will be revealed in us.
현재의 고난은 장차 우리에게 나타날 영광과 족히 비교할 수 없도다(롬 8:18).

4. the + 형용사; 복수 보통명사

the dead, the sick, the blind, the deaf, the rich, the poor, the unemployed, the young, the old, the handicapped, the mentally ill

구어체에서는 보통 the old 대신 old people, the young 대신 young people을 쓴다.

"The + 형용사"는 소유격과 함께 쓸 수 없다.
The problems of the blind. 혹은 blind people's problems (o)
The blind's problems (x)

The righteous will live by faith.
의인이 믿음으로 살리라(갈 3:11).

(The righteous = righteous people)

He has filled **the hungry** with good things but has sent **the rich** away empty.
주리는 자를 좋은 것으로 배 불리셨으며 부자를 공수로 보내셨도다(눅 1:53).

The blind receive sight, **the lame** walk, those who have leprosy are cured, **the deaf** hear, **the dead** are raised, and the good news is preached to **the poor**.
소경이 보며 앉은뱅이가 걸으며 문둥이가 깨끗함을 받으며 귀머거리가 들으며 죽은 자가 살아나며 가난한 자에게 복음이 전파된다(눅 7:22).

Blessed are **the meek**, for they will inherit the earth.
온유한 자는 복이 있나니 저희가 땅을 기업으로 받을 것임이요(마 5:5).

But they will have to give account to him who is ready to judge **the living** and **the dead**.
저희가 산 자와 죽은 자 심판하기를 예비하신 자에게 직고하리라(벧전 4:5).

the + 형용사 = 추상명사

You must distinguish between **the holy** and **the common**, between **the unclean** and **the clean**,
그리하여야 너희가 거룩하고 속된 것을 분별하며 부정하고 정한 것을 분별하고(레 10:10).

B. 수사

1. 복수의 숫자 뒤에서 hundred, thousand, million, dozen은 단수로 쓴다

Five hundred pounds
Hundreds of pounds (수백 파운드)
Several thousand times
It cost thousands.

형용사로 쓸 때도 단수로 쓴다.
A five-pound note, a three-mile walk, six two-hour lessons, a four-month-old baby

Noah was six **hundred** years old when the floodwaters came on the earth.
홍수가 땅에 있을 때에 노아가 육백 세라(창 7:6).

There were about six hundred **thousand** men on foot, besides women and children.
유아 외에 보행하는 장정이 육십만 가량이요(출 12:37).

thousands of; 수천의
Will the LORD be pleased with **thousands** of rams, with ten thousand rivers of oil?
여호와께서 천천의 숫양이나 만만의 강수 같은 기름을 기뻐하실까(미 6:7).

2. 서수사에는 the를 붙임

And there was evening, and there was morning – **the** first day
저녁이 되며 아침이 되니 이는 첫째 날이니라(창 1:5).

In **the** last days, God says, I will pour out my Spirit on all people.
하나님이 가라사대 말세에 내가 내 영으로 모든 육체에게 부어 주리니(행 2:17).

The word of the LORD came to Jonah **a** second time. (a second time = again)

1) 분수

1/8 one eighth,

3/7 three sevenths,

2/5 two fifths,

11/16 eleven sixteenths

2) 1 이하의 분수는 단수

Three quarters of a ton is too much.

One and a half hours

1.3 metres

Abram gave him a tenth of everything.

3) 소수

0.125 nought point one two five

3.7 three point seven

4) 숫자

(1) 백과 십 단위 사이에 and

560 five hundred **and** sixty

6,478 six thousand four hundred **and** seventy eight

(2) 숫자 0

nought(영국식), zero(미국식)로 읽는다.

한 자리 숫자씩 끊어 읽을 때는 oh(알파벳 O처럼)로 읽는다. 온도에서는 zero로 읽는다.

My account number is four one three **oh** six.

Zero degrees Centigrade is thirty-two degrees Fahrenheit.

(3) 전화번호

한 자리씩 읽는다. 같은 숫자가 겹치면 double을 쓴다.

706 2245 seven oh six double two four five

(4) 왕, 왕비
Henry the Eighth (Not; Henry Eight)
Louis the Fourteenth

(5) 사람의 수; there are + 숫자 + of + 대명사
There are only **seven of us** here today.
There were **twelve of us** in my family.

(6) 계산
2 + 2 = 4 two and two is/are four (informal)
two plus two equals four (formal)
7 − 4 = 3 four from seven is three (informal)
seven minus four equals three (formal)
3 x 4 = 12 three fours are twelve (informal)
three multiplied by four equals twelve (formal)
9 ÷ 3 = 3 nine divided by three equals three

3. 배수사

You travel about on sea and land to make one proselyte; and when he becomes one, you make him **twice as much** a son of hell **as** yourselves.
너희는 교인 하나를 얻기 위하여 바다와 육지를 두루 다니다가 생기면 너희보다 배나 더 지옥 자식이 되게 하는도다(마 23:15).

Take **double** the amount of silver with you, for you must return the silver that was put back into the mouths of your sacks.
너희 손에 돈을 배나 가지고 너희 자루 아구에 도로 넣어 온 그 돈을 다시 가지고 가라(창 43:12).

C. 고유형용사

국민을 나타내는 단어 the English, the French, the Swiss, the Japanese 등은 어미에 s가 붙이지 않는다.
그러나 the Koreans, the Americans, the Greeks 등은 어미에 s를 붙인다.

Leave us alone; let us serve **the Egyptians**.
우리를 버려 두라. 우리가 애굽 사람을 섬길 것이라 (출 14:12).

D. 주의할 수량형용사

1. many a는 복수의 의미지만 단수 취급을 한다

Many a man claims to have unfailing love, but a faithful man who can find?
많은 사람은 각기 자기의 인자함을 자랑하나니 충성된 자를 누가 만날 수 있으랴 (잠 20:6).

Play the harp well, sing **many a** song, so that you will be remembered.
기묘한 곡조로 많은 노래를 불러서 너를 다시 기억케 하라 (사 23:16).

2. few는 부정, a few는 긍정의 뜻

The harvest is plentiful but the workers are **few**.
추수할 것은 많되 일군은 적으니 (마 9:37).

A few days later, when Jesus again entered Capernaum, the people heard that he had come home.
수일 후에 예수께서 다시 가버나움에 들어가시니 집에 계신 소문이 들린지라 (막 2:1).

For John baptized with water, but in **a few** days you will be baptized with the Holy Spirit.
요한은 물로 세례를 베풀었으나 너희는 몇 날이 못 되어 성령으로 세례를 받으리라 (행 1:5).

not a few = many

only a few = but few ; 약간

When they were **only a few** men in number, Very few, and strangers in it.
때에 저희 인수가 적어 매우 영성하며 그 땅에 객이 되어(시 105:12).

3. as much; 동량의

Each one gathered **as much** as he needed.
각기 식량대로 거두었더라(출 16:18).

as much as to say = as if to say

so much = 그 정도의

not so much A as B; A라기보다는 B이다

If anyone has caused grief, he has **not so much** grieved me **as** he has grieved all of you.
근심하게 한 자가 있었을지라도 나를 근심하게 한 것이 아니요 어느 정도 너희 무리를 근심하게 한 것이니
(고후 2:5).

not A so much as B

not so much as = not even

not much = 너무 ~은 아니다

4. a little은 긍정, little은 부정의 뜻

When he had gone **a little** farther, he saw James son of Zebedee and his brother John in a boat, preparing their nets.
조금 더 가시다가 세베대의 아들 야고보와 그 형제 요한을 보시니 저희도 배에 있어 그물을 깁는데(막 1:19).

He who gathered much did not have too much, and he who gathered **little** did not have too **little**.
많이 거둔 자도 남지 아니하였고 적게 거둔 자도 모자라지 아니하였느니라(고후 8:15).

I know that you have **little** strength, yet you have kept my word and have not denied my name. 내가 네 행위를 아노니 네가 적은 능력을 가지고도 내 말을 지키며 내 이름을 배반치 아니하였도다 (계 3:8).

the little
not a little = much
little better than = as good as
little short of = almost

E. big, large, great

1. big

구어체에서 주로 사용한다.

We have a **big** new house.
Get your **big** feet off my flowers.
That's a really **big** improvement.
You're making a **big** mistake.

2. large

Large + concrete noun, great + abstract noun; 문어체에서 주로 사용한다.

It was a **large** house, situated neat the river.
I'm afraid my daughter has rather **large** feet.
Her work showed a **great** improvement last year.

3. great

1) 불가산 명사에는 great만 쓸 수 있다.

There was **great** confusion about the dates. (Not; big confusion)
I felt **great** excitement as the meeting came nearer.

2) great의 다른 의미

Famous, important
Do you think Napoleon was really a **great** man?
Newton was probably the **greatest** scientist who ever lived.

3) Wonderful(구어체)

I've had a **great** idea.
"How's the new job?" "**Great**."
It's a **great** car.

F. small / little

1. small

size에만 관련된다(반대말; big, large)

Could I have a **small bag**, please?
You're too **small** to be a policeman.

2. little

size에 감정이 개입된 경우에 쓰인다.

Poor little thing. Come here and let me look after you.

What's he like? Oh, he's a **funny little** man.
What's that **nasty little** boy doing in our garden?
They've bought a **pretty little** house in the country.

G. 부사처럼 생긴 형용사

Friendly, lovely, lonely, ugly, cowardly, likely, unlikely
She gave me a friendly smile.
Her singing was lovely.

이런 형용사는 부사가 없다. 다른 방법으로 부사의 의미를 나타내야 한다.

She smiled at me in a friendly way. (Not; She smiled at me friendly.)
He gave a silly laugh. (Not; He laughed silly.)

Daily, weekly, monthly, yearly, early는 형용사/부사이다.

It's a daily paper. It comes out daily.
An early train. I got up early.

연습 문제

1. Prepare the way for the Lord, make _____ paths for him.
   1) straight   2) straightly   3) straighten   4) straightness

2. Blessed are _____, for they will inherit the earth.
   1) the meekness   2) the meeks   3) the meek   4) meek

   Many are the victims she has brought down: **her slain** are a mighty throng.
   대저 그가 많은 사람을 상하여 엎드러지게 하였나니 그에게 죽은 자가 허다하니라(잠 7:26).

3. _____ are the merciful, for they will be shown mercy.
   1) Blesses   2) Blessings   3) The bless   4) Blessed

4. Do not murder, and anyone who murders will be _____ to judgment.
   1) subject   2) object   3) subjected   4) objected

5. But I tell you that anyone who is angry with his brother will be _____ to judgment.
   1) subject   2) object   3) subjected   4) objected

6. And do not swear by your head, for you cannot make even one hair _____.
   1) a white or a black   2) the white or black   3) the white or the black   4) white or black

7. If you love those who love you, _____ reward will you get?
   1) what   2) which   3) why   4) how

8. So when you give to _____, do not announce it with trumpets.
   1) the need   2) the needs   3) the needy   4) needy

9. When you fast, do not look _____ as the hypocrites do, for they disfigure their faces to show men they are fasting.
   1) somber   2) somberly   3) merry   4) clean

10. Lord, if you are willing, you can make me _____.
    1) cleanly   2) cleanest   3) clean   4) cleanness

11. My servant lies at home _____ and in terrible suffering.
    1) paralyzed   2) paralyzing   3) paralyze   4) paralysis

12. "Go! It will be done just as you believed it would." And his servant was healed at that _____ hour.
    1) such   2) very   3) just   4) some

On that very day Noah and his sons entered the ark.

But I have raised you up for this **very** purpose, that I might show you my power and that my name might be proclaimed in all the earth.
네가 너를 세웠음은 나의 능력을 네게 보이고 내 이름이 온 천하에 전파되게 하려 하였음이니라 (출 9:16).

13. So don't be afraid; you are _____ more than many sparrows.
    1) worth   2) worthy   3) worthless   4) worthness

14. Anyone who does not take his cross and follow me is not _____ of me.
    1) worth   2) worthy   3) worthless   4) worthness

I call to the LORD, who is worthy of praise, and I am saved from my enemies.

15. To what can I compare this generation? They are _____ children sitting in the marketplaces and calling out to others.
    1) liking   2) likely   3) like   4) alike

16. I praise you, Father, Lord of heaven and earth, because you have hidden these things from the wise and learned, and revealed them to _____ children.
    1) little   2) a little   3) a few   4) the most

17. He entered the house of God, and he and his companions ate the _____ bread.
    1) consecrate   2) consecration   3) consecrated   4) consecrating

18. Then they bought him a _____ man who was blind and mute, and Jesus healed him, so that he could both talk and see.
    1) demon-possessed   2) demon-possessing   3) demon possessed   4) demon possessing

19. _____ Judean countryside and all the people of Jerusalem went out to him. 4
    1) Whole   2) Whole the   3) Whole of   4) The whole

Lot looked up and saw that the whole plain of the Jordan was well watered.
Then the woman, knowing what had happened to her, came and fell at his feet and, trembling with fear, told him **the whole** truth.

20. Let us go somewhere else--to the _____ villages--so I can preach there also.
    1) nearly   2) nearing   3) nearby   4) near

21. Jesus asked them, "Which is lawful on the Sabbath: to do good or to do evil, to save life or to kill?" But they remained _____.
    1) silentness   2) silent   3) silently   4) silence

22. But whoever blasphemes against the Holy Spirit will never be forgiven; he is _____ of an eternal sin.
    1) guilty   2) guilt   3) guiltiness   4) guilted

23. He tore the chains apart and broke the irons on his feet. No one was _____ to subdue him.
    1) strong enoughly   2) strong enough   3) strongly enough   4) enoughly strong

I am sending you grain, new wine and oil, enough to satisfy you fully.

There will not be room enough for them.

24. And a woman was there who had been _____ to bleeding for twelve years.
   1) subjugated   2) damaged   3) subjected   4) subject

25. Don't you see that nothing that enters a man from the outside can make him _____?
   1) unclean   2) uncleanly   3) uncleanness   4) uncleaned

26. He even makes _____ hear and the mute speak.
   1) the deafen   2) the deaf   3) deaf   4) the deafs

27. _____ good is it for a man to gain the whole world, yet forfeit his soul?
   1) That   2) Whose   3) Which   4) What

28. But a poor widow came and put in two very small copper coins, _____ only a fraction of a penny.
   1) worthless   2) worth of   3) worth   4) worthy

29. But they had no children, because Elizabeth was _____.
   1) barred   2) barren   3) unable   4) impotent

30. When the devil had finished all this tempting, he left him until an _____ time.
   1) opportune   2) abrupt   3) enough   4) designated

31. News about him spread through _____ countryside.
   1) whole   2) whole the   3) whole of   4) the whole

32. No one after drinking old wine wants the new, for he says, '_____ is better.'
   1) The old   2) Old   3) The new   4) New

You are responsible for the wrong I am suffering.

33. The harvest is plentiful, but the workers are _____.
   1) little   2) few   3) many   4) least

34. Jesus, _____ as he was from the journey, sat down by the well.
    1) tired   2) tiring   3) tires   4) tireless

35. The Jews were amazed and asked, "How did this man get _____ learning without having studied?"
    1) so   2) as   3) such   4) such a

36. Our friend Lazarus has fallen _____; but I am going there to wake him up.
    1) sleep   2) asleep   3) sleepy   4) sleepness

37. _____ were Peter, John, James and Andrew.
    1) Those presented   2) Those presenting   3) The present   4) Those present

38. When they heard this, they were _____ and gnashed their teeth at him.
    1) furious   2) frightened   3) worried   4) interested

39. Men committed indecent acts with other men, and received in themselves the _____ penalty for their perversion.
    1) due   2) proper   3) exact   4) hard

40. One man considers one day more sacred than another; another man considers every day _____.
    1) alike   2) like   3) likely   4) likeness

41. I gave you milk, not solid food, for you were not yet _____ for it.
    1) readily   2) already   3) ready   4) readiness

42. Don't you know that _____ yeast works through the whole batch of dough?
    1) small   2) a little   3) little   4) not a little

43. Is it possible that there is nobody among you _____ to judge a dispute between believers?
    1) wise enough   2) wise enoughly   3) enoughly wise   4) enough wise

44. Everything is _____ for me--but not everything is beneficial.
   1) permit   2) permissible   3) permission   4) permitting

45. But since there is so _____ immorality, each man should have his own wife, and each woman her own husband.
   1) a lot   2) little   3) much   4) many

46. Bad company corrupts _____ character.
   1) good   2) bad   3) better   4) best

47. What is seen is temporary, but what is unseen is _____.
   1) short   2) shortness   3) eternity   4) eternal

48. Each one may receive what is _____ him for the things done while in the body, whether good or bad.
   1) due to   2) due   3) a due   4) dueness

49. But they did not understand what he meant and _____ ask him about it.
   1) were afraid of   2) were afraid to   3) afraid of   4) afraid to

   It was hidden from them, so that they did not grasp it, and they were afraid to ask him about it.

50. I will ask you one question. Answer me, and I will tell you by _____ authority I am doing these things.
   1) what   2) an   3) his   4) my

51. I have spoken to you of earthly things and you do not believe; how then will you believe if I speak of _____ things?
   1) heavenly   2) heaven   3) havened   4) hell

A man finds joy in giving an apt reply-- and how good is a **timely** word!
사람은 그 입의 대답으로 말미암아 기쁨을 얻나니 때에 맞은 말이 얼마나 아름다운고 (잠 15:23).

52. Noah was a righteous man, _____ among the people of his time, and he walked with God.

 1) blameless   2) blame   3) blamed   4) blaming

53. The earth was _____ in God's sight and was full of violence.

 1) benevolent   2) benign   3) corrupt   4) compassionate

54. This is how they made the pleasant land _____.

 1) desolate   2) desolation   3) to desolate   4) desolator

정답

1) 1, 2) 3, 3) 4, 4) 1, 5) 1, 6) 4, 7) 1, 8) 3, 9) 1, 10) 3
11) 1, 12) 2, 13) 1, 14) 2, 15) 3, 16) 1, 17) 3, 18) 1, 19) 4, 20) 3
21) 2, 22) 1, 23) 2, 24) 4, 25) 1, 26) 2, 27) 4, 28) 3, 29) 2, 30) 1
31) 4, 32) 1, 33) 2, 34) 1, 35) 3, 36) 2, 37) 4, 38) 1, 39) 1, 40) 1
41) 3, 42) 2, 43) 1, 44) 2, 45) 3, 46) 1, 47) 4, 48) 2, 49) 2, 50) 1
51) 1, 52) 1, 53) 3, 54) 1

숙어

devote oneself to; 헌신하다 (give oneself to)
Instead, I **devoted myself to** the work on this wall. All my men were assembled there for the work; we did not acquire any land.
도리어 이 성 역사에 힘을 다하며 땅을 사지 아니하였고, 나의 모든 종자도 모여서 역사를 하였으며(느 5:16).

For Ezra had **devoted himself to** the study and observance of the Law of the LORD, and to teaching its decrees and laws in Israel.
에스라가 여호와의 율법을 연구하여 준행하며 율례와 규례를 이스라엘에게 가르치기로 결심하였더라 (스 7:10).

die of; ~으로 죽다
A third of your people will **die of** the plague or perish by famine inside you; a third will fall by the sword outside your walls; and a third I will scatter to the winds and pursue with drawn sword.
너희 가운데서 삼분지 일은 온역으로 죽으며 기근으로 멸망할 것이요 삼분지 일은 너희 사방에서 칼에 엎드러 질 것이며 삼분지 일은 내가 사방에 흩고 또 그 뒤를 따라 칼을 빼리라 (겔 5:12).

* 비교
For through the law I **died to** the law so that I might live for God.
내가 율법으로 말미암아 율법을 향하여 죽었나니 이는 하나님을 향하여 살려 함이니라 (갈 2:19).

different from (to, that); ~와 다른, 별개의
You're very **different from** your brother.
difficulty with (something), **difficulty (in)** doing something; ~으로 곤란을 받고 있다
I'm having **difficulty with** my travel arrangements.
You won't have much **difficulty (in)** getting to know people in Italy.

disappointed with (somebody); ~에 실망하다
My father never showed if if he was **disappointed with** me.

disappointed with/at/about (something); ~에 실망하다
you must be pretty **disappointed with/at/about** your exam results.

discussion about (something); 에 대한 토론
We had a long **discussion about** politics.

distinguish A from B; A와 B를 구별하다
But solid food is for the mature, who by constant use have trained themselves to **distinguish** good **from** evil.
단단한 식물은 장성한 자의 것이니 저희는 지각을 사용하므로 연단을 받아 선악을 분변하는 자들이니라 (히 5:14).

No one could **distinguish** the sound of the shouts of joy **from** the sound of weeping, because the people made so much noise. And the sound was heard far away.
백성의 크게 외치는 소리가 멀리 들리므로 즐거이 부르는 소리와 통곡하는 소리를 백성들이 분변치 못하였느니라 (스 3:10).

divide into (Not; in); 갈라지다, 쪼개지다
The book is **divided into** three parts.

do away with; 제거하다, 죽이다 (abolish, get rid of, destroy)
For we know that our old self was crucified with him so that the body of sin might be **done away with**, that we should no longer be slaves to sin—
우리가 알거니와 우리 옛 사람이 예수와 함께 십자가에 못 박힌 것은 죄의 몸이 멸하여 다시는 우리가 죄에게 종 노릇하지 아니하려 함이니 (롬 6:6).

Then Christ would have had to suffer many times since the creation of the world. But now he has appeared once for all at the end of the ages to **do away with** sin by the sacrifice of himself.
그리하면 그가 세상을 창조할 때부터 자주 고난을 받았어야 할 것이로되 이제 자기를 단번에 제사로 드려 죄를 없게 하시려고 세상 끝에 나타나셨느니라 (히9:26).

They were haughty and did detestable things before me. Therefore I **did away with** them as you have seen.
거만하여 가증한 일을 내 앞에서 행하였음이라. 그러므로 내가 보고 곧 그들을 없이 하였느니라 (겔 16:50).

7. 형용사 비교
(形容詞 比較)

A. 원급 (동등 비교)

1. As + 형용사/부사 + as + 명사/대명사/절

She is **as tall as** her brother.
Can a man run **as fast as** a horse?
It's not **as good as** I expected.

2. 구어체에서 as + 목적격 인칭대명사

She doesn't sing as well as **me**.

3. 문어체에서 as + 주어 + 동사

She doesn't sing as well as **I do**.

I am still **as strong today as** the day Moses sent me out
모세가 나를 보내던 날과 같이 오늘날 오히려 강건하니(수 14:11).

I'm just **as vigorous** to go out to battle now **as I was** then.
나의 힘이 그때나 이제나 일반이라 싸움에나 출입에 감당할 수 있사온즉(수 14:11).

Your wound is **as deep as** the sea.
너의 파괴됨이 바다 같이 크니(아 2:13).

It has become **as dry as** a stick.
막대기 같이 말랐으니(아 4:8).

He is as greedy as the grave.
그는 사망 같아서 족한 줄을 모르고(합 2:5).

Be **as shrewd as** snakes and **as innocent as** doves.
너희는 뱀같이 지혜롭고 비둘기같이 순결하라(마 10:16).

His head and hair were white like wool, **as white as** snow.
그 머리와 털의 희기가 흰 양털 같고 눈 같으며(계 1:14).

Half(twice, three times, etc.) as ~ as ~
The green one isn't **half as good as** the blue one.
A color TV is **twice as expensive as** a black and white.

B. 비교급 (우열 비교)

The punishment of my people is **greater than** that of Sodom.
내 백성의 죄가 소돔의 죄악보다 중하도다(아 4:6).

But now they are **blacker than** soot.
이제는 그 얼굴이 숯보다 검고(아 4:8).

How much **more valuable** is a man **than** a sheep!
사람이 양보다 얼마나 더 귀하냐(마 12:12).

Their horses are **swifter than** leopards, **fiercer than** wolves at dusk.
그 말은 표범보다 빠르고 저녁 이리보다 사나우며(합 1:8).

1. the 비교급 + of the two

Which is taller, Henry or Tom. Henry is **the taller of the two**.

2. 동일인의 성질 비교

He is **more** clever than wise.

3. 라틴어 비교급

But I do not think I am in the least **inferior to** those "super-apostles."

내가 지극히 큰 사도들보다 부족한 것이 조금도 없는 줄 생각하노라(고후 11:5).

After you, another kingdom will rise, **inferior to** yours. Next, a third kingdom, one of bronze, will rule over the whole earth.
왕의 후에 왕만 못한 다른 나라가 일어날 것이요, 세째로 또 놋 같은 나라가 일어나서 온 세계를 다스릴 것이며 (단 2:39).

So he became as much **superior to** the angels as the name he has inherited is **superior to** theirs.
저가 천사보다 얼마큼 뛰어남은 저희보다 더욱 아름다운 이름을 기업으로 얻으심이니(히 1:4).

4. 이중 비교급; 변화를 나타냄

I'm getting **fatter and fatter**.
We're going **more and more** slowly.

5. The 비교급 ~ the 비교급; 두 사물이 함께 변화하는 것을 나타냄

The older I get, the happier I am.
The more dangerous it is, the more I like it.
The more I study, the less I learn.

6. 비교급 강조: very 대신 much/far

My boyfriend is **much/far** older than me.
Russian is **much/far** more difficult than Spanish.

7. 기타 비교급을 수식하는 단어들

very much nicer
a lot happier
rather more quickly
a little less expensive
a bit easier

Is your mother **any** better?
She looks **no** older than her daughter.

C. 최상급

1. the

It's **the best** book I have ever lead.

Though it is **the smallest** of all your seeds, yet when it grows, it is **the largest** of garden plants and becomes a tree
이는 모든 씨보다 작은 것이로되 자란 후에는 나물보다 커서 나무가 되매(마 13:32).

2. even의 뜻을 가지는 최상급

The wisest man does not know everything.

3. 절대 최상급

1) a most = a very

It is **a most** holy part of the offerings made to the LORD by fire.
이는 여호와의 화제 중에 지극히 거룩한 것이니라(레 2:3).

2) most people: 대부분의 사람

3) the most: 가장 ~한

The king went to Gibeon to offer sacrifices, for that was **the most** important high place.
이에 왕이 제사하러 기브온으로 가니 거기는 산당이 큼이라(왕상 3:4).

You are **the most** excellent of men and your lips have been anointed with grace.
왕은 인생보다 아름다와 은혜를 입술에 머금으니 (시 45:2).

4. 최상급 다음의 지명에는 of 보다는 in을 쓴다

I'm the happiest man **in** the world.

5. 명사를 쓰지 않고 최상급을 쓸 수 있다

You're **the nicest** of all.
Which one do your think is **the best**?

6. 같은 최상급의 내용을 나타내는 비교 형식

1) 부정 주어 + so + 원급 + as ~

In all Israel there was **not** a man **so** highly praised for his handsome appearance **as** Absalom.
온 이스라엘 가운데 압살롬같이 아름다움으로 크게 칭찬받는 자가 없었으니 (삼하 14:25).

2) 부정 주어 + 비교급 + than ~

I tell you, among those born of women there is **no** one **greater than** John.
내가 너희에게 말하노니 여자가 낳은 자 중에 요한보다 큰 이가 없도다 (눅 7:28).

3) 비교급 + than any other + 단수명사

You will be blessed **more than any other** people; none of your men or women will be childless, nor any of your livestock without young.

You will be blessed **more than any other** people.
네가 복을 받음이 만민보다 우승하여 (신 7:14).

He was **wiser than any other** man.
저는 모든 사람보다 지혜로와서 (왕상 4:31).

Now I know that the LORD is **greater than all other gods**, for he did this to those who had treated Israel arrogantly."
이제 내가 알았도다 여호와는 모든 신보다 크시므로 이스라엘에게 교만히 행하는 그들을 이기셨도다 (출 18:11).

4) 최상급 + of all (the) + 복수명사

The LORD did not set his affection on you and choose you because you were more numerous than other peoples, for you were the **fewest of all peoples**.
여호와께서 너희를 기뻐하시고 너희를 택하심은 너희가 다른 민족보다 수효가 많은 연고가 아니라 너희는 모든 민족 중에 가장 적으니라(신 7:7).

Never mind about your belongings, because the **best of all** Egypt will be yours.
또 너희의 기구를 아끼지 말라. 온 애굽 땅의 좋은 것이 너희 것임이니라(창 45:20).

연습 문제

1. It is like a mustard seed, which is _____ seed you plant in the ground.
   1) smaller   2) the smaller   3) smallest   4) the smallest

2. She had suffered a great deal under the care of many doctors and had spent all she had, yet instead of getting better she grew _____.
   1) worse   2) bad   3) good   4) worst

3. Jesus commanded them not to tell anyone. But the more he did so, the _____ they kept talking about it.
   1) better   2) faster   3) most   4) more

4. His clothes became dazzling white, _____ than anyone in the world could bleach them.
   1) white   2) whiter   3) whitest   4) the whitest

5. This poor widow has put more into the treasury than all _____.
   1) others   2) other   3) the others   4) the other

6. One _____ than I will come, the thongs of whose sandals I am not worthy to untie.
   1) more powerful   2) powerfuler   3) most powerful   4) powerful

7. The one who is least in the kingdom of God is _____ than he.
   1) great   2) greater   3) more great   4) the greatest

8. When the wine was gone, Jesus' mother said to him, "They have no ____ wine."
   1) more   2) better   3) most   4) much

7. 형용사 비교(形容詞 比較)   149

9. We must obey God _____ than men.
   1) just   2) often   3) rather   4) mostly

10. I am sending you out like sheep among wolves. Therefore be as shrewd as snakes and as _____ as doves.
    1) innocently   2) innocent   3) evil   4) better

    They made their hearts as hard as flint.
    Surely I will redeem them; they will be as numerous as before.

11. Terror and dread will fall upon them. By the power of your arm they will be as still _____ a stone-- until your people pass by, O LORD, until the people you bought pass by.
    1) as   2) so   3) of   4) like
    놀람과 두려움이 그들에게 미치매 주의 팔이 큼을 인하여 그들이 돌같이 고요하였사오되 여호와여 주의 백성이 통과하기까지 곧 주의 사신 백성이 통과하기까지였나이다 (출 15:16).

12. This is what the LORD has commanded: 'Each one is to gather _____ he needs. Take an omer for each person you have in your tent.'
    1) as much so   2) so much as   3) as much as   4) as much
    여호와께서 이같이 명하시기를 너희 각 사람의 식량대로 이것을 거둘지니 곧 너희 인수대로 매명에 한 오멜씩 취하되 각 사람이 그 장막에 있는 자들을 위하여 취할지니라 하셨느니라 (출 16:16).

13. On the sixth day they are to prepare what they bring in, and that is to be twice _____ much as they gather on the other days.
    1) as   2) so   3) very   4) that
    제 육 일에는 그들이 그 거둔 것을 예비할지니 날마다 거두던 것의 갑절이 되리라 (출 16:5).

14. "Come now, let us reason together," says the LORD. "Though your sins are like scarlet, they shall be _____ white as snow: though they are red as crimson, they shall be like wool.
    1) same   2) as   3) so   4) like
    여호와께서 말씀하시되 오라, 우리가 서로 변론하자 너희 죄가 주홍 같을지라도 눈과 같이 희어질 것이요, 진홍 같이 붉을지라도 양털 같이 되리라 (사1:18).

15. Then he said to the man, "Stretch out your hand." So he stretched it out and it was completely restored, just as sound _____ the other.
   1) than   2) so   3) of   4) as

16. Jesus commanded them not to tell anyone. But the more he did so, _____ they kept talking about it.
   1) the more   2) more   3) the much   4) much
   예수께서 저희에게 경계하사 아무에게라도 이르지 말라 하시되 경계 하실수록 저희가 더욱 널리 전파하니 (막 7:36).

   But **the more** they were oppressed, **the more** they multiplied and spread; so the Egyptians came to dread the Israelites and worked them ruthlessly.
   그러나 학대를 받을수록 더욱 번식하고 창성하니 애굽 사람이 이스라엘 자손을 인하여 근심하여 (출 2:12).

17. If what was fading away came with glory, how _____ greater is the glory of that which lasts!
   1) very   2) much   3) as   4) rather

정답
1) 4, 2) 1, 3) 4, 4) 2, 5) 3, 6) 1, 7) 2, 8) 1, 9) 3, 10) 2
11) 1, 12) 3, 13) 1, 14) 2, 15) 4, 16) 1 17) 2

숙어

do good; 이익이 되다
But I tell you who hear me: Love your enemies, **do good** to those who hate you.
그러나 너희 듣는 자에게 내가 이르노니 너희 원수를 사랑하며 너희를 미워하는 자를 선대하며 (눅 6:27).

do harm; 해를 끼치다
Love **does** no **harm** to its neighbor. Therefore love is the fulfillment of the law.
사랑은 이웃에게 악을 행치 아니하나니 그러므로 사랑은 율법의 완성이니라 (롬 13:10).

draw up; (문서를) 작성하다, 끌어올리다, 다가오다
Many have undertaken to **draw up** an account of the things that have been fulfilled among us, just as they were handed down to us by those who from the first were eyewitnesses and servants of the word.
우리 중에 이루어진 사실에 대하여 처음부터 말씀의 목격자 되고 일군 된 자들의 전하여 준 그대로 내력을 저술하려고 붓을 든 사람이 많은지라 (눅 1:1-2).

dream of (= think of, imagine); 몽상하다, 환상에 잠기다
I often **dreamed of** being famous when I was younger.

dream about; 꿈을 꾸다
What does it mean if you **dream about** mountains?

dress in (Not; with); 옷을 입히다
Who's the woman **dressed in** green?

drive into; 몰아넣다
Paul **drove into** a tree again yesterday.

eager to; 간절히 ~ 하고 싶어하는 (impatient)
Therefore, my brothers, be **eager to** prophesy, and do not forbid speaking in tongues.

그런즉 내 형제들아 예언하기를 사모하며 방언 말하기를 금하지 말라(고전 14:39).

example of (Not; for); 견본, 보기, 전례
Sherry is an **example of** a fortified wine.

face to face; 얼굴을 맞대고
I hope to see you soon, and we will talk **face to face**. Peace to you.
속히 보기를 바라노니 또한 우리가 면대하여 말하리라(요3 1:14).

fall(come) short of; ~에 미치지 않다:
for all have sinned and **fall short of** the glory of God,
모든 사람이 죄를 범하였으매 하나님의 영광에 이르지 못하더니(롬 3:23).

for a while; 잠시, 당분간
In the days when the judges ruled, there was a famine in the land, and a man from Bethlehem in Judah, together with his wife and two sons, went to live **for a while** in the country of Moab.
사사들의 치리하던 때에 그 땅에 흉년이 드니라 유다 베들레헴에 한 사람이 그 아내와 두 아들을 데리고 모압 지방에 가서 우거하였는데(룻 1:1).

for nothing; 거저, 무료로, 까닭 없이, 부질없이
For he is God's servant to do you good. But if you do wrong, be afraid, for he does not bear the sword **for nothing**. He is God's servant, an agent of wrath to bring punishment on the wrongdoer.
그는 하나님의 사자가 되어 네게 선을 이루는 자니라 그러나 네가 악을 행하거든 두려워하라 그가 공연히 칼을 가지지 아니하였으니 곧 하나님의 사자가 되어 악을 행하는 자에게 진노하심을 위하여 보응하는 자니라 (롬 13:4).

for one's sake; ~을 위하여
That is why, **for Christ's sake**, I delight in weaknesses, in insults, in hardships, in persecutions, in difficulties. For when I am weak, then I am strong.
그러므로 내가 그리스도를 위하여 약한 것들과, 능욕과, 궁핍과, 핍박과, 곤란을 기뻐하노니 이는 내가 약할 그 때에 곧 강함이니라(고후 12:10).

for the sake of; ~을 위하여

Jesus replied, "And why do you break the command of God **for the sake of** your tradition?
대답하여 가라사대 너희는 어찌하여 너희 유전으로 하나님의 계명을 범하느뇨 (마 15:3).

free from; ~이 없는, ~을 면한

For rulers hold no terror for those who do right, but for those who do wrong. Do you want to be **free from** fear of the one in authority? Then do what is right and he will commend you.
관원들은 선한 일에 대하여 두려움이 되지 않고 악한 일에 대하여 되나니 네가 권세를 두려워하지 아니하려느냐 선을 행하라 그리하면 그에게 칭찬을 받으리라 (롬 13:3).

8. 동사(動詞)
Verb

동사는 주어의 동작이나 상태를 서술하며 시제(tense), 법(mood), 태(voice), 인칭, 수에 따라 다른 형태를 갖추며, 또한 동명사(gerund), 분사(participle), 부정사(infinitive)로 변환될 수 있다.

동사는 구문(structure)상 특색으로 주어와 결합하여 영어의 기본 문형인 "주어 + 동사"를 이룬다. 동사는 목적어의 유무에 따라 타동사와 자동사로 분류되지만 대부분의 동사는 타동사로 쓰일 수도 있고 자동사로 쓰일 수도 있으며, 꼭 타동사로 쓰인다든지 반드시 자동사로만 쓰이는 동사는 그리 많지 않다. 동사의 종류에 따라 다음의 다섯 가지 문형을 만들어 낸다.

A. 문형에 따른 동사의 종류

1. 1형식 문형; S + V (완전자동사), 보어와 목적어가 없음

stop, come, disappear, talk, think, reason, remain, return 등

Immediately her bleeding **stopped** and she felt in her body that she was freed from her suffering.
이에 그의 혈루 근원이 곧 마르매 병이 나은 줄을 몸에 깨달으니라(막 5:29).

when perfection **comes**, the imperfect **disappears**.
온전한 것이 올 때에는 부분적으로 하던 것이 폐하리라(고전 13:10).

When I was a child, I **talked** like a child, I **thought** like a child, I **reasoned** like a child.
내가 어렸을 때에는 말하는 것이 어린 아이와 같고 깨닫는 것이 어린 아이와 같고 생각하는 것이 어린 아이와 같다가(고전 13:11).

And now these three **remain**: faith, hope and love. But the greatest of these is love.
그런즉 믿음, 소망, 사랑, 이 세 가지는 항상 있을 것인데 그 중에 제일은 사랑이라(고전 13:13).

When his time of service was completed, he **returned** home.
그 직무의 날이 다 되매 집으로 돌아가니라(눅 1:23).

2. 2형식 문형; S + V(불완전자동사) + C, 주격 보어가 있음

1) 주어와 형용사를 연결하여 주어의 성질을 설명하게 하는 동사
Be, look, seem, appear, sound, smell, taste, feel, remain

Love **is** patient, love **is** kind.
사랑은 오래 참고, 사랑은 온유하며(고전 13:4).

She **looks** nice.
She **looks** like her mother.
You **look** as if you've had a bad day.
Her perfume **smells** nice.

Her voice **sounds** nice.
You **sound** unhappy. What's the matter?
비교 ; That **sounds like** Arthur coming upstairs.

Her skin **feels** nice.

You **seem angry** about something. (seem + 형용사)
She **seems** nice.
I spoke to a man who **seemed to be the boss**. (seem to be + 명사)
Ann **seems to have** a new boyfriend. (seem + to 부정사)
North Wales **seems like** a good place for a holiday. (seem like)

All a man's ways **seem** innocent to him, but motives are weighed by the LORD.
사람의 행위가 자기 보기에는 모두 깨끗하여도 여호와는 심령을 감찰하시느니라(잠 16:2).

2) 변화에 대하여 설명하는 2형식 동사
It's **becoming** colder.
It's **getting** colder. (구어체)
It's **growing** colder. (문어체)
The leaves are **turning** brown. (문어체)

The leaves are **going** brown. (구어체)

3) 변화하지 않는 것에 대하여 설명하는 2형식 동사
They **remained** silent.
저희가 잠잠하거늘 (막 3:4).

I hope you will always **remain** so charming.
How does she **stay** so young?
Keep calm.

3. 3형식 문형; S + V (완전타동사) + O, 목적어가 1개 있음

We must **discuss** your plans.
She **married** a friend of her sister's
He's clever. But he **lacks** experience.

If any of you **lacks** wisdom.
너희 중에 누구든지 지혜가 부족하거든 (약 1:5).

He will **baptize** you with the Holy Spirit and with fire.
그는 성령과 불로 너희에게 세례를 주실 것이요 (마 3:11).

So the king **gave** the order, and they **brought** Daniel and **threw** him into the lions' den.
이에 왕이 명하매 다니엘을 끌어다가 사자 굴에 던져 넣는지라 (단 6:16).

1) 직접 목적어만 갖는 동사; explain, suggest, describe
I **explained** my problem to her.
Can you **explain** (to me) how to get to your house?
He **suggested** getting a job in a bank. (Not; He suggested me to get a job ---)
My uncle **suggested** that I should get a job in a bank.
Please **describe** your wife to us. (Not; Please describe us your wife.)

2) Marry/divorce

She **married** a professor. (Not; She married with a professor.)
Will you **marry** me?
He is going to **divorce** his wife.

3) 구어체에서 목적어가 없으면 get married / get divorced를 쓴다.

Lulu and Joe **got married** last week.
When are you going to **get married**?
The Robinsons are **getting divorced**.

4) Get/be married to + 목적어

She **got married to** her childhood sweetheart.
I've **been married to** her for 3 years and I still don't know what goes on inside her head.

4. 4형식 문형; S + V(완전타동사; 수여동사) + I.O. + D.O., 목적어가 2개 있음

Bring, buy, cost, give, leave, lend, make, offer, owe, pass, pay, promise, read, refuse, send, show, take, tell, write

He **gave** his wife a camera for Christmas.
Can you **send** me the bill?
I'll **lend** you some.

When she sat down with the harvesters, he **offered** her some roasted grain.
룻이 곡식 베는 자 곁에 앉으니 그가 볶은 곡식을 주매(룻 2:14).

The dragon **gave** the beast his power and his throne and great authority.
용이 자기의 능력과 보좌와 큰 권세를 그에게 주었더라(계 13:2).

5. 5형식 문형; S + V(불완전타동사) + O + C, 목적격 보어가 있음

The rain made the grass wet.
Let's paint the door red.

She ate all she wanted and **had** some left over.
룻이 배불리 먹고 남았더라(룻 2:14).

On the seventh day the priest is to examine him, and if it is spreading in the skin, the priest shall **pronounce** him unclean; it is an infectious skin disease.
칠일만에 제사장이 그를 진찰할지니 만일 병이 크게 피부에 퍼졌으면 그는 그를 부정하다 진단할 것은 문둥병의 환처임이니라(레 13:27).

From now on all generations will **call** me blessed.
이제 후로는 만세에 나를 복이 있다 일컬으리로다(눅 1:48).

The LORD will not **leave** the guilty unpunished.
죄인을 결코 사하지 아니하시느니라(나 1:3).

1) make가 그 용법에 따라 자동사 혹은 타동사가 되는 예

(1) 완전자동사
They **made** for the land. 그들은 육지를 향했다.
It **makes** against his advantage. 그것은 그에게 불이익이 된다.

(2) 불완전자동사
You will be **made** rich in every way so that you can be generous on every occasion, and through us your generosity will result in thanksgiving to God.
너희가 모든 일에 부요하여 너그럽게 연보를 함은 저희로 우리로 말미암아 하나님께 감사하게 하는 것이라(고후 9:11).

(3) 완전타동사
Let us **make** man in our image, in our likeness
우리의 형상을 따라 우리의 모양대로 우리가 사람을 만들고(창 1:26).

The spiritual man **makes** judgments about all things
신령한 자는 모든 것을 판단하나 (고전 2:15).

(4) 수여동사
So **make** yourself an ark of cypress wood;
너는 잣나무로 너를 위하여 방주를 짓되 (창 6:14).

(5) 불완전타동사
And do not swear by your head, for you cannot **make** even one hair white or black.
네 머리로도 말라 이는 네가 한 터럭도 희고 검게 할 수 없음이라 (마 5:36).

See, I lay in Zion a stone that causes men to stumble and a rock that **makes** them fall
보라 내가 부딪히는 돌과 거치는 반석을 시온에 두노니 (롬 9:33).

I will **make** you very fruitful
내가 너로 심히 번성케 하리니 (창 17:6).

B. 타동사의 목적어

1. 목적어의 의미; 동사의 동작이 미치는 사람이나 물건

1) 동작의 직접 대상
But during the night an angel of the Lord opened **the doors** of the jail and brought them out.
주의 사자가 밤에 옥문을 열고 끌어내어 (행 5:19).

2) 동작의 결과
But the man who had received the one talent went off, dug **a hole** in the ground and hid his master's money.
한 달란트 받은 자는 가서 땅을 파고 그 주인의 돈을 감추어 두었더니 (마 25:18).

3) 동족 목적어

Your old men will **dream dreams**.
너희의 늙은이들은 꿈을 꾸리라(행 2:17).

I have **fought** the good **fight**.
내가 선한 싸움을 싸우고(딤후 4:7).

4) 재귀 목적어

Then the prophet went and stood by the road waiting for the king. He disguised **himself** with his headband down over his eyes.
선지자가 가서 수건으로 그 눈을 가리워 변형하고 길가에서 왕을 기다리다가(왕상 20:38).

5) 상호 목적어

Come, let us go down and confuse their language so they will not understand **each other**.
자, 우리가 내려가서 거기서 그들의 언어를 혼잡케 하여 그들로 서로 알아듣지 못하게 하자(창 11:7).

6) 두 개의 직접 목적어를 취하는 동사; forgive, save, envy

I ask you to **forgive** your brothers the sins and the wrongs they committed in treating you so badly.
이제 바라 건대 그 허물과 죄를 용서하라(창 50:17).

2. 목적어의 형식

1) 간접 목적어와 직접 목적어

The woman you put here with me--she gave **me some fruit** from the tree, and I ate it.
하나님이 주셔서 나와 함께 하게 하신 여자 그가 그 나무 실과를 내게 주므로 내가 먹었나이다(창 3:12).

2) 부정사만 목적어로 취하는 동사

wish, hope, decide, care, choose, determine, pretend, refuse 등

Though one **wished to dispute** with him, he could not answer him one time out of a thousand.
사람이 하나님과 쟁변하려 할지라도 천 마디에 한 마디도 대답하지 못하리라(욥 9:3).

He **hoped to see** him perform some miracle.
무엇이나 이적 행하심을 볼까(눅 23:8).

So they **decided to use** the money to buy the potter's field as a burial place for foreigners.
의논한 후 이것으로 토기장이의 밭을 사서 나그네의 묘지를 삼았으니(마 27:7).

And if you **care to accept** [it,] he himself is Elijah, who was to come.
만일 너희가 즐겨 받을 진 대 오리라 한 엘리야가 곧 이 사람이니라(마 11:14).

Since they hated knowledge and did not **choose to fear** the LORD,
대저 너희가 지식을 미워하며 여호와 경외하기를 즐거워하지 아니하며(잠 1:29).

I am **determined to be** wise, but this was beyond me.
내가 지혜자가 되리라 하였으나 지혜가 나를 멀리하였도다(전 7:23).

Go to bed and **pretend to be** ill.
침상에 누워 병든 체하다가(삼하 13:5).

If you **refuse to let** them go, I will plague your whole country with frogs.
네가 만일 보내기를 거절하면 내가 개구리로 너의 온 지경을 칠지라(출 8:2).

3) 동명사만 목적어로 취하는 동사

mind, enjoy, give up, avoid, finish, escape, admit, deny, consider, practice, risk, miss, postpone, resist, excuse, put off 등

Saul will **give up searching** for me anywhere in Israel, and I will slip out of his hand.
사울이 이스라엘 온 경내에서 나를 수색하다가 절망하리니 내가 그 손에서 벗어나리라 하고(삼상 27:1).

On that day I will punish all who **avoid stepping** on the threshold, who fill the temple of their gods with violence and deceit.
그 날에 문턱을 뛰어 넘어서 강포와 궤휼로 자기 주인의 집에 채운 자들을 내가 벌하리라(습 1:9).

I'll draw water for your camels too, until they have **finished drinking**.
당신의 약대도 위하여 물을 길어 그것들로 배불리 마시게 하리이다(창 24:19).

How will you **escape being** condemned to hell?
너희가 어떻게 지옥의 판결을 피하겠느냐(마 23:33).

They could not **risk being** seen entering the city.
사람이 볼까 두려워하여 감히 성에 들어가지 못하고(삼하 17:17).

4) 절이 목적어

I tell you **that** if two of you on earth agree about anything you ask for, it will be done for you by my Father in heaven.
너희에게 이르노니 너희 중에 두 사람이 땅에서 합심하여 무엇이든지 구하면 하늘에 계신 내 아버지께서 저희를 위하여 이루게 하시리라(마 18:19).

C. 보어의 형식

1. 주격 보어

1) 명사

If it is **a boy**, kill him; but if it is **a girl**, let her live.
남자 여든 죽이고 여자 여든 그는 살게 두라(출 1:16).

2) 대명사

All the churches will know that I am **he** who searches hearts and minds
모든 교회가 나는 사람의 뜻과 마음을 살피는 자인 줄 알지라(계 2:23).

3) 형용사

It tasted as sweet as honey in my mouth, but when I had eaten it, my stomach turned **sour**.
내 입에는 꿀같이 다나 먹은 후에 내 배에서는 쓰게 되더라(계 10:10).

4) 부사

The period of his separation is **over**.

그의 몸을 구별한 기간이 끝났다(민 6:13).

5) 구

All who rely on observing the law are **under a curse**
율법 행위에 속한 자들은 저주 아래 있나니(갈 3:10).

The poison of vipers is **on their lips**.
그 입술에는 독사의 독이 있고(롬 3:13).

6) to 부정사

He seems **to be** advocating foreign gods.
이방 신들을 전하는 사람인가보다(행 17:18).

2. 목적격 보어

1) 형용사

Try to get it **clean**.
Cut the bread **thin**.
Keep him **warm**.
You left the house **dirty**.

I will strike her children **dead**.
나는 그녀의 자녀를 쳐서 죽이겠다(계 2:23).

2) 현재분사

I saw a mighty angel **proclaiming** in a loud voice
나는 힘 있는 천사가 큰 음성으로 외치는 것을 보았다(계 5:2).

3) to 부정사

(1) to 부정사를 목적격 보어로 취하는 동사들

Advise, allow, ask, (can't) bear, cause, encourage, expect, get, hate, help, invite, like, mean, need, order, persuade, prefer, remind, teach, tell, want, wan, wish

She didn't **want** me **to go** (Not; She didn't want that I go.)

I didn't **ask** you **to pay** for the meal.

I do not **want** you **to be** ignorant of the fact

너희가 알지 못하기를 내가 원치 아니하노니(고전 10:1).

The demons begged Jesus, "Send us among the pigs; **allow** us **to go** into them."

이에 간구하여 가로되 우리를 돼지에게로 보내어 들어가게 하소서 하니(막 5:12).

For I **command** you today **to love** the LORD your God, **to walk** in his ways, and **to keep** his commands, decrees and laws; then you will live and increase.

곧 내가 오늘날 너를 명하여 네 하나님 여호와를 사랑하고 그 모든 길로 행하며 그 명령과 규례와 법도를 지키라 하는 것이라 그리하면 네가 생존하며 번성할 것이요(신 30:16).

(2) Tell; inform, order의 의미인 경우

① tell + 사람

She **told me** that she would be late. (Not; She told that ---)

I **told the children** to go away.

② Tell이 사람(목적어)을 취하지 않는 경우

tell the truth, tell a lie, tell the time(- know how to read a clock)

I don't think she is **telling the truth.**

He's seven years old and he still can't **tell the time.**

③ 비교; say + (to 사람)

She **said** that she would be late.

She **said** "Go away" to the children.

(3) Remind

① Remind + 목적어 + to 부정사

잊어버렸을지도 모르는 것을 생각나게 해 주다.

Please **remind me to post** these letters.
I **reminded her to send** her sister a birthday card.

② **Remind + 목적어 + of**
과거를 기억 나게 해 주다.

The smell of hay always **reminds me of** our old house in the country.
She **reminds me of** her mother.

4) 원형부정사

(1) 원형부정사를 목적격 보어로 취하는 동사들
let, make(사역동사); see, hear, feel, watch, notice(지각동사); help(기타)

She **lets** her children **do** what they want to.
I **made** them **give** me the money back.
I didn't **see** you **come** in.
I **heard** her **say** that she was tired.
Could you **help** me **push** the car?

5) 명사
They elected him **President**.
You have made me **a very happy man**.
Why do you call your brother **Piggy**?

6) 구
All the believers were together and had everything **in common**.
믿는 사람이 다 함께 있어 모든 물건을 서로 통용하고 (행 2:44).

연습 문제

1. I tell you that out of these stones God can _____ up children for Abraham.
   1) risen   2) stand   3) raise   4) rise

   I will surely raise my hand against them so that their slaves will plunder them.

2. Jesus _____ him, "Away from me, Satan!"
   1) told to   2) talked   3) said to   4) said

   He was astonished and said to those following him.
   I will look to see what he will say to me.

3. If your right eye causes you _____, gouge it out and throw it away.
   1) make sin   2) a sin   3) to sin   4) sin

4. Anyone who _____ his wife must give her a certificate of divorce.
   1) divorces to   2) divorces   3) divorces with   4) divorces from

5. Do not store up for yourselves treasures on earth, where moth and rust destroy, and where thieves _____ and steal.
   1) break   2) break out   3) break up   4) break in

6. Look at the birds of the air; they do not sow or reap or store away in barns, and yet your heavenly Father _____ them.
   1) feeds   2) feed   3) feeds on   4) feed on

7. See how the lilies of the field _____. They do not labor or spin.
   1) raise   2) feed   3) rise   4) grow

The thunder and hail **stopped**, and the rain no longer poured down on the land.
뇌성과 우박이 그치고 비가 땅에 내리지 아니하니라(출 9:33).

8. I do not deserve to have you _____ under my roof.
   1) come   2) came   3) to come   4) coming

9. I _____ my servant, 'Do this,' and he does it.
   1) tell to   2) talk   3) say to   4) say

10. When Jesus came into Peter's house, he saw Peter's mother-in-law _____ in bed with a fever.
    1) lying   2) lie   3) laying   4) lay

When he drank some of its wine, he became drunk and lay uncovered inside his tent.

11. Do not _____ that I have come to bring peace to the earth. I did not come to bring peace, but a sword.
    1) suppose   2) suppose with   3) suppose of   4) be supposed

12. From the days of John the Baptist until now, the kingdom of heaven has been forcefully advancing, and forceful men _____ hold of it.
    1) lie   2) lay   3) lied   4) lain

13. Looking for a reason to accuse Jesus, they _____ him, "Is it lawful to heal on the Sabbath?"
    1) asked on   2) asked of   3) asked to   4) asked

14. If any of you has a sheep and it falls into a pit on the Sabbath, will you not take hold of it and _____ it out?
    1) erect   2) push   3) lift   4) rise

As the waters increased they lifted the ark high above the earth.

15. A bruised reed he will not _____, and a smoldering wick he will not snuff out, till he leads justice to victory.
   1) break   2) break out   3) die   4) grow

16. Every kingdom divided against itself will be ruined, and every city or household divided against itself will not _____.
   1) deteriorate   2) raise   3) perish   4) stand

17. He who is not with me is against me, and he who does not _____ me scatters.
   1) gather   2) gather with   3) gather up   4) gather from

18. Men will have to give account on the day of judgment for every careless word they have _____.
   1) said to   2) told   3) spoken   4) talked

19. As he was scattering the seed, some fell along the path, and the birds came and _____.
   1) ate up it   2) ate it up   3) have eaten up it   4) have eaten it up

20. Other seed _____ among thorns, which grew up and choked the plants.
   1) fall   2) falled   3) fell   4) felled

   He lay down and fell into a deep sleep.
   Rain fell on the earth forty days and forty nights.

21. But since he has no root, he _____ only a short time. When trouble or persecution comes because of the word, he quickly falls away.
   1) lasts   2) lacks   3) prevails   4) overcomes

22. The kingdom of heaven is like a man who _____ good seed in his field.
   1) sewed   2) sew   3) sowed   4) sow

23. As evening _____, the disciples came to him and said, "This is a remote place, and it's already getting late.
   1) approached to   2) approached by   3) was approached   4) approached

24. He was with the wild animals, and angels _____ him.
   1) attended   2) attended at   3) was attended   4) attended to

25. Jesus could no longer _____ a town openly but stayed outside in lonely places.
   1) enter at   2) enter   3) enter into   4) enter in

   His sons' wives entered the ark to escape the waters of the flood.

26. Because of the crowd he told his disciples to have a small boat ready for him, to _____ the people from crowding him.
   1) have   2) keep   3) hold   4) take

   The path of life leads upward for the wise to **keep** him **from going** down to the grave.
   지혜로운 자는 위로 향한 생명 길로 말미암음으로 그 아래 있는 음부를 떠나게 되느니라(잠 15:24).

27. This man lived in the tombs, and no one could _____ him any more, not even with a chain.
   1) bind   2) bind on   3) bound   4) bound on

28. My little daughter is _____. Please come and put your hands on her so that she will be healed and live.
   1) dead   2) died   3) dieing   4) dying

   Everything on dry land that had the breath of life in its nostrils died.

29. He entered a house and did not want anyone _____ it.
   1) knowing   2) of knowing   3) to know   4) know

30. What are you arguing _____?
   1) them at   2) them on   3) with them about   4) with them away

31. "You deaf and mute spirit," he said, "I _____ you, come out of him and never enter him again."
   1) comment on   2) command   3) comment   4) command of

32. The boy _____ so much like a corpse that many said, "He's dead."
   1) looked   2) looked up   3) looked on   4) was looked

33. _____ were you arguing about on the road?
   1) Why   2) How   3) Where   4) What

34. Anyone who divorces his wife and _____ another woman commits adultery against her.
   1) marries to   2) is married   3) marries   4) marries with

35. Both of them were upright in the sight of God, _____ all the Lord's commandments and regulations blamelessly.
   1) observing   2) observing on   3) observing up   4) observing to

36. His mercy _____ those who fear him, from generation to generation.
   1) expands   2) extends   3) expands to   4) extends to

37. You will find a baby wrapped in cloths and _____ in a manger.
   1) lied   2) lieing   3) lying   4) laying

   How long will you **lie** there, you sluggard? When will you get up from your sleep?
   게으른 자여 네가 어느 때까지 눕겠느냐 네가 어느 때에 잠이 깨어 일어나겠느냐(잠 6:9).

38. _____ his hands on each one, he healed them.
   1) lain   2) lieing   3) lying   4) laying

39. Can you make the guests of the bridegroom _____ while he is with them?
   1) fast   2) to fast   3) fasted   4) fasting

40. Lord, don't trouble yourself, for I do not _____ to have you come under my roof.
    1) reserve   2) deserve   3) conserve   4) preserve

41. That is why I did not even _____ myself worthy to come to you.
    1) consider   2) remember   3) thought   4) mind

42. The blind receive sight, the lame walk, those who have leprosy are cured, the deaf hear, the dead are _____, and the good news is preached to the poor.
    1) lifting   2) raising   3) raised   4) risen

The waters rose and increased greatly on the earth.

43. Two men _____ money to a certain moneylender.
    1) owned   2) owed   3) are owed   4) borrowed

44. He _____ another man, "Follow me."
    1) told to   2) talked   3) said to   4) said

45. Stay in that house, eating and drinking whatever they give you, for the worker _____ his wages.
    1) deserves to   2) deserves   3) is deserved   4) preserves

46. He was in the world, and though the world was made through him, the world did not _____ him.
    1) recognize on   2) recognize to   3) recognize at   4) recognize

47. Destroy this temple, and I will _____ it again in three days.
    1) raise   2) rise   3) rise up   4) be raised

48. Here is a boy with five small barley loaves and two small fish, but how far will they _____ among so many?
    1) go   2) come   3) run   4) make

49. A strong wind was blowing and the waters _____.
   1) grew roughly   2) grew rough   3) became roughly   4) rough

50. Immediately the boat _____ the shore where they were heading.
   1) reached to   2) reached   3) was reached to   4) was reached

He reached out his hand and took the dove.

51. He _____ them bread from heaven to eat.
   1) presented   2) presented with   3) gave   4) gave to

LORD, you have assigned me my portion and my cup.
She conceived and bore him a son.

52. This is why I _____ you that no one can come to me unless the Father has enabled him.
   1) said   2) told   3) talked   4) spoke

53. Some wanted to seize him, but no one _____ a hand on him.
   1) laid   2) lied   3) lain   4) lay

Shem and Japheth took a garment and laid it across their shoulders.

54. The good shepherd _____ down his life for the sheep.
   1) lays   2) lies   3) gives   4) looks

55. The truth will set you _____.
   1) freedom   2) to free   3) free   4) freely

56. Can any of you prove me _____ of sin?
   1) to guilty   2) guiltiness   3) guilty   4) of guilty

57. We are not stoning you for any of these, replied the Jews, but for blasphemy, because you, a mere man, _____ God.
   1) claim as   2) claim to be   3) claim being   4) claim of

58. This sickness will not _____ death.
    1) end in   2) be ended in   3) end   4) be ended

59. The Lord your God will _____ up for you a prophet like me from among your own people.
    1) raise   2) rise   3) be raised   4) be risen

60. I long to see you so that I may _____ you some spiritual gift to make you strong.
    1) impart   2) be imparted   3) impart of   4) impart to

61. There is no difference, for all have sinned and _____ short of the glory of God.
    1) fall   2) reach   3) come   4) pull

62. Those who live according to the sinful nature have their minds **set** on what that nature _____.
    1) is desired   2) desires   3) desires to   4) desires of

63. If your enemy is hungry, _____ him; if he is thirsty, give him something to drink.
    1) feed up   2) feed to   3) feed   4) feed on

They do not sow or reap or store away in barns, and yet your heavenly Father feeds them.

64. Your forefathers ate manna and died, but he who _____ this bread will live forever.
    1) feeds on   2) feeds   3) feeds to   4) feeds up

The discerning heart seeks knowledge, but the mouth of a fool **feeds on** folly.
명철한 자의 마음은 지식을 요구하고 미련한 자의 입은 미련한 것을 즐기느니라(잠 15:14).

65. The hour has come for you to _____ from your slumber.
    1) wake up   2) awake up   3) awake   4) be wake

66. I will destroy the wisdom of the wise; the intelligence of the intelligent I will _____.
    1) be frustrated   2) frustrate   3) frustrate to   4) frustrate of

67. No eye has seen, no ear has heard, no mind has _____ what God has prepared for those who love him.
   1) conceived   2) conceived on   3) conceived up   4) conceived to

68. It is good for them to stay _____, as I am.
   1) marry   2) unmarried   3) to be unmarried   4) marriage

69. A husband must not _____ his wife.
   1) divorce   2) divorce with   3) divorce from   4) divorced with

70. Keeping God's commands is what _____.
   1) counts   2) is counted   3) counts on   4) is counted on

71. If what I eat causes my brother _____ sin, I will never eat meat again.
   1) fall   2) fall into   3) to fall   4) to fall into

72. For I am the least of the apostles and do not even _____ to be called an apostle, because I persecuted the church of God.
   1) reserve   2) deserve   3) conserve   4) preserve

73. They refreshed my spirit and yours also. Such men _____ recognition.
   1) reserve   2) deserve   3) conserve   4) preserve

74. _____ perfection, listen to my appeal, be of one mind, live in peace.
   1) Aim of   2) Aim to   3) Aim for   4) Aim

75. _____ each other's burdens, and in this way you will fulfill the law of Christ.
   1) Carry on   2) Carry out   3) Carry for   4) Carry

76. Neither circumcision nor uncircumcision means anything; what _____ is a new creation.
   1) counts   2) is counted   3) counts on   4) is counted on (완전자동사)

May your fountain be blessed, and may you **rejoice** in the wife of your youth.
네 샘으로 복되게 하라 네가 젊어서 취한 아내를 즐거워하라(잠 5:18).

There is a way that seems right to a man, but in the end it **leads** to death.
어떤 길은 사람의 보기에 바르나 필경은 사망의 길이니라(잠 16:25).

Fools **mock** at making amends for sin, but goodwill is found among the upright.
미련한 자는 죄를 심상히 여겨도 정직한 자 중에는 은혜가 있느니라(잠 14:9).

77. The spiritual man _____ judgments about all things, but he himself is not subject to any man's judgment.
    1) makes   2) takes   3) has   4) holds

78. The One enthroned in heaven laughs; the Lord _____ them.
    1) scoffs   2) scoffs at   3) is scoffing   4) is scoffing at

79. Their buyers slaughter them and go _____.
    1) punishment   2) to unpunished   3) to punish   4) unpunished

80. Go into the ark, you and your whole family, because I have found you _____ in this generation.
    1) a right   2) righteous   3) righteousness   4) rightly

81. He _____ seven more days and again sent out the dove from the ark.
    1) waited on   2) waited of   3) waited   4) waited for

82. I _____ my coat to a friend of my brother's, and I never saw it again.
    1) lent   2) borrowed   3) received   4) came

Lend me your comb for a minute, will you? (lend something to somebody, lend somebody something)
I borrowed a pound from my friend. (borrow something from somebody)
Can I borrow your bicycle?

83. This is a nice restaurant. Thanks for _____ me here.
   1) taking   2) passing   3) bringing   4) coming

bring; 말하는 사람이나 듣는 사람이 있는(있었던, 있을) 곳으로 움직일 때
Whre are those papers I asked for? I brought them to you when you were in Mr. Allen's office.
Can you bring the car to my house tomorrow?

take; 다른 장소로 움직일 때
Let's have another drink, and then I'll take you home.
I took the papers to John's office.
Can you take the car to the garage tomorrow?

84. Get up and call _____ your god! Maybe he will take notice of us, and we will not perish.
   1) for   2) at   3) out   4) on

Then Moses went up to God, and the LORD **called to** him from the mountain and said, "This is what you are to say to the house of Jacob and what you are to tell the people of Israel:
모세가 하나님 앞에 올라가니 여호와께서 산에서 그를 불러 가라사대 너는 이같이 야곱 족속에게 이르고 이스라엘 자손에게 고하라(출 19:3).

정답

1) 3, 2) 3, 3) 3, 4) 2, 5) 4, 6) 1, 7) 4, 8) 1, 9) 3, 10) 1
11) 1, 12) 2, 13) 4, 14) 3, 15) 1, 16) 4 17) 2, 18) 3, 19) 2, 20) 3
21) 1, 22) 3, 23) 4, 24) 1, 25) 2, 26) 2, 27) 1, 28) 4, 29) 3, 30) 3
31) 2, 32) 1, 33) 4, 34) 3, 35) 1, 36) 4, 37) 3, 38) 4, 39) 1, 40) 2
41) 1, 42) 3, 43) 2, 44) 3, 45) 2, 46) 4, 47) 1, 48) 1, 49) 2, 50) 2
51) 3, 52) 2, 53) 1, 54) 1, 55) 3, 56) 3, 57) 2, 58) 1, 59) 1, 60) 4
61) 1, 62) 2, 63) 3, 64) 1, 65) 1, 66) 2, 67) 1, 68) 2, 69) 1, 70) 1
71) 4, 72) 2, 73) 2, 74) 3, 75) 4, 76) 1, 77) 1, 78) 2, 79) 4, 80) 2
81) 3, 82) 1, 83) 3, 84) 4

숙어

from a distance; 멀리서
When he saw Jesus **from a distance**, he ran and fell on his knees in front of him.
그가 멀리서 예수를 보고 달려와 절하며(막 5:6).

from generation to generation; 대대로
His mercy extends to those who fear him, **from generation to generation**.
긍휼하심이 두려워하는 자에게 대대로 이르는도다(눅 1:50).

from the beginning; 애초부터
Therefore, since I myself have carefully investigated everything **from the beginning**, it seemed good also to me to write an orderly account for you, most excellent Theophilus,
그 모든 일을 근원부터 자세히 미루어 살핀 나도 데오빌로 각하에게 차례대로 써 보내는 것이 좋은 줄 알았노니(눅 1:3).

get(be, become) acquainted with; (사람과) 아는 사이다(사이가 되다), (사물을) 알고 있다, ~에 정통하다
Then after three years, I went up to Jerusalem to **get acquainted with** Peter and stayed with him fifteen days.
그 후 삼년 만에 내가 게바를 심방하려고 예루살렘에 올라가서 저와 함께 십 오일을 유할 쌔(갈 1:18).

get better; 병이 낫다
She had suffered a great deal under the care of many doctors and had spent all she had, yet instead of **getting better** she grew worse.
많은 의원에게 많은 괴로움을 받았고 있던 것도 다 허비하였으되 아무 효험이 없고 도리어 더 중하여졌던 차에(막 5:26).

get in(to) (a car, taxi, small boat); 타다

get out of (a car, taxi, small boat); 내리다
When I **get into** my car, I found the radio had been stolen.

Get out of my sight! Make sure you do not appear before me again!
너는 나를 떠나가고 스스로 삼가 다시 내 얼굴을 보지 말라 (출 10:28).

get on(to) (a bus, train, plane, ship); 타다

get off (a bus, train, plane, ship); 내리다
We'll be **getting off** the train in ten minutes.

One day when she came to Othniel, she urged him to ask her father for a field. When she **got off** her donkey, Caleb asked her, "What can I do for you?"
악사가 출가할 때에 그에게 청하여 자기 아비에게 밭을 구하자 하고 나귀에서 내리매 갈렙이 그에게 묻되 네가 무엇을 원하느냐 (수 15:18).

get(be) **rid of**; 제거하다, 없애다, ~을 벗어나다
Get rid of the old yeast that you may be a new batch without yeast.
새 덩어리가 되기 위하여 묵은 누룩을 내어 버리라 (고전 5:7).

But what does the Scripture say? "**Get rid of** the slave woman and her son, for the slave woman's son will never share in the inheritance with the free woman's son."
그러니 성경이 무엇을 말하느뇨 계집종과 그 아들을 내어 쫓으라. 계집종의 아들이 자유하는 여자의 아들로 더불어 유업을 얻지 못하리라 하였느니라 (갈 4:30).

The clothing, or the woven or knitted material, or any leather article that has been washed and **is rid of** the mildew, must be washed again, and it will be clean."
네가 빤 의복의 날에나, 씨에나, 무릇 가죽으로 만든 것에 그 색점이 벗어졌으면 그것을 다시 빨아야 정하리라 (레 13:58).

Get rid of the slave woman and her son.
계집종과 그 아들을 내어 쫓으라 (갈 4:30).

give an account of; ~을 설명하다
So then, each of us will **give an account of** himself to God.
이러므로 우리 각인이 자기 일을 하나님께 직고하리라(롬 14:12).

give birth to; ~을 낳다, 생산하다 (bear, produce)
You will be with child and **give birth to** a son, and you are to give him the name Jesus.
보라 네가 수태하여 아들을 낳으리니 그 이름을 예수라 하라(눅 1:31).

give in; (vi) 굴복하다, 양보하다 (vt) 제출하다, 공표하다
We did not **give in** to them for a moment, so that the truth of the gospel might remain with you.
우리가 일시라도 복종치 아니하였으니 이는 복음의 진리로 너희 가운데 항상 있게 하려 함이라(갈 2:5).

9. 시제(時制)
Tense

시제는 동사의 굴절형에 의해 과거, 현재, 미래의 시간 관계를 나타낼 뿐만 아니라 동작의 진행, 완료, 반복 등의 현상을 나타내는 것으로 현재형, 과거형, 미래형, 현재완료형, 과거완료형, 미래완료형이 있다.

A. 현재 시제

1. 현재 시제의 용법

1) 현재의 사실

I **go** to New York about three times a week.
My parents **live** near Paris.

I **hate** pride and arrogance, evil behavior and perverse speech.
나는 교만과 거만과 악한 행실과 패역한 입을 미워하느니라(잠 8:13).

I will hand over to you the people who **live** in the land and you will drive them out before you.
그 땅의 거민을 네 손에 붙이리니 네가 그들을 네 앞에서 쫓아낼지라(출 23:31).

2) 현재의 습관

They **eat** the bread of wickedness and drink the wine of violence.
불의의 떡을 먹으며 강포의 술을 마심이니라(잠 4:17).

3) 불변의 진리

The earth moves round the sun once a year.

4) 미래의 대용

(1) 왕래 발착 동사

come, arrive, depart, go, leave, meet, start, return, sail, ride 등은 미래를 나타내는 부사, 부사구와 함께 쓰여 미래를 나타낼 때가 많다.

The train **arrives** at 4:15.
I **start** work tomorrow.

One rumor **comes** this year, another the next, rumors of violence in the land and of ruler against ruler.
풍설은 이 해에도 있겠고 저 해에도 있으리라 경내에는 강포함이 있어 관원끼리 서로 치리라(렘 51:46).

(2) 시간과 조건을 나타내는 부사절의 현재

I'll phone you when I come back.
She won't come if you don't ask her.
I'll always love you whatever you do.

Hide yourselves there three days until they **return**, and then go on your way.
거기 사흘을 숨었다가 따르는 자들이 돌아간 후에 너희 길을 갈지니라(수 2:16).

But you will receive power when the Holy Spirit **comes** on you.
오직 성령이 너희에게 임하시면 너희가 권능을 받고(행 1:8).

(3) 명사절에서는 미래형

Moreover, no man knows when his hour **will** come.
대저 사람은 자기의 시기를 알지 못하나니(전 9:12).

(4) I hope 다음에 나오는 현재형은 미래

I hope she likes the flowers.
I hope the bus comes soon.

부정문에서는 not을 뒤에 나오는 동사에 붙인다.
I hope she doesn't wake up. (Not; I don't hope she wakes up.)

6) 역사적 사실

Caesar crosses the Rubicon.

7) 옛사람, 옛날 책에 쓰인 말을 인용할 때

Dryden says that none but the brave deserve(s) the fair.

B. 과거 시제

1. 규칙 활용; 어미 + ~ed

Stop stopped(단모음 + 자음)
Try tried(자음 + y)

2음절의 동사가 '단모음 + 단자음'으로 끝나고 액센트가 뒤 음절에 오면 자음을 중복하고 ~ed를 붙인다.
Omit omitted, prefer preferred, occur occurred
그러나 visited, offered, limited
picnic picnicked, mimic mimicked

2. 불규칙 활용; 어미에 ~ed를 붙이지 않는 다른 형태

1) 원형-과거-과거분사의 형태가 같은 경우(A-A-A형)

put – put – put   set – set – set
let – let – let   cut – cut – cut

2) 원형 -과거분사가 형태가 같고 과거만 다른 경우(A-B-A형)

come – came – come   run – ran – run
become – became – become

3) 과거 - 과거분사의 형태가 같은 경우(A-B-B형)

find – found – found   buy – bought – bought
catch – caught – caught   have – had – had

4) 원형-과거-과거분사의 형태가 모두 다른 경우(A-B-C형)

begin – began – begun   choose – chose – chosen
drive – drove – driven   go – went – gone

3. 과거 시제의 용법

1) 과거의 동작, 상태

For he **chose** us in him before the creation of the world to be holy and blameless in his sight.
곧 창세 전에 그리스도 안에서 우리를 택하사 우리로 사랑 안에서 그 앞에 거룩하고 흠이 없게 하시려고 (엡 1:4).

2) 과거의 습관적 동작

We **ate** and **drank** with you, and you **taught** in our streets.
우리는 주 앞에서 먹고 마셨으며 주는 또한 우리 길거리에서 가르치셨나이다 (눅 13:26).

would, used to로 과거의 습관을 나타낼 수 있다.

When all the flocks were gathered there, the shepherds **would** roll the stone away from the well's mouth and water the sheep. Then they **would** return the stone to its place over the mouth of the well.
모든 떼가 모이면 그들이 우물 아구에서 돌을 옮기고 양에게 물을 먹이고는 여전히 우물 아구 그 자리에 돌을 덮더라 (창 29:3).

They recognized him as the same man who **used to** sit begging at the temple gate called Beautiful.
그 본래 성전 미문에 앉아 구걸하던 사람인 줄 알고 (행 3:10).

3) 과거형이 과거완료를 대용

접속사 before가 시간의 순서를 나타내기 때문에 대용이 가능하다.
Keep my requirements and do not follow any of the detestable customs that **were practiced** before you came and do not defile yourselves with them.
그러므로 너희는 내 명령을 지키고 너희 있기 전에 행하던 가증한 풍속을 하나라도 좇음으로 스스로 더럽히지 말라 (레 18:30).

C. 미래 시제

1. 단순 미래

1) I shall (미 will)

The LORD is my shepherd, I **shall** not be in want.
여호와는 나의 목자시니 내가 부족함이 없으리로다(시 23:1).

It is not good for the man to be alone. I **will** make a helper suitable for him.
사람의 독처하는 것이 좋지 못하니 내가 그를 위하여 돕는 배필을 지으리라(창 2:18).

2) You will

You **will** be my witnesses in Jerusalem, and in all Judea and Samaria, and to the ends of the earth.
예루살렘과 온 유대와 사마리아 땅 끝까지 이르러 내 증인이 되리라(행 1:8).

3) He will

He **will** baptize you with the Holy Spirit and with fire.
그는 성령과 불로 너희에게 세례를 주실 것이요(눅 3:16).

But if you do not forgive men their sins, your Father **will** not forgive your sins.
너희가 사람의 과실을 용서하지 아니하면 너희 아버지께서도 너희 과실을 용서하지 아니하시리라(마 6:15).

If one of them falls into a clay pot, everything in it **will** be unclean, and you must break the pot.
그것 중 어떤 것이 어느 질그릇에 떨어지면 그 속에 있는 것이 다 부정하여지나니 너는 그 그릇을 깨뜨리라 (레 11:33).

Blessed are the merciful, for they **will** be shown mercy.
긍휼히 여기는 자는 복이 있나니 저희가 긍휼히 여김을 받을 것임이요(마 5:7).

2. 의문문

1) shall(미 will) I ~?

Then the LORD said, "**Shall** I hide from Abraham what I am about to do?"
여호와께서 가라사대 나의 하려는 것을 아브라함에게 숨기겠느냐(창 18:17).

So do not worry, saying, 'What **shall** we eat?' or 'What **shall** we drink?' or 'What **shall** we wear?'
그러므로 염려하여 이르기를 무엇을 먹을까 무엇을 마실까 무엇을 입을까 하지 말라(마 6:31).

Will I really have a child, now that I am old?
내가 늙었거늘 어떻게 아들을 낳으리요(창 18:13).

2) Will(혹은 shall) you ~?

Will you sweep away the righteous with the wicked?
주께서 의인을 악인과 함께 멸하시려나이까(창 18:23).

You serpents, you brood of vipers, how **shall** you escape the sentence of hell?
뱀들아 독사의 새끼들아 너희가 어떻게 지옥의 판결을 피하겠느냐(마 23:33).

3) Will he ~?

Will the Lord reject forever? **Will** he never show his favor again?
주께서 영원히 버리실까, 다시는 은혜를 베풀지 아니하실까(시 77:7).

D. 진행형

1. 종류

1) 현재 진행형

My father Saul **is looking** for a chance to kill you.
내 부친 사울이 너를 죽이기를 꾀하시느니라(삼상 19:2).

2) 과거 진행형

While he **was sleeping**, he took one of the man's ribs.
잠들매 그가 그 갈빗대 하나를 취하고(창 2:21).

Before the throne, seven lamps **were blazing**
보좌 앞에 일곱 등불 켠 것이 있으니(계 4:5).

3) 미래 진행형

But if you fail to do this, you **will be sinning** against the LORD
너희가 만일 그같이 아니하면 여호와께 범죄함이니(민 32:23).

"Go, worship the LORD your God," he said. "But just who **will be going**?"
바로가 그들에게 이르되 가서 너희 하나님 여호와를 섬기라 갈 자는 누구 누구뇨(출 10:8).

Any vow or obligation taken by a widow or divorced woman **will be binding** on her.
과부나 이혼당한 여자의 서원이나 무릇 그 마음을 제어하려는 서약은 지킬 것이니라(민 30:9).

2. 진행형의 의미

순간적인 동작의 계속의 뜻 외에 습관, 반복을 의미할 수 있다.

1) 현재를 포함하여 가까운 과거, 가까운 미래의 행동, 상태

We are all **waiting** for you. Hurry up!
What **are** you **doing**? I **am reading**.
I **am going** to a lot of parties these days.

It has always been my ambition to preach the gospel where Christ was not known, so that I would not **be building** on someone else's foundation.
또 내가 그리스도의 이름을 부르는 곳에는 복음을 전하지 않기로 힘썼노니 이는 남의 터 위에 건축하지 아니하려 함이라(롬 15:20).

(1) 현재 근방이 아닌 전 시간에 걸친 일반적 시간

현재형을 쓴다.

My sister **is living** at home for the moment. (around now)
You **live** in North London, don't you? (general time)

Why **is** that girl **standing** on the table?
Chetford Castle **stands** on a hill outside the town.

The leaves **are going** brown.
I **go** to the mountains about twice a year.

(2) 물리적인 느낌과 관계되는 동사(feel, hurt, ache 등)

현재형과 현재진행형의 의미가 같다.

How **do** you **feel**? = How **are** you **feeling**?
My head **aches**. = My head **is aching**.

(3) 진행형에 Always를 쓰면 very often의 의미

I'm **always losing** my keys.

She's **always** giving people things and doing things for people.

계획되지 않았던 일이 자주 일어날 때
I'm always meeting Mr. Bailiff in the supermarket. (accidental, unplanned)
When Alice comes to see me, **I always meet** her at the station. (regular, planned)
Her mother **was always arranging** little surprise picnics and outings. (unplanned)
When I was a child, we **always had** picnics on Saturdays in the summer. (regular, planned)

2) 미래
What **are you doing** tomorrow?

3) 변화
The weather **is getting** warmer.
The child **is getting** bigger every day.

4) 정신 활동이나 감각을 나타내는 동사는 진행형을 못 쓴다. 그러나 일시적인 동작과 동사의 뜻이 바뀔 때는 쓸 수 있다
Like, dislike, know, love, hate, prefer, want, wish
surprise, impress, please
believe, feel, imagine, know, mean, realize
recognize, remember, suppose, think, understand
hear, see, smell, sound, taste
weigh, belong to, contain, depend on, include, matter, need, owe, own, possess
appear, seem, be

I like this music. (Not; I'm liking this music.)
I see what you mean. (= understand)
We've got a problem. **I see**. (Not; I am seeing.)

See가 meet, interview, talk to의 뜻일 때는 진행형을 쓸 수 있다.
I am seeing the doctor at ten o'clock.
I'm seeing Miss Barnett at four o'clock.

While Jesus **was having** dinner at Matthew's house, many tax collectors and "sinners" came and ate with him and his disciples. (having = taking)
예수께서 마태의 집에서 앉아 음식을 잡수실 때에 많은 세리와 죄인들이 와서 예수와 그 제자들과 함께 앉았더니 (마 9:10).

5) can + see, hear, feel, smell, taste = 진행형의 뜻

I **can see** Susan coming. (Not; I am seeing ---)
I **can see** a rabbit over there.
I **can hear** somebody coming up the stairs.
What did you put in the stew? I **can taste** something funny.

6) be going to의 용법

(1) 미래

Bring in your idols to tell us what **is going to** happen.
이리 와서, 장차 무슨 일이 일어날 것인지, 우리에게 말하여 보아라 (사 41:22).

(2) 예언

This horde **is going to** lick up everything around us, as an ox licks up the grass of the field.
이 무리가 소가 밭의 풀을 뜯어 먹음같이 우리 사면에 있는 것을 다 뜯어 먹으리로다 (민 22:4).

(3) 작정

Herod **is going to** search for the child to kill him.
헤롯이 아기를 찾아 죽이려 하니 (마 2:13).

* 비교; **go**의 진행형

The one you testified about--well, he is baptizing, and everyone **is going to** him.
선생님이 증거하시던 자가 세례를 주매 사람이 다 그에게로 가더이다 (요 3:26).

E. 현재 완료

have + 과거분사의 형태이며, 현재에 있어서 동작의 완료, 현재까지의 경험, 과거 동작이 현재에 미치는 결과, 현재까지의 동작, 상태의 계속을 나타낸다.

현재완료는 명백히 과거를 나타내는 어구와는 같이 쓰이지 않는다.
just now는 과거의 문장에 just는 현재완료의 문장에 쓴다.

While he was saying this, a ruler came and knelt before him and said, "My daughter **has just died.**
예수께서 이 말씀을 하실 때에 한 직원이 와서 절하고 가로되 내 딸이 방장 죽었사오나(마 9:18).

yet는 의문문, 부정문에, already는 긍정문에 쓴다.
그러나 already가 의문문에 사용될 때는 놀람을 나타낸다.

1. 완료; "막 ~해 버렸다"

I have fought the good fight, **I have finished** the race, I have kept the faith.
내가 선한 싸움을 싸우고 나의 달려갈 길을 마치고 믿음을 지켰으니(딤후 4:7).

2. 경험; "이전에 ~한 적이 있다"

Go back and report to John what you **have seen** and heard.
너희가 가서 보고 들은 것을 요한에게 고하되(눅 7:22).

Nothing like this **has ever been seen** in Israel.(ever; 경험을 강조)
이스라엘 가운데서 이런 일을 본 때가 없다(마 9:33).

Have you **seen** this, son of man?
인자야 네가 보았느냐(겔 8:17).

3. 결과; "그 결과 지금은 ~하다"

The wall of Jerusalem is broken down, and its gates **have been burned** with fire.
예루살렘 성은 훼파되고 성문들은 소화되었다 (느 1:3).

Do not think that I **have come** to abolish the Law or the Prophets.
내가 율법이나 선지자나 폐하러 온 줄로 생각(하)지 말라 (마 5:17).

But if I drive out demons by the Spirit of God, then the kingdom of God **has come** upon you.
그러나 내가 하나님의 성령을 힘입어 귀신을 쫓아 내는 것이면 하나님의 나라가 이미 너희에게 임하였느니라 (마 12:28).

That the Gentiles, who did not pursue righteousness, **have obtained** it, a righteousness that is by faith.
의를 좇지 아니한 이방인들이 의를 얻었으니 곧 믿음에서 난 의요 (롬 9:30-31).

Look! Some of the Israelites **have come** here tonight to spy out the land.
보소서 이 밤에 이스라엘 자손 몇 사람이 땅을 탐지하러 이리로 들어 왔나이다 (수 2:2).

We saw his star in the east and **have come** to worship him.
우리가 동방에서 그의 별을 보고 그에게 경배하러 왔노라 (마 2:2).

4. 계속; "현재까지의 동작, 상태의 계속"

Master, we**'ve worked** hard all night and haven't caught anything.
선생이여, 우리들이 밤이 맞도록 수고를 하였으되 얻은 것이 없지마는 (눅 5:5).

5. 현재 시제의 대용

부사절에서 현재완료는 현재 시제의 대용이며, 한 사건이 시작되기 전에 다른 사건이 완료된 것을 강조한다.

I will telephone you after I have arrived.
After I had left school, I went to Pusan.

I'll draw water for your camels too, until they **have finished** drinking. (= finish)
당신의 약대도 위하여 물을 길어 그것들로 배불리 마시게 하리이다(창 24:19).

I tell you the truth, you will not get out until you **have paid** the last penny. (= pay)
진실로 네게 이르노니 네가 호리라도 남김이 없이 다 갚기 전에는 결단코 거기서 나오지 못하리라(마 5:26).

I hope to visit you while passing through and to have you assist me on my journey there, after I **have enjoyed** your company for a while. (= enjoy)
이는 지나가는 길에 너희를 보고 먼저 너희와 교제하여 약간 만족을 받은 후에 너희의 그리로 보내줌을 바람이라(롬 15:24).

F. 과거 완료

1. 동작이 일어난 순서

When he **opened** his eyes he **could** see nothing.
눈은 떴으나 아무 것도 보지 못하고(행 9:8).

When the Gentiles **heard** this, they **were** glad and **honored** the word of the Lord
이방인들이 듣고 기뻐하여 하나님의 말씀을 찬송하며(행 13:48).

2. 먼저 일어난 사건

After the crowd **had been** put outside, he went in and took the girl by the hand, and she got up.
무리를 내어 보낸 후에 예수께서 들어 가사 소녀의 손을 잡으시 매 일어나는지라(마 9:25).

3. 과거의 어떤 때를 기준하여 그때까지의 완료, 경험, 결과, 계속

1) 완료

Now the springs of the deep and the floodgates of the heavens **had been** closed, and the rain **had stopped** falling from the sky.
깊음의 샘과 하늘의 창이 막히고 하늘에서 비가 그치매(창 8:2).

2) 경험

They realized he **had seen** a vision in the temple, for he kept making signs to them but remained unable to speak.
백성들이 그 성소 안에서 이상은 본 줄 알았더라. 그가 형용으로 뜻을 표시하며 그냥 벙어리 대로 있더니 (눅 1:22).

3) 결과

She heard in Moab that the LORD **had come** to the aid of his people by providing food for them
그가 모압 지방에 있어서 여호와께서 자기 백성을 권고하사 그들에게 양식을 주셨다 함을 들었으므로(룻 1:6).

4) 계속

And when the demon was driven out, the man who **had been** mute spoke.
귀신이 쫓겨나고 벙어리가 말 하거늘(마 9:33).

4. no sooner ~ than, hardly(scarcely) ~ when(before)은 과거완료 쓰고, 주어의 도치에 주의

No sooner had they set their feet on the dry ground **than** the waters of the Jordan returned to their place and ran at flood stage as before.
그 발바닥으로 육지를 밟는 동시에 요단 물이 본 곳으로 도로 흘러 여전히 언덕에 넘쳤더라(수 4:18).

No sooner had Gideon died **than** the Israelites again prostituted themselves to the Baals.
기드온이 이미 죽으매 이스라엘 자손이 돌이켜 바알들을 음란하게 위하고(삿 8:33).

Yet **no sooner** is Zion in labor **than** she gives birth to her children.
그러나 시온은 구로하는 즉시에 그 자민을 순산하였도다 (사 66:8).

expect, intend, want, desire 등 소망의 뜻이 있는 동사가 과거완료로 쓰이면 이루지 못한 사실을 나타낸다.

When his accusers got up to speak, they did not charge him with any of the crimes I **had expected**.
원고들이 서서 나의 짐작하던 것 같은 악행의 사건은 하나도 제출치 아니하고 (행 25:18).

And if it does evil in my sight and does not obey me, then I will reconsider the good I **had intended** to do for it.
만일 그들이 나 보기에 악한 것을 행하여 내 목소리를 청종치 아니하면 내가 그에게 유익케 하리라 한 선에 대하여 뜻을 돌이키리라 (렘 18:10).

G. 미래 완료

will(또는 shall) + have + 과거분사의 형태이며 미래의 때를 나타내는 어구를 동반하여 그때까지의 완료, 경험, 계속 등을 나타낸다. 미래의 시점에서 비로본 과거를 의미한다.

1. 완료

But if you do warn the wicked man and he does not turn from his wickedness or from his evil ways, he will die for his sin; but you **will have saved** yourself.
네가 악인을 깨우치되 그가 그 악한 마음과 악한 행위에서 돌이키지 아니하면 그는 그 죄악 중에서 죽으려니와 너는 네 생명을 보존하리라 (겔 3:19).

And he made known to us the mystery of his will according to his good pleasure, which he purposed in Christ, to be put into effect when the times **will have reached** their fulfillment--to bring all things in heaven and on earth together under one head, even Christ.
그리스도 안에서 미리 세우신 하나님이 기뻐하시는 뜻을 따라, 하나님의 신비한 뜻을 우리에게 알려 주셨습니다. 하나님의 경륜은 때가 차면 하늘과 땅에 있는 모든 것을 그리스도 안에서 그분을 머리로 하여 통일시키는 것입니다(엡 1:9-10).

2. 경험

I **shall have visited** his house four times if I visit again.

3. 계속

He **will have been** in hospital for five days by next Saturday.

H. 불규칙 동사의 변화

1. H. 원형, 과거형, 과거분사형이 동일

Burst, cast, cost, cut, hit, hurt, let, put, read, set, shed, shut, split, spread, thrust

2. 과거, 과거분사형이 동일

bring brought bought
buy bought bought
fight fought fought
sell sold sold
bleed bled bled
feed fed fed
build built built
lay laid laid
pay paid paid
keep kept kept
catch caught caught
teach taught taught

wind wound wound
speed sped sped
lead led led
spend spent spent
hear heard heard
sleep slept slept
weep wept wept
hold held held
leave left left
lose lost lost
mean meant meant
shine shone(shined) shone(shined)
win won won

3. 서로 다른 것

begin began begun
drink drank drunk
rise rose risen
write wrote written
choose chose chosen
bite bit bitten
blow blew blown
shave shaved shaven
show showed shown
swim swam swum
sing sang sung
drive drove driven
strive strove striven
freeze froze frozen
weave wove woven
hide hid hidden
tear tore torn
fly flew flown

shake shook shaken
sow sowed sown
swell swelled swollen
tread trod trodden
wear wore worn

4. 원형과 과거분사형이 동일한 것

come came come
run ran run
lie lied lied, lie lay lain, lay laid laid
fall fell fallen, fell felled felled
find found found, found founded founded
wind wound wound, wound wounded wounded
saw sawed sawn, sow sowed sown, sew sewed sewn

연습 문제

1. And when the demon was driven out, the man who _____ mute spoke.
   1) have been   2) had been   3) were   4) would have been

   If you **had responded** to my rebuke, **I would have poured** out my heart to you and made my thoughts known to you.

   When Pharaoh saw that the rain and hail and thunder **had stopped**, he sinned again: He and his officials hardened their hearts.
   바로가 비와 우박과 뇌성의 그친 것을 볼 때에 다시 범죄하여 마음을 완강케 하니 그와 그 신하가 일반이라 (출 9:34).

2. When Herod realized that he _____ by the Magi, he was furious.
   1) have outwitted   2) have been outwitted   3) had outwitted   4) had been outwitted

3. I tell you the truth, you will not get out until you _____ the last penny.
   1) have paid   2) will have paid   3) will pay   4) paid

   Stay with my workers **until** they **finish** harvesting all my grain.

4. Those tending the pigs ran off and reported this in the town and countryside, and the people went out to see what _____.
   1) happens   2) had happened   3) happening   4) will happen

   Those who had seen it told the people what had happened to the demon-possessed man

5. On hearing of this, John's disciples came and took his body and _____ it in a tomb.
   1) lays   2) were laying   3) laid   4) have laid

6. He saw at the water's edge two boats, left there by the fishermen, who _____ their nets.

   1) washing   2) have washed   3) washes   4) were washing

7. Here a great number of disabled people _____ to lie--the blind, the lame, the paralyzed.

   1) used   2) use   3) were using   4) had used

8. Last year you _____ the first not only to give but also to have the desire to do so.

   1) have   2) had   3) were   4) are

9. They will be ashes under the soles of your feet on the day when I _____ these things.

   1) do   2) will do   3) had done   4) did

   See, I will send you the prophet Elijah before that great and dreadful day of the LORD comes.

10. Then he sent out a dove to see if the water had _____ from the surface of the ground.

    1) recede   2) to recede   3) receded   4) recession

정답

1) 2, 2) 4, 3) 1, 4) 2, 5) 3, 6) 4, 7) 1, 8) 3, 9) 1, 10) 3

숙어

good at; 능숙한, 유능한
Are you any **good at** tennis?

go on ~ing; 계속해서 ~ 하다
What shall we say, then? Shall we **go on sinning** so that grace may increase?
그런즉 우리가 무슨 말 하리요 은혜를 더하게 하려고 죄에 거하겠느뇨(롬 6:1).

Yours **go on eating** and drinking.
당신의 제자들은 먹고 마시나이다(눅 5:33).

go out; 꺼지다, 외출하다
The fire must be kept burning on the altar continuously; it must not **go out**.
불은 끊이지 않고 단 위에 피워 꺼지지 않게 할지니라(레 6:13).

hand over; 넘겨주다, 양도하다
This man was **handed over** to you by God's set purpose and foreknowledge; and you, with the help of wicked men, put him to death by nailing him to the cross.
그가 하나님의 정하신 뜻과 미리 아신 대로 내어준 바 되었거늘 너희가 법 없는 자들의 손을 빌어 못 박아 죽였으나(행 2:23).

have nothing to do with; ~와 관계가 없다
Have nothing to do with the fruitless deeds of darkness, but rather expose them.
너희는 열매 없는 어두움의 일에 참예하지 말고 도리어 책망하라(엡5:11).

the idea of ~ing (Not; the idea to ~); ~ 생각
I don't like **the idea of getting** married yet.

ill with; ~으로 병든, 아픈
The boss has been **ill with** flu this week.

impressed with/by; ~에 감동하다
I'm very **impressed with/by** your work.

in a heap; 무더기를 이루어
the water from upstream stopped flowing. It piled up **in a heap** a great distance away, at a town called Adam in the vicinity of Zarethan, while the water flowing down to the Sea of the Arabah (the Salt Sea) was completely cut off. So the people crossed over opposite Jericho.
곧 위에서부터 흘러내리던 물이 그쳐서 심히 멀리 사르단에 가까운 아담 읍 변방에 일어나 쌓이고 아라바의 바다 염해로 향하여 흘러가는 물은 온전히 끊어 지매 백성이 여리고 앞으로 바로 건널 쌔 (수 3:16).

in accordance with; ~에 따라서, ~와 일치하여
You are to determine the amount of lamb needed **in accordance with** what each person will eat.
각 사람의 식량을 따라서 너희 어린 양을 계산할 것이며 (출 12:4).

For by the grace given me I say to every one of you: Do not think of yourself more highly than you ought, but rather think of yourself with sober judgment, **in accordance with** the measure of faith God has given you.
내게 주신 은혜로 말미암아 너희 중 각 사람에게 말하노니 마땅히 생각할 그 이상의 생각을 품지 말고 오직 하나님께서 각 사람에게 나눠 주신 믿음의 분량대로 지혜롭게 생각하라 (롬 12:3).

in addition (to); ~외에 또
In addition, we are sending with them our brother who has often proved to us in many ways that he is zealous, and now even more so because of his great confidence in you.
또 저희와 함께 우리의 한 형제를 보내었노니 우리가 여러 가지 일에 그 간절한 것을 여러 번 시험하였거니와 이제 저가 너희를 크게 믿은고로 더욱 간절하니라 (고후 8:22).

By all this we are encouraged. **In addition to** our own encouragement, we were especially delighted to see how happy Titus was, because his spirit has been refreshed by all of you.
이로 인하여 우리가 위로를 받았고 우리의 받은 위로 위에 디도의 기쁨으로 우리가 더욱 많이 기뻐함은 그의 마음이 너희 무리를 인하여 안심함을 얻었음이니라 (고후 7:13).

He also brought the grain offering, took a handful of it and burned it on the altar **in addition to** the morning's burnt offering.
또 소제를 드리되 그 중에서 한 움큼을 취하여 아침 번제물에 더하여 단 위에 불사르고 (레 9:17).

All their neighbors assisted them with articles of silver and gold, with goods and livestock, and with valuable gifts, **in addition to** all the freewill offerings.

그 사면 사람들이 은 그릇과 황금과 기타 물건과 짐승과 보물로 돕고 그 외에도 예물을 즐거이 드렸더라 (스 1:6).

10. 조동사(助動詞)
Auxiliary verb

조동사는 단독으로 쓰이지 못하며 본동사와 결합하여 시제(tense), 법(mood), 태(voice) 등의 부가적 의미를 본동사에 부가한다. 부가되는 의미에 따라 조동사를 분류하면 다음과 같다.

- 시제(tense); be, have(had), will(would), shall(should), etc.
- 법(mood); will(would), shall(should), may(might), can(could), etc.
- 태(voice); be, get, become, etc.
- 강조, 의문, 부정 ; do(did)

A. may, might

1. 일반적 용법

1) 허가; can/could보다 더 정중함

May I put the TV on? Yes, of course you may.
I wonder if I might have a little more cheese?

You must distinguish between the unclean and the clean, between living creatures that may be eaten and those that may not be eaten.
부정하고 정한 것과 먹을 생물과 먹지 못할 생물을 분별한 것이니라 (레 11:47).

이미 내려진 허가/불허가에 대해서는 may/might를 쓰지 않고 can/could를 쓴다.
These days, children can do what they like.
I could read what I liked when I was a child.

2) 금지

may not, must not은 거의 같은 뜻이지만 must not을 많이 쓴다.

Students may not use the staff car park.

You **must not** go very far.
너무 멀리는 가지 말라(출 8;28).

When he asks, he **must** believe and **not** doubt
오직 믿음으로 구하고 조금도 의심하지 말라(약 1:6).

3) 현재의 추측

Where's Henry? He **may/could** be at Joe's place.
We **may** go camping this summer. (Not; We can go ---)

Not that I am looking for a gift, but I am looking for what **may be** credited to your account.
내가 선물을 구함이 아니요 오직 너희에게 유익하도록 과실이 번성하기를 구함이라(빌 4:17).

이런 의미로 의문문에서는 may를 쓰지 않는다.
Do you think you'll go camping this summer?
(Not; May you go camping this summer?)

4) 과거의 추측

Peter was very late. He **may lave missed** his train.
What was that noise? It **might have been** a cat.

When someone invites you to a wedding feast, do not take the place of honor, for a person more distinguished than you **may have been** invited. If so, the host who invited both of you will come and say to you, 'Give this man your seat.'
네가 누구에게나 혼인 잔치에 청함을 받았을 때에 상좌에 앉지 말라. 그렇지 않으면 너보다 더 높은 사람이 청함을 받은 경우에 너와 저를 청한 자가 와서 너더러 이 사람에게 자리를 내어 주라 하리니(눅 14:8-9).

The youth **may have come** from prison to the kingship, or he **may have been** born in poverty within his kingdom.
한 나라의 가난한 집안에서 태어나서 젊어서 감옥살이를 하다가도 임금자리에 오를 수 있다(전 4:14).

5) 가능; may = can

You **may** eat any animal that has a split hoof completely divided and that chews the cud.
짐승 중 무릇 굽이 갈라져 쪽발이 되고 새김질하는 것은 너희가 먹되(레 11:3).

On the first day hold a sacred assembly, and another one on the seventh day. Do no work at all on these days, except to prepare food for everyone to eat--that is all you **may** do.
너희에게 첫날에도 성회요 제 칠일에도 성회가 되리니 이 두 날에는 아무 일도 하지 말고 각인의 식물만 너희가 갖출 것이니라(출 12:16).

6) 시제의 일치

She said it might rain.

2. 특수 용법

1) 기원문

May your God, whom you serve continually, rescue you!
너의 항상 섬기는 네 하나님이 너를 구원하시리라(단 6:16).

may를 생략하는 경우가 있다.

(May) your kingdom come, **(may)** your will be done on earth as it is in heaven.
나라이 임하옵시며 뜻이 하늘에서 이룬 것같이 땅에서도 이루어지이다(마 6:10).

2) 목적; (so) that ~ may = in order that ~ may, "~하기 위하여"

Then take it to your father to eat, **so that** he **may** give you his blessing before he dies.
네가 그것을 가져 네 부친께 드려서 그로 죽으시기 전에 네게 축복하기 위하여 잡수시게 하라(창 27:10).

3) 양보; may ~ but, "비록 ~이라 해도", "과연 ~ 이지만"

4) 당연; may well = have good reason to, "~하는 것도 당연하다"

May as well = had better, "~하는 게 더 낫다
May as well ---- as ~, "~할 바에는 --- 하는 게 낫다."
"~ 하는 것은 --- 하는 것과 같다."

5) might; may보다 정중한 표현, 과거의 뜻은 없음

You **might** come to me tomorrow.
Might I ask you a question? (매우 정중한 표현으로 잘 사용하지 않음)

Abraham said to God, "If only Ishmael **might** live under your blessing!"
아브라함이 이에 하나님께 고하되 이스마엘이나 하나님 앞에 살기를 원하나이다(창 17:18).

May보다 가능성이 더 적을 때 쓴다.
I **may** go to Kwangju tomorrow. (50퍼센트 정도의 가능성이 있을 때)
She **might** come with me. (30퍼센트 정도의 가능성이 있을 때)

B. can, could

1. 능력, 가능; "～할 수 있다"

Who **can** join the club? Anybody who wants to.
But where in this remote place **can** anyone get enough bread to feed them?
It **could** be quite frightening if you were alone in our big old house.

I am glad I **can** have complete confidence in you.
내가 너희를 인하여 범사에 담대한 고로 기뻐하노라(고후 7:16).

2. 허가; "～해도 좋다"

Can I ask you something? Yes, of course you **can**.
Can I have some more tea?
You **can** go now if you want to.
When I was a child, I **could** watch TV whenever I wanted to.

On the fourth day they got up early and he prepared to leave, but the girl's father said to his son-in-law, "Refresh yourself with something to eat; then you **can** go."

나흘 만에 일찌기 일어나 떠나고자 하매 여자의 아비가 그 사위에게 이르되 떡을 조금 먹어 그대의 기력을 도운 후에 그대의 길을 행하라(삿 19:5).

3. 강한 추측

There's somebody at the door. Who **can** it be?
It **can't** be the postman. It's only seven o'clock. (축약형 부정: can't[/ka:nt/]).
The report **cannot** be true.

4. 제의

Can I carry your bag? Oh, thanks very much.

5. 요청

Can you put the children to bed? Yes, all right.
Could you lend me five dollars until tomorrow?

6. cannot have 과거분사 = 과거의 부정 추측; "~ 이었을 리가 없다"

That was a bad place to go skiing. You **could have broken** your leg.
Why did you throw the bottle out of the window? It **could have hit** somebody.

7. 공손한 말씨에는 could

Could I see you tomorrow evening?

8. remember, understand, speak, play는 can이 없어도 can의 의미가 있음

I (can) remember London during the war.
She speaks Greek.

I can't/don't understand.
Can/do you play the piano?

C. must, have to, had to

1. must의 용법

1) 필요, 의무; "~하여야 한다"

I really **must** stop smoking.
You **must** be here before eight o'clock.
Must I clean all the rooms?
Why **must** you always leave the door open?

It is required that those who have been given a trust **must** prove faithful.
맡은 자들에게 구할 것은 충성이니라 (고전 4:2).

2) 필연, 불가피; "반드시 ~한다"

All must die.

3) 금지(must not = mustn't)

You **mustn't** tell him. (= Don't tell him.)
You **mustn't** open this parcel before Christmas Day.

You **must not** eat fruit from the tree that is in the middle of the garden, and you **must not** touch it, or you will die.
동산 중앙에 있는 나무의 실과는 하나님의 말씀에 너희는 먹지도 말고 만지지도 말라 너희가 죽을까 하노라 (창 3:3).

There are some that only chew the cud or only have a split hoof, but you **must not** eat them.
새김질하는 것이나 굽이 갈라진 짐승 중에도 너희가 먹지 못할 것은 이러하니 (레 11:4).

If any brother has a wife who is not a believer and she is willing to live with him, he **must not** divorce her.
만일 어떤 형제에게 믿지 아니하는 아내가 있어 남편과 함께 살기를 좋아하거든 저를 버리지 말며(고전 7:12).

4) 추측; "~임에 틀림없다"

Mary keeps crying. She must have some problem.
There's the doorbell. It must be Henry.

5) 과거의 추측; "~했음에 틀림없다"

We went to Rome last month. That must have been nice.
I don't think he must have heard you. Call again.

What I did **must have become** known.
일이 탄로되었도다(출 2:14).

Something **must have happened** to David to make him ceremonially unclean.
그에게 무슨 사고가 있어서 부정한가 보다(삼상 20:26).

2. have to, had to의 용법

must와 have to는 정확하게 똑같은 뜻은 아니다.
Must는 명령을 하거나 명령을 받을 때 쓰며, 주로 말하는 사람이나 듣는 사람으로부터 명령이 나온다.
그에 비해서 have to는 법, 규칙, 협정 또는 제3자 등 외부에서부터 오는 명령이다.

I **must** stop smoking. (I want to.)
I **have to** stop smoking. (Doctor's orders)

This is a terrible party. We really **must** go home.
This is a lovely party, but we **have to** go home because of the babysitter.

I've got bad toothache. I **must** make an appointment with the dentist.
I can't come to work tomorrow morning because I **have to** see the dentist.

(I have an appointment.)

Must you wear dirty old jeans all the time? (= Is it personally important for you?)
Do you **have to** wear a tie at work? (= Is it a rule?)

1) have to = must, don't have to = neet not

Even if I **have to** die with you, I will never disown you.
내가 주와 함께 죽을 지언 정 주를 부인하지 않겠나이다(막 14:31).

You **don't have to** tell him. (= You can if you like, but it's not necessary.)
You **don't have to** wear a tie to work, but you **mustn't** wear jeans. (= Wear a tie or not, as you like. But no jeans.)

have to, had to의 의문문과 부정문 형식은 각각 두 가지다.

I will let you go; you **don't have to** stay any longer.
내가 너희를 보내리니 너희가 다시는 머물지 아니하리라(출 9;28).

2) had to는 must의 과거형이다.

I **had to** pay a big price for my citizenship.
나는 돈을 많이 들여 이 시민권을 얻었노라(행 22:28).

Each one **had to** provide supplies for one month in the year.
각기 일 년에 한 달씩 식물을 예비하였으니(왕상 4:7).

3) must의 미래 시제

A hot-tempered man must pay the penalty; if you rescue him, you **will have to** do it again.
노하기를 맹렬히 하는 자는 벌을 받을 것이라. 네가 그를 건져 주면 다시 건져 주게 되리라(잠 19:19).

But I tell you that men **will have to** give account on the day of judgment for every careless word they have spoken.
내가 너희에게 이르노니 사람이 무슨 무익한 말을 하든지 심판 날에 이에 대하여 심문을 받으리니(마 12:36).

4) 간접화법에서 must의 과거: had to 또는 must

5) 추측의 의미: must(had to는 사용할 수 없음)

D. will, shall

1. 주어의 의지를 나타내는 will

이때의 will은 [wil]하고 강하게 발음한다.

Can somebody help me? I will.
There's the doorbell. I'll go.
I really will stop smoking.

I **will** go and be a lying spirit in the mouths of all his prophets.
내가 나가서 거짓말하는 영이 되어 그 모든 선지자의 입에 있겠나이다(대하 18:21).

I **will** never blot out his name from the book of life
내가 그 이름을 생명책에서 반드시 흐리지 아니하고(계 3:5).

But because you say so, I **will** let down the nets.
말씀에 의지하여 내가 그물을 내리리이다(눅 5:5).

2. 말하는 사람의 의지를 나타내는 shall

If a man will not work, he **shall** not eat.
누구든지 일하기 싫어하거든 먹지도 말게 하라(살후 2:10).

But I am the LORD your God, who brought you out of Egypt. You **shall** acknowledge no God but me, no Savior except me.
그러나 네가 애굽 땅에서 나옴으로부터 나는 네 하나님 여호와라. 나밖에 네가 다른 신을 알지 말 것이라. 나

외에는 구원자가 없느니라 (호 13:4).

3. 상대방의 의지를 묻는 shall, will

Shall I carry your bag?
Shall we go out for lunch?
What **shall** we do?

Shall I go and get one of the Hebrew women to nurse the baby for you?
내가 가서 히브리 여인 중에서 유모를 불러 다 가 당신을 위하여 이 아이를 젖 먹이게 하리이까 (출 2:7).

She went out and said to her mother, "What **shall** I ask for?" "The head of John the Baptist," she answered.
저가 나가서 그 어미에게 말하되 내가 무엇을 구하리이까 그 어미가 가로되 세례 요한의 머리를 구하라 하니 (막 6:24).

Will you destroy the whole city because of five people?
오십 의인 중에 오 인이 부족할 것이면 그 오 인 부족함을 인하여 온 성을 멸하시리이까 (창 18:28).

4. will, shall의 특수 용법

1) 부드러운 명령, 제의

Will you send me the bill, please?
Will you come this way?
Will you have some more potatoes?
What **will** you have to drink?

2) 습성, 성격

She **will** sit talking to herself for hours.
When I was a child, I **would** get up early and go fishing on Saturdays. (과거)

3) 거부

But I know that the king of Egypt **will not** let you go unless a mighty hand compels him.
내가 아노니 강한 손으로 치기 전에는 애굽 왕이 너희의 가기를 허락(하).지 아니하다가(출 3:19).

4) 습관

He will often go to see his mother in the evening.

5) 추측

This will be your luggage.

6) 법률, 규칙

The priest **shall** bring it to the altar, wring off the head and burn it on the altar; its blood **shall** be drained out on the side of the altar.
제사장은 그것을 단으로 가져 다가 그 머리를 비틀어 끊고 단 위에 불사르고 피는 단 곁에 흘릴 것이며 (레 1:15).

The priest **shall** make atonement for him for his sin.
제사장은 그의 허물을 위하여 속죄할 지니라(레 5:6).

7) 예언

So I will stretch out my hand and strike the Egyptians with all the wonders that I will perform among them. After that, he **will** let you go.
내가 내 손을 들어 애굽 중에 여러 가지 이적으로 그 나라를 친 후에야 그가 너희를 보내리라(출 3:20).

E. Do

1. 부정문에서

Jesus replied, "They **do** not need to go away.
예수께서 가라사대 갈 것 없다(마 14:16).

Do not resist an evil person.
악한 자를 대적지 말라(마 5:39).

2. 의문문에서

Why **do** you quarrel with me? Why **do** you put the LORD to the test?
너희가 어찌하여 나와 다투느냐 너희가 어찌하여 여호와를 시험하느냐(출 17:2).

3. 강조의 조동사

I **do** think so.

4. 어순 도치

Never **did** I read such an interesting book.

5. 대동사

Did you see him lately? Yes, I **did**.

So when you give to the needy, do not announce it with trumpets, as the hypocrites **do** in the synagogues and on the streets, to be honored by men.
그러므로 구제할 때에 외식하는 자가 사람에게 영광을 얻으려고 회당과 거리에서 하는 것같이 너희 앞에 나팔을 불지 말라(마 6:2).

I will stand there before you by the rock at Horeb. Strike the rock, and water will come out of it for the people to drink. So Moses **did** this in the sight of the elders of Israel.
내가 거기서 호렙 산 반석 위에 너를 대하여 서리니 너는 반석을 치라 그것에서 물이 나리니 백성이 마시리라 모세가 이스라엘 장로들의 목전에서 그대로 행하니라(출 17:6).

F. would, should, ought to

1. would의 용법

will의 과거형으로 사용하며, will보다 부드러운 표현에도 쓴다.

1) 과거

I will be here at ten tomorrow. (현재)
She said that she **would** be there at ten the next day. (과거)

2) 과거의 거부

He won't do his homework. (현재)
He wouldn't do his homework. (과거)

But this time also Pharaoh hardened his heart and **would not** let the people go.
그러나 바로가 이 때에도 마음을 완강케 하여 백성을 보내지 아니하였더라(출 8:32).

3) 과거의 습관

She will talk to herself for hours. (현재)
She **would** talk to herself for hours. (과거)

Night and day among the tombs and in the hills he **would** cry out and cut himself with stones.
밤낮 무덤 사이에서나 산에서나 늘 소리지르며 돌로 제 몸을 상하고 있었더라(막 5:5).

4) 부드러운 요청

Will you open the window, please (정식 요청)

Would you open the window, please (부드러운 요청)

5) would = wish to

If anyone **would** come after me, he must deny himself and take up his cross and follow me.
아무든지 나를 따라 오려거든 자기를 부인하고 자기 십자가를 지고 나를 좇을 것이니라 (막 8:34).

So in everything, do to others what you **would** have them do to you.
그러므로 무엇이든지 남에게 대접을 받고자 하는 대로 너희도 남을 대접하라 (마 7:12).

2. should의 용법

1) 의무

People **should** drive more carefully.
You **shouldn't** say things like that to her.

In this matter no one **should** wrong his brother or take advantage of him.
이 일에 분수를 넘어서 형제를 해하지 말라 (살전 4:6).

The king **should** know that we went to the district of Judah, to the temple of the great God.
왕께 아시게 하나이다 우리가 유다도에 가서 지극히 크신 하나님의 전에 나아가 보온즉 (스 5:8).

But Moses said to God, "Who am I, that I **should** go to Pharaoh and bring the Israelites out of Egypt?"
이제 이스라엘 자손의 부르짖음이 내게 달하고 애굽 사람이 그들을 괴롭게 하는 학대도 내가 보았으니 (출 3:9).

2) 과거에 하지 않은 일 비평; "~했어야만 했는데"

I **should have phoned** him this morning, but I forgot.

Since its blood was not taken into the Holy Place, you **should have eaten** the goat in the sanctuary area, as I commanded.
그 피를 성소에 들여오지 아니하였으니 그 제육은 너희가 나의 명한 대로 거룩한 곳에서 먹었어야 할 것이니라 (레 10:18).

By lying to my people, who listen to lies, you have killed those who **should not have died** and have spared those who should not live.
거짓말을 지어서 죽지 아니할 영혼을 죽이고 살지 못할 영혼을 살리는도다(겔 13:19).

3) 이성적 판단

It is 다음에 necessary, important, proper, natural, right, well, good, wrong, rational 등이 올 때 종속절에 should를 쓴다. 이때의 should는 해석하지 않는다.

But it is more **necessary** for you that I remain in the body.
그러나 내가 육신에 거하는 것이 너희를 위하여 더 유익하리라(빌 1:24).

4) 감정적 판단

It is 다음에 strange, curious, odd, wonderful, surprising, regrettable, a pity 등이 오면 종속절에 should를 쓴다.

5) 관용적 사용

insist, suggest, propose, demand, order, desire, wish, request 등의 동사 다음에 계속되는 that절 내에 should가 관용적으로 쓰인다. 그러나 미국 영어에서는 이 should를 빼고 원형을 많이 쓴다.

(Jesus) **ordered** that the men **be** put outside for a little while.
명하사 사도들을 잠간 밖에 나가게 하고(행 5:34).

All agreed that the king **should** issue an edict and enforce the decree
관원이 의논하고 왕에게 한 율법을 세우며 한 금령을 정하실 것을 구하려 하였는데(단 6:7).

Then King Nebuchadnezzar fell prostrate before Daniel and paid him honor and ordered that an offering and incense **be** presented to him.
이에 느부갓네살 왕이 엎드려 다니엘에게 절하고 명하여 예물과 향품을 그에게 드리게 하니라(단 2:46).

He shall **order** that the contaminated article **be** washed.
제사장은 명하여 그 색점 있는 것을 빨게 하고(레 13:54).

6) why should

(1) 이유를 모르겠다는 의미
Why should it get colder when you go up to mountain? You're getting nearer the sun.

(2) 화가 났다는 의미
Why should I? / how should I know?
Open the window. Why should I?
What's Susan's phone number? How should I know?

7) so that ---- should(혹은 might); "~하도록"
I lent him the book so that he should study the subject.

8) 추측
Henry should be here soon. He left home at six.
We're spending the winter in Miami. That should be nice.

9) If I were you, I should ~; 충고할 때
If I were you, I should get that car serviced.
I shouldn't worry if I were you.

때때로 If I were you를 생략한다.
I should get that car serviced.
I shouldn't worry.

3. ought 의 용법

to부정사와 함께 쓰여서 should와 거의 같은 뜻이지만 외부의 규칙, 법률, 도덕적 의무 등에 관해 나타낼 때는 ought를 많이 쓴다. must보다는 약하다.

1) 의무
What time ought I to arrive?
I really ought to phone my friend.

Everybody **ought** to give five per cent of their income to the Third World.

We do not know what we **ought** to pray for, but the Spirit himself intercedes for us with groans that words cannot express.
우리가 마땅히 빌 바를 알지 못하나 오직 성령이 말할 수 없는 탄식으로 우리를 위하여 친히 간구하시느니라 (롬 8:26).

ought의 부정 ; ought not ; People **ought not** to drive like that.

He gave them over to a depraved mind, to do what **ought not** to be done.
하나님께서 저희를 그 상실한 마음대로 내어 버려두사 합당치 못한 일을 하게 하셨으니 (롬 1:28).

2) 추측
He **ought** to be here soon – he left home at six.
We're spending the winter in Miami. That **ought** to be nice.
Tom **ought** to be at home now.
비교 ; Tom **must** be at home now. (확실함)

3) 충고
You **ought** to give up smoking.
비교 ; The doctor said I **must** give up smoking. (명령)

4) 과거
I told him that he **ought** to look for her.

5) ought to have + 과거분사 ; "~했어야만 했는데"
I **ought to have phoned** him this morning, but I gorgot.
She **ought to have arrived** at her office by now.

I have made a fool of myself, but you drove me to it. I **ought to have been** commended by you, for I am not in the least inferior to the "super-apostles," even though I am nothing.
내가 어리석은 자가 되었으나 너희에게 억지로 시킨 것이니 내가 너희에게 칭찬을 받아야 마땅하도다. 내가 아무 것도 아니나 지극히 큰 사도들보다 조금도 부족하지 아니하니라 (고후 12:11).

G. need, dare (감히 ~하다)

need, dare는 의문문, 부정문(do 없이)에서 조동사, 긍정문, 부정문(do와 함께)에서는 본동사의 역할을 한다.

1. need

1) 조동사

But they **need not** account for the money entrusted to them, because they are acting faithfully.
그러나 저희 손에 붙인 은을 회계하지 아니하였으니 이는 그 행하는 것이 진실함이었더라 (왕하 22:7).

2) 본동사

I **need to** be baptized by you, and do you come to me?
내가 당신에게 세례를 받아야 할 터인데 당신이 내게로 오시나이까 (마 3:14).

the priest is to examine him, and if the itch has spread in the skin, the priest does not **need to** look for yellow hair; the person is unclean.
제사장은 그를 진찰할지니 과연 옴이 피부에 퍼졌으면 누른 털을 찾을 것 없이 그는 부정하니라 (레 13:36).

2. dare

1) 조동사

Dare she tell him?
I **dare** not say what I think.

If any of you has a dispute with another, **dare** he take it before the ungodly for judgment instead of before the saints?
너희 중에 누가 다른 이로 더불어 일이 있는데 구태여 불의한 자들 앞에서 송사하고 성도 앞에서 하지 아니하느냐 (고전 6:1).

No one else **dared** join them, even though they were highly regarded by the people.
그 나머지는 감히 그들과 상종하는 사람이 없으나 백성이 칭송하더라 (행 5:13).

From then on no one **dared** ask him any more questions.
그 후에 감히 묻는 자가 없더라(막 12:34).

2) 본동사

He **dares** to say what he thinks.
She didn't **dare** to tell him.

현대 영어에서 dare는 보통 일반동사로 쓰며 특히 부정문에서는 일반동사로 많이 쓴다.

She does not **dare** to go out at night.
They didn't **dare** to open the door.

'I am the God of your fathers, the God of Abraham, Isaac and Jacob.' Moses trembled with fear and did not **dare to** look.
나는 네 조상의 하나님 즉 아브라함과 이삭과 야곱의 하나님이로라 하신대 모세가 무서워 감히 알아 보지 못하더라(행 7:32).

We **do not dare to** classify or compare ourselves with some who commend themselves.
우리가 어떤 자기를 칭찬하는 자로 더불어 감히 짝하며 비교할 수 없노라(고후 10:12).

Very rarely will anyone die for a righteous man, though for a good man someone might possibly **dare to** die.
의인을 위하여 죽는 자가 쉽지 않고 선인을 위하여 용감히 죽는 자가 혹 있거니와(롬 5:7).

But even the archangel Michael, when he was disputing with the devil about the body of Moses, did not **dare to** bring a slanderous accusation against him, but said, "The Lord rebuke you!"
천사장 미가엘이 모세의 시체에 대하여 마귀와 다투어 변론할 때에 감히 훼방하는 판결을 쓰지 못하고 다만 말하되 주께서 너를 꾸짖으시기를 원하노라 하였거늘(유 1:9).

They are so defiled with blood that no one **dares to** touch their garments.
그 옷이 피에 더러웠으므로 사람이 만질 수 없도다(아 4:14).

I dare say = I think probably / I suppose
I **dare say** it'll rain tomorrow.
I **dare say** you are ready for a walk.

H. used to

1. 과거의 습관

I **used to** smoke, but I've stopped.
She **used to** be very talkative.

Just as you **used to** offer the parts of your body in slavery to impurity and to ever-increasing wickedness, so now offer them in slavery to righteousness leading to holiness.
전에 너희가 너희 지체를 부정과 불법에 드려 불법에 이른 것같이 이제는 너희 지체를 의에게 종으로 드려 거룩함에 이르라(롬 6:19).

Don't you remember that when I was with you I **used to** tell you these things?
내가 너희와 함께 있을 때에 이 일을 너희에게 말한 것을 기억하지 못하느냐(살후2:5).

And all the believers **used to** meet together in Solomon's Colonnade.
믿는 사람이 다 마음을 같이하여 솔로몬 행각에 모이고(행 5:12).

2. 과거에 있어서의 계속적인 상태

Before certain men came from James, he **used to** eat with the Gentiles.
야고보에게서 온 어떤 이들이 이르기 전에 게바가 이방인과 함께 먹다가(갈 2:12).

But thanks be to God that, though you **used to** be slaves to sin, you wholeheartedly obeyed the form of teaching to which you were entrusted.
하나님께 감사하리로다. 너희가 본래 죄의 종이더니 너희에게 전하여 준 바 교훈의 본을 마음으로 순종하여 (롬 6:17).

As for you, you were dead in your transgressions and sins, in which you **used to** live
너희의 허물과 죄로 죽었던 너희를 살리셨도다(엡 2:1-2).

3. used to의 의문문, 부정문

Did you **use to** play football at school? (informal)
Used you **to** play football at school? (formal)

I **didn't use to** like opera, but now I do. (informal)
I **used not to** like opera, but now I do. (formal)

4. be used to 명사 혹은 ~ing; "~에 익숙하다"

I'**m used to** London traffic. I've lived here for six years.
At the beginning, I couldn't understand the Londoners, because I **wasn't used to** their accent.
I'**m used to driving** in London now, but it was hard at the beginning.
It was a long time before she **was** completely **used to working** with old people.

5. get(become) used to 명사 혹은 ~ing

You'll soon **get used to** living in the country.

연습 문제

1. If anyone _____ not welcome you or listen to your words, shake the dust off your feet when you leave that home or town.
   1) will   2) shall   3) has   4) did

   But Moses said to the LORD, "If the Israelites **will** not listen to me, why would Pharaoh listen to me, since I speak with faltering lips?
   모세가 여호와 앞에 고하여 가로되 이스라엘 자손도 나를 듣지 아니하였거든 바로가 어찌 들으리이까 나는 입이 둔한 자니이다(출 6:12).

2. Turn from your evil ways and your evil practices. But they _____ not listen or pay attention to me.
   1) shall   2) must   3) should   4) would

   When I called, they did not listen; so when they called, I would not listen.

   Yet Pharaoh's heart became hard and he would not listen to them, just as the LORD had said.
   그러나 바로의 마음이 강퍅하여 그들을 듣지 아니하니 여호와의 말씀과 같더라(출 7:13).

3. And from then on no one _____ ask him any more questions.
   1) dare   2) does   3) dare to   4) dared

   Get these out of here! How dare you turn my Father's house into a market!
   You were steeped in sin at birth; how dare you lecture us!
   Moses trembled with fear and did not dare to look.

4. I will repair its broken places, restore its ruins, and build it as it _____ be.
   1) used   2) used to   3) use   4) was used to

5. The fish in the Nile will die, and the river will stink; the Egyptians will not be able _____ its water.

   1) drinking   2) in drinking   3) to drink   4) drink

   하수의 고기가 죽고 그 물에서는 악취가 나리니 애굽 사람들이 그 물 마시기를 싫어하리라 (출 7:18).

6. Then Pharaoh summoned Moses and said, "Go, worship the LORD. Even your women and children _____ go with you; only leave your flocks and herds behind."

   1) ought   2) need   3) could   4) may

   바로가 모세를 불러서 이르되 너희는 가서 여호와를 섬기되 너희 양과 소는 머물러 두고 너희 어린 것은 너희와 함께 갈지니라 (출 10:24).

7. When Pharaoh let the people go, God did not lead them on the road through the Philistine country, though that was shorter. For God said, "If they face war, they _____ change their minds and return to Egypt."

   1) might   2) be   3) have to   4) should

   바로가 백성을 보낸 후에 블레셋 사람의 땅의 길은 가까울지라도 하나님이 그들을 그 길로 인도하지 아니하셨으니 이는 하나님이 말씀하시기를 이 백성이 전쟁을 보면 뉘우쳐 애굽으로 돌아갈까 하셨음이라 (출 13:17).

8. You _____ leave here and go to Judea, so that your disciples may see the miracles you do.

   1) ought   2) ought to   3) had   4) had to

   A man ought to examine himself before he eats of the bread and drinks of the cup.

9. Go and get your own straw wherever you can find it, but your work _____ be reduced at all.

   1) will   2) could not   3) will not   4) shall

   너희는 짚을 얻을 곳으로 가서 주우라 너희 일은 조금도 감하지 아니하리라 (출 5:11).

10. Though we live in the world, we do not wage war as the world _____.

    1) does   2) wage   3) has   4) can

    대동사
    He died, and so **did** the prophets.

And no one pours new wine into old wineskins. If he **does**, the wine will burst the skins, and both the wine and the wineskins will be ruined. No, he pours new wine into new wineskins. 새 포도주를 낡은 가죽부대에 넣는 자가 없나니 만일 그렇게 하면 새 포도주가 부대를 터뜨려 포도주와 부대를 버리게 되리라. 오직 새 포도주는 새 부대에 넣느니라(막 2:22).

정답
1) 1, 2) 4, 3) 4, 4) 2, 5) 3, 6) 4, 7) 1, 8) 2, 9) 3, 10) 1

숙어

in an instant; 눈 깜짝할 사이에
The devil led him up to a high place and showed him **in an instant** all the kingdoms of the world.
마귀가 또 예수를 이끌고 올라가서 순식간에 천하 만국을 보이며(눅 4:5).

in bundles; 덩어리로
Let both grow together until the harvest. At that time I will tell the harvesters: First collect the weeds and tie them **in bundles** to be burned; then gather the wheat and bring it into my barn.'"
둘 다 추수 때까지 함께 자라게 두어라. 추수 때에 내가 추수 군들에게 말하기를 가라지는 먼저 거두어 불사르게 단으로 묶고 곡식은 모아 내 곳간에 넣으라 하리라(마 13:30).

in charge of; ~을 맡고 있는
That same day Pharaoh gave this order to the slave drivers and foremen **in charge of** the people:
바로가 당일에 백성의 간역자들과 패장들에게 명하여 가로되(출 5:6).

independent of; ~로부터 독립하여, ~와 관계없이
She got a job so that she could be **independent of** her parents.

In fact; 사실상, 실제로, 사실은(as a matter of fact)
In fact, no one can enter a strong man's house and carry off his possessions unless he first ties up the strong man. Then he can rob his house.
사람이 먼저 강한 자를 결박(하).지 않고는 그 강한 자의 집에 들어가 세간을 늑탈치 못하리니 결박한 후에야 그 집을 늑탈하리라(막 3:27).

Now if it pleases the king, let a search be made in the royal archives of Babylon to see if King Cyrus did **in fact** issue a decree to rebuild this house of God in Jerusalem.
이제 왕이 선히 여기시거든 바벨론에서 왕의 국고에 조사하사 과연 고레스 왕이 조서를 내려 하나님의 이 전을 예루살렘에 건축하라 하셨는지 보시고(스 5:17).

in front of; ~의 앞에, ~의 정면에
Aaron threw his staff down **in front of** Pharaoh and his officials, and it became a snake.
아론이 바로와 그 신하 앞에 지팡이를 던졌더니 뱀이 된지라 (출 7:10).

When I saw that they were not acting in line with the truth of the gospel, I said to Peter **in front of** them all.
네가 유대인으로서 이방을 좇고 유대인답게 살지 아니하면서 어찌하여 억지로 이방인을 유대인답게 살게 하려느냐 하였노라 (갈 2:14).

Immediately he stood up **in front of** them, took what he had been lying on and went home praising God.
그 사람이 저희 앞에서 곧 일어나 누웠던 것을 가지고 하나님께 영광을 돌리며 자기 집으로 돌아가니 (눅 5:25).

in full 전부, 전액, 줄이지 않고, 고스란히, 자세히
I tell you the truth, they have received their reward **in full**.
진실로 너희에게 이르노니 저희는 자기 상을 이미 받았느니라 (마 6:2).

in harmony with; ~와 조화되어
Live **in harmony with** one another. Do not be proud,
서로 마음을 같이 하며 높은 데 마음을 두지 말고 (롬 12:16).

in need; ~필요로 하는, 부족한
Share with God's people who are **in need**. Practice hospitality.
성도들의 쓸 것을 공급하며 손 대접하기를 힘쓰라 (롬 12:13).

He answered, "Have you never read what David did when he and his companions were hungry and **in need**?
예수께서 가라사대 다윗이 자기와 및 함께 한 자들이 핍절되어 시장할 때에 한 일을 읽지 못하였느냐 (막 2:25).

in order to; ~ 할 목적으로
You have a fine way of setting aside the commands of God **in order to** observe your own traditions!
너희가 너희 유전을 지키려고 하나님의 계명을 잘 저버리는도다 (막 7:9).

in other words; 바꾸어 말하면

In other words, it is not the natural children who are God's children, but it is the children of the promise who are regarded as Abraham's offspring.

곧 육신의 자녀가 하나님의 자녀가 아니라 오직 약속의 자녀가 씨로 여기심을 받느니라(롬 9:8).

11. 태(態)
Voice

태는 동작의 관점 차이에 의해 생기는 동사의 형태상 구별로 능동태(active voice)와 수동태(passive voice)가 있으며, 수동태는 be + 과거분사로 이루어지고, be 동사가 아닌 get, become, grow, stand 등이 쓰여 수동태의 의미가 되는 수도 많다.

A. 태의 종류와 전환

1. 종류

- 능동태; 동작을 하는 쪽에 중점을 둠
- 수동태; 동작을 받는 쪽에 중점을 둠

2. 능동태에서 수동태로 전환하는 방법

- 주어; 능동태의 목적어가 됨
- 동사; be + 과거분사로
- by ~; 능동태의 주어가 by 뒤에 와서 부사구를 이룸

At that time Jesus came from Nazareth in Galilee and **was baptized by** John in the Jordan.
그 때에 예수께서 갈릴리 나사렛으로부터 와서 요단강에서 요한에게 세례를 받으시고(막 1:9).

B. 수동태의 시제

1. 현재

Give me my wife. My time **is completed**, and I want to lie with her.
내 기한이 찼으니 내 아내를 내게 주소서 내가 그에게 들어가겠나이다(창 29:21).

2. 과거

Thus the heavens and the earth **were completed** in all their vast array.
천지와 만물이 다 이루니라(창 2:1).

3. 미래

인칭에 따라 will, shall을 정한다.

He who overcomes **will**, like them, **be dressed** in white
이기는 자는 이와 같이 흰 옷을 입을 것이요(계 3:5).

C. 주의할 수동태

1. 4형식의 수동태

4형식 문장은 대개 간접 목적어를 주어로 하든지, 직접 목적어를 주어로 하여 2개의 수동태가 가능하다. 4형식의 수동태는 3형식 문장이다.

He gave me the book.
I was given the book by him.
The book was given (to) me by him.

4형식 문장이 반드시 2개의 수동태가 되는 것은 아니다. 4형식의 make, write, sell, send, sing, pass 등의 동사는 수동태가 하나뿐이다.

She made her child a doll.
A doll was made for her child by her.

I wrote him a letter.
A letter was written him by me.

2. 5형식의 수동태

5형식 문장을 수동태로 고쳐 쓰면 2형식의 문장이 된다.

They elected him President.
He was elected President.

일반인을 나타내는 we, you, one, they, people, someone, somebody등은 수동태에서는 보통 생략된다.

3. 보어가 원형부정사인 수동태

술부 동사가 지각동사 또는 사역동사일 경우, 원형부정사는 수동태에서는 to 있는 부정사로 된다.

We saw him enter the theater.
He was seen to enter the theater.

4. 동작의 행위를 나타내는 전치사

능동문의 주어는 수동태에서 대개 전치사구로 나타나는데 그 때의 대표적인 전치사는 by 이지만, 동사에 따라 다른 전치사가 오는 경우가 있다.

The earth will **be filled with** the knowledge of the glory of the LORD, as the waters cover the sea.
대저 물이 바다를 덮음 같이 여호와의 영광을 인정하는 것이 세상에 가득하리라(합 2:14).

연습 문제

1. Then Jesus was led by the Spirit into the desert to be tempted _____ the devil.
   1) from   2) by   3) of   4) to

   Jesus came from Galilee to the Jordan to be baptized by John.
   Be careful not to do your acts of righteousness before men, to be seen by them.

2. Ask and it will be given to you; seek and you will find; knock and the door will _____ to you.
   1) be opened   2) be open   3) open   4) opened

3. Still other seed fell on good soil, where it produced a crop--a hundred, sixty or thirty times what _____.
   1) sew   2) was sowed   3) was sewn   4) was sown

4. All who touched him _____.
   1) healed   2) have healed   3) were healed   4) was healed

5. Anyone who curses his father or mother must _____ to death.
   1) be put   2) put   3) be to put   4) have been put

6. The people were amazed _____ his teaching, because he taught them as one who had authority.
   1) from   2) of   3) at   4) with

   The chiefs of Edom will be terrified, the leaders of Moab will **be seized with** trembling, the people of Canaan will melt away;
   에돔 방백이 놀라고 모압 영웅이 떨림에 잡히며 가나안 거민이 다 낙담하나이다 (출 15:15).

7. Just then a man in their synagogue who _____ an evil spirit cried out.
   1) possessed of   2) was possessed from   3) was possessed by   4) was possessed with

8. And no one pours new wine into old wineskins. If he does, the wine will burst the skins, and both the wine and the wineskins will _____.
   1) be ruined   2) ruined   3) be ruin   4) be ruinously

9. John, the man I beheaded, _____ from the dead!
   1) have been raised   2) has been raised   3) has raised   4) has been risen

10. At this, the man's ears were opened, his tongue _____ and he began to speak plainly.
    1) was loosened   2) loosen   3) was loosen   4) loose

11. Then his eyes were opened, his sight _____, and he saw everything clearly.
    1) were relieved   2) relieved   3) was restored   4) restored

12. Not one stone here will _____ another; every one will be thrown down.
    1) leave to   2) leave on   3) be left to   4) be left on

13. While they were there, the time came for the baby _____.
    1) to born   2) to be born   3) to bear   4) born

14. Every firstborn male is to _____ to the Lord.
    1) be consecrated   2) consecrate   3) be confiscated   4) confiscate

15. He and all his companions _____ the catch of fish they had taken.
    1) were astonished by   2) were astonished at   3) astonished by   4) astonished at

16. And he _____, because some were saying that John had been raised from the dead.
    1) was perplexed   2) perplexed   3) was cried   4) amuzed

17. Just then his disciples returned and _____ find him talking with a woman.
    1) surprised to   2) surprised by   3) were surprised to   4) were surprised at

18. Gather the pieces that _____ over. Let nothing be wasted.
    1) are left   2) left   3) leave   4) is left

19. Abraham believed God, and it _____ him as righteousness.
    1) was credited to   2) was credited for   3) credited to   4) credited for

20. When a man works, his wages are not _____ him as a gift, but as an obligation.
    1) delivered on   2) delivered to   3) credited on   4) credited to

21. The man who plants and the man who waters have one purpose, and each will _____ according to his own labor.
    1) be award   2) rewarded   3) be rewarded   4) reward

22. The body is a unit, though it is _____ many parts.
    1) made up by   2) made up of   3) made by   4) made of

23. The entire law _____ a single command: Love your neighbor as yourself.
    1) is summed up by   2) is summed up in   3) summed up in   4) summed up by

24. And I--in righteousness I will see your face; when I awake, I will be satisfied _____ seeing your likeness.
    1) with   2) by   3) of   4) to

The LORD was grieved that he had made man on the earth, and his heart was filled with pain.
I am going to put an end to all people, for the earth is filled with violence because of them.
All peoples on earth will be blessed through you.

25. These men are not _____, as you suppose. It's only nine in the morning!
    1) drank   2) drunk   3) drinking   4) to drink

26. A city on a hill cannot be _____.
    1) hide   2) to hide   3) have hid   4) hidden

정답

1) 2, 2) 1, 3) 4, 4) 3, 5) 1, 6) 3, 7) 3, 8) 1, 9) 2, 10) 1
11) 3, 12) 4, 13) 2, 14) 1, 15) 2, 16) 1 17) 3, 18) 1, 19) 1, 20) 4
21) 3, 22) 2, 23) 2, 24) 1, 25) 2, 26) 4

숙어

in proportion to; ~에 비례하여
We have different gifts, according to the grace given us. If a man's gift is prophesying, let him use it **in proportion to** his faith.
우리에게 주신 은혜대로 받은 은사가 각각 다르니 혹 예언이면 믿음의 분수대로 (롬 12:6).

in pursuit of; ~을 추구하여, ~을 얻고자
So the men set out **in pursuit of** the spies on the road that leads to the fords of the Jordan, and as soon as the pursuers had gone out, the gate was shut.
그 사람들은 요단 길로 나루턱까지 따라갔고, 그 따르는 자들이 나가자 곧 성문을 닫았더라 (수 2:7).

in regard to; ~와 관련하여
He must make restitution for what he has failed to do **in regard to** the holy things, add a fifth of the value to that and give it all to the priest, who will make atonement for him with the ram as a guilt offering, and he will be forgiven.
성물에 대한 범과를 갚되 그것에 오분 일을 더하여 제사장에게 줄 것이요, 제사장은 그 속건제의 수양으로 그를 위하여 속한즉 그가 사함을 얻으리라 (레 5:16).

But the Israelites acted unfaithfully **in regard to** the devoted things; Achan son of Carmi, the son of Zimri, the son of Zerah, of the tribe of Judah, took some of them. So the LORD's anger burned against Israel.
이스라엘 자손들이 바친 물건을 인하여 범죄하였으니, 이는 유다 지파 세라의 증손 삽디의 손자 갈미의 아들 아간이 바친 물건을 취하였음이라. 여호와께서 이스라엘 자손들에게 진노하시니라 (수 7:1).

insist on; 주장하다, 우기다, 강요하다
Henry's father **insisted on** paying.

in spite of; ~에도 불구하고
In spite of all this, I never demanded the food allotted to the governor, because the demands were heavy on these people.

비록 이같이 하였을지라도 내가 총독의 녹을 요구하지 아니하였음은 백성의 부역이 중함이니라 (느 5:18).

in the end; 결국, 마침내
In the end she is bitter as gall, sharp as a double-edged sword.
나중은 쑥 같이 쓰고 두 날 가진 칼같이 날카로우며 (잠 5:4).

interest in / interested in; ~에 대한 관심(이 있는)
When did your **interest in** social work begin?
Not many people are **interested in** grammar.

in turn; 차례로
I **in turn** will laugh at your disaster; I will mock when calamity overtakes you.
너희가 재앙을 만날 때에 내가 웃을 것이며 너희에게 두려움이 임할 때에 내가 비웃으리라 (잠 1:26).

inquire about; ~에 관하여 묻다
When Moses **inquired about** the goat of the sin offering and found that it had been burned up, he was angry with Eleazar and Ithamar, Aaron's remaining sons, and asked,
모세가 속죄제 드린 염소를 찾은즉 이미 불살랐는지라. 그가 아론의 남은 아들 엘르아살과 이다말에게 노하여 가로되 (레 10:16).

interfere with; 방해하다, 훼방하다
Do not **interfere with** the work on this temple of God. Let the governor of the Jews and the Jewish elders rebuild this house of God on its site.
하나님의 전 역사를 막지 말고 유다 총독과 장로들로 하나님의 이 전을 본처에 건축하게 하라 (스 6:7).

keep away from; 피하다
I urge you, brothers, to watch out for those who cause divisions and put obstacles in your way that are contrary to the teaching you have learned. **Keep away from** them.
형제들아 내가 너희를 권하노니 너희 교훈을 거스려 분쟁을 일으키고 거치게 하는 자들을 살피고 저희에게서 떠나라 (롬 16:17).

But **keep away from** the devoted things, so that you will not bring about your own destruction by taking any of them. Otherwise you will make the camp of Israel liable to destruction and bring trouble on it.

너희는 바칠 물건을 스스로 삼가라. 너희가 그것을 바친 후에 그 바친 어느 것이든지 취하면 이스라엘 진으로 바침이 되어 화를 당케 할까 두려워 하노라(수 6:18).

In the name of the Lord Jesus Christ, we command you, brothers, to **keep away from** every brother who is idle and does not live according to the teaching you received from us.
형제들아 우리 주 예수 그리스도의 이름으로 너희를 명하노니 규모 없이 행하고 우리에게 받은 유전대로 행하지 아니하는 모든 형제에게서 떠나라(살후 3:16).

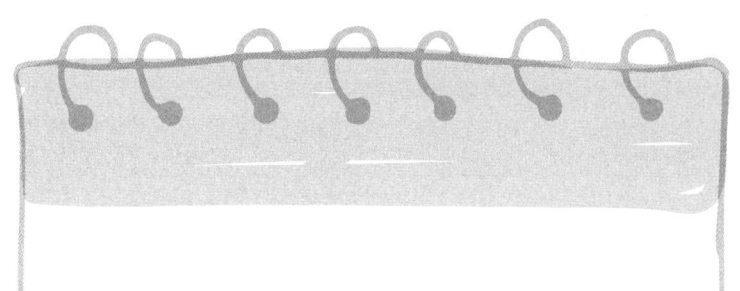

12. 법(法)
Mood

말하는 사람의 심리 태도에 의한 동사의 표현 형식을 법이라 하며, 직설법(indicative mood), 명령법(imperative mood), 가정법(subjunctive mood)이 있다.

A. 법의 종류

1. 법의 종류

1) 직설법; 사실을 사실 그대로 객관적으로 나타냄

Their throats are **open** graves.
저희 목구멍은 열린 무덤이요(롬 3:13).

2) 명령법; 명령, 요구, 간청, 권유 등 화자의 의지(will)를 나타냄

Worship the Lord your God, and **serve** him only.
주 너의 하나님께 경배하고 다만 그를 섬기라(마 4:10).

Treat younger men as brothers
젊은이를 형제에게 하듯 하고(딤전 5:1).

Do not be afraid, Daniel.
다니엘아 두려워하지 말라(단 10:12).

Prepare the way for the Lord, **make** straight paths for him.
주의 길을 예비하라, 그의 첩경을 평탄케 하라(마 3:3).

3) 가정법; 사실을 사실 그대로가 아니라 화자의 주관적인 생각을 투입하여 감정적인 색채를 나타냄

I wish that all men were as I am.
나는 모든 사람이 나와 같기를 원하노라(고전 7:7).

B. 명령법의 형식과 용법

명령법은 동사의 원형을 사용한다. 명령은 상대방에게 하므로 주어 you를 생략하는 것이 보통이지만, 특히 상대방의 주의를 끌려고 할 때는 사용한다.

Jesus replied, "They do not need to go away. **You** give them something to eat."
예수께서 가라사대, 갈 것 없다 너희가 먹을 것을 주라(마 14:16).

1. 명령법 + and

But **seek** first his kingdom and his righteousness, **and** all these things will be given to you as well.
너희는 먼저 그의 나라와 그의 의를 구하라 그리하면 이 모든 것을 너희에게 더하시리라(마 6:33).

Ask and it will be given to you; **seek and** you will find; **knock and** the door will be opened to you.
구하라 그러면 너희에게 주실 것이요 찾으라 그러면 찾을 것이요 문을 두드리라 그러면 너희에게 열릴 것이니 (마 7:7).

Be faithful, even to the point of death, **and** I will give you the crown of life.
네가 죽도록 충성하라 그리하면 내가 생명의 면류관을 네게 주리라(계 2:10).

2. 명령법 + or

Do not judge, **or** you too will be judged.
비판을 받지 아니하려 거든 비판하지 말라(마 7:1).

3. let's 형식의 명령법

1) 1인칭, 3인칭에 관하여 명령, 허가 또는 권유하는 형식

Let's have a ride. (= I think we should have a ride.)
Let's go home, shall we?

Let my people go, so that they may worship me.
내 백성을 보내라 그들이 나를 섬길 것이라 (출 10:3).

Let your "Yes" be yes, and your "No," no, or you will be condemned.
오직 너희의 그렇다 하는 것은 그렇다 하고, 아니라 하는 것은 아니라 하여 죄 정함을 면하라 (약 5:12).

Let it be so now.
이제 허락하라 (마 3:15).

2) Let's의 부정 두 가지

Let's not get angry. (더 정확한 표현으로 여겨지고 있음)
Don't let's get angry.

C. 가정법의 종류와 용법

1. 종류

1) 가정법 현재

현재 혹은 미래에 대한 단순한 가정

If the trumpet does not sound a clear call, who will get ready for battle?
만일 나팔이 분명치 못한 소리를 내면 누가 전쟁을 예비하리요 (고전 14:8).

Let us not become weary in doing good, for at the proper time we will reap a harvest if we do not give up.
우리가 선을 행하되 낙심하지 말지니 피곤하지 아니하면 때가 이르매 거두리라 (갈 6:9).

If anyone hears my voice and opens the door, I will come in and eat with him, and he with me.
누구든지 내 음성을 듣고 문을 열면 내가 그에게로 들어가 그로 더불어 먹고 그는 나로 더불어 먹으리라 (계 3:20).

2) 가정법 과거; 현재 사실에 반대되는 상황을 가정

If I **were** still trying to please men, I **would** not be a servant of Christ.
내가 지금까지 사람의 기쁨을 구하는 것이었더면 그리스도의 종이 아니니라(갈 1:10).

Instead, you welcomed me **as if I were** an angel of God, **as if I were** Christ Jesus himself.
오직 나를 하나님의 천사와 같이 또는 그리스도 예수와 같이 영접하였도다(갈 4:14).

Do not rebuke an older man harshly, but exhort him **as if** he **were** your father.
늙은이를 꾸짖지 말고 권하되 아비에게 하듯 하며(딤전 5:1).

3) 가정법 과거완료; 과거 사실에 반대되는 상황을 가정

Lord, if you **had been** here, my brother **would not have died**.
주께서 여기 계셨더면 내 오라비가 죽지 아니하였겠나이다(요 11:32).

4) 가정법 미래; 미래에 대한 매우 불확실한 상황을 가정

Even if I **should** choose to boast, I **would** not be a fool, because I would be speaking the truth.
내가 만일 자랑하고자 하여도 어리석은 자가 되지 아니할 것은 내가 참말을 함이라(고후 12:6).

2. 용법

1) 가정법 현재의 용법

(1) 현재 혹은 미래에 대한 불확실한 가정, 상상 혹은 소망을 나타냄

If you do not repent, I will come to you and remove your lampstand from its place.
만일 그리하지 아니하고 회개치 아니하면 내가 네게 임하여 네 촛대를 그 자리에서 옮기리라(계 2:5).

(2) 주장, 명령, 희망, 요구, 기대, 제안 등을 나타내는 구문에서 should를 빼고 원형만을 쓸 수 있음

David took up this lament concerning Saul and his son Jonathan, and **ordered** that the men of Judah **be taught** this lament of the bow
다윗이 이 슬픈 노래로 사울과 그 아들 요나단을 조상하고 명하여 그것을 유다 족속에게 가르치라 하였으니 (삼하 1:17-18).

(3) 미래에 대한 기원

Long live the king!
왕이여 만세(삼하 16:16).

(4) 명령문을 사용한 양보

May the LORD deal with me, **be it ever so** severely, if anything but death separates you and me.
만일 내가 죽는 일 외에 어머니와 떠나면 여호와께서 내게 벌을 내리시고 더 내리시기를 원하나이다(룻 1:17).

2) 가정법 미래의 용법

(1) 미래에 대한 강한 의심을 나타내며, 인칭에 상관없이 should를 쓴다

And if the ear **should** say, "Because I am not an eye, I do not belong to the body," it would not for that reason cease to be part of the body.
또 귀가 이르되 나는 눈이 아니니 몸에 붙지 아니하였다 할지라도 이로 인하여 몸에 붙지 아니한 것이 아니니 (고전 12:16).

(2) 주어의 의지

In that case you **would** have to leave this world
만일 그리하려면 세상 밖으로 나가야 할 것이라(고전 5:10).

3) 가정법 과거; 현재 사실에 반대되는 가정

If I **were** still trying to please men, I would not be a servant of Christ.
내가 지금까지 사람의 기쁨을 구하는 것이었더면 그리스도의 종이 아니니라(갈 1:10).

Why not? Because they pursued it not by faith but as if it **were** by works.
어찌 그러하뇨 이는 저희가 믿음에 의지하지 않고 행위에 의지함이라(롬 9:32).

Even if these three men--Noah, Daniel and Job--**were** in it, they could save only themselves by their righteousness.
비록 노아, 다니엘, 욥, 이 세사람이 거기 있을지라도 그들은 자기의 의로 자기의 생명만 건지리라(겔 14:14).

(1) if가 생략되어 were가 앞에 나옴

Were I to speak and tell of them, they would be too many to declare.

내가 들어 말하고자 하나 주의 앞에 베풀 수도 없고, 그 수를 셀 수도 없나이다(시 40:5).

(2) I wish ----- 가정법
I wish that all men **were** as I am.
나는 모든 사람이 나와 같기를 원하노라(고전 7:7).

(3) as if ---- 가정법

① as if = as though
She talks **as if** she **was** rich. (But she isn't.)

② 문어체에서는 was 대신 were
Instead, you welcomed me **as if I were** an angel of God, **as if I were** Christ Jesus himself.
오직 나를 하나님의 천사와 같이 또는 그리스도 예수와 같이 영접하였도다(갈 4:14).

Do not rebuke an older man harshly, but exhort him **as if** he **were** your father.
늙은이를 꾸짖지 말고 권하되 아비에게 하듯 하며(딤전 5:1).

Some of you have become arrogant, **as if I were** not coming to you.
어떤 이들은 내가 너희에게 나아가지 아니할 것같이 스스로 교만하여졌으나(고전 4:18).

If those who are not circumcised keep the law's requirements, will they not be regarded **as though** they **were** circumcised?
그런즉 무할례자가 율법의 제도를 지키면 그 무할례를 할례와 같이 여길 것이 아니냐(롬 2:26).

Why do you stare at us **as if** by our own power or godliness we **had made** this man walk?
우리 개인의 권능과 경건으로 이 사람을 걷게 한 것처럼 왜 우리를 주목하느냐(행 3:12).

Circumcision has value if you observe the law, but if you break the law, you have become **as though** you **had not been** circumcised.
네가 율법을 행한즉 할례가 유익하나 만일 율법을 범한즉 네 할례가 무할례가 되었느니라(롬 2:25).

(4) it is time ~ 가정법; 당연, 필요
It's **time** you **went** to bed. (= It's time that you should go to bed.)

It's time she washed that dress.
I'm getting tired. It's time we went home.

(5) 가정법을 포함하는 관용 표현

① **had better ~ 원형부정사**; "~하는 게 좋다"
You **had better** work hard.

② **I would rather, I had rather~**; "차라리 ~하고 싶다"
I **would rather** die **than** have anyone deprive me of this boast.
내가 차라리 죽을 지언 정 누구든지 내 자랑하는 것을 헛된 데로 돌리지 못하게 하리라 (고전 9:15).

③ **As it were**; "말하자면"
She is, **as it were**, a grown-up baby.

4) 가정법 과거완료

(1) 과거 사실에 반대되는 가정
Would the LORD **have been** pleased if I **had eaten** the sin offering today?
오늘 내가 속죄 제육을 먹었더면 여호와께서 어찌 선히 여기셨으리요 (레 10:19).

If the miracles that were performed in you **had been performed** in Tyre and Sidon, they **would have repented** long ago in sackcloth and ashes.
너희에게서 행한 모든 권능을 두로와 시돈에서 행하였더면 저희가 벌써 베옷을 입고 재에 앉아 회개하였으리라 (마 11:21).

None of the rulers of this age understood it, for **if** they **had**, they **would not have crucified** the Lord of glory.
이 지혜는 이 세대의 관원이 하나도 알지 못하였나니 만일 알았더면 영광의 주를 십자가에 못 박지 아니 하였으리라 (고전 2:8).

If it were not for his advice, I would make a mistake.
if it were not for ~ ; "~이 없다면", "~이 아니라면"
if it had not been for ~; "~이 없었다면", "~이 아니었다면"

(2) I wish + 가정법 과거완료; 과거에 실현하지 못한 소망
I wish I had worked harder in my youth.

(3) I had hoped; 실현되지 못한 소망
I had hoped that Peter would become a doctor, but he wasn't good enough at science.

(4) 조건절은 가정법 과거완료이지만 주절이 가정법 과거가 되는 경우가 있다. 과거의 결과가 현재에 영향을 미칠 수 있기 때문이다
If he had become the prime minister, our country would be much better now.

D. 조건문에 쓰이는 접속사

unless = if ~ not

He who prophesies is greater than one who speaks in tongues, **unless** he interprets, so that the church may be edified.
방언을 말하는 자가 만일 교회의 덕을 세우기 위하여 통역하지 아니하면 예언하는 자만 못하니라(고전 14:5).

No widow may be put on the list of widows **unless** she is over sixty.
과부로 명부에 올릴 자는 나이 육십이 덜 되지 아니하고(딤전 5:9).

Do not entertain an accusation against an elder **unless** it is brought by two or three witnesses.
장로에 대한 송사는 두 세 증인이 없으면 받지 말 것이요(딤전 5:19).

Do you not realize that Christ Jesus is in you--**unless**, of course, you fail the test?
예수 그리스도께서 너희 안에 계신 줄을 너희가 스스로 알지 못하느냐 그렇지 않으면 너희가 버리운 자니라 (고후 13:5).

How foolish! What you sow does not come to life **unless** it dies.
어리석은 자여 너의 뿌리는 씨가 죽지 않으면 살아나지 못하겠고(고전 15:36).

How can they preach **unless** they are sent?
보내심 받지 아니하였으면 어찌 전파하리요(롬 10:15).

provided (that), providing (that) = if, if ~ only
supposing (that), suppose = if

Suppose I go to the Israelites and say to them, 'The God of your fathers has sent me to you,' and they ask me, 'What is his name?' Then what shall I tell them?
내가 이스라엘 자손에게 가서 이르기를 너희 조상의 하나님이 나를 너희에게 보내셨다 하면 그들이 내게 묻기를 그의 이름이 무엇이냐 하리니 내가 무엇이라고 그들에게 말하리이까 (출 3:13).

granted (that), granting (that) = even if
Granting that it is late, we should continue our discussion.

on condition (that), in case (that) = if
so long as = if only

E. 조건절의 대용 어구

1. but for, without

1) but for ~ = without ~ = if it were not for ~ ; "~이 없으면"

But for the sun, we could not live.
But for your help, I should have failed.

2) but for, without의 뜻은 주절에 의하여 결정됨

(1) 가정법 과거
If it were not for your assistance, this project would fail.

(2) 가정법 과거완료
If it had not been for your assistance, this project would have failed.

2. 조건의 뜻을 포함하는 부정사와 분사

It would have been better for us **to serve** the Egyptians than to die in the desert!
애굽 사람을 섬기는 것이 광야에서 죽는 것보다 낫겠노라(출 14:12).

3. 주어에 조건의 뜻이 내포되어 있는 경우

A true friend would not say such a thing.

4. 조건의 뜻을 포함하는 부사어구

Repent therefore! **Otherwise**, I will soon come to you and will fight against them with the sword of my mouth.
그러므로 회개하라 그리하지 아니하면 내가 네게 속히 임하여 내 입의 검으로 그들과 싸우리라(계 2:16).

연습 문제

1. And if someone _____ to sue you and take your tunic, let him have your cloak as well. 1
   1) wants   2) will want   3) wanted   4) have wanted

2. If the miracles that were performed in you had been performed in Sodom, it _____ to this day. 1
   1) would have remained   2) has remained   3) would remained   4) should have remained

가정법 과거완료의 예문
If you had been here, my brother would not have died.
I would not have known what coveting really was if the law had not said, "Do not covet."
None of the rulers of this age understood it, for if they had, they would not have crucified the Lord of glory.

3. If you _____ what these words mean, 'I desire mercy, not sacrifice,' you would not have condemned the innocent. 3
   1) knew   2) knows   3) had known   4) have known

4. How can anyone enter a strong man's house and carry off his possessions _____ he first ties up the strong man?
   1) if   2) if not   3) unless   4) though

Unless the LORD Almighty had left us some survivors, we would have become like Sodom, we would have been like Gomorrah.
만군의 여호와께서 우리를 위하여 조금 남겨 두지 아니하셨더면 우리가 소돔 같고 고모라 같았었으리로다 (사1:9).

5. If I just _____ his clothes, I will be healed. 3
   1) should touch   2) have touched   3) touch   4) touched

가정법 현재의 예문

If anyone wants to be first, he must be the very last, and the servant of all.
Salt is good, but if it loses its saltiness, how can you make it salty again?
And if she divorces her husband and marries another man, she commits adultery.
If anyone keeps my word, he will never see death.
If her husband dies, she is released from the law of marriage.
If one part suffers, every part suffers with it; if one part is honored, every part rejoices with it.

6. No one could perform the miraculous signs you are doing if God _____ not with him. 1
   1) were   2) was   3) is   4) are

7. If God _____ your Father, you would love me. 1
   1) were   2) was   3) is   4) are

가정법 과거의 예문

If this man were not from God, he could do nothing.
If you were blind, you would not be guilty of sin.

8. Circumcision has value if you observe the law, but if you break the law, you have become _____ you had not been circumcised.
   1) as   2) if   3) though   4) as though

They will be as though I had not rejected them.
It will be as though a man fled from a lion only to meet a bear.

9. ___ you do not forgive men their sins, your Father will not forgive your sins. 1
   1) If   2) So   3) Since   4) Though

10. From now on those who have wives should live as if they _____ none.
    1) have   2) had   3) had have   4) would have

11. If I speak in the tongues of men and of angels, but _____ not love, I am only a resounding gong or a clanging cymbal.
    1) had   2) have   3) were   4) was

12. It is fine to be zealous, _____ the purpose is good.
    1) so   2) even   3) provided   4) though

13. If anyone _____ God's temple, God will destroy him; for God's temple is sacred, and you are that temple.
    1) destroy   2) destroyed   3) had destroyed   4) destroys

14. Return to me, _____ I will return to you.
    1) but   2) and   3) so   4) that

Strike the shepherd, and the sheep will be scattered.

정답

1) 1, 2) 1, 3) 3, 4) 3, 5) 3, 6) 1, 7) 1, 8) 4, 9) 1, 10) 2
11) 2, 12) 3, 13) 4, 14) 2

숙어

keep A from ~ing; A가 ~하는 것을 막다

Because of the crowd he told his disciples to have a small boat ready for him, to **keep** the people **from crowding** him.
예수께서 무리의 에워싸 미는 것을 면키 위하여 작은 배를 등대하도록 제자들에게 명하셨으니 (막 3:9).

To **keep** me **from becoming** conceited because of these surpassingly great revelations, there was given me a thorn in my flesh, a messenger of Satan, to torment me.
여러 계시를 받은 것이 지극히 크므로 너무 자고(自高)하지 않게 하시려고 내 육체에 가시 곧 사단의 사자를 주셨으니 이는 나를 쳐서 너무 자고하지 않게 하려 하심이니라 (고후 12:7).

The people were looking for him and when they came to where he was, they tried to **keep** him **from leaving** them.
무리가 찾다가 만나서 자기들에게 떠나시지 못하게 만류하려 하매 (눅 4:42).

Now these things occurred as examples to **keep** us **from** setting our hearts on evil things as they did.
그런 일은 우리의 거울이 되어 우리로 하여금 저희가 악을 즐긴 것 같이 즐기는 자가 되지 않게 하려 함이니 (고전 10:6).

keep ~ing; ~을 계속하다

He **kept making** signs to them but remained unable to speak.
그가 형용으로 뜻을 표시하며 그냥 벙어리 대로 있더니 (눅 1:22).

keep on ~ing; ~을 계속하다

Is he to **keep on emptying** his net, destroying nations without mercy?
그가 그물을 떨고는 연하여 늘 열국을 살륙함이 옳으니이까 (합 1:17).

When you pray, do not **keep on babbling** like pagans, for they think they will be heard because of their many words.

기도할 때에 이방인과 같이 중언부언하지 말라. 저희는 말을 많이 하여야 들으실 줄 생각하느니라(마 6:7).

He **kept on preaching** in the synagogues of Judea.
갈릴리 여러 회당에서 전도하시더라(눅 4:44).

lack in; 모자라다, 결핍하다
Never be **lacking in** zeal, but keep your spiritual fervor, serving the Lord.
부지런하여 게으르지 말고 열심을 품고 주를 섬기라(롬 12:11).

last of all; 최후로
Then he appeared to James, then to all the apostles, and **last of all** he appeared to me also, as to one abnormally born.
그 후에 야고보에게 보이셨으며 그 후에 모든 사도에게와 맨 나중에 만삭되지 못하여 난 자 같은 내게도 보이셨느니라(고전 15:7,8).

In fact, none of the seven left any children. **Last of all**, the woman died too.
일곱이 다 후사가 없었고 최후에 여자도 죽었나이다(막 12:22).

laugh at; 비웃다
I hate being **laughed at**.

But they **laughed at** him. After he put them all out, he took the child's father and mother and the disciples who were with him, and went in where the child was.
저희가 비웃더라 예수께서 저희를 다 내어 보내신 후에 아이의 부모와 또 자기와 함께 한 자들을 데리시고 아이 있는 곳에 들어가사(막 5:40).

Her enemies looked at her and **laughed at** her destruction.
대적은 보고 그 황적함을 비웃도다(아 1:7).

lay hold of; ~을 붙잡다
From the days of John the Baptist until now, the kingdom of heaven has been forcefully advancing, and forceful men **lay hold of** it.
세례 요한의 때부터 지금까지 천국은 침노를 당하나니 침노하는 자는 빼앗느니라(마 11:12).

lay siege to; ~을 포위(공격) 하다

Then lay siege to it: Erect siege works against it, build a ramp up to it, set up camps against it and put battering rams around it.

그 성읍을 에워싸되 운제를 세우고 토둔을 쌓고 진을 치고 공성퇴를 둘러 세우고 (겔 4:2).

13. 부정사(不定詞)
Infinitive

부정사에는 동사의 원형에 to를 붙이는 to 부정사와 동사 원형을 그대로 쓰는 원형부정사가 있다.

A. to 부정사의 용법

1. 명사적 용법; 주어로 쓰임

For to me, **to live** is Christ and **to die** is gain.
이는 내게 사는 것이 그리스도니 죽는 것도 유익함이니라(빌 1:21).

2. 형용사적 용법; 명사, 대명사를 수식

When her people fell into enemy hands, there was no one **to help** her.
백성이 대적의 손에 빠지나 돕는 자가 없고(애 1:7).

3. 부사적 용법; 동사를 수식

The devil will put some of you in prison **to test** you
마귀가 장차 너희 가운데서 몇 사람을 옥에 던져 시험을 받게 하리니(계 2:10).

4. 독립부정사

To be sure, Elijah does come first, and restores all things.
엘리야가 과연 먼저 와서 모든 것을 회복하거니와(막 9:12).

B. 명사적 to 부정사

1. 주어의 역할

주어로서 to 부정사가 문두에 오는 일은 드물며, 그 대신 형식주어 it를 쓴다.

For to me, **to live** is Christ and **to die** is gain.
이는 내게 사는 것이 그리스도니 죽는 것도 유익함이니라(빌 1:21).

2. 보어의 역할

1) 주격 보어

To fear the LORD is **to hate** evil.
여호와를 경외하는 것은 악을 미워하는 것이라(잠 8:13).

The wisdom of the prudent is **to give** thought to their ways, but the folly of fools is deception.
슬기로운 자의 지혜는 자기의 길을 아는 것이라도 미련한 자의 어리석음은 속이는 것이니라(잠 14:8).

2) 목적격 보어

And if your eye causes you **to sin**, pluck it out. It is better for you to enter the kingdom of God with one eye than to have two eyes and be thrown into hell,
만일 네 눈이 너를 범죄케 하거든 빼어버리라 한 눈으로 하나님의 나라에 들어가는 것이 두 눈을 가지고 지옥에 던지우는 것보다 나으니라(마 9:47).

3. 목적어의 역할

His disciples were hungry and began **to pick** some heads of grain and eat them.
제자들이 시장하여 이삭을 잘라먹으니(마 12:1).

But when they arrived, he began **to draw** back and separate himself from the Gentiles because he was afraid of those who belonged to the circumcision group.

저희가 오매 그가 할례자들을 두려워하여 떠나 물러가매(갈 2:12).

How long will you refuse **to humble** yourself before me?
네가 어느 때까지 내 앞에 겸비치 아니하겠느냐(출 10:3).

4. 의문사 + to 부정사 = 명사구

Now go; I will help you speak and will teach you **what to say**. (목적어)
이제 가라. 내가 네 입과 함께 있어서 할 말을 가르치리라(출 4:12).

At that time you will be given **what to say** (목적어).
그때에 무슨 말할 것을 주시리니(마 10:19).

If you, then, though you are evil, know **how to give** good gifts to your children. (목적어)
너희가 악한 자라도 좋은 것으로 자식에게 줄 줄 알거든(마 7:11).

But when they arrest you, do not worry about **what to say** or **how to say it**. (전치사의 목적어)
너희를 넘겨 줄 때에 어떻게 또는 무엇을 말할까 염려치 말라(마 10:19).

C. 형용사적 to 부정사

1. 수식되는 명사가 부정사의 의미상의 주어가 될 경우

Do you have a key **to open** this door?

They have divine power **to demolish** strongholds.
하나님 앞에서 견고한 진을 파하는 강력이라(고후 10:4).

Where can I find anyone **to comfort** you?
내가 어디서 너를 위로할 자를 구하리요(나 3:7).

2. 수식되는 명사가 부정사의 의미상의 목적어가 될 경우

I need some more work **to do**

Give us water **to drink**.
우리에게 물을 주어 마시게 하라(출 17:2).

3. 부정사와 관계대명사; 전치사 + 관계대명사 + to 부정사에서 관계대명사가 빠지면, 전치사는 뒤에

I have no house to live in. (= I have no house in which to live.)
Give me a chair to sit in. (= Give me a chair I which to sit.)

4. It's time

It's time **to buy** a new car.
It's time for you **to go** to bed.

5. be + to의 용법(주격 보어)

1) 예정; "~하기로 되어 있다"
문어체로 계획이나 약속 등의 사무적인 행위를 나타낼 때 쓴다.

The president **is to** visit Korea next month.
We **are to** get a 10 per cent wage rise in June.

If a carcass falls on any seeds that **are to** be planted, they remain clean.
이것들의 주검이 심을 종자에 떨어질지라도 그것이 정하거니와(레 11:37).

The son who **is to** succeed him as anointed priest shall prepare it.
이 소제는 아론의 자손 중 기름 부음을 받고 그를 이어 제사장 된 자가 드릴 것이요(레 6:22).

And if you are to judge the world, are you not competent to judge trivial cases?
세상도 너희에게 판단을 받겠거든 지극히 작은 일 판단하기를 감당치 못하겠느냐(고전 6:2).

Moses answered, "We will go with our young and old, with our sons and daughters, and with our flocks and herds, because we are to celebrate a festival to the LORD."
모세가 가로되 우리가 여호와 앞에 절기를 지킬 것인즉 우리가 남녀 노소와 우양을 데리고 가겠나이다 (출 10:9).

2) 의무; "~하여야 한다(명령)"
부모가 아이들에게 쓰는 말

You are to eat all your supper before you watch TV.
She can go to the party, but she's not to be back late.

Then they are to take some of the blood and put it on the sides and tops of the doorframes of the houses where they eat the lambs.
양을 먹을 집 문 좌우 설주와 인방에 바르고(출 12:7).

It is the LORD's regular share and is to be burned completely.
영원한 규례로 여호와께 온전히 불사를 것이니(레 6:22).

You will be with child and give birth to a son, and you are to give him the name Jesus.
보라 네가 수태하여 아들을 낳으리니 그 이름을 예수라 하라(눅 1:31).

3) 운명; "~할 운명이다"
I was never to meet my family again.

4) 가능; "~할 수 있다"
No one is to enter the room without a pass card.

5) 의도; "~하려면"
If you are to pass the exam, you must study hard.

D. 부사적 to 부정사

1. 목적: "~하기 위하여"

Then Jesus was led by the Spirit into the desert **to be** tempted by the devil.
그 때에 예수께서 성령에게 이끌리어 마귀에게 시험을 받으러 광야로 가사(마 4:1).

After leaving them, he went up on a mountainside **to pray**.
무리를 작별하신 후에 기도하러 산으로 가시다(막 6:46).

Then Pharaoh's daughter went down to the Nile **to bathe**
바로의 딸이 목욕하러 하수로 내려오고(출 2:5).

She saw the basket among the reeds and sent her slave girl **to get** it.
그가 갈대 사이에 상자를 보고 시녀를 보내어 가져다가(출 2:5).

So I have come down **to rescue** them from the hand of the Egyptians and **to bring** them up out of that land into a good and spacious land, a land flowing with milk and honey.
내가 내려와서 그들을 애굽인의 손에서 건져내고 그들을 그 땅에서 인도하여 아름답고 광대한 땅 젖과 꿀이 흐르는 땅에 이르려 하노라(출 3:8).

2. 결과; "~해서 ~하다"

Cush was the father of Nimrod, who grew **to be** a mighty warrior on the earth.
구스가 또 니므롯을 낳았으니 그는 세상에 처음 영걸이라(창 10:8).

3. 원인; "~하니"(감정의 원인)

I'm pleased **to see** you.
He was surprised **to get** her letter.

Jethro was delighted **to hear** about all the good things the LORD had done for Israel in rescu-

ing them from the hand of the Egyptians.
이드로가 여호와께서 이스라엘에게 모든 은혜를 베푸사 애굽 사람의 손에서 구원하심을 기뻐하여(출 18:9).

In addition to our own encouragement, we were especially delighted **to see** how happy Titus was, because his spirit has been refreshed by all of you.
우리의 받은 위로 위에 디도의 기쁨으로 우리가 더욱 많이 기뻐함은 그의 마음이 너희 무리를 인하여 안심함을 얻었음이니라(고후 7:13).

They were pleased **to do** it, and indeed they owe it to them.
저희가 기뻐서 하였거니와 또한 저희는 그들에게 빚진 자니(롬 15:27).

4. 이유, 판단의 근거; "~을 보니"

He must be foolish **to say** like that.

5. 조건; "만일 ~이면"

I should be happy **to go** with you.

6. 형용사 또는 부사를 수식

His accident is not easy **to understand**.
She is very nice **to talk** to.

They are almost ready **to stone** me.
그들이 얼마 아니면 내게 돌질하겠나이다(출 17:4).

If you do this and God so commands, you will be able **to stand** the strain, and all these people will go home satisfied.
그대가 만일 이 일을 하고 하나님께서도 그대에게 인가하시면 그대가 이 일을 감당하고 이 모든 백성도 자기 곳으로 평안히 가리라(출 18:23).

Who is worthy **to break** the seals and open the scroll?
누가 책을 펴며 그 인을 떼기에 합당하냐(계 5:2).

E. 독립부정사

to begin with = 우선
strange to say = 이상한 이야기지만
to make a long story short = 간단히 말해서
to make matters worse = 설상가상으로
not to speak of = ~은 말할 것도 없이
to be sure = 확실히

F. 완료부정사

1. 단순부정사일 때

부정사의 시제는 본동사와 동일 시제 또는 나중 시제이다.

Beware of turning to evil, which you seem **to prefer** to affliction.
삼가 악으로 치우치지 말라 네가 환난보다 이것을 택하였느니라(욥 36:21).

2. 완료부정사일 때

부정사의 시제는 본동사보다 앞선다.

One of the heads of the beast seemed **to have had** a fatal wound, but the fatal wound had been healed.
그의 머리 하나가 상하여 죽게 된 것 같더니 그 죽게 되었던 상처가 나으매(계 13:3).

소망의 동사가 포함된 과거완료 다음에 단순부정사를 써도 이루지 못한 사실을 나타낼 수 있다.

And if it does evil in my sight and does not obey me, then I will reconsider the good **I had intended to do** for it.
만일 그들이 나 보기에 악한 것을 행하여 내 목소리를 청종치 아니하면 내가 그에게 유익케 하리라 한 선에 대하여 뜻을 돌이키리라(렘 18:10).

G. 부정사의 의미상 주어

부정사의 의미상 주어는 문중의 한 말이 겸용할 경우와 특히 명시할 경우, 그리고 생략될 경우가 있다.

1. 주어가 의미상 주어

I have had a dream that troubles me and I want **to know** what it means.
내가 꿈을 꾸고 그 꿈을 알고자 하여 마음이 번민하도다(단 2:3).

2. 목적어가 의미상 주어

And now, brothers, we want **you to know** about the grace that God has given the Macedonian churches.
형제들아 하나님께서 마게도냐 교회들에게 주신 은혜를 우리가 너희에게 알게 하노니(고후 8:1).

I would like **you** to be free from concern.
너희가 염려 없기를 원하노라(고전 7:32).

But even if he does not, we want **you to** know, O king, that we will not serve your gods or worship the image of gold you have set up.
그리 아니하실지라도 왕이여 우리가 왕의 신들을 섬기지도 아니하고 왕의 세우신 금신상에게 절하지도 아니할 줄을 아옵소서(단 3:18).

I want **you to give** me right now the head of John the Baptist on a platter.
세례 요한의 머리를 소반에 담아 곧 내게 주기를 원하옵나이다(막 6:25).

I would like **every one of you to speak** in tongues.
나는 너희가 다 방언 말하기를 원하나(고전 14:5).

For Jesus had commanded **the evil spirit to come out** of the man.
이는 예수께서 이미 더러운 귀신을 명하사 이 사람에게서 나오라 하셨음이라(눅 8:29).

3. for + 목적어 + 부정사; 목적어는 부정사의 의미상 주어

They camped at Rephidim, but there was no water **for the people to drink**.
르비딤에 장막을 쳤으나 백성이 마실 물이 없는지라(출 17:1).

Master, it is good **for us to be** here.
주여, 우리가 여기 있는 것이 좋사오니(눅 9:33).

It is proper **for us to do** this to fulfill all righteousness.
우리가 이와 같이 하여 모든 의를 이루는 것이 합당하니라(마 3:15).

It is better **for you to lose** one part of your body than for your whole body to be thrown into hell.
네 백체 중 하나가 없어지고 온 몸이 지옥에 던지우지 않는 것이 유익하며(마 5:29).

What good is it **for a man to gain** the whole world, yet forfeit his soul?
사람이 만일 온 천하를 얻고도 제 목숨을 잃으면 무엇이 유익하리요(막 8:36).

It is enough **for the student to be** like his teacher, and the servant like his master.
제자가 그 선생 같고 종이 그 상전 같으면 족하도다 집 주인을 바알세불이라 하였거든 하물며 그 집 사람들이랴(마 10:25).

because it is impossible **for the blood of bulls and goats to take** away sins.
이는 황소와 염소의 피가 능히 죄를 없이 하지 못함이라(히 10:4).

Is it a trivial matter **for the house of Judah to do** the detestable things they are doing here?
유다 족속이 여기서 행한 가증한 일을 적다 하겠느냐(겔 8:17).

4. 동사, 형용사가 관용구로서 for 아닌 다른 전치사를 수반할 때, 의미상 주어를 유도하기 위해 for + 목적어의 for를 쓸 필요는 없다

1) 부정사의 의미상 주어가 일반인일 때는 명시하지 않음

It is not good **to punish** an innocent man, or **to flog** officials for their integrity.
의인을 벌하는 것과 귀인을 정직하다고 때리는 것이 선치 못하니라(잠 17:26).

It is not right **to take** the children's bread and toss it to their dogs.
자녀의 떡을 취하여 개들에게 던짐이 마땅치 아니하니라(막 7:27).

2) Of + 목적어 + 부정사로 부정사의 의미상 주어를 나타냄

이 문형에는 careful, careless, good, foolish, honest, kind, nice, silly, rude 등 사람의 성격을 나타내는 형용사가 쓰인다.

H. 원형부정사

원형부정사는 will/would, shall/should, can/could, may/might, do, must 등의 조동사와 같이 쓰이며 다음과 같은 용법으로 활용된다.

1. 지각동사(see, watch, hear) 뒤에서

See, watch, hear + 목적어 + 원형부정사; 완료된 행위에 대하여
See, watch, hear + 목적어 + 현재분사; 진행중 행위에 대하여

I **saw** Mary **cross** the road and disappear into the post office.
I looked out of the window and **saw** Mary **crossing** the road.

When you hear them **sound** a long blast on the trumpets
제사장들이 양각나팔을 길게 울려 불어서 그 나팔 소리가 너희에게 들릴 때에는(수 6:5).

When the Lamb opened the third seal, I heard the third living creature **say**, "Come!"
세째 인을 떼실 때에 내가 들으니 세째 생물이 말하되 오라 하기로(계 6:5).

2. 사역동사 뒤에서

The devil led him to Jerusalem and **had** him **stand** on the highest point of the temple.
또 이끌고 예루살렘으로 가서 성전 꼭대기에 세우고(눅 4:9).

Have all the people **give** a loud shout; then the wall of the city will collapse and the people will go up, every man straight in.
백성은 다 큰 소리로 외쳐 부를 것이라 그리하면 그 성벽이 무너져 내리리니 백성은 각기 앞으로 올라갈지니라 하시매(수 6:5).

In the same way, let your light **shine** before men, that they may see your good deeds and praise your Father in heaven.
저희로 너희 착한 행실을 보고 하늘에 계신 너희 아버지께 영광을 돌리게 하라(마 5:16).

I will let you **go** to offer sacrifices to the LORD your God in the desert
내가 너희를 보내리니 너희가 너희 하나님 여호와께 광야에서 희생을 드릴 것이나(출 8:28).

He even makes the deaf **hear** and the mute **speak**.
귀머거리도 듣게 하고 벙어리도 말하게 한다(막 7:37).

I would rather have you **prophesy**
특별히 예언하기를 원하노라(고전 14:5).

I will make those who commit adultery with her **suffer** intensely, unless they repent of her ways.
또 그로 더불어 간음하는 자들도 만일 그의 행위를 회개치 아니하면 큰 환난 가운데 던지고(계 2:22).

Come up and **help** me **attack** Gibeon.
내게로 올라와 나를 도우라 우리가 기브온을 치자(수 10:4).

3. Cannot but 원형 = "~ 하지 않을 수 없다"

She cannot but cry.

4. Do nothing but 원형 = "~하기만 한다"

He did nothing but work.

5. Had better 원형 = "~하는 게 좋다"

You had better study hard to pass the examination.

6. 2개의 to 부정사가 and, or, except, but, than으로 연결될 때 뒤의 것은 원형부정사를 쓴다

I'd like to lie down **and go** to sleep.
Do you want to eat now **or wait** till later?
We had nothing to do **except look** at the garden.
I'll do anything **but work** on a farm.
It's easier to do it yourself **than explain** to somebody else how to do it.

I. 기타

1. too ~ to

I am **too** old **to** have another husband.
나는 늙었으니 남편을 두지 못할지라(룻 1:12).

Your eyes are **too** pure **to look** on evil.
주께서는 눈이 정결하시므로 악을 참아 보지 못하시며 (합 1:13).

2. enough to

No one was strong **enough to subdue** him.
그리하여 아무도 저를 제어 할 힘이 없는지라 (막 5:4).

3. 부정사의 부정; 부정어(never, not)를 부정사 앞에 놓는다

I have told the men **not to touch** you.
내가 그 소년들에게 명하여 너를 건드리지 말라 하였느니라 (룻 2:9).

Daniel resolved **not to defile** himself with the royal food and wine.
다니엘은 뜻을 정하여 왕의 진미와 그의 마시는 포도주로 자기를 더럽히지 아니하리라 하고 (단 1:8).

Be careful **not to neglect** this matter.
너희는 삼가서 이 일에 게으르지 말라 (스 4:22).

4. 대부정사; 부정사의 반복을 피하기 위해 to만 쓰는 것

I can give it to anyone I want **to** (give).
나의 원하는 자에게 주노라 (눅 4:6).

Don't collect any more than you are required **to** (collect).
정한 세 외에는 늑징치 말라 (눅 3:13).

5. 능동형으로 수동태의 의미를 나타내는 부정사

This house is **to let**.
He is **to blame**.

연습 문제

1. Then the devil took him to the holy city and had him _____ on the highest point of the temple.
   1) to stand   2) stand   3) standing   4) stood

   But let all who take refuge in you be glad; let them ever sing for joy.
   Immediately Jesus made the disciples get into the boat and go on ahead of him to the other side.
   Let it be so now; it is proper for us to do this to fulfill all righteousness.

   I will harden his heart so that he will not let the people go.
   내가 그의 마음을 강퍅케 한즉 그가 백성을 놓지 아니하리니 (출 4:21).

2. When the disciples saw him _____ on the lake, they were terrified.
   1) walking   2) to walk   3) walked   4) walks

   We saw a man driving out demons in your name and we tried to stop him, because he is not one of us.

3. He saw heaven being torn open and the Spirit _____ on him like a dove.
   1) to descend   2) descending   3) descended   4) being descended

4. Herod himself had given orders to have John arrested, and he had him _____ and put in prison.
   1) bind   2) to bind   3) bounded   4) bound

5. She went home and found her child _____ on the bed, and the demon gone.
   1) lying   2) lay   3) laying   4) lied

6. Is it lawful for a man _____ his wife?
   1) divorced   2) divorce with   3) to divorce   4) divorce

7. Moses permitted a man _____ a certificate of divorce and send her away.
   1) write   2) written   3) of writing   4) to write

8. Therefore what God has joined together, let man not _____.
   1) be separated   2) separate   3) separated   4) to separate

Have only the men **go**; and worship the LORD, since that's what you have been asking for.
너희 남정만 가서 여호와를 섬기라 이것이 너희의 구하는 바니라(출 10:11).

The LORD **made** an east wind **blow** across the land all that day and all that night.
여호와께서 동풍을 일으켜 온 낮과 온 밤에 불게 하시니(출 10:13).

Then Jesus directed them to **have** all the people **sit** down in groups on the green grass.
제자들을 명하사 그 모든 사람으로 떼를 지어 푸른 잔디 위에 앉게 하시니(막 6:39).

9. Some men came carrying a paralytic on a mat and tried _____ him into the house to lay him before Jesus.
   1) take   2) of taking   3) to take   4) taking of

10. He ordered them not _____ anyone what had happened.
    1) to tell   2) tell   3) telling   4) told

Teacher, I beg you to look at my son, for he is my only child.
I begged your disciples to drive it out, but they could not.
The tempter came to him and said, "If you are the Son of God, tell these stones to become bread."
I want you to give me right now the head of John the Baptist on a platter.
If someone forces you to go one mile, go with him two miles.

She begged Jesus to drive the demon out of her daughter.
자기 딸에게서 귀신 쫓아 주시기를 간구하거늘(막 7:26).

11. He gave them power and authority _____ out all demons.
    1) drive   2) drove   3) to drive   4) to have driven

형용사적 용법

The LORD provided a great fish to swallow Jonah.
Have you any right to be angry?
You will have plenty to eat, until you are full.

12. Get up, take the child and his mother and go to the land of Israel, for those who were trying _____ the child's life are dead.
    1) taking   2) to take   3) take   4) took

13. John tried to deter him, saying, "I need _____ baptized by you, and do you come to me?"
    1) to be   2) being   3) be   4) to

명사적 용법

I will command the serpent to bite them.

14. Again they tried _____ him, but he escaped their grasp.
    1) seizing   2) to seize of   3) to seize   4) seize

When Pharaoh stubbornly **refused to** let us go, the LORD killed every firstborn in Egypt, both man and animal.

15. He touched her hand and the fever left her, and she got up and began _____ on him.
    1) wait   2) herself waiting   3) waited   4) to wait

to 부정사와 동명사를 목적어로 함께 취하는 동사

As John's disciples were leaving, Jesus began to speak to the crowd about John.
Coming to his hometown, he began teaching the people in their synagogue

16. The LORD confides in those who fear him; he makes his covenant _____ to them.
    1) know   2) known   3) to know   4) knowing

17. I will wait patiently ___ the day of calamity to come on the nation invading us.

　　1) on　　2) for　　3) in　　4) at

18. I will so increase your descendants that they will be _____ numerous to count.

　　1) too　　2) so　　3) as　　4) very

You are **too** heavy a burden for me **to** carry alone.

19. 용법이 틀린 것은?

　　1) Foxes have holes and birds of the air have nests, but the Son of Man has no place to lay his head.
　　2) He became hungry and wanted something to eat, and while the meal was being prepared, he fell into a trance.
　　3) They picked up stones to stone him.
　　4) Yet to all who received him, to those who believed in his name, he gave the right to become children of God

20. 용법이 틀린 것은?

　　1) You refuse to come to me to have life.
　　2) They do not need to go away.
　　3) You give them something to eat.
　　4) The disciples, each according to his ability, decided to provide help for the brothers living in Judea.

21. They do not know _____ to do right.

　　1) as　　2) which　　3) how　　4) you

22. I have determined _____ good again.

　　1) doing　　2) do　　3) done　　4) to do

정답

1) 2, 2) 1, 3) 2, 4) 4, 5) 1, 6) 3, 7) 4, 8) 2, 9) 3, 10) 1
11) 3, 12) 2, 13) 1, 14) 3, 15) 4, 16) 2 17) 2, 18) 1, 19) 3, 20) 3
21) 3, 22) 4

숙어

listen to; 귀를 기울이다, 귀담아 듣다
If you don't **listen to** people, they won't **listen to** you.

look at (= point one's eyes at); ~을 보다, 자세히 보다, 고찰하다
Stop **looking at** me like that.

look after (= take care of); ~에 주의하다, ~을 보살피다
Thanks for **looking after** me when I was ill.
Will you **look after** the children while I'm out?

look down on; 경멸하다
The man who eats everything must not **look down on** him who does not.
먹는 자는 먹지 않는 자를 업신여기지 말고(롬 14:3).

You should not **look down on** your brother in the day of his misfortune.

look for (try to find); 찾다, 기다리다
Can you help me **look for** my keys?
What are you doing down there? **Looking for** my book.

When they found him, they exclaimed: "Everyone is **looking for** you!"
만나서 가로되 모든 사람이 주를 찾나이다(막 1:37).

Jews demand miraculous signs and Greeks **look for** wisdom,
유대인은 표적을 구하고 헬라인은 지혜를 찾으나(고전 1:22).

look forward to; ~을 기대하다
Coming up to them at that very moment, she gave thanks to God and spoke about the child to all who were **looking forward to** the redemption of Jerusalem.

마침 이 때에 나아와서 하나님께 감사하고 예루살렘의 구속됨을 바라는 모든 사람에게 이 아기에 대하여 말하니라(눅 2:38).

look over; ~을 대충 훑어보다

Then Joshua son of Nun secretly sent two spies from Shittim. "Go, **look over** the land," he said, "especially Jericho." So they went and entered the house of a prostitute [2] named Rahab and stayed there.
눈의 아들 여호수아가 싯딤에서 두 사람을 정탐으로 가만히 보내며 그들에게 이르되, 가서 그 땅과 여리고를 엿보라 하매, 그들이 가서 라합이라 하는 기생의 집에 들어가 거기서 유숙하더니(수 2:1).

make atonement for; 속죄하다

He shall burn all the fat on the altar as he burned the fat of the fellowship offering. In this way the priest will **make atonement for** the man's sin, and he will be forgiven.
그 모든 기름은 화목제 희생의 기름같이 단 위에 불사를지니 이같이 제사장이 그 범한 죄에 대하여 그를 위하여 속죄한즉 그가 사함을 얻으리라(레 4:26).

Why didn't you eat the sin offering in the sanctuary area? It is most holy; it was given to you to take away the guilt of the community by **making atonement for** them before the LORD.
이 속죄제 희생은 지극히 거룩하거늘 너희가 어찌하여 거룩한 곳에서 먹지 아니하였느뇨 이는 너희로 회중의 죄를 담당하여 그들을 위하여 여호와 앞에 속하게 하려고 너희에게 주신 것이니라(레 10:17).

make effort to; 노력하다, 애쓰다

Let us therefore **make** every **effort to** do what leads to peace and to mutual edification.
이러므로 우리가 화평의 일과 서로 덕을 세우는 일을 힘쓰나니(롬 14:19).

make fun of; 놀리다

Some, however, **made fun of** them and said, "They have had too much wine."
또 어떤 이들은 조롱하여 가로되 저희가 새 술이 취하였다 하더라(행 2:13).

make much of; ~을 중요시하다, 이해하다

I am talking to you Gentiles. Inasmuch as I am the apostle to the Gentiles, I **make much of** my ministry
내가 이방인인 너희에게 말하노라 내가 이방인의 사도인 만큼 내 직분을 영광스럽게 여기노니(롬 11:13).

make the most of; ~을 최대한 이용하다

Be very careful, then, how you live--not as unwise but as wise, **making the most of** every opportunity, because the days are evil.

그런즉 너희가 어떻게 행할 것을 자세히 주의하여 지혜 없는 자같이 말고, 오직 지혜 있는 자같이 하여 세월을 아끼라 때가 악하니라 (엡5:15,16).

14. 동명사(動名詞)
Gerund

동명사는 명사적 성격과 동사적 성격을 동시에 갖고 있으며, 현재분사와 같이 동사+ing의 형태지만, 동명사가 명사의 역할을 하는데 비해 현재분사는 형용사의 역할을 하는 차이가 있다.

a **dancing** master (동명사)
a **dancing** girl (현재분사)

동명사의 명사적 성격 ; 명사처럼 관사, 소유대명사, 지시대명사, 형용사가 동명사 앞에 올 수 있고, 전치사의 목적어가 될 수도 있다.

동명사의 동사적 성격 ; 동사의 경우처럼 부사가 동명사를 수식할 수 있고, 타동사의 경우에는 목적어를 취할 수 있고, 자체의 주어를 가질 수도 있으며 시제형과 수동형을 가질 수도 있다.

A. 동명사의 명사적 성질

1. 주어

Casting the lot settles disputes and keeps strong opponents apart.
제비 뽑는 것은 다툼을 그치게 하여 강한 자 사이에 해결케 하느니라(잠 18:18).

Starting a quarrel is like breaching a dam: so drop the matter before a dispute breaks out.
다투는 시작은 방축에서 물이 새는 것 같은즉 싸움이 일어나기 전에 시비를 그칠 것이니라
(잠 17:14).

2. 보어

All the ways of the LORD are **loving** and faithful for those who keep the demands of his covenant.
여호와의 모든 길은 그 언약과 증거를 지키는 자에게 인자와 진리로다(시 25:10).

3. Finish의 목적어

Just as he finished **making** the offering, Samuel arrived, and Saul went out to greet him.
번제 드리기를 필하자 사무엘이 온지라 사울이 나가 맞으며 문안하매(삼상 13:10).

4. 전치사 for의 목적어

You are no longer to supply the people with straw for **making** bricks.
너희는 백성에게 다시는 벽돌 소용의 짚을 전과 같이 주지 말고(출 5:7).

5. 현재분사는 동사와 형용사의 역할

You also, like **living** stones, are being built into a spiritual house to be a holy priesthood, offering spiritual sacrifices acceptable to God through Jesus Christ.
너희도 산 돌같이 신령한 집으로 세워지고 예수 그리스도로 말미암아 하나님이 기쁘게 받으실 신령한 제사를 드릴 거룩한 제사장이 될지니라(벧전 2:5).

B. 동명사의 완료형

1. 완료형 동명사; 과거에 대하여 말함

I'm sure of his **being** a man of ability.
I'm sure of his **having been** a man of ability in his youth.

Somebody is sure/certain of ~ing; I am talking about somebody's feeling.
Before the game she was **sure/certain of winning**. (she felt sure.)
Somebody is sure/certain to; I am talking about my own feeling.
Before the game she was **sure/certain to win**. (I felt sure.)

2. Sorry for/about ~ing; 과거의 사실

I'm **sorry for/about waking** you up.
= I'm sorry to have woken you up.
= I'm sorry that I woke you up.

3. Sorry to 부정사; 현재, 미래의 사실

Sorry to disturb you. Could I speak to you for a moment?
I'm **sorry to tell** you that you failed the exam.

C. 동명사의 의미상 주어

1. 주어 Jesus와 일치

When Jesus had finished **saying** these things, the crowds were amazed at his teaching,
예수께서 이 말씀을 마치시매 무리들이 그 가르치심에 놀레니(미 7:28).

2. you가 주어

He has heard **your grumbling** against him.
여호와께서 너희가 자기를 향하여 원망함을 들으셨음이라(출 16:7).

D. 동명사와 부정사

1. 동명사와 부정사 어느 쪽이든 목적어로 취할 수 있는 동사

begin, start, continue, like, love, hate, prefer, attempt, intend, try, remember, forget, can't bear

How old were you when you **started to play/playing** the piano?
She **began to play/playing** the guitar when she was six.
I **hate to work/working** at weekends.
I **intend to tell/telling** her what I think.

She got up at once and **began to wait** on them.
여자가 곧 일어나 저희에게 수종드니라(눅 4:39).

Thinking he was in their company, they traveled on for a day. Then they began **looking** for him among their relatives and friends.
동행 중에 있는 줄로 생각하고 하룻길을 간 후 친족과 아는 자 중에서 찾되(눅 2:44).

But when they arrived, he **began to draw** back and separate himself from the Gentiles because he was afraid of those who belonged to the circumcision group.
저희가 오매 그가 할례자들을 두려워하여 떠나 물러가매(갈 2:12).

So the elders of the Jews **continued to build** and **prosper** under the preaching of Haggai the prophet and Zechariah, a descendant of Iddo.
유다 사람의 장로들이 선지자 학개와 잇도의 손자 스가랴의 권력으로 인하여 전 건축할 일이 형통한지라(스 6:14).

2. 목적어를 동명사로 썼을 때와 부정사로 썼을 때 뜻이 다른 경우

remember, forget

3. 동명사를 쓰면 과거의 사실을 나타냄

I still **remember buying** my first packet of cigarettes.
I'll never **forget meeting** the Queen.

4. To 부정사를 쓰면 미래의 사실을 나타냄

Did you **remember to buy** my cigarette?
You mustn't **forget to go** and meet Mr. Lewis at the station tomorrow.

Like
I **like climbing** mountains. (좋아하는 것)
I **like to start** work early in the morning. (선택, 습관)

5. 동명사만을 목적어로 취하는 동사

admit, allow, avoid, consider, delay, deny, dislike, enjoy, escape, excuse, feel like, finish, forgive, give up, go, imagine, keep, mind, miss, practice, postpone, practice, put off, regret, risk, suggest, stop, try, understand

I **dislike arguing** about money.
Forgive my interrupting you.
Let's **go swimming**.
I can't **understand his being** so late.

After Jesus had **finished instructing** his twelve disciples, he went on from there to teach and preach in the towns of Galilee.
예수께서 열 두 제자에게 명하시기를 마치시고, 이에 저희 여러 동네에서 가르치시며 전도하시려고 거기를 떠나 가시니라(마 11:1).

They finished building the temple according to the command of the God of Israel and the decrees of Cyrus, Darius and Artaxerxes, kings of Persia.
이스라엘 하나님의 명령과 바사왕 고레스와 다리오와 아닥사스다의 조서를 좇아 전을 건축하며 필역하되 (스 6:14).

When Naomi realized that Ruth was determined to go with her, she **stopped urging** her.
나오미가 룻의 자기와 함께 가기로 굳게 결심함을 보고 그에게 말하기를 그치니라 (룻 1:18).

Day after day, in the temple courts and from house to house, they never **stopped teaching** and **proclaiming** the good news that Jesus is the Christ.
저희가 날마다 성전에 있든지 집에 있든지 예수는 그리스도라 가르치기와 전도하기를 쉬지 아니하니라 (행 5:42).

This fellow never stops **speaking** against this holy place and against the law.
이 사람이 이 거룩한 곳과 율법을 거스려 말하기를 마지 아니하는도다 (행 6:13).

I stopped smoking. (smoking이 stop의 목적어)
I stopped (work) to smoke. (to smoke는 목적을 나타내는 부사적 용법)

1) regret

(1) 동명사(과거의 사실)
I don't regret telling her what I thought, even if it made her angry.

(2) To 부정사; 현재의 사실(부사적 용법)
British rail regret to announce that the 15:15 train will leave ten minutes late.

2) Allow
Allow 다음에 간접목적어가 있으면 to 부정사를 쓴다.
We don't **allow smoking** in the lecture room.
We don't **allow people to smoke** in the lecture room.

3) Try

(1) 동명사; make an experiment, do something to see what will happen
I **tried sending** her flowers, **giving** her presents, **writing** her letters; but she still wouldn't speak to me.

(2) To 부정사; make an effort (부사적 용법)
I **tried to write** a letter, but my hands were too cold to hold a pen.

4) Mind
dislike, be annoyed by, object to의 뜻으로 의문문, 부정문에 주로 쓴다.
I don't **mind** you **coming** in late if you don't wake me up.
Would you **mind opening** the window? (= Please open the window.)
Would you **mind my opening** the window? (= Can I open the window?)
Do you **mind** people **smoking** in the kitchen? (담배 피우는 것을 허락할 때는 No, 불허할 때는 Yes 라고 대답함)

6. 부정사만을 목적어로 취하는 동사

wish, hope, care, choose, determine, expect, refuse, decide, mean, plan, beg

Do you wish **to be** enslaved by them all over again?
다시 저희에게 종 노릇 하려 하느냐(갈 4:9).

I hope **to visit** you and talk with you face to face, so that our joy may be complete.
너희에게 가서 면대하여 말하려 하니 이는 너희 기쁨을 충만케 하려 함이라(요이 1:12).

But our fathers refused **to obey** him. Instead, they rejected him and in their hearts turned back to Egypt.
우리 조상들이 모세에게 복종치 아니하고자 하여 거절하며 그 마음이 도리어 애굽으로 행하여(행 7:39).

Recalling your tears, I long **to see** you, so that I may be filled with joy.
네 눈물을 생각하여 너 보기를 원함은 내 기쁨이 가득하게 하려함이니(딤후1:4).

E. 동명사의 관용적 용법

there is no ~ing = it is impossible to ~

But you multiply remedies in vain; **there is no healing** for you.
네가 많은 의약을 쓸지라도 무효하여 낫지 못하리라(렘 46:11).

it is no use (or good) ~ing = it is of no use to ~ = there is no use in ~ing
It's no use expecting her to say thank-you.
It's no good talking to him. He never listens.

cannot help ~ing = cannot (choose) but + 원형
For we **cannot help speaking** about what we have seen and heard.
우리는 보고 들은 것을 말하지 아니할 수 없다 하니(행 4:20).

of one's own ~ing = 과거분사 + by oneself
This is the tree of my own planting.

on ~ing = as soon as
On hearing this, Jesus said, "It is not the healthy who need a doctor, but the sick.
예수께서 들으시고 이르시되 건강한 자에게는 의원이 쓸데 없고 병든 자에게라야 쓸데 있느니라(마 9:12).

it goes without saying that ~ = it is needless to say that ~
It goes without saying that she will stop smoking.

feel like ~ing = feel inclined to ~
make a point of ~ing = make it a rule to ~
be worth ~ing = be worth while to 원형(혹은 동명사)
be on the point of ~ing = be about to ~
come near ~ing = nearly escape ~ing
be far from ~ing = be never ~
what do you say to ~ing? = let's ~

need, want 다음에 오는 동명사는 수동의 의미

Your hair needs cutting. (= ---- needs to be cut.)

The car wants servicing. (= ---- wants to be serviced.)

Afraid of ~ing = afraid to 부정사

I'm not afraid of telling/to tell her the truth.

단, 사고에 관해 말할 때는 afraid of ~ing를 쓴다.
I don't like to drive fast because I'm afraid of crashing.

전치사 to 다음

I look forward to seeing you.

I'm not used to getting up early.

I prefer riding to walking.

To가 to 부정사의 to가 아니라 전치사인지를 확인하려면 to 다음에 명사를 넣어서 뜻이 통하면 이때의 to는 전치사이다.

I want to your letter. (x, to 부정사)

I'm looking forward to your letter. (o, 전치사)

연습 문제

1. When Jesus had finished _____ these things, the crowds were amazed at his teaching.
   1) to say   2) say   3) saying of   4) saying

   After Jesus had finished instructing his twelve disciples, he went on from there to teach and preach in the towns of Galilee.
   Stop judging by mere appearances, and make a right judgment.
   The LORD scattered them from there over all the earth, and they stopped building the city.

2. He kept _____ signs to them but remained unable to speak.
   1) making   2) make   3) to make   4) made

   For forty days the flood kept coming on the earth
   It kept flying back and forth until the water had dried up from the earth.

3. Who of you by _____ can add a single hour to his life?
   1) to worry   2) worrying   3) worried   4) worrisome

4. It is better _____ you to enter the kingdom of God with one eye than to have two eyes and be thrown into hell.
   1) for   2) of   3) to   4) that

5. A woman was there who had been subject _____ for twelve years, but no one could heal her.
   1) to bleed   2) bleed   3) to bleeding   4) bleeding

6. We cannot help _____ about what we have seen and heard.
   1) to speak   2) of speaking   3) speaking   4) speak

7. I consider that our present sufferings are not worth _____ with the glory that will be revealed in us.

   1) comparing   2) to compare   3) compare   4) of comparing

8. Eat anything sold in the meat market without _____ questions of conscience.

   1) raising   2) to raise   3) rising   4) to rise

9. Come back to your senses as you ought, and stop _____.

   1) sinning   2) to sin   3) sinned   4) of sinning

10. And all the Egyptians dug along the Nile to get _____ water, because they could not drink the water of the river.

    1) drunken   2) drink   3) to drink   4) drinking

    애굽 사람들은 하수 물을 마실 수 없으므로 하숫가를 두루 파서 마실 물을 구하였더라(출 7:24).

If you hold to my teaching, you are really my disciples.
Everyone who heard him was amazed at his understanding and his answers.

다음의 현재분사와 비교해 보세요
He saw the Spirit of God **descending** like a dove and **lighting** on him.
Then the woman, **seeing** that she could not go unnoticed, came **trembling** and fell at his feet.

11. They will throw them into the fiery furnace, where there will be weeping and _____ of teeth.

    1) gnashing   2) gnash   3) to gnash   4) gnashed

12. As Jesus was getting into the boat, the man who had been demon-possessed begged _____ with him.

    1) going   2) gone   3) to go   4) go

정답

1) 4, 2) 1, 3) 2, 4) 1, 5) 3, 6) 3, 7) 1, 8) 1, 9) 1, 10) 4
11) 1, 12) 3

숙어

make up for; 만회하다, 완전하게 하다
because he almost died for the work of Christ, risking his life to **make up for** the help you could not give me.
저가 그리스도의 일을 위하여 죽기에 이르러도 자기 목숨을 돌아보지 아니한 것은 나를 섬기는 너희의 일에 부족함을 채우려 함이니라(빌 2:30).

make up one's mind; 결심하다
Therefore let us stop passing judgment on one another. Instead, **make up your mind** not to put any stumbling block or obstacle in your brother's way.
그런즉 우리가 다시는 서로 판단하지 말고 도리어 부딪힐 것이나 거칠 것으로 형제 앞에 두지 아니할 것을 주의하라(롬 14:13).

But the man who has settled the matter in his own mind, who is under no compulsion but has control over his own will, and who has **made up his mind** not to marry the virgin--this man also does the right thing.
그러나 그 마음을 굳게 하고 또 부득이한 일도 없고 자기 뜻대로 할 권리가 있어서 그 처녀 딸을 머물러 두기로 마음에 작정하여도 잘 하는 것이니라(고전 7:37).

marriage to, get married to (Not; with); ~와 결혼(하다)
Her **marriage to** Philip didn't last very long.
How long have you been **married to** Maria.

not ~ at all; 전혀 ~ 하지 않다
But I tell you, Do **not** swear **at all**: either by heaven, for it is God's throne:
나는 너희에게 이르노니 도무지 맹세하지 말지니 하늘로도 말라 이는 하나님의 보좌임이요(마 5:34).

nothing but; 단지 ~ 만
"Please test your servants for ten days: Give us **nothing but** vegetables to eat and water to drink.

청하오니 당신의 종들을 열흘 동안 시험하여 채식을 주어 먹게 하고 물을 주어 마시게 한 후에(단 1:12).

on ~ing; ~ 하자마자
On coming to the house, they saw the child with his mother Mary, and they bowed down and worshiped him. Then they opened their treasures and presented him with gifts of gold and of incense and of myrrh.
집에 들어가 아기와 그 모친 마리아의 함께 있는 것을 보고 엎드려 아기께 경배하고 보배합을 열어 황금과 유향과 몰약을 예물로 드리니라(마 2:11).

on account of; (어떤 이유) 때문에
And your fame spread among the nations **on account of** your beauty, because the splendor I had given you made your beauty perfect, declares the Sovereign LORD.
네 화려함을 인하여 네 명성이 이방인 중에 퍼졌음은 내가 네게 입힌 영화로 네 화려함이 온전함이니라 나 주 여호와의 말이니라(겔 16:14).

Blessed is the man who does not fall away **on account of** me."
누구든지 나를 인하여 실족하지 아니하는 자는 복이 있도다(마 11:6).

on ons's behalf; ~을 대신하여, ~을 위하여
He is to lay his hand on the head of the burnt offering, and it will be accepted **on his behalf** to make atonement for him.
그가 번제물의 머리에 안수할지니 그리하면 열납되어 그를 위하여 속죄가 될 것이라(레 1:4).

on one's knees; 무릎을 꿇고
A man with leprosy came to him and begged him **on his knees**, "If you are willing, you can make me clean."
한 문둥병자가 예수께 와서 꿇어 엎드리어 간구하여 가로되 원하시면 저를 깨끗케 하실 수 있나이다(막 1:40).

on behalf of; ~을 대신하여, ~을 위하여
For I tell you that Christ has become a servant of the Jews **on behalf of** God's truth, to confirm the promises made to the patriarchs
내가 말하노니 그리스도께서 하나님의 진실하심을 위하여 할례의 수종자가 되셨으니 이는 조상들에게 주신 약속들을 견고케 하시고(롬 15:8).

15. 분사(分詞)
Participle

Smoking, drinking, talking 등은 동사지만 형용사나 명사로 쓸 수도 있다. 동사처럼 일정한 시제와 형태를 갖고 있고 또한 형용사적인 성격도 갖고 있을 때 분사라고 하며, 명사로 쓰일 때는 동명사(Gerunds)라고 한다.

분사로 쓰일 때
You're **smoking** too much these days.
There was a **smoking** cigarette end in the ashtray.

동명사로 쓰일 때
Smoking is bad for your health.

A. 분사의 형용사적 용법

분사는 형용사처럼 직접 명사에 부가하여 수식어로서 사용된다.

1. 현재분사는 능동적 의미, 과거분사는 수동적 의미

I thought the lesson was **interesting**.
I was **interested** in the lesson. (Not; I was interesting in the lesson.)

Susan's party was pretty **boring**.
I went home early because I felt **bored**. (Not; because I felt boring.)

It was an **exciting** story.
When I read it I felt **excited**.

The explanation was **confusing**. I got **confused**.
It was a **tiring** day. It made me **tired**.

Why should any **living** man complain when punished for his sins?
살아 있는 사람은 자기 죄로 벌을 받나니 어찌 원망하랴(애 3:39).

This is the **written** account of Adam's life.
아담 자손의 계보가 이러하니라 (창 5:1).

Stolen water is sweet; food **eaten** in secret is delicious!
도적질한 물이 달고 몰래 먹는 떡이 맛이 있다 하는도다 (잠 9:17).

2. 예외; 능동적 의미를 가지는 과거분사

Fallen rocks, a **retired** army officer, a **grown-up** daughter, an **escaped** prosoner

3. 분사가 보어, 목적어 혹은 부사적 수식어구를 동반할 때는 통상 명사 뒤에

A river **watering** the garden flowed from Eden.
강이 에덴에서 발원하여 동산을 적시고 (창 2:10).

He went and lived in a town **called** Nazareth.
나사렛이란 동네에 와서 사니 (마 2:23).

He saw two brothers, Simon **called** Peter and his brother Andrew.
두 형제 곧 베드로라 하는 시몬과 그 형제 안드레가 (마 4:18).

Those **controlled** by the sinful nature cannot please God.
육신에 있는 자들은 하나님을 기쁘시게 할 수 없느니라 (롬 8:8).

Cursed is everyone who does not continue to do everything **written** in the Book of the Law.
누구든지 율법 책에 기록된 대로 온갖 일을 항상 행하지 아니하는 자는 저주 아래 있는 자라 (갈 3:10).

A voice of one **calling** in the desert
광야에 외치는 자의 소리 (마 3:3).

4. 분사가 대명사를 수식할 때는 단독일 때도 뒤에

These were the clans of Reuben; those **numbered** were 43,730.
이는 르우벤 가족들이라 계수함을 입은 자가 사만 삼천칠백삼십 명이요 (민 26:7).

B. 보어로서의 분사

분사도 형용사처럼 보어로서 주어 혹은 목적어를 서술적으로 수식한다.

1. 주격 보어로서

She cried **looking** her mother.

2. 목적격 보어로서

I looked, and I saw a windstorm **coming** out of the north.
내가 보니 북방에서부터 폭풍과 큰 구름이 오는데 (겔 1:4).

If you do not tell me what my dream was and interpret it, I will **have** you **cut** into pieces and your houses **turned** into piles of rubble.
너희가 만일 꿈과 그 해석을 나로 알게 하지 아니하면 너희 몸을 쪼갤 것이며 너희 집으로 거름 터를 삼을 것이요 (단 2:5).

So he **had** the ark of the LORD **carried** around the city, circling it once. Then the people returned to camp and spent the night there.
여호와의 궤로 성을 한번 돌게 하니라 무리가 진에 돌아와서 진에서 자니라 (수 6:11).

C. 분사구문

분사가 유도하는 구가 주문을 부서적으로 수식할 때, 그 분사구를 분사구문이라 한다.

1. 시간

Confessing their sins, they were baptized by him in the Jordan River.
자기들의 죄를 자복하고 요단강에서 그에게 세례를 받더니 (마 3:6).

Confessing their sins, = After they confessed their sins

Coming to his hometown, he began teaching the people in their synagogue, and they were amazed.
고향으로 돌아가사 저희 회당에서 가르치시니 저희가 놀라 가로되 이 사람의 이 지혜와 이런 능력이 어디서 났느뇨 (마 13:54).

These are the visions I saw **while lying** in my bed: I looked, and there before me stood a tree in the middle of the land. Its height was enormous.
내가 침상에서 나의 뇌 속으로 받은 이상이 이러하니라. 내가 본즉 땅의 중앙에 한 나무가 있는데 고가 높더니 (단 4:10).

2. 이유

Furious with rage, Nebuchadnezzar summoned Shadrach, Meshach and Abednego. So these men were brought before the king,
느부갓네살 왕이 노하고 분하여 사드락과 메삭과 아벳느고를 끌어 오라 명하매 드디어 그 사람들을 왕의 앞으로 끌어온지라 (단 3:13).

And, once **made perfect**, he became the source of eternal salvation for all who obey him
온전하게 되었은 즉 자기를 순종하는 모든 자에게 영원한 구원의 근원이 되시고 (히 5:9).

Terrified at her torment, they will stand far off and cry: "'Woe! Woe, O great city, O Babylon, city of power! In one hour your doom has come!'
그 고난을 무서워하여 멀리 서서 가로되 화 있도다 화 있도다 큰 성 견고한 성 바벨론이여. 일시간에 네 심판이 이르렀다(계 18:10).

Filled with compassion, Jesus reached out his hand and touched the man. "I am willing," he said. "Be clean!"
예수께서 민망히 여기사 손을 내밀어 저에게 대시며 가라사대 내가 원하노니 깨끗함을 받으라 하신대(막 1:41).

3. 조건

Turning to the right, you will find the post-office.

4. 양보

Admitting what you say, I still don't believe it.

5. 부대상황(동시상황)

이것은 원래 주격 보어인데, 주절의 동작이 행해질 때의 주어의 상황을 나타낸다.

He went out and began to talk freely, **spreading** the news.
그 사람이 나가서 이 일을 많이 전파하여 널리 퍼지게 하니(막 1:45).

Both of them were upright in the sight of God, **observing** all the Lord's commandments and regulations blamelessly.
이 두 사람이 하나님 앞에 의인이니 주의 모든 계명과 규례대로 흠이 없이 행하더라(눅 1:6).

The apostles left the Sanhedrin, **rejoicing** because they had been counted worthy of suffering disgrace for the Name.
사도들은 그 이름을 위하여 능욕 받는 일에 합당한 자로 여기심을 기뻐하면서 공회 앞을 떠나니라(행 5:41).

They will walk with me, **dressed** in white, for they are worthy.
흰 옷을 입고 나와 함께 다니리니 그들은 합당한 자인 연고라(계 3:4).

If he does, the new piece will pull away from the old, **making the tear worse**.
만일 그렇게 하면 기운 새것이 낡은 그것을 당기어 해어짐이 더하게 되느니라 (막 2:21).

He is to wring its head from its neck, not **severing** it completely,
그 머리를 목에서 비틀어 끊고 몸은 아주 쪼개지 말며 (레 5:8).

You trampled the sea with your horses, churning the great waters.
주께서 말을 타시고 바다 곧 큰 물의 파도를 밟으셨나이다 (합 3:15).

D. 분사구문의 시제

1. 분사구문이 나타내는 시간은 주절의 술부 동사의 시제와 일치하지만, 그 보다 앞선 시제를 나타낼 때는 having + 과거분사를 쓴다

And **having been warned** in a dream not to go back to Herod, **they** returned to their country by another route.
꿈에 헤롯에게로 돌아가지 말라 지시하심을 받아 다른 길로 고국에 돌아가니라 (마 2:12).

2. 분사구문의 뜻이 때, 이유, 조건 등 어느 것인지 혼동을 방지하기 위해, 해당 접속사를 분사구문의 앞에 부가할 경우가 있다

By faith Abraham, **when called** to go to a place he would later receive as his inheritance, obeyed and went, even though he did not know where he was going.
믿음으로 아브라함은 부르심을 받았을 때에 순종하여 장래 기업으로 받을 땅에 나갈새 갈 바를 알지 못하고 나갔으며 (히 11:8).

Yet **when planted**, it grows and becomes the largest of all garden plants, with such big branches that the birds of the air can perch in its shade.
심긴 후에는 자라서 모든 나물보다 커지며 큰 가지를 내니 공중의 새들이 그 그늘에 깃들일 만큼 되느니라 (막 4:32).

E. 독립분사구문

분사구문에는 의미상 주어가 있다. 이것이 주문의 주어와 같을 때는 나타낼 필요가 없지만, 다를 때는 분사 앞에 분사의 주어를 첨가해 나타내 주어야 한다.

1. 때

The sun having risen, we started our journey.

2. 이유

The meeting over, we were at leisure.

3. 조건

We shall stop demonstration, our request permitted.

4. 부대상황

I was playing football, my son sleeping in the house.

F. 무인칭 독립분사구문

Abraham reasoned that God could raise the dead, and **figuratively speaking**, he did receive Isaac back from death.
저가 하나님이 능히 죽은 자 가운데서 다시 살리실 줄로 생각한 지라. 비유컨대 죽은 자 가운데서 도로 받은 것이니라(히 11:19).

strictly speaking = if we speak strictly = 엄격히 말해서
judging from ~ = if we judge from ~ = ~으로 판단하건대
generally speaking = if we speak generally = 일반적으로 말해서
talking all things into consideration = 만사를 고려하면

G. 부대상황

1. with + 목적어 + 분사

부대상황을 나타내는 독립분사구문에 with를 붙이면 묘사적인 효과를 나타낸다. 이때 목적어와 분사는 주어, 술어의 관계가 있다.

When they came to the home of the synagogue ruler, Jesus saw a commotion, **with** people **crying and wailing** loudly.
회당장의 집에 함께 가사 훤화함과 사람들의 울며 심히 통곡함을 보시고(막 5:38).

Then, at the evening sacrifice, I rose from my self-abasement, **with** my tunic and cloak **torn**, and fell on my knees with my hands spread out to the LORD my God
저녁 제사를 드릴 때에 내가 근심 중에 일어나서 속옷과 겉옷을 찢은 대로 무릎을 꿇고 나의 하나님 여호와를 향하여 손을 들고(스 9:5).

And he ordered the people, "Advance! March around the city, **with** the armed guard **going** ahead of the ark of the LORD."
또 백성에게 이르되 나아가서 성을 돌되 무장한 자들이 여호와의 궤 앞에 행할지니라(수 6:7).

Is it proper for a woman to pray to God **with** her head **uncovered**?
여자가 쓰지 않고 하나님께 기도하는 것이 마땅하냐(고전 11:13).

And every woman who prays or prophesies **with** her head **uncovered** dishonors her head
무릇 여자로서 머리에 쓴 것을 벗고 기도나 예언을 하는 자는 그 머리를 욕되게 하는 것이니(고전 11:5).

2. 보어로 부사구가 쓰였다.

I myself am a man under authority, **with** soldiers **under me**.
나도 남의 수하에 있는 사람이요 내 아래도 군사가 있으니(마 8:9).

At this, she bowed down **with** her face **to the ground**.
룻이 땅에 엎드려 절하며(룻 2:10).

Then the cherubim, **with** the wheels **beside them**, spread their wings, and the glory of the God of Israel was above them.

때에 그룹들이 날개를 드는데 바퀴도 그 곁에 있고 이스라엘 하나님의 영광도 그 위에 덮였더니 (겔 11:22).

연습 문제

1. _____ warned in a dream not to go back to Herod, they returned to their country by another route.
   1) To be 2) That 3) Having been 4) Having

   Having been warned in a dream, he withdrew to the district of Galilee

2. _____ their sins, they were baptized by him in the Jordan River.
   1) Confessed 2) To confess 3) Being confessing 4) Confessing

   All at once he followed her like an ox going to the slaughter, like a deer stepping into a noose till an arrow pierces his liver, like a bird darting into a snare, little **knowing** it will cost him his life.
   소년이 곧 그를 따랐으니 소가 푸주로 가는 것 같고 미련한 자가 벌을 받으려고 쇠사슬에 매이러 가는 것과 일반이라 필경은 살이 그 간을 뚫기까지에 이를 것이라. 새가 빨리 그물로 들어가되 그 생명을 잃어버릴 줄을 알지 못함과 일반이니라 (잠 7:22,23).

3. You brood of vipers! Who warned you to flee from the _____ wrath?
   1) came 2) coming 3) to come 4) come

4. _____ fasting forty days and forty nights, he was hungry.
   1) After 2) Since 3) So 4) That

5. _____ Nazareth, he went and lived in Capernaum.
   1) Left 2) To be left 3) Leaving 4) Leave

6. _____ on from there, he saw two other brothers.
   1) Go 2) Went 3) Gone 4) Going

   Going on from that place, he went into their synagogue.

7. They were in a boat with their father Zebedee, _____ their nets.
   1) prepare   2) preparing   3) prepared   4) for preparing of

8. There is nothing _____ that will not be disclosed, or hidden that will not be made known.
   1) to conceal   2) conceal   3) concealed   4) concealing

   Nothing green remained on tree or plant in all the land of Egypt.
   애굽 전경에 나무나 밭의 채소나 푸른 것은 남지 아니하였더라 (출 10:15).

   And the LORD said to Moses, "Stretch out your hand over Egypt so that locusts will swarm over the land and devour everything **growing** in the fields, everything **left** by the hail."
   여호와께서 모세에게 이르시되 네 손을 애굽 땅 위에 들어 메뚜기로 애굽 땅에 올라와서 우박에 상하지 아니한 밭의 모든 채소를 먹게 하라 (출 10:12).

9. If the home is _____ , let your peace rest on it; if it is not, let your peace return to you.
   1) deserve   2) deserving   3) deserved   4) being deserved

10. Many followed him, and he healed all their sick, _____ them not to tell who he was.
    1) warned   2) warn   3) warning   4) to warn

    He produces a crop, yielding a hundred, sixty or thirty times what was sown.
    He fell to the ground and rolled around, foaming at the mouth.
    They saw Jesus approaching the boat, walking on the water.

11. The good man brings good things out of the good _____ up in him.
    1) to store   2) stored   3) store   4) storage

12. While Jesus was still talking to the crowd, his mother and brothers stood outside, _____ to speak to him.
    1) wanting   2) wanted   3) to want   4) want

13. You will be ever hearing but never understanding; you will be ever seeing but never _____.

    1) looking   2) perceiving   3) watching   4) catching

14. For this people's heart has become _____; they hardly hear with their ears, and they have closed their eyes.

    1) calloused   2) callous   3) to callous   4) callousing

15. Again, the kingdom of heaven is like a merchant _____ for fine pearls.

    1) to look   2) looked   3) looking   4) look

16. Taking the five loaves and the two fish and _____ up to heaven, he gave thanks and broke the loaves.

    1) looked   2) looks   3) to look   4) looking

17. And when the men of that place recognized Jesus, they sent word to all the _____ country.

    1) surrounded   2) surrounding   3) surround   4) surrounding of

18. Yet when _____, it grows and becomes the largest of all garden plants.

    1) planted   2) planting   3) plant   4) to be planted

19. _____ him, they asked him for a sign from heaven.

    1) Testing   2) Test   3) To be tested   4) To test

20. So they hurried off and found Mary and Joseph, and the baby, who was _____ in the manger.

    1) laying   2) lying   3) lied   4) lay

    Immediately he stood up in front of them, took what he had been lying on and went home praising God.

21. The punishment _____ on him by the majority is sufficient for him.

    1) to be inflicted   2) to inflict   3) inflicted   4) infliction

22. We are hard pressed on every side, but not _____; perplexed, but not in despair.
   1) crushed   2) to crush   3) crush   4) crushing

23. In the synagogue there was a man _____ by a demon, an evil spirit.
   1) possessing   2) possessed   3) possess   4) possessment

24. They have tracked me down, they now surround me, _____ eyes alert, to throw me to the ground.
   1) both   2) their   3) with   4) by

I see a solid gold lampstand with a bowl at the top.
There before me were two women, with the wind in their wings.
Once again men and women of ripe old age will sit in the streets of Jerusalem, each with cane in hand because of his age.

25. All the nations will call you _____, for yours will be a delightful land.
   1) bless   2) blessed   3) blessing   4) blesses

26. God saw how corrupt the earth had become, for all the people on earth had _____ their ways.
   1) to corrupt   2) corrupted   3) corruption   4) corrupting

27. Anyone who marries the _____ woman commits adultery.
   1) divorce   2) divorced   3) to divorce   4) divorcement

28. Settle matters quickly with your adversary who is _____ you to court.
   1) take   2) took   3) taken   4) taking

정답

1) 3, 2) 4, 3) 2, 4) 1, 5) 3, 6) 4, 7) 2, 8) 3, 9) 2, 10) 3
11) 2, 12) 1, 13) 2, 14) 1, 15) 3, 16) 4, 17) 2, 18) 1, 19) 4, 20) 2
21) 3, 22) 1, 23) 2, 24) 3, 25) 2, 26) 2, 27) 2, 28) 4

숙어

on the contrary; 반대로
On the contrary, "It is through Isaac that your offspring will be reckoned."
오직 이삭으로부터 난 자라야 네 씨라 칭하리라 하셨으니(롬 9:7).

On the contrary, they have divine power to demolish strongholds.
오직 하나님 앞에서 견고한 진을 파하는 강력이라(고후 10:4).

on the way; ~ 하는 중에
Settle matters quickly with your adversary who is taking you to court. Do it while you are still with him **on the way**, or he may hand you over to the judge, and the judge may hand you over to the officer, and you may be thrown into prison.
너를 송사하는 자와 함께 길에 있을 때에 급히 사화하라. 그 송사하는 자가 너를 재판관에게 내어주고 재판관이 관예에게 내어주어 옥에 가둘까 염려하라(마 5:25).

pay attention to; ~에 유의하다
Why do you look at the speck of sawdust in your brother's eye and **pay no attention to** the plank in your own eye?
어찌하여 형제의 눈 속에 있는 티는 보고 네 눈 속에 있는 들보는 깨단지 못하느냐(마 7:3).

Make the work harder for the men so that they keep working and **pay no attention to** lies.
그 사람들의 고역을 무겁게 함으로 수고롭게 하여 그들로 거짓말을 듣지 않게 하라(출 5:9).

pay for(something) (Not; pay something); 지불하다, 빚 등을 갚다
Excuse me, sir. You haven't **paid for** your ticket.

plead with; 탄원하다, 간청하다
Three times I **pleaded with** the Lord to take it away from me.
이것이 내게서 떠나기 위하여 내가 세 번 주께 간구하였더니(고후 12:8).

pleased with (somebody); 좋아하는, 만족스러운
The boss is very **pleased with** you.

pleased with/at/about (something); 좋아하는, 만족스러운
I wasn't very **pleased with/at/about** my test results.

polite to (Not; with); 공손한, 품위 있는
Try to be **polite to** your uncle for once.

prevent A from ~ing; 예방하다, 지키다, 보호하다
The noise of your party **prevented** me **from sleeping**.

proof of (Not; for); ~의 증거
I want **proof of** your love. Lend me some money.

provide A with B; A에게 B를 공급하다
and he had **provided** him **with** a large room formerly used to store the grain offerings and incense and temple articles, and also the tithes of grain, new wine and oil prescribed for the Levites, singers and gatekeepers, as well as the contributions for the priests.
도비야를 위하여 한 큰 방을 갖추었으니 그 방은 원래 소제물과 유향과 또 기명과 레위 사람들과 노래하는 자들과 문지기들에게 십일조로 주는 곡물과 새 포도주와 기름과 또 제사장들에게 주는 거제물을 두는 곳이라 (느 13:5).

And the people of any place where survivors may now be living are to **provide** him **with** silver and gold, with goods and livestock, and with freewill offerings for the temple of God in Jerusalem.
무릇 그 남아있는 백성이 어느 곳에 우거하였든지 그곳 사람들이 마땅히 은과 금과 기타 물건과 짐승으로 도와주고 그 외에도 예루살렘 하나님의 전을 위하여 예물을 즐거이 드릴지니라 (스 1:4).

put out; 끄다 (turn out)
Do not **put out** the Spirit's fire;
성령을 소멸치 말며 (살전 5:19).

put(bring) to shame; 체면을 손상시키다, 창피 주다, 모욕하다

I lay a stone in Zion, a chosen and precious cornerstone, and the one who trusts in him will never be **put to shame**.

내가 택한 보배롭고 요긴한 모퉁이 돌을 시온에 두노니, 저를 믿는 자는 부끄러움을 당치 아니하리라 하였으니 (벧전 2:6).

put ~ to the test; ~을 시험하다

Do not **put** the Lord your God **to the test**.

주 너의 하나님을 시험치 말라(눅 4:12).

16. 일치와 화법
(一致와 話法)

A. 주어와 술어동사의 일치

The number of those who ate **was** about five thousand men, besides women and children.
먹은 사람은 여자와 아이 외에 오천 명이나 되었더라(마 14:21).

The **number** of the mounted troops **was** two hundred million. I heard their number.
마병대의 수는 이만만이니 내가 그들의 수를 들었노라(계 9:16).

Your father and I **have** been anxiously searching for you.
네 아버지와 내가 근심하여 너를 찾았노라(눅 2:48).

1. 집합명사; 단수 취급, 군집명사; 복수 취급

Their cavalry **gallops** headlong.
그 기병은 원방에서부터 빨리 달려오는 기병이라(합 1:8).

2. either A or B, neither A nor B는 통상 B에 술부 동사 일치

Once the crowd realized that **neither** Jesus **nor** his disciples **were** there, they got into the boats and went to Capernaum in search of Jesus.
무리가 거기 예수도 없으시고 제자들도 없음을 보고 곧 배들을 타고 예수를 찾으러 가버나움으로 가서 (요 6:24).

3. Not only A but also B = B as well as A

Not only A but also B; 술부 동사가 뒤의 B에 일치
B as well as A; 술부 동사가 앞의 B에 일치

They risked their lives for me. **Not only** I **but** all the churches of the Gentiles **are** grateful to them.
저희는 내 목숨을 위하여 자기의 목이라도 내어 놓았나니 나뿐 아니라 이방인의 모든 교회도 저희에게 감사하 느니라(롬 16:4).

4. 형식은 복수지만 내용상 단수 취급을 하는 예

분수는 뒤에 오는 말에 따라서 수가 결정된다.
A third of the living creatures in the sea died, and a third of the ships **were** destroyed.
바다 가운데 생명 가진 피조물들의 삼분의 일이 죽고 배들의 삼분의 일이 깨어지더라 (계 8:9).

5. 동일인

The poet and novelist **is** present at the conference.

6. 수량의 일치

1) every, each는 단수

Give an order now to bring your livestock and everything you have in the field to a place of shelter, because the hail will fall on **every** man and animal that **has** not been brought in and **is** still out in the field, and they will die.
이제 보내어 네 생축과 네 들에 있는 것을 다 모으라. 사람이나 짐승이나 무릇 들에 있어서 집에 돌아오지 않은 자에게는 우박이 그 위에 내리리니 그것들이 죽으리라 하셨다 하라 (출 9:19).

2) neither는 단수

Neither of my sisters **is** married.

그러나 구어체에서는 복수도 가능하다.
Neither of my sisters **are** married.

3) a lot of/lots of + 단수 명사 + 단수 동사

A lot of time **is** needed to learn a language.
There **is** a lot of coffee in the pot.

4) a lot of/lots of + 복수 명사 + 복수 동사

A lot of my friends **think** there's going to be a war.
Lots of people **live** in the country and work in Ulsan.

A lot of us **want** to change our jobs.

5) A lot of/lots of는 구어체에서 주로 쓰며, 문어체에서는 다음 표현들이 쓰인다.

6) a great deal of + 단수 명사,

He has spent **a great deal of** time in the Far East.

7) a large number of + 복수 명사

We have **a large number of** problems to solve.

8) plenty of + 단/복수 명사

Thirty years ago there were **plenty of** jobs; now there are very few.

B. 시제의 일치

1. 시제 일치의 예외

1) 보편적 진리

Columbus **proved** that the earth **is** round.

2) 현재의 습관

She **said** that she **goes** to school at seven in the morning.

3) 과거로부터 현재 혹은 미래에 계속 관계가 미칠 때

She said he is now in London.
The earth **goes** round the sun. > He proved that the earth **goes/went** round the sun.
How old **are** you? > I asked how old you **are/were**.

4) 역사적 사실은 항상 과거 시제로

The historian told us that the Civil War **broke** out in 1861.

5) 가정법

She said that she **would** visit her friend if she **were** not ill.

6) must, need, ought to는 그대로

He said he **must** go home at once.
I told him that he **need** not worry over the problem.

C. 화법

1. 평서문의 전달

1) 전달 동사

say는 say
say to는 tell
그 외의 동사는 그대로

2) 피전달문; that 절로 한다

인칭, 지시대명사, 부사(구)는 전달자의 입장에서 적절히 바꾼다.

3) 시제의 변화

Will you marry me? > I asked him if he would marry me.
You look nice. > I told her she looked nice.
I'm learning French. > She said she was learning French.
I've forgotten. > He said he had forgotten.
John phoned. > She told me that John had phoned.

4) 평서문

He said (that) he wanted to go home.
구어체에서는 that을 생략할 수 있다.

5) 화법 전환에 따른 어구 변화

Bill (토요일에); I don't like this party. I want to go home.
Peter (일요일에); Bill said **he didn't** like **the** party, **and he** wanted to go home.

now > then
today > that day
tomorrow > next day 혹은 the following day
yesterday > the day before, 혹은 the previous day
last night > the night before 혹은 the previous night
ago > before,
this > that
these > those
here > there

2. 의문문의 전달

1) 전달 동사: ask, inquire

2) 의문사(who, what, how 등)가 있는 의문문은 의문사 + 평서문

She asked me **what my name was**.
He asked **where I was** going.
I asked **where the President and his wife were** staying.

3) 의문사가 없는 의문문은 if(whether) + 평서문

She asked me **if/whether** I wanted anything to eat.
The driver asked **if/whether** I wanted the town center.
I don't know **if/whether** I can help you.

3. 명령문의 전달

1) 전달 동사
tell, ask, beg, order, command, bid, advise, request, forbid + 목적어 + to 부정사

2) Let가 유도하는 명령문
그 내용에 따라서 suggest(or propose) that ~ should, 혹은 offer, ask to be allowed 등을 쓴다.

3) 요청을 나타낼 때; ask(beg)
The lady downstairs has **asked us to be** quiet after nine o'clock.

4) 충고를 나타낼 때; tell(advise)
I **advised Lucy to go** to the police.
I **advised Andrew to be** careful.
I **advise you to think** again before you decide which one to buy.
The policeman **told me not to park** there.
He **told me to be** quiet. (Not; He said me ---)

5) 제안을 할 때
전달 동사를 suggest 혹은 propose로 바꾸고 전달 내용을 that 절로 하여 should를 넣는다. 이 should를 빼고 동사 원형을 써도 된다.

She **suggested** that we (**should**) pay the bill.

연습 문제

1. So he got up, took the child and his mother and _____ to the land of Israel.
   1) going   2) to go   3) went   4) go

2. Blessed are you when people insult you, _____ you and falsely say all kinds of evil against you because of me.
   1) to persecute   2) persecute   3) persecuting   4) persecuted

3. It is no longer good for anything, except to be thrown out and _____ by men.
   1) trampled   2) to trample   3) trampling   4) trample

4. Everyone who asks receives; he who seeks finds; and to him who _____, the door will be opened.
   1) is knocking   2) knocks   3) knock   4) knocked

5. And even the very hairs of your head _____ all numbered.
   1) are   2) is   3) has   4) have

6. Go back and _____ to John what you hear and see.
   1) to report   2) reporting   3) reported   4) report

7. A wicked and adulterous generation asks for a miraculous _____!
   1) signature   2) signatures   3) sign   4) signs

8. Peter got down out of the boat, _____ on the water and came toward Jesus.
   1) walking   2) to walk   3) walked   4) walk

9. He foams at the mouth, gnashes his teeth and _____ rigid.
   1) becomes   2) become   3) became   4) becoming

10. His winnowing fork is in his hand to clear his threshing floor and _____ the wheat into his barn.

   1) gathering   2) to gather   3) gather   4) gathered

11. Blessed are you who _____ now, for you will be satisfied.

   1) hunger   2) hungers   3) hungry   4) hungered

12. She is not dead but _____.

   1) sleeps   2) to sleep   3) sleep   4) asleep

13. Not until halfway through the Feast did Jesus go up to the temple courts and _____ to teach.

   1) began   2) to begin   3) begin   4) beginning

14. On the contrary, those parts of the body that _____ weaker are indispensable.

   1) seems to be   2) seem to be   3) seems be   4) seems

15. It is better for you to enter life maimed than with two hands _____ into hell, where the fire never goes out.

   1) go   2) to go   3) going   4) goes

16. A large herd of pigs _____ feeding on the nearby hillside.

   1) were   2) was   3) has   4) have

   마침 거기 돼지의 큰 떼가 산 곁에서 먹고 있는지라(막 5:11).

정답

1). 3,   2). 2,   3). 1,   4). 2,   5). 1,   6). 4,   7). 3,   8). 3,   9). 1,   10). 2
11). 1,   12). 4,   13). 3,   14). 2,   15). 2,   16). 2

숙어

put to the sword; (특히 승자가). 칼로 죽이다, 대학살을 하다
The LORD also gave that city and its king into Israel's hand. The city and everyone in it Joshua **put to the sword**. He left no survivors there. And he did to its king as he had done to the king of Jericho.
여호와께서 또 그 성읍과 그 왕을 이스라엘의 손에 붙이신지라. 칼날로 그 성읍과 그 중의 모든 사람을 쳐서 멸하여 한 사람도 남기지 아니하였으니 그 왕에게 행한 것이 여리고 왕에게 행한 것과 일반이었더라(수 19:30).

put up with; 참다
"O unbelieving and perverse generation," Jesus replied, "how long shall I stay with you and **put up with** you? Bring your son here."
예수께서 대답하여 가라사대 믿음이 없고 패역한 세대여 내가 얼마나 너희와 함께 있으며 너희를 참으리요 네 아들을 이리로 데리고 오라 하시니(눅 9:41).

reason for (Not; of); ~의 이유
Nobody knows the **reason for** the accident.

regard as; ~으로 여기다, 간주하다
All the peoples of the earth are **regarded as** nothing.
땅의 모든 거민을 없는 것 같이 여기시며(단 4:35).

remind A of B; A에게 B를 생각나게 하다
She **reminds** me **of** a girl I was at school with.

responsibility for / responsible for; 책임(있는)
Who's **responsible for** the shopping this week?

result in; 귀착하다, 끝나다
What benefit did you reap at that time from the things you are now ashamed of? Those things **result in** death!

너희가 그 때에 무슨 열매를 얻었느뇨 이제는 너희가 그 일을 부끄러워하나니 이는 그 마지막이 사망이니라 (롬 6:21).

You will be made rich in every way so that you can be generous on every occasion, and through us your generosity will **result in** thanksgiving to God.
너희가 모든 일에 부요하여 너그럽게 연보를 함은 저희로 우리로 말미암아 하나님께 감사하게 하는 것이라 (고후 9:11).

rid A of B; A에서 B를 없애다
But now you must **rid yourselves of** all such things as these: anger, rage, malice, slander, and filthy language from your lips.
이제는 너희가 이 모든 것을 벗어버리라. 곧 분과 악의와 훼방과 너희 입의 부끄러운 말이라(골 3:8).

Therefore, **rid yourselves of** all malice and all deceit, hypocrisy, envy, and slander of every kind.
그러므로 모든 악독과 모든 궤휼과 외식과 시기와 모든 비방하는 말을 버리고(벧전 2:1).

rude to; 실례가 되는, 모욕하는
Lisa was pretty **rude to** my family last weekend.

rule over; 지배(통치)하다
And again, Isaiah says, "The Root of Jesse will spring up, one who will arise to **rule over** the nations; the Gentiles will hope in him."
또 이사야가 가로되 이새의 뿌리 곧 열방을 다스리기 위하여 일어나시는 이가 있으리니 열방이 그에게 소망을 두리라 하였느니라(롬 15:12).

run into (= meet); ~와 우연히 만나다, ~에 빠지다
I **ran into** a friend at Victoria Station this morning.

search for (= look for); 찾다, 구하다
The customs were **searching for** drugs at the airport.

When his parents saw him, they were astonished. His mother said to him, "Son, why have you treated us like this? Your father and I have been anxiously **searching for** you."

그 부모가 보고 놀라며 그 모친은 가로되 아이야 어찌하여 우리에게 이렇게 하였느냐 보라 네 아버지와 내가 근심하여 너를 찾았노라(눅 2:48).

Though you search for your enemies, you will not find them. Those who wage war against you will be as nothing at all.
네가 찾아도 너와 싸우던 자들을 만나지 못할 것이요 너를 치는 자들은 아무 것도 아닌 것 같이, 허무한 것 같이 되리니(사 41:12).

17. 부사(副詞)
Adverb

부사는 동사, 형용사, 부사, 문 전체를 수식하여 시간, 정도, 장소, 방법, 원인 등을 나타내며, 그 외 관계대명사처럼 관계절을 유도하는 관계부사와 의문문을 유도하는 의문부사로 쓰이는 것이 있다.

A. 부사의 용법

1. 부사와 형용사

1) 형용사 + ly
They rose **greatly** on the earth.

2) 형용사와 꼴이 같은 부사
hard, long, high, early, enough, near, much, well, ill 등

3) 형용사와 같은 꼴의 부사에 ly를 붙여 다른 뜻의 부사가 되는 예
high(높이) highly(매우), near(가까이) nearly(거의), dear(비싸게) dearly(마음으로부터), late(늦게) lately(최근에), direct(곧바로), directly(즉시)

4) 어미 ly가 있는 부사와 없는 부사의 뜻이 같을 때
go slow = go slowly

5) 명사구가 부사의 역할을 할 때
See you **next Monday**. (tomorrow morning, yesterday afternoon, etc.)
The meeting is **this Thursday**.
Come **any day** you like.
The party lasted **all night**.
Why don't you come round (on) **Monday evening**?
What time does the train arrive?
They planted corn **the same way** their ancestors used to 500 years ago. (this way, another way, etc.)

I'm going **home**.
Is anybody **home**?

2. 부사의 기능

1) 동사를 수식

She sang **beautifully**. (Not; beautiful)
We'll have to think **quickly**. (Not; quick)
She danced **happily** into the room. (Not; happy)
I don't remember that evening very **well**. (Not; very good)

When his time of service was completed, he returned **home**.
그 직무의 날이 다 되매 집으로 돌아가니라(눅 1:23).

Master, we've worked hard **all night** and haven't caught anything.
선생이여 우리들이 밤이 맞도록 수고를 하였으되 얻은 것이 없지마는(눅 5:5).

Many times it had seized him.
귀신이 가끔 이 사람을 붙잡으므로(눅 8:29).

2) 형용사를 수식

It's **terribly** cold today. (Not; terrible cold)
This steak is very **badly** cooked. (Not; bad cooked)
They are playing **unusually** fast. (Not; unusual fast)

Be **very** careful, then, how you live--not as unwise but as wise, making the most of every opportunity, because the days are evil. (부사 very는 형용사 careful을 수식)
그런즉 너희가 어떻게 행할 것을 자세히 주의하여 지혜 없는 자같이 말고 오직 지혜 있는 자같이 하여 세월을 아끼라 때가 악하니라(엡 5:15, 16).

The camel, though it chews the cud, does not have a split hoof; it is **ceremonially** unclean for you.

약대는 새김질은 하되 굽이 갈라지지 아니하였으므로 너희에게 부정하고 (레 11:4).

3) 부사(구,절)를 수식

I enjoyed it **very much**.
He was **madly** in love with her.
I had lived **long** before he came.

4) (대)명사를 수식

I am **quite** a stranger here.
You **alone** know it.

5) 문장 전체를 수식

Happily he did not die. (cf. He did not die happily.)

B. 부사의 위치

1. 일반 원칙

1) 부사는 동사와 목적어 사이에는 두지 않는다

I **very much** like my job. (Not; I like very much my job.)
She speaks Korean **well**. (Not; She speaks well Korean.)

2) 부사는 문장의 앞, 중간, 뒤에 올 수 있다

Yesterday something very strange happened.
My brother **completely** forgot my birthday.
He got dressed **quickly**.

3) 대개의 부사구는 문장 중간에 올 수 없다

He got dressed **in a hurry**. (Not; He in a hurry got dressed.)

4) 문장 앞에 두는 경우; 절을 연결시키는 부사

However, then, nest, besides, anyway

Some of us wanted to change the system; **however**, not everybody agreed.

I worked without stopping until five o'clock. **Then** I went home.

Next, I want to say something about the future.

happily, angrily, quickly, terribly, beautifully, badly, nicely, well, fast, slowly, noisily, quietly, softly

2. 양태 부사(adverbs of manner); "어떻게"

happily, angrily, quickly, terribly, beautifully, badly, nicely, well, fast, slowly, noisily, quietly, soly

1) 일반적으로 동사의 뒤에 놓는다

News about him spread **quickly** over the whole region of Galilee.
예수의 소문이 곧 온 갈릴리 사방에 퍼지더라(막 1:28).

But since they have no root, they last only a short time. When trouble or persecution comes because of the word, they **quickly** fall away.
그 속에 뿌리가 없어 잠간 견디다가 말씀을 인하여 환난이나 핍박이 일어나는 때에는 곧 넘어지는 자요(막 4:17).

2) 목적어가 있으면 목적어 뒤에 놓는데 동사 앞에 둘 때도 있다

The father spread his arms **abroad**.
그 아버지는 자기의 팔을 넓게 펼쳤다.

3) 강조하기 위해 문두에 놓는다

Well do I know how treacherous you are; you were called a rebel from birth.
네가 궤휼하고 궤휼하여 모태에서부터 패역한 자라 칭함을 입은 줄 내가 알았음이라(사 48:8).

3. 빈도 부사, 정도 부사, 확실성의 부사, 완전성의 부사

• 빈도 부사

always, usually, generally, normally, often, frequently, ever, sometimes, occasionally, rarely, forever, ever, never, seldom

• 정도 부사

just, even, only, mainly, mostly, still, yet, already, also, or, neither, nor

• 확실성의 부사

certainly, definitely, clearly, obviously, probably, really

• 완전성의 부사

completely, practically, almost, nearly, quite, rather, partly, scarcely, hardly, sort of, kind of

1) 일반 동사 앞에

(1) 빈도 부사

We **usually** go to church on Sunday.
It **sometimes** gets very windy here.

(2) 정도 부사

Your bicycle **just** needs some oil.
She **neither** said thank-you **nor** looked at me.
When I was fourteen, I **already** knew that I wanted to be a doctor.
I **still** remember your first birthday.

단, yet는 문미에 온다.
She hasn't gone **yet**.
I haven't done the shopping **yet**.

too, as well은 같은 뜻으로 주로 문미에 온다.
She not only sings; she plays the piano **as well**.
We all went to China last year. He came **too**.

Too, as well은 문맥에 따라 다른 부분을 가리킬 수 있다.
We have meetings on Sundays as well.
- as well이 문맥에 따라 각각 we, have meetings, on Sundays을 가리킬 수 있다. 말할 때는 가리키는 부분을 강조하여 표시한다.

(3) 확실성의 부사
He **probably** thinks you don't like him.
I **certainly** feel better today.

단, perhaps, maybe는 보통 문두에 온다.

(4) 완전성의 부사
I **kind of** hope she wins.

For this people's heart has become calloused; they **hardly** hear with their ears, and they have closed their eyes.
이 백성들의 마음이 완악하여져서 그 귀는 듣기에 둔하고 눈은 감았으니 (마 13:15).

2) be 동사, 조동사 뒤에

(1) 빈도 부사
My boss is **often** bad-tempered.
I am **seldom** late for work.
I have **never** seen a whale.
You can **always** come and stay with us if you want to.
Have you **ever** played American football?

The one who trusts in him will **never** be put to shame.
저를 믿는 자는 부끄러움을 당치 아니하리라 (벧전 2:6).

The Lord will punish men for all such sins, as we have **already** told you and warned you.
우리가 너희에게 미리 말하고 증거한 것과 같이 이 모든 일에 주께서 신원하여 주심이니라 (살전 4:6).

I have already cursed them, because you have not set your heart to honor me.
내가 이미 저주하였나니 이는 너희가 그것을 마음에 두지 아니하였음이니라(말 2:2).

Jesus could no longer enter a town openly but stayed outside in lonely places.
예수께서 다시는 드러나게 동네에 들어가지 못하시고 오직 바깥 한적한 곳에 계셨으나(막 1:45).

조동사가 두 개일 경우에는 앞의 조동사 뒤에 둔다.
We have **never** been invited to one of their parties.
She must **sometimes** have wanted to run away.

usually, normally, often, frequently, sometimes, occasionally는 강조하기 위해 문두에 올 수 있으나 always, never, rarely, seldom, ever는 문두에 올 수 없다.
Sometimes I think I'd like to live somewhere else.
Usually I get up early.
Not; Always I get up early. Never I get up early.

그러나 명령문에서는 always, never가 문두에 올 수 있다.
Always look in your mirror before starting to drive.
Never ask her about her marriage.

(2) 정도 부사

He has **even** been to Antarctica.
I am **only** going for two days.
She is my teacher, but she is **also** my friend.
The people at the meeting were **mainly** scientists.
She's **still** asleep.
It's **still** raining.
When is Sally going to come? She's **already** here.
You must go to Amman. I've **already** been.

His wife Elizabeth was also a descendant of Aaron.
그 아내는 아론의 자손이니 이름은 엘리사벳이라(눅 1:5).

Must they **also** fill the land with violence and continually provoke me to anger?
그들이 강포로 이 땅에 채우고 또 다시 내 노를 격동하고(겔 8:17).

He is to bring them to the priest, who shall **first** offer the one for the sin offering.
제사장에게로 가져 갈 것이요, 제사장은 그 속죄 제물을 먼저 드리되(레 5:8).

(3) 확실성의 부사

It will **probably** rain this evening.
The train has **obviously** been delayed.

He will **certainly** not lose his reward.
그 사람이 결단코 상을 잃지 아니하리라(마 10:42).

Everyone who is **fully** trained will be like his teacher.
무릇 온전케 된 자는 그 선생과 같으리라(눅 6:40).

(4) 완전성의 부사

I have completely forgotten your name.
Sally can practically read.
It is almost dark.
The house is partly ready.

There some people brought to him a man who was deaf and could **hardly** talk.
사람들이 귀먹고 어눌한 자를 데리고 예수께 나아와(막 7:32).

think, believe, suppose, imagine의 부정은 첫 번째 동사에 not을 붙인다.
I don't think you've met my son. (Not; I think you've not met my son.)
I don't believe she's at home.

Hope의 경우는 틀림
I hope it doesn't rain. (Not; I don't hope it rains.)

4. 타동사 + 부사의 결합

1) 명사가 목적어일 때; 타동사+부사+목적어 = 타동사+목적어+부사

She threw down the book. = She threw the book down.
He put on his coat. = He put his coat on.
She threw it down. (Not; She threw down it.)
He put it on. (Not; He put on it.)

영어 문장은 문미에 중요한 정보를 위치시키는 경향이 있기 때문에 이미 알고 있는 대명사는 문미에 놓지 않는다.

How can anyone enter a strong man's house and **carry off his possessions** unless he first ties up the strong man?
사람이 먼저 강한 자를 결박하지 않고야 어떻게 그 강한 자의 집에 들어가 그 세간을 늑탈하겠느냐(마 12:29).

carry off his possessions = carry his possessions off

The priest shall bring it to the altar, **wring off** the head and burn it on the altar.
제사장은 그것을 단으로 가져다가 그 머리를 비틀어 끊고 단 위에 불사르고(레 1:15).

The LORD has **taken away** your punishment, he has **turned back** your enemy.
여호와가 너의 형벌을 제하였고 너의 원수를 쫓아내었으며(습 3:15).

2) 대명사가 목적어일 때; 타동사+대명사+부사의 어순

And if your right hand causes you to sin, **cut it off** and **throw it away**.
또한 만일 네 오른손이 너로 실족케 하거든 찍어 내버리라(마 5:30).

If your right eye causes you to sin, **gouge it out** and **throw it away**.
만일 네 오른눈이 너로 실족케 하거든 빼어 내버리라(마 5:29).

I am **sending you out** like sheep among wolves.
내가 너희를 보냄이 양을 이리 가운데 보냄과 같도다(마 10:16).

"Stretch out your hand." So he **stretched it out**.
손을 내밀라 하시니 저가 내밀매(마 12:13).

The Spirit **lifted me up** between earth and heaven.
주의 신이 나를 들어 천지 사이로 올리시고(겔 8:3).

Again, take a few of these and throw them into the fire and **burn them up**.
또 그 가운데서 얼마를 가져 불에 던져 사르라(겔 5:4).

자동사 + 전치사의 결합형과 혼동하지 말 것

So he bent **over** her and rebuked the fever, and it left her.
예수께서 가까이 서서 열병을 꾸짖으신대 병이 떠나고(눅 4:39).

5. enough

1) 수식하는 말 뒤에 둔다

You have stayed long **enough** at this mountain.
너희가 이 산에서 거한 지 오래니(신 1:6).

What man is wise **enough** to understand this?
지혜가 있어서 이 일을 깨달을 만한 자가 누구며(렘 9:12).

2) enough; 형용사

When he had cut **enough** wood for the burnt offering, he set out for the place God had told him about.
번제에 쓸 나무를 쪼개어 가지고 떠나 하나님의 자기에게 지시하시는 곳으로 가더니(창 22:3).

3) enough; 명사

However many his children, their fate is the sword; his offspring will never have **enough** to eat.
그 자손이 번성하여도 칼을 위함이요 그 후에는 식물에 배부르지 못할 것이며(욥 27:14).

그 위치가 자유롭게 변한다. 관계가 가장 밀접한 말 가까이에 놓는 것이 원칙이다.

And if you greet **only** your brothers, what are you doing more than others?
또 너희가 너희 형제에게만 문안하면 남보다 더하는 것이 무엇이냐(마 5:47).

If I **only** touch his cloak, I will be healed.
그 겉옷만 만져도 구원을 받겠다(마 9:21).

Only in his hometown and in his own house is a prophet without honor.
선지자가 자기 고향과 자기 집 외에서는 존경을 받지 않음이 없느니라(마 13:57).

7. fairly, quite, rather, pretty

1) 강조의 순서

not > fairly > quite > rather(pretty) > very nice

2) fairly

누군가에게 fairly clever 혹은 fairly nice라고 해도 그 사람은 그다지 좋아하지 않을 것이다.
How was the film? **Fairly** good. Not the best one I've seen this year.
I speak Greek **fairly** well – enough for most everyday purposes.

3) Quite

fairly 보다 조금 강함

How was the film? **Quite** good. You ought to go.
He's been Greece for two years, so he speaks Greek **quite** well.
It was a good party. I **quite** enjoyed myself.

4) Rather

quite보다 강함(more than is usual, more than was expected, more than is wanted)

How was the film? **Rather** good. I was surprised.

He speaks Greek **rather** well. People often think he is Greek.
I think I'll put the heating on. It's **rather** cold.
I **rather** like gardening.

5) Pretty

rather와 비슷하며 구어체에서만 쓰인다.

How are you feeling? **Pretty** tired. I'm going to bed.

C. 의문부사와 관계부사

1. 의문부사의 접속 용법

의문문을 유도하는 의문 부사가 종속절 혹은 종속구를 유도하는 접속의 역할을 한다.

If you, then, though you are evil, know **how to give** good gifts to your children, how much more will your Father in heaven give good gifts to those who ask him!
너희가 악한 자라도 좋은 것으로 자식에게 줄 줄 알거든 하물며 하늘에 계신 너희 아버지께서 구하는 자에게 좋은 것으로 주시지 않겠느냐(마 7:11).

2. 관계부사의 용법

관계부사 where, when, why, how는 부사와 접속사의 역할을 하는데, 전치사 + which로 바꿔 쓸 수 있다.

1) where = 장소의 관계부사 = in which, on which 등

He went home to his upstairs room **where** the windows opened toward Jerusalem.
(다니엘이). 자기 집에 돌아가서는 그 방의 예루살렘으로 향하여 열린 창에서(단 6:10).

Watch the field **where** the men are harvesting, and follow along after the girls.
그들의 베는 밭을 보고 그들을 따르라(룻 2:9).

When they arrived, they went upstairs to the room **where** they were staying.
들어가 저희 유하는 다락에 올라 가니 (행 1:13).

2) when = 시간의 관계부사 = on which, at which 등

Noah was six hundred years old **when** the floodwaters came on the earth.
홍수가 땅에 있을 때에 노아가 육백 세라 (창 7:6).

* 비교; when의 생략

The day you see my face you will die.
내 얼굴을 보는 날에는 죽으리라 (출 10:28).

3) why = 이유의 관계부사 = for which

Now this was the reason **why** he rebelled against the king.
저가 손을 들어 왕을 대적하는 까닭은 이러하니라 (왕상 11:27).

Meanwhile, the people were waiting for Zechariah and wondering **why** he stayed so long in the temple.
백성들이 사가랴를 기다리며 그의 성소 안에서 지체함을 기이히 여기더니 (눅 1:21).

I must preach the good news of the kingdom of God to the other towns also, because that is **why** I was sent.
내가 다른 동네에서도 하나님의 나라 복음을 전하여야 하리니, 나는 이 일로 보내심을 입었노라 (눅 4:43).

4) how = 방법의 관계부사

the way how는 피해야 할 용법이다. The way 혹은 how만을 쓰든지, the way that 혹은 the way in which를 쓴다.

This is **how** you are to eat it: with your cloak tucked into your belt, your sandals on your feet and your staff in your hand. Eat it in haste; it is the LORD's Passover.
너희는 그것을 이렇게 먹을지니 허리에 띠를 띠고 발에 신을 신고 손에 지팡이를 잡고 급히 먹으라 이것이 여호와의 유월절이니라 (출 12:11).

3. 관계부사로서의 that

that은 관계부사로 when, how, why, where 대신 쓰이며, 형용사절을 유도한다. 이 that은 때로 생략된다.

She died on the day **that** I arrived.; that은 when의 대용

4. 관계부사의 계속적 용법

관계부사 when, where는 관계대명사와 마찬가지로 계속적 용법이 있다.

1) ~, where = ~, and there

They will throw them into the fiery furnace, **where** there will be weeping and gnashing of teeth.
풀무 불에 던져 넣으리니 거기서 울며 이를 갊이 있으리라 (마 13:42).

In visions of God he took me to Jerusalem, to the entrance to the north gate of the inner court, **where** the idol that provokes to jealousy stood.
하나님의 이상 가운데 나를 이끌어 예루살렘으로 가서 안뜰로 들어가는 북향한 문에 이르시니 거기는 투기의 우상 곧 투기를 격발케 하는 우상의 자리가 있는 곳이라 (겔 8:3).

2) ~, when = ~, and then

By faith Abel offered God a better sacrifice than Cain did. By faith he was commended as a righteous man, **when** God spoke well of his offerings. And by faith he still speaks, even though he is dead.
믿음으로 아벨은 가인보다 더 나은 제사를 하나님께 드림으로 의로운 자라 하시는 증거를 얻었으니, 하나님이 그 예물에 대하여 증거하심이라. 저가 죽었으나 그 믿음으로써 오히려 말하느니라 (히 11:4).

They were looking intently up into the sky as he was going, **when** suddenly two men dressed in white stood beside them.
올라가실 때에 제자들이 자세히 하늘을 쳐다보고 있는 데 흰 옷 입은 두 사람이 저희 곁에 서서 (행 1:10).

A man was going down from Jerusalem to Jericho, **when** he fell into the hands of robbers.
어떤 사람이 예루살렘에서 여리고로 내려가다가 강도를 만나매 (눅 10:30).

5. 명사절을 유도하는 관계부사

관계부사는 선행사를 갖지 않고 명사절을 유도한다.

1) 목적절

He asked them **where** the Christ was to be born.
그리스도가 어디서 나겠느뇨 물으니 (마 2:4).

But now see **how** dry and moldy it is.
보소서 이제 말랐고 곰팡이 났으며 (수 9:12).

2) 보어절

That is **why** the Israelites cannot stand against their enemies.
그러므로 이스라엘 자손들이 자기 대적을 능히 당치 못하고 (수 7:12).

Woe to you when all men speak well of you, for that is **how** their fathers treated the false prophets.
모든 사람이 너희를 칭찬하면 화가 있도다. 저희 조상들이 거짓 선지자들에게 이와 같이 하였느니라 (눅 6:26).

3) 전치사의 목적절

The people were looking for him and when they came to **where he was**, they tried to keep him from leaving them.
무리가 찾다가 만나서 자기들에게 떠나시지 못하게 만류하려 하매 (눅 4:42).
(- where he was는 전치사 to의 목적어)

6. 복합관계부사; wherever, whenever, however는 그 자체가 선행사를 포함하여 부사절을 이끈다

1) wherever = to any place that

2) however

No king, **however great and mighty**, has ever asked such a thing of any magician or enchanter or astrologer.

크고 권력 있는 왕이 이런 것으로 박수에게나 술객에게나 갈대아 술사에게 물은 자가 절대로 있지 아니하였나이다(단 2:10).

however great and mighty = no matter how great and might

3) whenever = at any time when

Consider it pure joy, my brothers, **whenever** you face trials of many kinds
내 형제들아 너희가 여러 가지 시험을 만나거든 온전히 기쁘게 여기라(약 1:2).

And **whenever** you are thirsty, go and get a drink from the water jars the men have filled.
목이 마르거든 그릇에 가서 소년들의 길어 온 것을 마실지니라(룻 2:9).

D. 부사의 비교

1. 단음절어의 부사는 -er, -est를 붙여 비교급, 최상급을 표시한다

ly로 끝나면 more, most를 붙여 비교급, 최상급을 표시한다.

불규칙 변화;
well better best, ill badly worse, much more most,
far farther farthest, far further, furthest, little less least

부사의 최상급 앞에는 the를 안 붙여도 된다.

2. the + 비교급, the + 비교급

전반은 부사절이며, 이 the는 in what degree의 뜻인 관계부사이다. 그리고 후반은 주절이며, 이 the는 in that degree의 뜻인 지시부사이다.

E. 주의할 부사의 용법

1. very 와 much

1) very는 원급, 현재분사를 수식한다

Since you cannot do this **very** little thing, why do you worry about the rest?
그런즉 지극히 작은 것이라도 능치 못하거든 어찌 그 다른 것을 염려하느냐(눅 12:26).

The LORD was **very** angry with your forefathers.
나 여호와가 무리의 열조에게 심히 진노하였느니라(슥 1:2).

2) much는 비교급, 과거분사, 동사를 수식한다

Are you not **much** more valuable than they?
너희는 이것들보다 귀하지 아니하냐(마 6:26).

2. 유도부사 there

문두에서 동사를 이끄는 역할을 한다. Be 동사의 경우가 흔하다. 이 there는 [더]로 약하게 발음한다.

There is no fear in love.
사랑 안에 두려움이 없고(요일 4:18).

And it will come about in that day, that every place where **there** used to be a thousand vines, valued at a thousand shekels of silver, will become briars and thorns.
그날에는 천 주에 은 일천 개의 가치 되는 포도나무 있던 곳마다 질려와 형극이 날 것이라(사 7:23).

3. not; 단어, 표현, 구 등을 부정으로 만든다

Not surprisingly, we missed the train. (Not; No surprisingly ---)
The students went on strike, but **not the teachers**.
I can see you tomorrow, but **not on Thursday**.
I have **not** received his answer.

1) No + 명사; not a + 명사, not any + 명사

No teachers went on strike. (= There were not any teachers on strike.)
I telephoned, but there was **no answer**. (= not an answer.)
No smoking

2) Not a 또는 not any가 아닌 No를 써야 하는 경우

문장의 첫머리에서
No cigarette is completely harmless. (Not; Not any cigarette ---)
No tourists ever come to our village.

3) 부정을 강조할 때

I can't get there. There's **no** bus. (there's not a bus보다 강조하는 표현)
Sorry I can't stop. I have **no** time.
There were **no** letters for you this morning, I am afraid.
Nobody came. (Not; Not anybody came.)
I saw nobody. (I didn't see anybody보다 강조하는 표현)

(1) I think not

Think, believe, suppose, imagine, hope 등의 동사에서
Will it rain? I hope **not**.
Do you think she will go? I think **not**.

(2) 부분 부정

Dear friends, do **not** believe **every** spirit, but test the spirits to see whether they are from God.
사랑하는 자들아 영을 다 믿지 말고 오직 영들이 하나님께 속하였나 시험하라 (요일 4:1).

no more와 not any more

no more; 수량이나 정도에 관해 말할 때 (how much)

There's **no more** bread.

She's **no more** a great singer than I am.

not any more; 시간에 관해 말할 때 (=no longer, not ~ any longer)

I **no longer** support the Conservative Party. (Not; no more ---)

This **can't** go on **any longer**.

She **doesn't** live here **any more**.

4. too either

Also, too, as well은 부정 구문에서는 잘 쓰이지 않고 대신 not ~ either, neither, nor 를 쓴다.

He is there too – He isn't there either.

I like you as well. – I don't like you either.

I do too. – Nor do I.

Drink, and I'll water your camels **too**.
마시라 내가 당신의 약대에게도 마시우리라 (창 24:46).

For if God did not spare the natural branches, he will not spare you **either**.
하나님이 원 가지들도 아끼지 아니하셨은 즉 너도 아끼지 아니하시리라 (롬 11:21).

1) do, say, think 등의 목적어로서 대명사처럼 쓰인 so

But because you say **so**, I will let down the nets.
말씀에 의지하여 내가 그물을 내리리이다 (눅 5:5).

Do you think we'll have good weather? I hope so.

It that Alex? I think so.

Did you lose? I'm afraid so.

Will it rain? I hope not. (= I don't expect so.)

2) 정말 그러하다

so + 주어 + (조)동사의 형태로 앞의 서술을 강조함

3) ~도 또한 그러하다

so + 조동사 + 주어 ; so는 also의 의미가 됨

Jane can dance beautifully, and **so** can her sister.
"I have lost the address." "**So** have I."
I was tired. **So** were the others.
"I have a headache." "**So** have I."
"I like milk." "**So** do I."

If the root is holy, **so** are the branches.
뿌리가 거룩한즉 가지도 그러하니라(롬 11:16).

Jesus got up and went with him, and **so** did his disciples.
예수께서 일어나 따라 가시매 제자들도 가더니(마 9:19).

4) 그러므로, 따라서(therefore)

Go to the hills **so** the pursuers will not find you.
두렵건대 따르는 사람들이 너희를 만날까 하노니 너희는 산으로 가서(수 2:16).

6. 기타

1) home

home 앞에는 전치사 to를 쓰지 않는다.
I think I will go home.
She came home late.
Is anybody home? (= at home)

2) indeed

very를 강조하기 위해 쓴다.

Thank you **very** much **indeed**.
I was **very** pleased **indeed** to hear from you.
He was driving **very** fast **indeed**.

Very가 없이는 indeed를 쓰지 않는다.
He was driving fast indeed. (x)

연습 문제

1. But I tell you that anyone who looks at a woman _____ has already committed adultery with her in his heart.
   1) lustfully   2) lustful   3) lust   4) to lust

2. Where your treasure is, _____ your heart will be also.
   1) then   2) so   3) there   4) where

3. Are you not _____ more valuable than they?
   1) much   2) so   3) many   4) very

   How much more valuable is a man than a sheep!

4. Jesus reached _____ his hand and touched the man.
   1) to   2) out   3) of   4) on

* 타동사 + 부사

    Because you say so, I will let **down** the nets.
    He rebukes the sea and dries it **up**
    Pick me **up** and throw me into the sea.
    To the roots of the mountains I sank down; the earth beneath barred me **in** forever.
    They declared a fast, and all of them, from the greatest to the least, put **on** sackcloth.
    He spread **out** his hands toward the LORD

    Take your staff and stretch **out** your hand over the waters of Egypt--over the streams and canals, over the ponds and all the reservoirs.
    네 지팡이를 잡고 네 팔을 애굽의 물들과 하수들과 운하와 못과 모든 호수 위에 펴라(출 7:19).

    A perverse man stirs **up** dissension, and a gossip separates close friends.
    패려한 자는 다툼을 일으키고 말장이는 친한 벗을 이간하느니라(잠 16:28).

* 비교; 자동사 + 부사

After many days had gone **by**, the Jews conspired to kill him.

5. The crowd was amazed and said, "Nothing like this has _____ been seen in Israel."
   1) ever   2) never   3) yet   4) already

6. Whoever acknowledges me before men, I will _____ acknowledge him before my Father in heaven.
   1) also   2) scarcely   3) never   4) still

7. When the wheat sprouted and formed heads, _____ the weeds also appeared.
   1) so   2) already   3) still   4) then

8. The people were all _____ amazed that they asked each other.
   1) very   2) so   3) much   4) more

9. So many gathered that there was no room left, not _____ outside the door, and he preached the word to them.
   1) often   2) on   3) even   4) of

Still other seed fell on good soil. It came up, grew and produced a crop, multiplying thirty, sixty, or **even** a hundred times.
더러는 좋은 땅에 떨어지매 자라 무성하여 결실하였으니, 삼십 배와 육십 배와 백배가 되었느니라 (막 4:8).

10. Some of them were looking for a reason to accuse Jesus, _____ they watched him closely to see if he would heal him on the Sabbath.
    1) that   2) also   3) so   4) as

11. A furious squall came up, and the waves broke over the boat, so that it was _____ swamped.
    1) nearly   2) near to   3) near   4) near at

12. Some people brought to him a man who was deaf and could _____ talk
    1) hard   2) hardly   3) ever   4) nicely

13. When I broke the five loaves for the five thousand, _____ many basketfuls of pieces did you pick up?
    1) how   2) so   3) what   4) where

14. I must preach the good news of the kingdom of God to the other towns also, because that is _____ I was sent.
    1) how   2) what   3) when   4) why

15. Master, we've worked _____ all night and haven't caught anything.
    1) hardly   2) hard   3) hardness   4) little

16. John's disciples often fast and pray, and _____ do the disciples of the Pharisees.
    1) such   2) like   3) so   4) as

    If the root is holy, so are the branches.

17. When a flood came, the torrent struck that house but could not shake it, because it was _____ built.
    1) well   2) good   3) best   4) badly

18. What good is it for a man to gain the whole world, and _____ lose or forfeit his very self?
    1) so   2) to   3) yet   4) also

19. But we know where this man is from; when the Christ comes, no one will know _____ he is from.
    1) that   2) where   3) when   4) how

    Bear in mind that the LORD has given you the Sabbath; that is **why** on the sixth day he gives you bread for two days. Everyone is to stay **where** he is on the seventh day; no one is to go out.
    볼지어다 여호와가 너희에게 안식일을 줌으로 제 육일에는 이틀 양식을 너희에게 주는 것이니, 너희는 각기 처소에 있고 제 칠일에는 아무도 그 처소에서 나오지 말지니라(출 16:29).

20. A short while _____ the Jews tried to stone you, and yet you are going back there?
    1) ago   2) before   3) after   4) since

21. Our fathers refused to obey him. _____, they rejected him and in their hearts turned back to Egypt.
    1) Instead of   2) So   3) But   4) Instead

22. _____ a wretched man I am! Who will rescue me from this body of death?
    1) So   2) What   3) Why   4) How

23. The night is nearly over; the day is _____ here.
    1) almost   2) most   3) already   4) not

24. Do not think about _____ to gratify the desires of the sinful nature.
    1) how   2) what   3) why   4) something

25. The man who thinks he knows something does not ____ know as he ought to know.
    1) still   2) already   3) also   4) yet

Therefore disaster will overtake him in an instant; he will **suddenly** be destroyed--without remedy.
그러므로 그 재앙이 갑자기 임한즉 도움을 얻지 못하고 당장에 패망하리라 (잠 6:15).

26. By this gospel you are saved, if you hold firmly to the word I preached to you. _____, you have believed in vain.
    1) So   2) Likewise   3) Otherwise   4) On the contrary

The Egyptians urged the people to hurry and leave the country. "For **otherwise**," they said, "we will all die!"
애굽 사람들은 말하기를 우리가 다 죽은 자가 되도다 하고 백성을 재촉하여 그 지경에서 속히 보내려 하므로 (출 12:33).

27. Since death came through a man, the resurrection of the dead comes _____ through a man.
    1) also   2) yet   3) still   4) almost

28. If the part of the dough offered as firstfruits is holy, _____ the whole batch is holy.
    1) then   2) there   3) so   4) such

   then; 그러면(부사)

29. But _____ you give to the needy, do not let your left hand know what your right hand is doing.
    1) that   2) what   3) when   4) where

30. Some fell on rocky places, _____ it did not have much soil.
    1) which   2) what   3) that   4) where

   Take care of them until the fourteenth day of the month, when all the people of the community of Israel must slaughter them at twilight.
   이달 십사일까지 간직하였다가 해질 때에 이스라엘 회중이 그 양을 잡고(출 12:6).

31. We found the jail _____ locked.
    1) to secure   2) secured   3) to secure   4) securely

32. Send the crowds away, _____ they can go to the villages and buy themselves some food.
    1) as   2) so   3) for   4) for

33. First go and be reconciled to your brother; _____ come and offer your gift.
    1) then   2) so   3) after   4) late

34. It scarcely _____ leaves him and is destroying him.
    1) but   2) rather   3) ever   4) never

35. To the LORD I cry _____, and he answers me from his holy hill.
    1) aloud   2) aloudly   3) loud   4) noisy

Why do you now cry aloud?

Beside the gates leading into the city, at the entrances, she cries **aloud**.

The woman Folly is **loud**: she is undisciplined and without knowledge.
미련한 계집이 떠들며 어리석어서 아무 것도 알지 못하고 (잠 9:13).

36. Day _____ day they pour forth speech; night _____ night they display knowledge.
    1) after   2) before   3) of   4) from

37. People staggered from town to town for water but did not get _____.
    1) enough drink   2) enough to drink   3) drink enough   4) to enough drink

enough; 명사
You eat, but never have enough.

38. That is _____ it was called Babel --because there the LORD confused the language of the whole world.
    1) reason   2) why   3) because   4) for

This is why I sacrifice to the LORD the first male offspring of every womb and redeem each of my firstborn sons.

39. Do not take _____ any gold or silver or copper in your belts.
    1) through   2) back   3) along   4) on

정답

1) 1, 2) 3, 3) 1, 4) 2, 5) 1, 6) 1, 7) 4, 8) 2, 9) 3, 10) 3
11) 1, 12) 2, 13) 1, 14) 4, 15) 2, 16) 3, 17) 1, 18) 3, 19) 2, 20) 1
21) 4, 22) 2, 23) 1, 24) 1, 25) 4, 26) 3, 27) 1, 28) 1, 29) 3, 30) 4
31) 4, 32) 2, 33) 1, 34) 3, 35) 1, 36) 1, 37) 2, 38) 2, 39) 3

숙어

search (= look through, look everywhere in/on); 찾다, 수색하다
They **searched** everybody's luggage.
They **searched** the man in front of me from head to foot.

Send A for B; A를 데리러(가지러) B를 보내다
After this, Joseph **sent for** his father Jacob and his whole family, seventy-five in all.
요셉이 보내어 그 부친 야곱과 온 친족 일흔 다섯 사람을 청하였더니(행 7:14).

separate A from B; A에서 B를 떼다, 잘라내다
Who shall **separate** us **from** the love of Christ? Shall trouble or hardship or persecution or famine or nakedness or danger or sword?
누가 우리를 그리스도의 사랑에서 끊으리요 환난이나 곤고나 핍박이나 기근이나 적신이나 위협이나 칼이랴(롬 8:35).

set(lay, make) an ambush; 복병을 배치해 두다
with these orders: "Listen carefully. You are to **set an ambush** behind the city. Don't go very far from it. All of you be on the alert.
그들에게 명하여 가로되 너희는 성읍 뒤로 가서 성읍을 향하고 매복하되 그 성읍에 너무 멀리 하지 말고 다 스스로 예비하라(수 8:4).

shocked by / at; 깜짝 놀란
I was terribly **shocked by/at** the news of Peter's accident.

shout at; 외치다, 큰 소리를 내다
If you don't stop **shouting at** me I'll run away
shout to; 큰 소리로 부르다
Mary **shouted to** us to come in and swim.

smile at; 미소 짓다
If you **smile at** me like that I'll give you anything you want.

sorry about (something that has happened); 유감스러운
I'm **sorry about** your exam results.

sorry for/about (something that one has done); 유감스러운
I'm **sorry for/about** breaking the window.

speak well of ~; ~을 좋게 말하다
Woe to you when all men **speak well of** you, for that is how their fathers treated the false prophets.
모든 사람이 너희를 칭찬하면 화가 있도다. 저희 조상들이 거짓 선지자들에게 이와 같이 하였느니라 (눅 6:26).

All **spoke well of** him and were amazed at the gracious words that came from his lips. "Isn't this Joseph's son?" they asked.
저희가 다 그를 증거하고 그 입으로 나오는 바 은혜로운 말을 기이히 여겨 가로되 이 사람이 요셉의 아들이 아니냐 (눅 4:22).

stand for; ~을 나타내다
The field is the world, and the good seed **stands for** the sons of the kingdom. The weeds are the sons of the evil one,
밭은 세상이요, 좋은 씨는 천국의 아들들이요, 가라지는 악한 자의 아들들이요 (마 13:38).

Fine linen, bright and clean, was given her to wear. (Fine linen **stands for** the righteous acts of the saints.)
그에게 허락하사 빛나고 깨끗한 세마포를 입게 하셨은 즉 이 세마포는 성도들의 옳은 행실이로다 (계 19:8).

suffer from; 고통 받다
My wife is **suffering from** hepatitis.

sum up; 합계하다
So in everything, do to others what you would have them do to you, for this **sums up** the Law and the Prophets.

그러므로 무엇이든지 남에게 대접을 받고자 하는 대로 너희도 남을 대접하라 이것이 율법이요 선지자니라 (마 7:12).

surprised at / by; 놀란
Everybody was **surprised at/by** the weather.

18. 전치사(前置詞)
Preposition

전치사는 대체로 명사 또는 대명사 앞에 위치하여 형용사 및 부사구를 구성한다. 전치사의 목적어가 될 수 있는 것은 명사, 대명사뿐만 아니라 구, 절, 동명사 등 명사 상당어구도 있다.

A. 전치사의 용법

1. 전치사의 목적어

전치사 뒤에 오는 말은 모두 목적격이 되어야 한다.

1) 명사, 대명사

It is easier **for** a camel to go through the eye of a needle than **for** a rich man to enter the kingdom of God.
약대가 바늘귀로 나가는 것이 부자가 하나님의 나라에 들어가는 것보다 쉬우니라 하신대(막 10:25).

Son, why have you treated us **like** this?
아이야 어찌하여 우리에게 이렇게 하였느냐(눅 2:48).

His splendor was **like** the sunrise.
그 광명이 햇빛 같고(합 3:4).

2) 동명사

I have killed a man **for** wounding me.
나의 창상을 인하여 내가 사람을 죽였고(창 4:23).

3) 구

It is no longer good for anything, **except** to be thrown out and trampled by men.
후에는 아무 쓸데 없어 다만 밖에 버리워 사람에게 밟힐 뿐이니라(마 5:13).
(to be thrown out and trampled by men은 except의 목적어)

For you know very well that the day of the Lord will come **like** a thief in the night.
주의 날이 밤에 도적같이 이를 줄을 너희 자신이 자세히 앎이라 (살전 5:2).

If he offers it **as** an expression of thankfulness
만일 그것을 감사하므로 드리거든 (레 7:12).

He is to bring **as** an offering for his sin a tenth of an ephah of fine flour for a sin offering.
만일 힘이 산비둘기 둘이나 집비둘기 둘에도 미치지 못하거든 그 범과를 인하여 고운 가루 에바 십분 일을 예물로 가져다가 속죄 제물로 드리되 (레 5:11).

4) 절

The sun rises and the sun sets, and hurries back **to** where it rises.
해는 떴다가 지며 그 떴던 곳으로 빨리 돌아가고 (전 1:5).

5) 기타

Let us behave decently, **as** in the daytime, not in orgies and drunkenness.

But if anyone regards something **as** unclean, then for him it is unclean.
다만 속되게 여기는 그 사람에게는 속되니라 (롬 14:14).

Their hearts will be glad **as** with wine.
포도주를 마심 같이 마음이 즐거울 것이요 (슥 10:7).

The people still came to him **from** everywhere. (부사)
사방에서 그에게로 나아오더라 (막 1:45).

I will destroy your horses **from** among you and demolish your chariots.

2. 전치사의 위치

전치사는 그 목적어 앞에 노는 것이 정상적인 위치이지만 가끔 목적어에서 떨어지는 경우가 있다.

1) 전치사가 문미에 오는 경우

(1) 의문사가 전치사의 목적어가 될 때
What are you looking **at**?
Who did you go **with**?

Where do you come **from**? What is your country? **From** what people are you?
어디서 왔으며 고국이 어디며 어느 민족에 속하였느냐(욘 1:8).

(2) 관계대명사를 생략할 때
There's the house (that) I told you **about**.
You remember the boy I was going out **with**?

You will not leave the bed you are lying **on**.
네가 올라간 침상에서 내려오지 못할지라(왕하 1:4).

2) 비교; 격식을 갖추어서 쓸 때는 전치사를 의문사나 관계사 앞에 쓴다
To whom is that letter addressed?
She met a man **with whom** she had been friendly years before.
On which flight is the general traveling?

With what can I compare you, O Daughter of Jerusalem?
무엇으로 네게 비유할꼬 처녀 시온이여(애 2:13).

To what can I liken you, that I may comfort you.
내가 무엇으로 네게 비교하여 너를 위로 할꼬(애 2:13).

3) to 부정사 문장에서
It's boring place **to live in**.

I need something **to write with**.

4) 수동태 문장에서

I hate being laughed **at**.
They took him to hospital yesterday and he's already been operated **on**.

3. 합성전치사(전치사구); 낱말이 둘 이상 모여 한 개의 전치사에 해당하는 구실을 한다

1) instead of; "~ 대신에"

Light has come into the world, but men loved darkness **instead of** light because their deeds were evil.
빛이 세상에 왔으되 사람들이 자기 행위가 악하므로 빛보다 어두움을 더 사랑한 것이니라(요 3:19).

2) because of , on account of; "~ 때문에"

Because of thirst the infant's tongue sticks to the roof of its mouth
젖먹이가 목말라서 혀가 입천장에 붙음이여(아 4:4).

4. "전치사 + 목적어"의 역할

1) of value = valuable

Their father had given them many gifts of silver and gold and articles **of value**, as well as fortified cities in Judah.
그 부친이 저희에게는 은금과 보물과 유다 견고한 성읍들을 선물로 후히 주었고(대하 21:3).

2) 보어가 되는 형용사구

For physical training is **of some value**, but godliness has value for all things, holding promise for both the present life and the life to come.
육체의 연습은 약간의 유익이 있으나 경건은 범사에 유익하니 금생과 내생에 약속이 있느니라(딤전 4:8).

of some value = some valuable

Not many of you were wise by human standards; not many were influential; not many were **of noble birth**.
육체를 따라 지혜 있는 자가 많지 아니하며 능한 자가 많지 아니하며 문벌 좋은 자가 많지 아니하도다
(고전 1:26).

3) ten miles = for ten miles[부사구]

시간, 거리, 방법, 정도를 나타낼 때는 전치사 없이 부사구의 역할을 한다. 이런 부사구를 부사적 대격이라고 한다.

When they had rowed **three or three and a half miles**, they saw Jesus approaching the boat, walking on the water; and they were terrified.
제자들이 노를 저어 십여 리쯤 가다가 예수께서 바다 위로 걸어 배에 가까이 오심을 보고 두려워하거늘
(요 6:19).

4) the same size as that는 그 앞에 전치사 of가 생략되어 있다.

연령, 크기, 모양, 색채, 가격, 직업 등을 나타낼 때는 of를 생략할 때가 많다. 이것을 형용사적 대격이라 한다.

B. 장소의 전치사

1. at

1) 좁은 장소

It's very hot **at** the center of the earth.
Turn right **at** the next traffic lights.

2) 넓은 장소라도 한 점으로 생각한다면 at을 사용할 수 있다

You have to change trains **at** London.
The plane stops for an hour **at** Seoul.
Let's meet **at** the station.

There's good film at the cinema in Market Street.
At the cinema, at the theatre, at a party, at university

Here I am! I stand at the door and knock
볼지어다 내가 문 밖에 서서 두드리노니 (계 3:20).

2. in

1) 넓은 장소

I don't think he's in his office.
Let's go for a walk in the woods.
I last saw her in the car park.

2) 거리 이름

She lives in Albert Street.

3) 기타

at home/school/work/university/college
in a picture, in the sky, in bed/hospital/prison/church
on a page

So we arrived in Jerusalem, where we rested three days.
이에 예루살렘에 이르러 거기서 삼 일을 유하고 (스 8:32).

3. on

1) 평면에 접촉한 '위에'

Come on, supper is on the table.
I'd prefer that picture on the other wall.
There's a big spider on the ceiling.
She lives in a flat on the third floor.

You are the light of the world. A city **on** a hill cannot be hidden.
너희는 세상의 빛이라 산 위에 있는 동네가 숨기우지 못할 것이요(마 5:14).

But the seed **on** good soil stands for those with a noble and good heart, who hear the word, retain it, and by persevering produce a crop.
좋은 땅에 있다는 것은 착하고 좋은 마음으로 말씀을 듣고 지키어 인내로 결실하는 자니라(눅 8:15).

I will cast her **on** a bed of suffering
내가 그를 침상에 던질 터이요(계 2:22).

2) 선 '위의'

His house is on the way from the town to the park.

Bus, plane, train에 대해서 on/off를 쓴다.
He's arriving on the 3:15 train.
There's no room on the bus; let's get off again.

4. above

1) ~ 보다 높은 '위에, 위쪽에'(higher than)

A student is not **above** his teacher, but everyone who is fully trained will be like his teacher.
제자가 그 선생보다 높지 못하나 무릇 온전케 된 자는 그 선생과 같으리라(눅 6:40).

2) 한 사물이 다른 사물의 직접 위에 붙어 있지 않을 때

We have got a little house above the lake(not over).

3) 수직 측량에서

above zero (for temperature), above sea-level, above average

5. over; 떨어져 '바로 위에' ~ 보다 높은(higher than)

Darkness was **over** the surface of the deep.
흑암이 깊음 위에 있고(창 1:2).

They stumbled **over** the stumbling stone.
부딪힐 돌에 부딪혔느니라(롬 9:32).

So he bent **over** her and rebuked the fever, and it left her.
예수께서 가까이 서서 열병을 꾸짖으신대 병이 떠나고(눅 4:39).

1) 한 사물이 다른 사물을 덮을 때

There is cloud over the mountain.

2) Across(가로질러)와 같은 뜻으로

Electricity cables stretch over/across the fields.
The plane was flying over/across the Channel.

3) More than의 의미로 쓴다.

How old are you? Over thirty.
He's over two meters tall.
There were over fifty people at the party.

4) above/over 둘 다 higher than의 의미로 쓰임

The snow came up above/over our knees.
There's a spider on the ceiling above/over your head.

6. beneath

1) 접해서 '바로 밑에': beneath 대신 under도 쓴다

The seeds are shriveled **beneath** the clods.
씨가 흙덩이 아래서 썩어졌고(욜 1:17).

2) Below; 보다 낮은 '아래쪽'(lower than)

Jonah had gone **below** deck, where he lay down and fell into a deep sleep.
요나는 배 밑층에 내려가서 누워 깊이 잠이 든지라(욘 1:5).

3) Under; 떨어져 '바로 아래에'

No one lights a lamp and puts it in a place where it will be hidden, or **under** a bowl.
누구든지 등불을 켜서 움 속에나 말 아래 두지 아니하고 등경 위에 두나니(눅 11:33).

Even the dogs **under** the table eat the children's crumbs.
상 아래 개들도 아이들의 먹던 부스러기를 먹나이다(막 7:28).

7. behind; ~의 뒤에

When I became a man, I put childish ways **behind** me.
장성한 사람이 되어서는 어린 아이의 일을 버렸노라(고전 13:11).

8. after; ~뒤를 쫓아

Elisha then left his oxen and ran **after** Elijah.
저가 소를 버리고 엘리야에게로 달려가서(왕상 19:20).

9. near; ~의 가까이, ~에 가깝게

Heal the sick who are there and tell them, 'The kingdom of God is **near** you.'
거기 있는 병자들을 고치고 또 말하기를 하나님의 나라가 너희에게 가까이 왔다 하라(눅 10:9).

10. opposite; ~의 맞은 편에

Then two scoundrels came and sat **opposite** him.
때에 비류 두 사람이 들어와서 그 앞에 앉고(왕상 21:13).

Jesus sat down **opposite** the place where the offerings were put.
예수께서 연보궤를 대하여 앉으사(막 12:41).

11. between

1) 둘 '사이에' 혹은 명확하게 구분되는 사람들/사물 '사이에'

I will put enmity **between** you and the woman
내가 너로 여자와 원수가 되게 하고(창 3:15).

Our house is **between** the wood, the river and the village.

2) Divide between, share between + 단수 명사

Divide between (혹은 among), share between (혹은 among) + 복수 명사
He **divided** his money **between** his wife, his daughter and his sister.
I **shared** the food **between/among** all my friends.

12. among; 셋 이상 '사이에' 혹은 구분할 수 없는 사람들/사물 '사이에'

His house is hidden among the trees.

Fools mock at making amends for sin, but goodwill is found **among** the upright.
미련한 자는 죄를 심상히 여겨도 정직한 자 중에는 은혜가 있느니라(잠 14:9).

Whoever wants to become great **among** you must be your servant,
너희 중에 누구든지 크고자 하는 자는 너희를 섬기는 자가 되고(막 8:43).

The apostles performed many miraculous signs and wonders **among** the people.
사도들의 손으로 민간에 표적과 기사가 많이 되매(행 5:12).

13. in; ~의 안에(상태)

Come over here. Have some bread and dip it **in** the wine vinegar.
이리로 와서 떡을 먹으며 네 떡 조각을 초에 찍으라(룻 2:14).

Do not take along any gold or silver or copper **in** your belts;
너희 전대에 금이나 은이나 동이나 가지지 말고(마 10:9).

14. into; ~의 안으로(운동)

They were casting a net **into** the lake, for they were fishermen.
바다에 그물 던지는 것을 보시니 저희는 어부라(마 4:18).

15. out of; ~안에서 밖으로(운동)

And the priests came up **out of** the river carrying the ark of the covenant of the LORD.
여호와의 언약궤를 멘 제사장들이 요단 가운데서 나오며(수 4:18).

16. along; 긴 것을 따라서

Her attendants were walking **along** the river bank.
시녀들은 하숫가에 거닐 때에(출 2:5).

17. across; (평면을) 횡단하여, 교차하여 (운동)

After he had sent them **across** the stream, he sent over all his possessions.
그들을 인도하여 시내를 건네며 그 소유도 긴니고(창 32:23).

It took him six weeks to walk across the desert.
I walked across the ice.
I drove across the desert.
The river is too wide to swim across.

18. Over; (높은 것을) 넘어 (운동)

Why is that woman climbing over the wall?

19. through; (3차원의 공간을) 관통하여, 꿰뚫고 (주변에는 물건이 꽉 차 있음)

Now they grope **through** the streets like men who are blind.
저희가 거리에서 소경 같이 방황함이여(아 4:14).

I walked through the crowd to the museum.
I walked through the wood.
We drove through several towns.

20. to; ~으로(도착 지점)

The devil led him up **to** a high place.
마귀가 또 예수를 이끌고 올라가서(눅 4:5).

21. for; ~을 목표로 하여(방향)

So Peter and the other disciple started **for** the tomb.
베드로와 그 다른 제자가 나가서 무덤으로 갈 쌔(요 20:3).

22. from; ~으로부터(출발점)

"If you are the Son of God," he said, "throw yourself down **from** here"
네가 만일 하나님의 아들이어든 여기서 뛰어 내리라(눅 4:9).

23. (a)round

We all sat **round** the table.
I walked **round** the car and looked at the wheels.
Where do you live? Just **round** the cornor.
We walked **round** the old part of the town.
Can I look **round**?
Could you pass the cups **round**, please?

24. around와 about

불명확한 동작이나 장소를 표현함(here and there, somewhere near, in different parts of).
The children were running **around/about** everywhere.
Stop standing **around/about** and do some work.
Where's John? Somewhere **around/about**.
Stop fooling **around/about**. We are late.

Approximately, not exactly의 뜻으로
There were **around/about** thirty people there.
What time shall I come? **Around/about** eight.

25. 기타

beyond; ~의 저쪽에, ~을 지나서

Do not go **beyond** what is written.
기록한 말씀 밖에 넘어가지 말라(고전 4:6).

C. 때의 전치사

1. at; 정확한 시각, 밤, 정오

I usually get up **at** six o'clock.
I will meet you at 4:30
Phone me **at** lunch time.

1) 휴가 전체를 말할 때

Are you going away **at** Easter? (Christmas, New Year, Thanksgiving)

At mealtime Boaz said to her
식사할 때에 보아스가 룻에게 이르되 (룻 2:14).

At that time Jesus went through the grainfields on the Sabbath.
그 때에 예수께서 안식일에 밀밭 사이로 가실 쌔 (마 12:1).

2. on; 날짜, 정한 시간

I'll phone you **on** Thursday.
My birthday is **on** October 18th.
They are having a party **on** Christmas Day.

1) 미국 영어에서는 이 때의 on을 생략하기도 한다

I'm seeing her Monday morning.

2) 반복적 행위를 나타낼 때는 on을 생략하지 않는다

We usually go to see Granny **on** Sundays.

Which is lawful **on** the Sabbath: to do good or to do evil, to save life or to kill?
안식일에 선을 행하는 것과 악을 행하는 것 생명을 구하는 것과 죽이는 것 어느 것이 옳으냐 (막 3:4).

On the seventh day, march around the city seven times, with the priests blowing the trumpets.
제 칠일에는 성을 일곱번 돌며 제사장들은 나팔을 불 것이며 (수 6:4).

3. in: 하루의 부분, 월, 계절, 해, 세기 등 비교적 긴 시간

I work best in the morning.
Three o'clock in the afternoon.
We usually go out in the evening.
It happened in the week after Christmas.
I was born in March.
He died in 1953.
Our house was built in the 19th Century.

* 예외

at night

See you on Monday morning. (어떤 날의 아침/점심 등을 말할 때)

It was on a cold afternoon in early spring. (아침/점심을 묘사할 때)

In the days when the judges ruled, there was a famine in the land.
사사들의 치리하던 때에 그 땅에 흉년이 드니라(룻 1:1).

If a man loudly blesses his neighbor early **in** the morning, it will be taken as a curse.
이른 아침에 큰 소리로 그 이웃을 축복하면 도리어 저주같이 여기게 되리라(잠 27:14).

next, last, this, one, any, each, every, some, all 앞에서는 전치사를 쓰지 않는다

See you next week.

Are you free this morning?

Let's meet one day.

Come any time.

I'm at home every evening.

We stayed all day.

Yesterday, the day before yesterday, tomorrow, the day after tomorrow 앞에서도 전치사를 쓰지 않는다.

What are you doing the day after tomorrow?

4. in; 현재부터 ~이 지나면

For John baptized with water, but **in** a few days you will be baptized with the Holy Spirit.
요한은 물로 세례를 베풀었으나 너희는 몇 날이 못되어 성령으로 세례를 받으리라(행 1:5).

5. within; ~ 이내에

If you can give me the answer **within** the seven days of the feast, I will give you thirty linen garments and thirty sets of clothes.
잔치하는 칠 일 동안에 너희가 능히 그것을 풀어서 내게 고하면 내가 베옷 삼십 벌과 겉옷 삼십 벌을 너희에게 주리라(삿 14:12).

6. after; (과거부터) ~ 후에

Then **after** three years, I went up to Jerusalem to get acquainted with Peter and stayed with him fifteen days.
그 후 삼년 만에 내가 게바를 심방하려고 예루살렘에 올라가서 저와 함께 십 오일을 유할쌔 (갈 1:18).

7. before; ~ 전에

I must move my car before nine o'clock.

* **비교**

in front of; (장소) ~ 앞에
It's parked in front of the post office. (Not; before the post office)

8. till (until); ~까지 (계속)

Wait **until** two o'clock.
Can I stay here **until** the weekend?
I'll have to keep the watch **until** Saturday.

The one who touches any such thing will be unclean **till** evening.
곧 이런 것에 접촉된 자는 저녁까지 부정하니 (레 22:6).

9. by; ~까지는 (완료)

You'll have to leave **by** Monday midday at the latest.
Can you repair my watch **by** Tuesday?

Come to me in Jezreel **by** this time tomorrow.
내일 이맘때에 이스르엘에 이르러 내게 나아오라 (왕하 10:6).

10. since; ～이래 죽(과거부터 현재까지 계속), 시제는 현재완료로

I have known him **since** Tuesday.
I've been here **since** July.

Since the first day that you set your mind to gain understanding and to humble yourself before your God, your words were heard, and I have come in response to them.
네가 깨달으려 하여 네 하나님 앞에 스스로 겸비케 하기로 결심하던 첫 날부터 네 말이 들으신 바 되었으므로 내가 네 말로 인하여 왔느니라(단 10:12).

11. from; ～부터(어느 때의 기점)

A glorious throne, exalted **from** the beginning, is the place of our sanctuary.
영화로우신 보좌여 원시부터 높이 계시며 우리의 성소이시며(렘 17:12).

12. for; ～ 동안(기간); 현재완료로 쓸 수도 있다

I've known her **for** three days.
I've been here **for** a month.

My father was in hospital **for** six weeks.
After that, he must be set free **for** a short time.
그 후에는 반드시 잠깐 놓이리라(계 20:3).

13. during; ～중에(상태의 계속)

My father was in hospital **during** the summer.
It rained **during** the night **for** two or three hours.
I'll call in and see you **for** a few minutes **during** the afternoon.

He who gathers crops in summer is a wise son, but he who sleeps **during** harvest is a disgraceful son.
여름에 거두는 자는 지혜로운 아들이나 추수 때에 자는 자는 부끄러움을 끼치는 아들이니라(잠 10:5).

14. through; ~ 동안 죽 (처음부터 끝까지)

For the LORD is good and his love endures forever; his faithfulness continues **through** all generations.
대저 여호와는 선하시니 그 인자하심이 영원하고 그 성실하심이 대대에 미치리로다 (시 100:5).

D. 원인, 이유의 전치사

1. from; 직접적 원인

More of them died **from** the hailstones than were killed by the swords of the Israelites.
이스라엘 자손의 칼에 죽은 자보다 우박에 죽은 자가 더욱 많았더라 (수 10:11).

2. through; 간접적, 소극적인 원인

You also died to the law **through** the body of Christ.
너희도 그리스도의 몸으로 말미암아 율법에 대하여 죽임을 당하였으니 (롬 7:4).

3. die of; ~으로 죽다 (사망, 병의 원인)

Those killed by the sword are better off than those who **die of** famine.
칼에 죽은 자가 주려 죽은 자보다 나음은 (애 4:9).

4. at; ~을 보고, 듣고 (기쁘다. 슬프다, 놀라다 등 감정의 원인)

When Jesus had finished saying these things, the crowds were amazed **at** his teaching,
예수께서 이 말씀을 마치시매 무리들이 그 가르치심에 놀래니 (마 7:28).

All spoke well of him and were amazed **at** the gracious words that came from his lips. "Isn't this Joseph's son?" they asked.
저희가 다 그를 증거하고 그 입으로 나오는 바 은혜로운 말을 기이히 여겨 가로되 이 사람이 요셉의 아들이 아니냐 (눅 4:22).

5. over; ～에 대하여 (기뻐하다. 슬프다, 웃다, 울다 등 감정의 원인)

As he approached Jerusalem and saw the city, he wept **over** it.
가까이 오사 성을 보시고 우시며(눅 19:41).

6. with; ～으로

When Zechariah saw him, he was startled and was gripped **with** fear.
사가랴가 보고 놀라며 무서워하니(눅 1:12).

7. for, out of; ～ 때문에

They waste away **for** lack of food from the field.
토지 소산이 끊어지므로 점점 쇠약하여 감이로다(아 4:9).

Christ died **for** our sins according to the Scriptures
성경대로 그리스도께서 우리 죄를 위하여 죽으시고(고전 15:3).

The lips of the righteous nourish many, but fools die **for** lack of judgment.
의인의 입술은 여러 사람을 교육하나 미련한 자는 지식이 없으므로 죽느니라(잠 10:20).

Some preach Christ **out of** envy and rivalry, but others **out of** goodwill.
어떤 이들은 투기와 분쟁으로 어떤 이들은 착한 뜻으로 그리스도를 전파하나니(빌 1:15).

E. 원료, 재료의 전치사

1. of; 재료가 제품이 되어도 원형을 잃지 않을 때 쓰인다

John's clothes were **made of** camel's hair, and he had a leather belt around his waist. His food was locusts and wild honey.
이 요한은 약대 털옷을 입고 허리에 가죽띠를 띠고 음식은 메뚜기와 석청이었더라(마 3:4).

The head of the statue was **made of** pure gold, its chest and arms **of** silver, its belly and thighs **of** bronze,
그 우상의 머리는 정금이요 가슴과 팔들은 은이요 배와 넓적다리는 놋이요(단 2:32).

The wall was **made of** jasper, and the city **of** pure gold, as pure as glass.
그 성곽은 벽옥으로 쌓였고, 그 성은 정금인데 맑은 유리 같더라(계 21:18).

John wore clothing **made of** camel's hair, with a leather belt around his waist, and he ate locusts and wild honey.
요한은 약대털을 입고 허리에 가죽띠를 띠고 메뚜기와 석청을 먹더라(막 1:6).

2. From; 재료가 제품이 되어 원형을 잃어버릴 때 쓰인다

Who is this coming up from the desert like a column of smoke, perfumed with myrrh and incense made **from** all the spices of the merchant?
연기 기둥과도 같고 몰약과 유향과 장사의 여러 가지 향품으로 향기롭게도 하고 거친 들에서 오는 자가 누구인고(아 3:6).

3. In; write, speak, paint, carve 등의 동사와 같이 쓰여 재료를 나타낸다

I put this **in** human terms because you are weak in your natural selves.
너희 육신이 연약하므로 내가 사람의 예대로 말하노니(롬 6:19).

F. 수단, 도구의 전치사

1. with; 사용되는 도구를 나타낸다

The weapons we fight **with** are not the weapons of the world
우리의 싸우는 병기는 육체에 속한 것이 아니오(고후 10:4).

I baptize you **with** water for repentance.
나는 너희로 회개케 하기 위하여 물로 세례를 주거니와 (마 3:11).

2. Through; 중개를 나타낸다

In love he predestined us to be adopted as his sons **through** Jesus Christ.
그 기쁘신 뜻대로 우리를 예정하사 예수 그리스도로 말미암아 자기의 아들들이 되게 하셨으니 (엡 1:5).

For **through** the law I died to the law so that I might live for God.
내가 율법으로 말미암아 율법을 향하여 죽었나니 이는 하나님을 향하여 살려 함이니라 (갈 2:19).

3. By; 수단을 나타낸다

Hiram king of Tyre replied **by** letter to Solomon.
두로 왕 후람이 솔로몬에게 답장하여 가로되 (대하 2:11).

4. in

in pen, **in** pencil, **in** ink
Please fill in the form **in** ink.

5. 박탈의 of

They defraud a man **of** his home, a fellowman **of** his inheritance.
밭들을 탐하여 빼앗고 집들을 탐하여 취하니 (미 2:2).

G. 기타

Except / except for; all, any, every, no, anything, anybody, anyone, anywhere, everything, everybody, nothing, whole 등 전체를 나타내는 단어 뒤에 쓸 수 있다.

He ate everything on the plate except (for) beans.
He ate the whole meal except (for) the beans.
He ate the meal except for the beans. (Not; except the beans)

I've cleaned all the rooms except (for) the bathroom.
I've cleaned the whole house except (for) the bathroom.
I've cleaned the house except for the bathroom. (Not; except the bathroom)

전치사 및 접속사 앞에서는 except를 쓴다.
It's the same everywhere **except** in Seoul.
She's beautiful **except** when she smiles.

A book **by** Joyce, a concerto **by** Mozart, a film **by** Fassbinder (Not; of)

연습 문제

1. You oppress the righteous and take bribes and you deprive the poor _____ justice in the courts. 1
   1) of   2) from   3) to   4) off

2. _____ coming to the house, they saw the child with his mother Mary. 2
   1) In   2) On   3) At   4) By

3. So he got up, took the child and his mother _____ the night and left for Egypt. 1
   1) during   2) for   3) while   4) by

   But during the night an angel of the Lord opened the doors of the jail and brought them out.
   During those days another large crowd gathered.
   He ate nothing during those days, and at the end of them he was hungry.

   A woman who becomes pregnant and gives birth to a son will be ceremonially unclean for seven days, just as she is unclean **during** her monthly period.
   여인이 잉태하여 남자를 낳으면 그는 칠일 동안 부정하리니 곧 경도할 때와 같이 부정할 것이며(레 12:2).

4. John's clothes were made _____ camel's hair. 3
   1) by   2) in   3) of   4) from

5. He had a leather belt _____ his waist. 4
   1) in   2) by   3) at   4) around

   He will baptize you with the Holy Spirit and with fire.

6. Do not put the Lord your God _____ the test. 3
   1) in   2) at   3) to   4) on

7. From that time _____ Jesus began to preach, "Repent, for the kingdom of heaven is near.
   1) by   2) with   3) on   4) to

8. As Jesus was walking _____ the Sea of Galilee, he saw two brothers.
   1) nearly   2) beside   3) in   4) besides

9. _____ once they left their nets and followed him.
   1) At   2) On   3) In   4) From

10. Blessed are those who are persecuted _____ righteousness, for theirs is the kingdom of heaven.
    1) due   2) owing   3) because of   4) because

All men will hate you because of me, but he who stands firm to the end will be saved.

11. It is better _____ you to lose one part of your body than for your whole body to be thrown into hell.
    1) to   2) for   3) of   4) on

12. Give to the one who asks you, and do not turn away from the one who wants to borrow _____ you.
    1) from   2) to   3) of   4) at

13. _____ my account you will be brought before governors and kings as witnesses to them and to the Gentiles.
    1) In   2) At   3) To   4) On

14. Look! Your disciples are doing what is unlawful _____ the Sabbath. 1
    1) on   2) in   3) at   4) for

15. When an evil spirit comes _____ a man, it goes through arid places seeking rest and does not find it.
    1) to   2) out of   3) from   4) with

He reached down from on high and took hold of me; he drew me out of deep waters.

For Jesus had said to him, "Come out of this man, you evil spirit!"
이는 예수께서 이미 저에게 이르시기를 더러운 귀신아 그 사람에게서 나오라 하셨음이라(막 5:8).

As soon as they **got out of** the boat, people recognized Jesus.
배에서 내리니 사람들이 곧 예수신 줄을 알고(막 6:54).

16. Let both grow together _____ the harvest.
    1) still   2) since   3) though   4) until

17. I will utter things hidden _____ the creation of the world.
    1) by   2) beside   3) since   4) to

18. The angels will come and separate the wicked _____ the righteous.
    1) from   2) to   3) on   4) at

19. I will send my messenger _____ you, who will prepare your way.
    1) out of   2) ahead of   3) from   4) in

20. John wore clothing made of camel's hair, _____ a leather belt around his waist, and he ate locusts and wild honey.
    1) on   2) with   3) by   4) as

21. And a voice came from heaven: "You are my Son, whom I love; _____ you I am well pleased."
    1) by   2) for   3) with   4) on

22. Simon's mother-in-law was in bed _____ a fever.
    1) with   2) on   3) in   4) by

23. A man with leprosy came to him and begged him _____ his knees.
    1) on   2) in   3) to   4) with

24. He could not do any miracles there, _____ lay his hands on a few sick people and heal them. 1
    1) except   2) and   3) beside   4) so

The disciples had forgotten to bring bread, except for one loaf they had with them in the boat.

25. He presented it ____ the girl, and she gave it to her mother. 4
    1) on   2) with   3) for   4) to

26. Have salt in yourselves, and be at peace _____ each other. 1
    1) with   2) on   3) at   4) for

27. Seeing ____ the distance a fig tree in leaf, he went to find out if it had any fruit.
    1) on   2) in   3) by   4) of

28. When he reached it, he found _____ leaves, because it was not the season for figs.
    1) something   2) any   3) nothing but   4) none

except의 의미로 all, none, every, any, no, everything, everybody, nothing, nobody, anywhere등 다음에 but을 쓴다.
He eats nothing but hamburgers.
Everybody's here but George.
I've finished all the jobs but one.
I will accept nothing but what my men have eaten and the share that belongs to the men who went with me.
That child does nothing but watch TV. (but + 동사원형)
My friend Jackie lives next door but one. (=two houses from me)

29. Love your neighbor _____ yourself.
    1) as   2) for   3) with   4) by

The LORD their God will save them on that day as the flock of his people.

30. You are right in saying that God is one and there is no other _____ him.

   1) but   2) than   3) from   4) beside

   Why does this fellow talk like that? He's blaspheming! Who can forgive sins **but** God alone?

31. She gave birth _____ her firstborn, a son.

   1) of   2) to   3) on   4) by

32. Glory to God in the highest, and on earth peace to men _____ whom his favor rests.

   1) in   2) at   3) to   4) on

33. Man does not live _____ bread alone.

   1) on   2) in   3) from   4) at

34. As he _____ the town gate, a dead person was being carried out.

   1) reach to   2) arrive   3) approached to   4) approached

35. An argument started among the disciples _____ which of them would be the greatest.

   1) as from   2) as   3) as to   4) as of

36. Heal the sick who are there and tell them, 'The kingdom of God is __ you.'

   1) nearly   2) near   3) near of   4) at near

   He spoke these words while teaching in the temple area near the place where the offerings were put.

   Then they came to Elim, where there were twelve springs and seventy palm trees, and they camped there **near** the water.
   그들이 엘림에 이르니 거기 물샘 열 둘과 종려 칠십 주가 있는지라. 거기서 그들이 그 물 곁에 장막을 치니라 (출 15:27).

37. They stripped him _____ his clothes.

   1) of   2) from   3) by   4) off

38. _____ the beginning was the Word, and the Word was with God, and the Word was God. 3

   1) By   2) As   3) In   4) On

39. This is the verdict: Light has come into the world, but men loved darkness _____ light because their deeds were evil.

   1) instead   2) instead of   3) despite of   4) beside

40. He testifies _____ what he has seen and heard, but no one accepts his testimony.

   1) from   2) to   3) in   4) on

41. This woman was caught _____ the act of adultery. 4

   1) on   2) to   3) around   4) in

42. They were using this question as a trap, in order to have a basis _____ accusing him. 1

   1) for   2) to   3) as   4) on

43. May I ask why you sent _____ me?

   1) from   2) with   3) for   4) to

44. Now these things occurred as examples to keep us _____ setting our hearts on evil things as they did.

   1) from   2) to   3) on   4) with

   I have kept myself from being a burden to you in any way, and will continue to do so.
   Who cut in on you and kept you from obeying the truth?
   I have been blameless before him and have kept myself from sin.
   I will prevent pests from devouring your crops.

45. I brought you my son, who is possessed by a spirit that has robbed him _____ speech.

   1) into   2) by   3) from   4) of

46. Ascribe to the LORD the glory _____ his name; worship the LORD in the splendor of his holiness.
   1) due   2) due to   3) owing   4) owe to

47. My name will be great _____ the nations, from the rising to the setting of the sun. 1
   1) among   2) between   3) with   4) at

And you will again see the distinction between the righteous and the wicked, between those who serve God and those who do not. (둘 사이에)

Whenever they have a dispute, it is brought to me, and I decide **between** the parties and inform them of God's decrees and laws."
그들이 일이 있으면 내게로 오나니 내가 그 양편을 판단하여 하나님의 율례와 법도를 알게 하나이다 (출 18:16).

48. The mountains melt beneath him and the valleys split apart, _____ wax before the fire, _____ water rushing down a slope.
   1) as   2) like   3) due to   4) by

Like a gold ring in a pig's snout is a beautiful woman who shows no discretion.
아름다운 여인이 삼가지 아니하는 것은 마치 돼지 코에 금고리 같으니라 (잠 11:22).

49. As _____ the days when you came out of Egypt, I will show them my wonders. 3
   1) at   2) though   3) in   4) on

In the last days the mountain of the LORD's temple will be established as chief among the mountains
I will make the sun go down at noon and darken the earth in broad daylight.
At dawn the next day God provided a worm, which chewed the vine so that it withered.

50. They trample on the heads of the poor as _____ the dust of the ground and deny justice to the oppressed.
   1) by   2) upon   3) if   4) from

From inside the fish Jonah prayed to the LORD his God.

51. Now there was a famine in the land, and Abram went down to Egypt to live there _____ because the famine was severe.
   1) for a while   2) contemporary   3) instead   4) despite

정답

1) 1, 2) 2, 3) 1, 4) 3, 5) 4, 6) 3, 7) 3, 8) 2, 9) 1, 10) 3
11) 2, 12) 1, 13) 4, 14) 1, 15) 2, 16) 4, 17) 3, 18) 1, 19) 2, 20) 2
21) 3, 22) 1, 23) 1, 24) 1, 25) 4, 26) 1, 27) 2, 28) 3, 29) 1, 30) 1
31) 2, 32) 4, 33) 1, 34) 4, 35) 3, 36) 2, 37) 1, 38) 3, 39) 2, 40) 2
41) 4, 42) 1, 43) 3, 44) 1, 45) 4, 46) 1, 47) 1, 48) 2, 49) 3, 50) 2
51) 1

숙어

take along; 지니다
Do not **take along** any gold or silver or copper in your belts;
너희 전대에 금이나 은이나 동이나 가지지 말고(마 10:9).

take(have) charge of; ~을 맡다, 담임하다
A man will seize one of his brothers at his father's home, and say, "You have a cloak, you be our leader: **take charge of** this heap of ruins!"
혹시 사람이 그 아비의 집에서 그 형제를 붙잡고 말하기를 너는 의복이 오히려 있으니 우리 관장이 되어 이 멸망을 네 수하에 두라 할 것이면(사3:6).

take courage; 용기를 내다
But Jesus immediately said to them: "**Take courage**! It is I. Don't be afraid."
예수께서 즉시 일러 가라사대, 안심하라 내니 두려워 말라(마 14:27).

take heart; 용기를 내다
Jesus turned and saw her. "**Take heart**, daughter," he said, "your faith has healed you." And the woman was healed from that moment.
예수께서 돌이켜 그를 보시며 가라사대, 딸아 안심하라 네 믿음이 너를 구원하였다 하시니 여자가 그 시로 구원을 받으니라(마 9:22).

take hold of; 붙잡다
He said to them, "If any of you has a sheep and it falls into a pit on the Sabbath, will you not **take hold of** it and lift it out?
예수께서 가라사대 너희 중에 어느 사람이 양 한 마리가 있어 안식일에 구덩이에 빠졌으면 붙잡아 내지 않겠느냐(마 12:11).

take into account; 고려하다
If any household is too small for a whole lamb, they must share one with their nearest neighbor, having **taken into account** the number of people there are.

그 어린 양에 대하여 식구가 너무 적으면 그 집의 이웃과 함께 수를 따라서 하나를 취하며(출 12:4).

For before the law was given, sin was in the world. But sin is not **taken into account** when there is no law.
죄가 율법 있기 전에도 세상에 있었으나 율법이 없을 때에는 죄를 죄로 여기지 아니하느니라(롬 5:13).

take off; 벗다, 이륙하다
Then he is to **take off** these clothes and put on others, and carry the ashes outside the camp to a place that is ceremonially clean.
그 옷을 벗고 다른 옷을 입고 그 재를 진 바깥 정결한 곳으로 가져 갈 것이요(레 6:11).

take offense at; 성내다
And they **took offense at** him. But Jesus said to them, "Only in his hometown and in his own house is a prophet without honor."
예수를 배척한지라 예수께서 저희에게 말씀하시되, 선지자가 자기 고향과 자기 집 외에서는 존경을 받지 않음이 없느니라 하시고(마 13:57).

take one's place; ~에 대신하다
I would have liked to keep him with me so that he could **take your place** in helping me while I am in chains for the gospel.
저를 내게 머물러 두어 내 복음을 위하여 갇힌 중에서 너 대신 나를 섬기게 하고자 하나(몬 1:13).

take pains; (대단히) 수고하다
For we are **taking pains** to do what is right, not only in the eyes of the Lord but also in the eyes of men.
이는 우리가 주 앞에서만 아니라 사람 앞에서도 선한 일에 조심하려 함이라(고후 8:21).

take part in (Not; at); 참가하다
I don't want to **take part in** any more conferences.

19. 접속사(接續詞)
Conjunction

접속사는 문장 중에서 낱말(word), 구(phrase), 절(clause) 등을 연결한다.
2개 이상의 단어로 구성된 접속사를 상관접속사라고 하며, 문법적 기능에 따라 대등접속사, 종속접속사로 구분한다.

A. 대등접속사

문법적으로 대등한 관계에 있는 낱말, 구, 절 등을 연결한다.

1. 부가

1) 2개 이상을 묶을 때 and를 마지막 단어 앞에 놓는다

Bread and cheese.
We drank, talked and danced.

He causes his sun to rise on the evil and the good, and sends rain on the righteous and the unrighteous.
하나님이 그 해를 악인과 선인에게 비취게 하시며, 비를 의로운 자와 불의한 자에게 내리우심이니라 (마 5:45).

2) 2단어로 된 표현에서 보통 짧은 단어를 먼저 쓴다

Young and pretty, cup and saucer

3) 몇 가지 표현은 고착되어서 순서를 바꿀 수 없다

Hands and knees, knife and fork, bread and butter, fish and chips

4) 명사 앞의 형용사들은 and로 연결하지 않는다

Thanks for your nice long letter. (Not; nice and long letter)
A tall dark handsome man

그러나 형용사가 같은 물건의 다른 부분을 가리킬 때는 and를 쓸 수 있다.
Red and yellow socks, a metal and glass table.

5) 회화체에서 Try(wait, go) to 대신에 try(wait, go) and를 쓴다

Try and eat something. You will feel better if you do.
I'll **try and** phone you tomorrow morning.

그러나 tries, tried, trying에서는 and를 쓰지 않고 to를 쓴다.
I tried to eat something. (Not; I tried and eat something.)

6) 보통 wait and see를 쓰며 wait to see를 쓰지 않는다

What's for lunch? – Wait and see.

Come and, go and, run and, hurry up and, stay and는 and 대신 to를 쓸 수 있는데 단 목적의 to 부정사에 한하며 모든 시제에서 쓸 수 있다.

Come **and** have a drink.
Stay **and** have dinner.
Hurry up **and** open the door.
He often **comes and** spends the evening with us.
She **stayed and** played with the children.

Go **and** make a careful search for the child.
가서 아기에 대하여 자세히 알아보고 (마 2:8).

But come **and** put your hand on her, and she will live.
오셔서 그 몸에 손을 얹으소서. 그러면 살겠나이다 (마 9:18).

7) 명령문 + and (and; 그러면)

"Come, follow me," Jesus said, "**and** I will make you fishers of men."
말씀하시되 나를 따라 오너라 내가 너희로 사람을 낚는 어부가 되게 하리라 (마 4:19).

8) both ~ and ~

both와 and 다음에 같은 종류의 단어들을 쓴다.

She's both pretty and clever (형용사)

I spoke to both the director and his secretary (명사)
(Not; I both spoke to the director and his secretary.)
She both plays the piano and sings. (동사)
(Not; She both plays the piano and she sings.)

Praise our God, all you his servants, you who fear him, **both** small **and** great!
하나님의 종들 곧 그를 경외하는 너희들아 무론 대소하고 다 우리 하나님께 찬송하라 (계 19:5).

You cannot serve **both** God **and** Money.
너희가 하나님과 재물을 겸하여 섬기지 못하느니라 (마 6:24).

9) as well as ~ 뿐만 아니라
He has a car **as well as** a motorbike.
She's clever **as well as** beautiful.

(1) As well as 다음에 동사가 올 때는 동명사가 온다
As well as breaking his leg, he hurt his arm. (Not; As well as he broke his leg, ---)
Smoking is dangerous, **as well as** making you smell bad.

(2) 차이 비교
She sings **as well as** playing the piano. (= She not only plays, but also sings.)
She sings **as well as** she plays the piano. (= Her singing is as good as her playing.)

Judah will be besieged **as well as** Jerusalem.
예루살렘이 에워 싸일 때에 유다에까지 미치리라 (슥 12:2).

(3) not only ~ but (also) ---- = ~ 뿐만 아니라 --- 도 역시
He is the atoning sacrifice for our sins, and **not only** for ours **but also** for the sins of the whole world.
저는 우리 죄를 위한 화목 제물이니 우리만 위할 뿐 아니요, 온 세상의 죄를 위하심이라 (요일 2:2).

For we are taking pains to do what is right, **not only** in the eyes of the Lord **but also** in the eyes of men.
이는 우리가 주 앞에서만 아니라 사람 앞에서도 선한 일에 조심하려 함이라 (고후 8:21).

2. 반대

They come to you in sheep's clothing, **but** inwardly they are ferocious wolves.
양의 옷을 입고 너희에게 나아오나 속에는 노략질하는 이리라(마 7:15).

Everything is permissible for me **but** I will not be mastered by anything.
모든 것이 내게 가하나 내가 아무에게든지 제재를 받지 아니하리라(고전 6:12).

I have **not** come to abolish them **but** to fulfill them. (not ~ but ~)
폐하러 온 것이 아니요 완전케 하려 함이로다(마 5:17).

He went in and said to them, "Why all this commotion and wailing? The child is **not** dead **but** asleep."
들어가서 저희에게 이르시되 너희가 어찌하여 훤화하며 우느냐 이 아이가 죽은 것이 아니라 잔다 하시니 (막 5:39).

I tell you, among those born of women there is no one greater than John; **yet** the one who is least in the kingdom of God is greater than he.
내가 너희에게 말하노니 여자가 낳은 자 중에 요한보다 큰 이가 없도다 그러나 하나님의 나라에서는 극히 작은 자라도 저보다 크니라 하시니(눅 7:28).

You are the salt of the earth. **But** if the salt loses its saltiness, how can it be made salty again?
(But = However)
너희는 세상의 소금이니 소금이 만일 그 맛을 잃으면 무엇으로 짜게 하리요(마 5:13).

3. 선택

1) or, either ~ or ~, whether(if) ~ or ~, neither ~ nor ~

(1) 보통 whether 대신 if를 쓸 수 있다
I'm not sure **whether/if** I'll have time.
I asked **whether/if** she had any letters for me.

(2) 그러나 or가 있으면 whether를 많이 쓴다
Let me know **whether** you can come **or** not.

(3) Discuss 다음에는 whether만 쓴다
We **discussed whether** we should close the shop.

If he cannot afford a lamb, he is to bring two doves **or** two young pigeons to the LORD as a penalty for his sin.
만일 힘이 어린 양에 미치지 못하거든 그 범과를 속하기 위하여 산비둘기 둘이나 집비둘기 새끼 둘을 여호와께로 가져 가되 (레 5:7).

"Do not judge, **or** you too will be judged. (or; 그렇지 않으면)
비판을 받지 아니하려거든 비판하지 말라 (마 7:1).

"No one can serve two masters. **Either** he will hate the one and love the other, **or** he will be devoted to the one and despise the other.
한 사람이 두 주인을 섬기지 못 할 것이니, 혹 이를 미워하며 저를 사랑하거나 혹 이를 중히 여기며 저를 경히 여김이라 (마 6:24).

The LORD will do nothing, **either** good **or** bad.
여호와께서는 복도 내리지 아니하시며 화도 내리지 아니하시리라 (습 1:12).

So, because you are lukewarm--**neither** hot **nor** cold--I am about to spit you out of my mouth.
네가 이같이 미지근하여 더웁지도 아니하고 차지도 아니하니 내 입에서 너를 토하여 내치리라 (계 3:16).

Neither their silver **nor** their gold will be able to save them on the day of the LORD's wrath.
그들의 은과 금이 여호와의 분노의 날에 능히 그들을 건지지 못할 것이며 (습 1:18).

Whether it was in the body **or** out of the body I do not know--God knows.
그가 몸 안에 있었는지 몸 밖에 있었는지 나는 모르거니와 하나님은 아시느니라 (고후 12:2).

But Peter and John replied, "Judge for yourselves **whether** it is right in God's sight to obey you rather than God.
베드로와 요한이 대답하여 가로되 하나님 앞에서 너희 말 듣는 것이 하나님 말씀 듣는 것보다 옳은가 판단하라 (행 4:19).

Examine yourselves to see **whether** you are in the faith (or not).
너희가 믿음에 있는가 너희 자신을 시험하고 너희 자신을 확증하라(고후 13:5).

4. 이유

My grace is sufficient for you, **for** my power is made perfect in weakness.
내 은혜가 네게 족하도다. 이는 내 능력이 약한 데서 온전하여짐이라(고후 12:9).

Blessed are those who mourn, **for** they will be comforted.
애통하는 자는 복이 있나니 저희가 위로를 받을 것임이요(마 5:4).

Be joyful always; pray continually; give thanks in all circumstances, **for** this is God's will for you in Christ Jesus.
항상 기뻐하라. 쉬지 말고 기도하라 범사에 감사하라 이는 그리스도 예수 안에서 너희를 향하신 하나님의 뜻이니라(살전 5:16~18).

B. 종속접속사

명사절(주어절, 술어절, 동격절), 전치사절, 부사절, 관계사절 등 여러 종류의 종속절을 주절에 연결시킨다.

1. 명사절

I did not realize **that** he was the high pries. (realize의 목적어 역할)
나는 그가 대제사장인 줄 알지 못하였노라(행 23:5).

We cannot hide from our lord the fact **that** since our money is gone and our livestock belongs to you, there is nothing left for our lord except our bodies and our land. (동격의 명사절)
우리가 주께 숨기지 아니하나이다. 우리의 돈이 다하였고, 우리의 짐승 떼가 주께로 돌아갔사오니 주께 낼 것이 아무것도 남지 아니하고 우리의 몸과 전지뿐이라(창 47:18).

2. 부사절

1) 때

when, as, while, after, before, since, till, as long as, the moment 등

(1) As/when/while A was happening, B happened.
어떤 사건이 발생했을 때, 1개의 다른 더 긴 행위가 진행된다.

As I was walking down the street I saw him driving a car.
The telephone rang **when** I was having a bath.
While they were playing cards, somebody broke into the house.
Please don't interrupt me **when** I'm speaking.
I often get good ideas **while** I'm shaving.

(2) while A was happening/happened, B was happening/happened.
2개의 긴 행위가 동시에 진행된다.

While you were reading the paper, I was working.
I cooked supper **while** he watched TV.
After supper, I wash up **while** she puts the children to bed.

(3) As A happened, B happened.
2개의 짧은 행위가 동시에 진행된다.

As I opened my eyes I heard a strange voice.
The doorbell rang just **as** I picked up the phone.

When he came out, he could not speak to them.
그가 나와서 저희에게 말을 못하니(눅 1:22).

When his parents saw him, they were astonished.
그 부모가 보고 놀라며(눅 2:48).

Seven days passed **after** the LORD struck the Nile.
여호와께서 하수를 치신 후 칠일이 지나니라(출 7:25).

Before certain men came from James, he used to eat with the Gentiles.
야고보에게서 온 어떤 이들이 이르기 전에 게바가 이방인과 함께 먹다가(갈 2:12).

How can the guests of the bridegroom mourn **while** he is with them?
혼인집 손님들이 신랑과 함께 있을 동안에 슬퍼할 수 있느뇨(마 9:15).

(4) no sooner ~ than = hardly(or scarcely) ~ when(or before)

No sooner had they set their feet on the dry ground **than** the waters of the Jordan returned to their place and ran at flood stage as before.
그 발바닥으로 육지를 밟는 동시에 요단 물이 본 곳으로 도로 흘러 여전히 언덕에 넘쳤더라(수 4:18).

As soon as you hear the sound of the horn, flute, zither, lyre, harp, pipes and all kinds of music, you must fall down and worship the image of gold that King Nebuchadnezzar has set up.
너희는 나팔과 피리와 수금과 삼현금과 양금과 생황과 및 모든 악기 소리를 들을 때에 엎드리어 느부갓네살 왕의 세운 금신상에게 절하라(단 3:5).

As soon as you began to pray, an answer was given, which I have come to tell you, for you are highly esteemed. Therefore, consider the message and understand the vision:
이 네 나라 마지막 때에 패역자들이 가득할 즈음에 한 왕이 일어나리니 그 얼굴은 엄장하며 궤휼에 능하며 (단 8:23).

As soon as you find him, report to me, so that I too may go and worship him.
찾거든 내게 고하여 나도 가서 그에게 경배하게 하라(마 2:8).

As long as the heir is a child, he is no different from a slave, although he owns the whole estate.
유업을 이을 자가 모든 것의 주인이나 어렸을 동안에는 종과 다름이 없어서(갈 4:1, 2).

And they have power to turn the waters into blood and to strike the earth with every kind of plague **as often as** they want.
또 권세를 가지고 물을 변하여 피되게 하고, 아무 때든지 원하는 대로 여러 가지 재앙으로 땅을 치리로다 (계 11:6).

2) 장소

as far as(~까지), where 등

Your branches spread **as far as** the sea.
너의 가지가 바다를 넘어 야셀 바다까지 뻗었더니(렘 48:32).

3) 원인, 이유

because, since, now that = since, as(~이므로, ~함에 따라)
not ~ because ---- = "----라고 해서 ~ 하지는 않다"

(1) 이유가 가장 중요한 개념일 때에는 because로 시작되는 절이 뒤쪽으로 간다

Why am I leaving? I'm leaving because I'm fed up.

But perfect love drives out fear, **because** fear has to do with punishment.
온전한 사랑이 두려움을 내어 쫓나니 두려움에는 형벌이 있음이라(요일 4:18).

(2) as, since는 이유가 가장 중요한 개념이 아닐 경우에나 이미 알려진 개념일 경우에 쓴다(Since가 좀 더 문어체임)

As it is raining again, we shall have to stay at home.
Since he had not paid his bill, his electricity was cut off.

As the men were leaving Jesus, Peter said to him.
두 사람이 떠날 때에 베드로가 예수께 여짜오되(눅 9:33).

As he was praying, the appearance of his face changed
기도하실 때에 용모가 변화되고(눅 9:29).

Since you have given me land in the Negev, give me also springs of water.
아버지께서 나를 남방 땅으로 보내시오니 샘물도 내게 주소서(수 15;19).

But **since** he has no root, he lasts only a short time
그 속에 뿌리가 없어 잠시 견디다가(마 13:21).

4) 목적

that ~ may = so that ~ may = in order that ~ may
lest ~ should = so that ~ may not 등

Perseverance must finish its work **so that** you **may** be mature and complete, not lacking anything.
인내를 온전히 이루라 이는 너희로 온전하고 구비하여 조금도 부족함이 없게 하려 함이라(약 1:4).

Now if we are children, then we are heirs--heirs of God and co-heirs with Christ, if indeed we share in his sufferings **in order that** we **may** also share in his glory.
자녀이면 또한 후사 곧 하나님의 후사요 그리스도와 함께 한 후사니, 우리가 그와 함께 영광을 받기 위하여 고난도 함께 받아야 될 것이니라(롬 8:17).

We did not give in to them for a moment, **so that** the truth of the gospel **might** remain with you.
우리가 일시라도 복종치 아니하였으니 이는 복음의 진리로 너희 가운데 항상 있게 하려 함이라(갈 2:5).

Therefore I will boast all the more gladly about my weaknesses, **so that** Christ's power **may** rest on me.
이러므로 도리어 크게 기뻐함으로 나의 여러 약한 것들에 대하여 자랑하리니 이는 그리스도의 능력으로 내게 머물게 하려 함이라(고후 12:9).

For Christ did not send me to baptize, but to preach the gospel--not with words of human wisdom, **lest** the cross of Christ be emptied of its power.
그리스도께서 나를 보내심은 세례를 주게 하려 하심이 아니요 오직 복음을 전케 하려 하심이니 말의 지혜로 하

지 아니함은 그리스도의 십자가가 헛되지 않게 하려 함이라(고전 1:17).

5) 결과
so ~ that, such ~ that 등

These men have power to shut up the sky **so that** it will not rain during the time they are prophesying.
저희가 권세를 가지고 하늘을 닫아 그 예언을 하는 날 동안 비 오지 못하게 하고(계 11:6).

At Iconium Paul and Barnabas went as usual into the Jewish synagogue. There they spoke **so** effectively **that** a great number of Jews and Gentiles believed.
이에 이고니온에서 두 사도가 함께 유대인의 회당에 들어가 말하니 유대와 헬라의 허다한 무리가 믿더라 (행 14:1).

Therefore I will boast all the more gladly about my weaknesses, **so that** Christ's power may rest on me.
이러므로 도리어 크게 기뻐함으로 나의 여러 약한 것들에 대하여 자랑하리니 이는 그리스도의 능력으로 내게 머물게 하려 함이라(고후 12:9).

Instead, he puts it on a stand, **so that** those who come in can see the light.
등경 위에 두나니 이는 들어가는 자들로 그 빛을 보게 하려 함이라(눅 8:16).

6) 조건
unless, in case, provided, providing, suppose, supposing 등

I will not let you go **unless** you bless me.
당신이 내게 축복하지 아니하면 가게 하지 아니하겠나이다(창 32:26).

It is fine to be zealous, **provided** the purpose is good, and to be so always and not just when I am with you.
좋은 일에 대하여 열심으로 사모함을 받음은 내가 너희를 대하였을 때뿐 아니라 언제든지 좋으니라(갈 4:18).

7) 양보

though, although, if, for all, with all, even if, even though 등

(1) though와 although는 같은 뜻으로 though는 회화체이며, 강조하기 위해 even though를 쓰나 even although는 쓰지 않는다

Though it is the smallest of all your seeds, yet when it grows, it is the largest of garden plants and becomes a tree, so that the birds of the air come and perch in its branches.
이는 모든 씨보다 작은 것이로되 자란 후에는 나물보다 커서 나무가 되매 공중의 새들이 와서 그 가지에 깃들이느니라(마 13:32).

Even though my illness was a trial to you, you did not treat me with contempt or scorn.
너희를 시험하는 것이 내 육체에 있으되 이것을 너희가 업신여기지도 아니하며 버리지도 아니하고(갈 4:14).

Though가 회화체에서 however의 의미로 문미에 쓰일 수 있다.
"Nice day." "Yes. Bit cold, though."
as 앞에 형용사, 부사, 명사(관사 뺌)가 나오면 양보일 때가 많다.

8) 비교, 양태

as, as if, as though 등

Be sure to allocate this land to Israel for an inheritance, **as** I have instructed you.
나의 명한 대로 그 땅을 이스라엘에게 분배하여 기업이 되게 하되(수 13:6).

As the body without the spirit is dead, **so** faith without deeds is dead.
영혼 없는 몸이 죽은 것같이 행함이 없는 믿음은 죽은 것이니라(약 2:26).

But **just as** he who called you is holy, **so** be holy in all you do.
오직 너희를 부르신 거룩한 자처럼 너희도 모든 행실에 거룩한 자가 되라(벧전 1:15).

When I saw him, I fell at his feet **as though** dead.
내가 볼 때에 그 발 앞에 엎드러져 죽은 자같이 되매(계 1:17).

Dear friends, do not be surprised at the painful trial you are suffering, **as though** something strange were happening to you.
사랑하는 자들아 너희를 시련 하려고 오는 불 시험을 이상한 일 당하는 것같이 이상히 여기지 말고(벧전 4:12).

It is just **as though** her head were shaved.
이는 머리 민 것과 다름이 없음이니라(고전 11:5).

연습 문제

1. Go and make a careful search for the child. As soon as you find him, report to me, _____ I too may go and worship him.
   1) but   2) so that   3) like   4) though

   Let your light shine before men, that they may see your good deeds and praise your Father in heaven.
   Spread your protection over them, that those who love your name may rejoice in you.
   Let us go down and confuse their language so they will not understand each other.
   Say you are my sister, so that I will be treated well for your sake.
   Their possessions were so great that they were not able to stay together.

   But take this staff in your hand **so** you can perform miraculous signs with it.
   너는 이 지팡이를 손에 잡고 이것으로 이적을 행할지니라 (출 4:17).

   My son, pay attention to my wisdom, listen well to my words of insight, **that** you may maintain discretion and your lips may preserve knowledge.
   내 아들아 내 지혜에 주의하며 내 명철에 네 귀를 기울여서 근신을 지키며 네 입술로 지식을 지키도록 하라 (잠 1:1,2).

2. They were casting a net into the lake, _____ they were fishermen.
   1) so   2) why   3) though   4) for

   Stay there until I tell you, for Herod is going to search for the child to kill him.

   Then Jesus asked him, "What is your name?" "My name is Legion," he replied, "for we are many."
   이에 물으시되 네 이름이 무엇이냐 가로되 내 이름은 군대니 우리가 많음이니이다 하고 (막 5:9).

3. _____ Jesus was baptized, he went up out of the water.
   1) As soon as   2) While   3) And   4) That

   Some people are like seed along the path, where the word is sown. As soon as they hear it, Satan comes and takes away the word that was sown in them.
   말씀이 길가에 뿌리웠다는 것은 이들이니 곧 말씀을 들었을 때에 사단이 즉시 와서 저희에게 뿌리운 말씀을 빼앗는 것이요(막 4:15).

4. Do not think that I have come to abolish the Law or the Prophets; I have not come to abolish them _____ to fulfill them.
   1) and   2) but   3) as   4) than

   It is not the healthy who need a doctor, but the sick.

5. I tell you the truth, you will not finish going through the cities of Israel _____ the Son of Man comes.
   1) before   2) that   3) so   4) but

6. A student is not above his teacher, _____ a servant above his master.
   1) nor   2) neither   3) but   4) and

   Eat unleavened bread during those seven days; nothing with yeast in it is to be seen among you, **nor** shall any yeast be seen anywhere within your borders.
   칠일 동안에는 무교병을 먹고 유교병을 너희 곳에 있게 하지 말며, 네 지경 안에서 누룩을 네게 보이지도 말게 하며(출 13:7).

7. Rather, be afraid of the One who can destroy _____ soul and body in hell.
   1) a   2) either   3) both   4) the

   I will remove both the prophets and the spirit of impurity from the land.
   I am surely going to destroy both them and the earth.

8. John came neither eating _____ drinking.
   1) nor   2) and   3) or   4) but

I was neither a prophet nor a prophet's son.

Moses said to the LORD, "O Lord, I have never been eloquent, **neither** in the past **nor** since you have spoken to your servant. I am slow of speech and tongue."
모세가 여호와께 고하되 주여, 나는 본래 말에 능치 못한 자라 주께서 주의 종에게 명하신 후에도 그러하니 나는 입이 뻣뻣하고 혀가 둔한 자니이다 (출 4:10).

Neither the pillar of cloud by day nor the pillar of fire by night left its place in front of the people.
낮에는 구름 기둥, 밤에는 불기둥이 백성 앞에서 떠나지 아니하니라 (출 13:22).

9. Come to me, all you who are weary and burdened, _____ I will give you rest.
   1) then   2) and   3) so   4) for

10. Anyone who speaks a word against the Son of Man will be forgiven, but anyone who speaks against the Holy Spirit will not be forgiven, _____ in this age or in the age to come.
   1) as   2) both   3) either   4) neither

11. Such large crowds gathered around him _____ he got into a boat and sat in it.
   1) that   2) this   3) how   4) why

12. But when the sun came up, the plants were scorched, and they withered _____ they had no root.
   1) so   2) because   3) that   4) why

13. These people honor me with their lips, _____ their hearts are far from me.
   1) so   2) but   3) and   4) that

Some trust in chariots and some in horses, but we trust in the name of the LORD our God.

14. Whenever you enter a house, stay there _____ you leave that town.
   1) while   2) by   3) when   4) until

15. As _____ as the sound of your greeting reached my ears, the baby in my womb leaped for joy.
   1) early   2) soon   3) good   4) well

16. Put out into deep water, _____ let down the nets for a catch.
   1) and   2) but   3) for   4) that

17. No good tree bears bad fruit, _____ does a bad tree bear good fruit.
   1) but   2) so   3) nor   4) though

   I did not receive it from any man, nor was I taught it.

18. Send the crowd away _____ they can go to the surrounding villages and countryside and find food and lodging.
   1) so   2) though   3) therefore   4) but

19. The light shines in the darkness, _____ the darkness has not understood it.
   1) but   2) and   3) for   4) since

20. _____ you do not know him, I know him.
   1) But   2) As   3) Because   4) Though

21. _____ John never performed a miraculous sign, all that John said about this man was true.
   1) As soon as   2) Though   3) As   4) That

22. It contained all kinds of four-footed animals, _____ reptiles of the earth and birds of the air.
   1) though   2) by   3) as well as   4) so

23. By law a married woman is bound to her husband as _____ as he is alive.
   1) long   2) well   3) soon   4) good

   The law has authority over a man only as long as he lives.

As long as the heir is a child, he is no different from a slave, although he owns the whole estate.

As long as Moses held up his hands, the Israelites were winning, but whenever he lowered his hands, the Amalekites were winning.
모세가 손을 들면 이스라엘이 이기고, 손을 내리면 아말렉이 이기더니 (출 17:11).

24. Therefore, it is necessary to submit to the authorities, not only because of possible punishment _____ because of conscience.
    1) but also   2) also   3) and   4) as well as

25. _____ I am not physically present, I am with you in spirit.
    1) As   2) Even though   3) For   4) As long as

26. Unlike so many, we do not peddle the word of God for profit. _____, in Christ we speak before God with sincerity, like men sent from God.
    1) On the contrary   2) Neither   3) As well   4) Meanwhile

27. If you keep on biting and devouring each other, watch out _____ you will be destroyed by each other.
    1) and   2) or   3) but   4) so

28. Let us not become weary in doing good, _____ at the proper time we will reap a harvest if we do not give up.
    1) while   2) for   3) Although   4) or

29. Kiss the Son, _____ he be angry and you be destroyed in your way, for his wrath can flare up in a moment.
    1) lest   2) unless   3) if   4) though

30. Two-thirds will be struck down and perish; _____ one-third will be left in it.
    1) yet   2) and   3) already   4) despite

31. The LORD will go out and fight against those nations, _____ he fights in the day of battle.
   1) so   2) but   3) as   4) though

   They will mourn for him **as** one mourns for an only child, and grieve bitterly for him as one grieves for a firstborn son.
   As vinegar to the teeth and smoke to the eyes, so is a sluggard to those who send him.
   게으른 자는 그 부리는 사람에게 마치 이에 초 같고 눈에 연기 같으니라(잠 10:26).

   But Moses said to the LORD, "**Since** I speak with faltering lips, why would Pharaoh listen to me?"
   모세가 여호와 앞에서 고하되 나는 입이 둔한 자이오니 바로가 어찌 나를 들으리이까(출 6:30).

   Hail fell and lightning flashed back and forth. It was the worst storm in all the land of Egypt **since** it had become a nation.
   우박의 내림과 불덩이가 우박에 섞여 내림이 심히 맹렬하니, 애굽 전국에 그 개국 이래로 그 같은 것이 없던 것이라(출 9:24).

32. For seven days no yeast is to be found in your houses. And whoever eats anything with yeast in it must be cut off from the community of Israel, _____ he is an alien or native-born.
    1) though   2) that   3) whether   4) and
    칠일 동안은 누룩을 너희 집에 있지 않게 하라. 무릇 유교물을 먹는 타국인이든지 본국에서 난 자든지 무론하고 이스라엘 회중에서 끊쳐지리니(출 12:19).

33. With many similar parables Jesus spoke the word to them, _____ they could understand.
    1) as many as   2) as much as   3) as though as   4) as though
    예수께서 이러한 많은 비유로 저희가 알아 들을 수 있는 대로 말씀을 가르치시되(막 4:33).

34. "How many loaves do you have?" he asked. "Go _____ see." When they found out, they said, "Five--and two fish."
    1) and   2) for   3) but   4) as
    이르시되 너희에게 떡 몇 개나 있느냐 가서 보라 하시니, 알아보고 가로되 떡 다섯 개와 물고기 두 마리가 있더이다 하거늘(막 6:38).

정답

1) 2, 2) 4, 3) 1, 4) 2, 5) 1, 6) 1, 7) 3, 8) 1, 9) 2, 10) 3
11) 1, 12) 2, 13) 2, 14) 4, 15) 2, 16) 1, 17) 3, 18) 1, 19) 1, 20) 4
21) 2, 22) 3, 23) 1, 24) 1, 25) 2, 26) 1, 27) 2, 28) 2, 29) 1, 30) 1
31) 3, 32) 3, 33) 2, 34) 1

숙어

take place; 일어나다, 개최되다
This will **take place** on the day when God will judge men's secrets through Jesus Christ, as my gospel declares.
곧 내 복음에 이른 바와 같이 하나님이 예수 그리스도로 말미암아 사람들의 은밀한 것을 심판하시는 그날이라 (롬 2:16).

They say that the resurrection has already **taken place**, and they destroy the faith of some.
부활이 이미 지나갔다 하므로 어떤 사람들의 믿음을 무너뜨리느니라(딤후2:18).

take pride in; ~을 자랑하다
The brother in humble circumstances ought to **take pride in** his high position. But the one who is rich should **take pride in** his low position, because he will pass away like a wild flower.
낮은 형제는 자기의 높음을 자랑하고 부한 형제는 자기의 낮아짐을 자랑할지니 이는 풀의 꽃과 같이 지나감이라(약 1:9-10).

take revenge; 복수하다
For jealousy arouses a husband's fury, and he will show no mercy when he **takes revenge**.
그 남편이 투기함으로 분노하여 원수를 갚는 날에 용서하지 아니하고(잠 6:34).

take to heart; 마음에 두다, 심히 서러워 하다
Blessed is the one who reads the words of this prophecy, and blessed are those who hear it and **take to heart** what is written in it, because the time is near.
이 예언의 말씀을 읽는 자와 듣는 자들과 그 가운데 기록한 것을 지키는 자들이 복이 있나니 때가 가까움이라(계 1:3).

think of / about; ~에 관해 생각하다, 숙고하다
I'm **thinking of** studying medicine.
I'm also **thought about** studying dentistry.

throw ~ at (aggressive); 던지다
Stop **throwing** stones **at** the cars.

throw ~ to (게임 등에서); 던지다
If you get the ball, **throw** it **to** me.

to be sure; 과연, 정말
To be sure, Elijah does come first, and restores all things.
엘리야가 과연 먼저 와서 모든 것을 회복하거니와(막 9:12).

to one's astonishment; 놀랍게도
He asked for a writing tablet, and **to everyone's astonishment** he wrote, "His name is John."
저가 서판을 달라 하여 그 이름은 요한이라 쓰매 다 기이히 여기더라(눅 1:63).

to the end; 끝까지
All men will hate you because of me, but he who stands firm **to the end** will be saved.
또 너희가 내 이름을 인하여 모든 사람에게 미움을 받을 것이나 나중까지 견디는 자는 구원을 얻으리라(마 10:22).

two by two; 둘씩
After this the Lord appointed seventy-two [40] others and sent them **two by two** ahead of him to every town and place where he was about to go.
이후에 주께서 달리 칠십 인을 세우사 친히 가시려는 각동 각처로 둘씩 앞서 보내시며(눅 10:1).

typical of (Not; for); 대표하는, 상징하는
The wine is **typical of** the region.

under construction; 공사 중
So this Sheshbazzar came and laid the foundations of the house of God in Jerusalem. From that day to the present it has been **under construction** but is not yet finished.
이에 이 세스바살이 이르러 예루살렘 하나님의 전 지대를 놓았고, 그 때로부터 지금까지 건축하여 오나 오히려 필역하지 못하였다(스 5:16).

20. 도치, 강조, 생략, 공통관계, 삽입, 동격

A. 도치

구문의 성질에 의한 도치
뜻을 강조하기 위한 도치 – 목적격, 보어, 부사(구)를 문두에 둔다.

Cursed are you above all the livestock and all the wild animals!
네가 모든 육축과 들의 모든 짐승보다 더욱 저주를 받아(창 3:14).

Never before had there been such a plague of locusts, nor will there ever be again.
이런 메뚜기는 전에도 없었고 후에도 없을러라(출 10:14).

1. 구문상의 도치

1) 의문문

Who will rescue me from this body of death?
이 사망의 몸에서 누가 나를 건져내랴(롬 7:24).

Where can you get this living water?
어디서 이 생수를 얻겠삽나이까(요 4:11).

2) 감탄문

What a ruin she has become, a lair for wild beasts!
어찌 이같이 황무하여 들짐승의 엎드릴 곳이 되었는고(습 2:15).

What a wretched man I am!
오호라 나는 곤고한 사람이로다(롬 7:24).

How beautiful are the feet of those who bring good news!
아름답도다 좋은 소식을 전하는 자들의 발이여 함과 같으니라(롬 10:15).

3) there is ~의 구문

Now **there lived** in that city **a man** poor but wise.
그 성읍 가운데 가난한 지혜자가 있어서 (전 9:15).

* 비교; there – **거기에**, **그곳에**

There the angel of the LORD appeared to him in flames of fire from within a bush. Moses saw that though the bush was on fire it did not burn up.
여호와의 사자가 떨기나무 불꽃 가운데서 그에게 나타나시니라. 그가 보니 떨기나무에 불이 붙었으나 사라지지 아니하는지라 (출 3:2).

4) 기원문

Long **may** he **live! May gold** from Sheba be given him. **May people** ever pray for him and bless him all day long.
저희가 생존하여 스바의 금을 저에게 드리며 사람들이 저를 위하여 항상 기도하고 종일 찬송하리로다 (시 72:15).

5) if가 생략된 조건문

Were I to count them, they would outnumber the grains of sand.
내가 세려고 할지라도 그 수가 모래보다 많도소이다 (시 139:18).

Should the raw flesh change and turn white, he must go to the priest.
그 난육이 변하여 다시 희어지면 제사장에게로 갈 것이요 (레 13:16).

6) scarcely ~ when ~; "~ 하자마자 곧 ~ 하다"

Scarcely had I passed them **when** I found the one my heart loves.
그들을 떠나자마자 마음에 사랑하는 자를 만나서 (아 3:4).

2. 목적어의 도치

1) 의문사가 목적어이다

What must I do to inherit eternal life?
내가 무엇을 하여야 영생을 얻으리이까(막 10:17).

2) 강조하기 위하여 목적어를 문두에 두었다

What I tell you in the dark, speak in the daylight; what is whispered in your ear, proclaim from the roofs.
내가 너희에게 어두운 데서 이르는 것을 광명한 데서 말하며, 너희가 귓속으로 듣는 것을 집 위에서 전파하라(마 10:27).

3) 목적어를 문두에 내고 강조하였으며, 조동사 did를 앞에 놓았다

3. 보어의 도치

1) 의문문

Who is that man in the field coming to meet us?
들에서 배회하다가 우리에게로 마주 오는 자가 누구뇨(창 24:65).

2) 감탄문

How happy your men must be!
복되도다 당신의 사람들이여(왕상 10:8).

3) 강조하기 위해 보어를 문두에 내놓았다.

"Blessed are the poor in spirit, for theirs is the kingdom of heaven.
심령이 가난한 자는 복이 있나니 천국이 저희 것임이요(마 5:3).

Rejoice and be glad, because great is your reward in heaven.
기뻐하고 즐거워하라 하늘에서 너희의 상이 큼이라(마 5:12).

4. 부사(구)의 도치

1) 강조하기 위해 부사어구가 앞에 나가 도치 구문을 만드는 예가 많은데, 특히 부정을 나타내는 어구에 많다

Under no circumstances can we accept cheques.
Hardly had I arrived when trouble started.

With pain you will give birth to children.
네가 수고하고 자식을 낳을 것이며(창 3:16).

Never again will he leave it
그가 결코 다시 나가지 아니하리라(계 3:12).

After me will come one who is more powerful than I, whose sandals I am not fit to carry.
내 뒤에 오시는 이는 나보다 능력이 많으시니 나는 그의 신을 들기도 감당치 못하겠노라(마 3:11).

2) neither, nor, so

I'm hungry. **So am I.**
I don't like Mozart. **Neither/nor do I.**

John's disciples often fast and pray, and **so do** the disciples of the Pharisees.
요한의 제자는 자주 금식하며 기도하고 바리새인의 제자들 또한 그리하되(눅 5:33).

3) only

Only then did I understand what she meant.
Not only did we lose our money, but we were also in danger of losing our lives.

4) Here/there + 동사 + 주어(명사)

Here comes Mrs. Foster. (Not; Here Mrs. Foster comes.)
There goes your brother.

5) Here/there + 주어(대명사) + 동사

Here she comes; There he goes.

6) 문어체

Under a tree was sitting the biggest man I have ever seen.
On the bed lay a beautiful young girl.

B. 강조

do, very, 부사(구), 어구반복
강조 구문 등에 의한 강조

1. 강조의 do

I **do** hope you will help us.
Do be careful, please!
Do be quiet, for God's sake!
Do sit down.
You are wrong. She **does** like you.

2. 강조의 very

And his servant was healed at that **very** hour.
그 시로 하인이 나으니라(마 8:13).

To this **very** hour we go hungry and thirsty, we are in rags, we are brutally treated, we are homeless.
바로 이 시간까지 우리가 주리고 목마르며 헐벗고 매맞으며 정처가 없고(고전 4:11).

Does not the **very** nature of things teach you that if a man has long hair, it is a disgrace to him,
만일 남자가 긴 머리가 있으면 자기에게 욕 되는 것을 본성이 너희에게 가르치지 아니하느냐(고전 11:14).

3. 강조의 부사구 on earth, in the world

There is not a man **on earth** who can do what the king asks!
세상에는 왕의 그 일을 보일 자가 하나도 없으므로 (단 2:10).

4. It is ~ that 구문

it is 다음에 놓이는 어구가 강조된다.

It is to us **that** this message of salvation has been sent.
이 구원의 말씀을 우리에게 보내셨거늘 (행 13:26).

5. 동일 어구 반복으로 강조

He looks **much, much** older.

6. 재귀대명사의 강조 용법

I myself will judge between the fat sheep and the lean sheep.
나 곧 내가 살진 양과 파리한 양 사이에 심판하리라 (겔 34:20).

C. 생략

품사가 거의 모두 다 생략될 수 있고 생략의 경우도 너무 많으나, 여기서는 대표적인 것만 예를 들겠다.

1. 주어 + be동사의 생략;

부사절이 as, though, if, when, while 등으로 유도될 때

(**As he was**) Aware of this, Jesus withdrew from that place.
예수께서 아시고 거기를 떠나가시니 (마 12:15).

2. 반복을 피하기 위한 생략

But small is the gate and narrow **(is)** the road that leads to life, and only a few find it.
생명으로 인도하는 문은 좁고 길이 협착하여 찾는 이가 적음이니라(마 7:14).

For I have not come to call the righteous, but **(come to call)** sinners."
내가 의인을 부르러 온 것이 아니요 죄인을 부르러 왔노라(마 9:13).

If anyone hears my voice and opens the door, I will come in and eat with him, and he **(will eat)** with me.
누구든지 내 음성을 듣고 문을 열면 내가 그에게로 들어가 그로 더불어 먹고 그는 나로 더불어 먹으리라 (계 3:20).

But many who are first will be last, and the last **(will be)** first.
그러나 먼저 된 자로서 나중 되고 나중 된 자로서 먼저 될 자가 많으니라(막 8:31).

3. 관용적 생략;

1) 관용어구, 일상 인사하는 말, 격언, 게시 용어 등에 많다

Woe to the city of oppressors!
포학한 그 성읍이 화 있을진저(습 3:1).

What a burden!
이 일이 얼마나 번폐스러운고(말 1:13).

2) 구어체 문장의 첫머리에서

Car's running badly. (= The car's -----)
Wife's on holiday. (= My wife's -----)
Couldn't understand a word. (= I couldn't -----)
Seen Joe? (= Have you seen Joe?)

D. 삽입

주어 + 동사, 구, 종속절의 삽입

1. 주문의 삽입; 대개 comma나 dash를 앞뒤에 찍는다

2. 의문문이나 관계사절 안에서 comma의 표시 없이 주문이 삽입되는 경우

Who **do you think** I am?
너희가 나를 누구로 생각하느냐(행 13:25).

I give a judgment as one who **by the Lord's mercy** is trustworthy.
주의 자비하심을 받아서 충성된 자가 되어 의견을 고하노니(고전 7:25).

Just as they were handed down to us by those who **from the first** were eyewitnesses and servants of the word.
처음부터 말씀의 목격자 되고 일군 된 자들의 전하여 준 그대로 내력을 저술하려고 붓을 든 사람이 많은지라 (눅 1:2).

3. 형용사절이나 부사절을 문중에 삽입하여 설명을 부가하는 경우

1) 형용사절

I will wipe mankind, **whom I have created,** from the face of the earth
나의 창조한 사람을 지면에서 쓸어버리되(창 6:7).

Israel, **who pursued a law of righteousness,** has not attained it.
의의 법을 좇아간 이스라엘은 법에 이르지 못하였으니(롬 9:30, 31).

I looked, and there **before me** was a black horse
내가 보니 검은 말이 나오는데(계 6:5).

2) 부사절

Nor **because they are his descendants** are they all Abraham's children.
또한 아브라함의 씨가 다 그 자녀가 아니라(롬 9:7).

Which of you, **if his son asks for bread**, will give him a stone?
너희 중에 누가 아들이 떡을 달라 하면 돌을 주며(마 7:9).

My son, **if** sinners entice you, do not give in to them.
내 아들아 악한 자가 너를 꾈지라도 좇지 말라(잠 1:10).

4. 구의 삽입

Anyone who prays to any god or man during the next thirty days, **except to you, O king**, shall be thrown into the lions' den.
이제부터 삼십일 동안에 누구든지 왕 외에 어느 신에게나 사람에게 무엇을 구하면 사자 굴에 던져 넣기로 한 것이니이다(단 6:7).

E. 동격

명사, 부정사, 전문 전체를 받는 어구, 명사절이 동격어로 쓰임

1. 명사가 동격의 역할

In those days **John the Baptist** came, preaching in the Desert of Judea.
그 때에 세례 요한이 이르러 유대 광야에서 전파하여 가로되(마 3:1).

When Arioch, **the commander of the king's guard** had gone out to put to death the wise men of Babylon.
왕의 시위대 장관 아리옥이 바벨론 박사들을 죽이러 나가매(단 2:14).

Why have I found such favor in your eyes that you notice **me--a foreigner**?
나는 이방 여인이어늘 당신이 어찌하여 내게 은혜를 베푸시며 나를 돌아보시나이까(룻 2:10).

Christ, **our Passover lamb**, has been sacrificed.
우리의 유월절 양 곧 그리스도께서 희생이 되셨느니라(고전 5:7).

2. 고딕체 부분의 문장 전체가 동격어

The time will come when the bridegroom will be taken from them; then they will fast.
그러나 신랑을 빼앗길 날이 이르리니 그 때에는 금식할 것이니라(마 9:15).

연습 문제

1. The _____ has not yet come for the LORD's house to be built.
   1) period   2) time   3) hour   4) man

   * 동격
   As the time approached for him to be taken up to heaven, Jesus resolutely set out for Jerusalem.

2. Woe _____ the worthless shepherd, who deserts the flock!
   1) for   2) from   3) to   4) is

   Woe to him who piles up stolen goods

3. Many of the people of Israel will _____ bring back to the Lord their God.
   1) me   2) him   3) he   4) his

   * 도치
   No longer will you be called Abram; your name will be Abraham.
   After me will come one more powerful than I
   Never again will I curse the ground because of man
   Rejoice in that day and leap for joy, because **great** is your reward in heaven.

4. Six days you are to gather it, but on the _____ day, the Sabbath, there will not be any.
   1) first   2) third   4) fifth   4) seventh
   육일 동안은 너희가 그것을 거두되 제 칠일은 안식일인즉 그날에는 없으리라(출 16:26).

5. I _____ have carefully investigated everything from the beginning.
   1) me   2) and myself   3) own   4) myself
   그 모든 일을 근원부터 자세히 미루어 살핀 나도(눅 1:3).

6. Who _____ you think you are?
   1) does   2) are   3) do   4) can

   의문문 안에서 comma 없이 삽입됨
   Who do the crowds say I am?
   I who speak to you am he.

7. You are no longer to supply the people with straw for making bricks; let them go and _____ their own straw.
   1) gather   2) to gather   3) gathering   4) gathers
   너희는 백성에게 다시는 벽돌 소용의 짚을 전과 같이 주지 말고 그들로 가서 스스로 줍게 하라 (출 5:7).

   They will be **enslaved** and **mistreated** four hundred years.
   Abram **brought** all these to him, **cut** them in two and **arranged** the halves opposite each other.

8. He is staying with Simon _____, whose house is by the sea.
   1) the tanner   2) tanner   3) tanning   4) the tanners

   Simon과 동격

9. The knowledge of the secrets of the kingdom of heaven has been given to you, but not _____ them.
   1) of   2) for   3) to   4) by

10. Do not work for food that spoils, but _____ food that endures to eternal life.
    1) to   2) of   3) for   4) as

정답
1) 2, 2) 3, 3) 3, 4) 4, 5) 4, 6) 3, 7) 1, 8) 1, 9) 3, 10) 3

숙어

wait on; 시중들다
She got up at once and began to **wait on** them.
여자가 곧 일어나 저희에게 수종드니라 (눅 4:39).

Watch out; 망보다, 경계하다
Watch out that you do not lose what you have worked for, but that you may be rewarded fully.
너희는 너희를 삼가 우리의 일한 것을 잃지 말고 오직 온전한 상을 얻으라 (요2 1:8).

Watch out for false prophets. They come to you in sheep's clothing, but inwardly they are ferocious wolves.
거짓 선지자들을 삼가라. 양의 옷을 입고 너희에게 나아오나 속에는 노략질하는 이리라 (마 7:15).

Watch out for those dogs, those men who do evil, those mutilators of the flesh.
개들을 삼가고 행악하는 자들을 삼가고 손할례당을 삼가라 (빌 3:2).

What is more; 게다가 (furthermore)
What is more, he was chosen by the churches to accompany us as we carry the offering, which we administer in order to honor the Lord himself and to show our eagerness to help.
이뿐 아니라, 저는 동일한 주의 영광과 우리의 원(願)을 나타내기 위하여 여러 교회의 택함을 입어 우리의 맡은 은혜의 일로 우리와 동행하는 자라 (고후 8:19).

with regard to; ~에 관하여는
You are sent by the king and his seven advisers to inquire about Judah and Jerusalem **with regard to** the Law of your God, which is in your hand.
너는 네 손에 있는 네 하나님의 율법을 좇아 유다와 예루살렘의 정형을 살피기 위하여 왕과 일곱 모사의 보냄을 받았으니 (스 7:14).

without a doubt; 물론, 틀림없이,

Then Peter came to himself and said, "Now I know **without a doubt** that the Lord sent his angel and rescued me from Herod's clutches and from everything the Jewish people were anticipating."

이에 베드로가 정신이 나서 가로되 내가 이제야 참으로 주께서 그의 천사를 보내어 나를 헤롯의 손과 유대 백성의 모든 기대에서 벗어나게 하신 줄 알겠노라 하여 (행 12:11).

without fail; 틀림없이, 반드시, 꼭

Whatever is needed--young bulls, rams, male lambs for burnt offerings to the God of heaven, and wheat, salt, wine and oil, as requested by the priests in Jerusalem--must be given them daily **without fail**,

또 그 수용물 곧 하늘의 하나님께 드릴 번제의 수송아지와, 수양과, 어린 양과, 또 밀과, 소금과, 포도주와, 기름을 예루살렘 제사장의 소청대로 영락없이 날마다 주어 (스 6:9).

독해 연습

1과

창 1:1~5

In the beginning God created the heavens and the earth. Now the earth was formless and empty, darkness was over the surface of the deep, and the Spirit of God was hovering over the waters. And God said, "Let there _____ light," and there was light. God saw that the light was good, and he separated the light from the darkness. God called the light "day," and the darkness he called "night." And there was evening, and there was morning--the first day.

* hover 공중을 떠돌다

1) is   2) be   3) are   4) can

힌트) 사역동사 let 다음에는 동사 원형이 온다.

태초에 하나님이 천지를 창조하시니라. 땅이 혼돈하고 공허하며 흑암이 깊음 위에 있고 하나님의 신은 수면에 운행하시니라. 하나님이 가라사대 빛이 있으라 하시매 빛이 있었고 그 빛이 하나님의 보시기에 좋았더라. 하나님이 빛과 어두움을 나누사 빛을 낮이라 칭하시고 어두움을 밤이라 칭하시니라 저녁이 되며 아침이 되니 이는 첫째 날이니라. 2

창 17:1~11

When Abram was ninety-nine years old, the LORD appeared to him and said, "I am God Almighty; walk before me and be blameless. I will confirm my covenant between 가)_____ and you and will greatly increase your numbers." Abram fell facedown, and God said to him, "As for me, this is my covenant with you: You will be the father of many nations. No longer will you be called Abram; your name will be Abraham, for I have made you a father of many nations. I will make you very 나)_____; I will make nations of you, and kings will come from you. I will establish my covenant as an everlasting covenant between me and you and your descendants after you for the generations to come, to be your God and the God of your descendants after you. The whole land of Canaan, where you are now an alien, I will give as an everlasting possession to you and your descendants after you; and I will be their God." Then God said to Abraham, "As for you, you must keep my covenant, you and your descendants after you for the generations to come. This is my covenant with you and your descendants after you, the covenant you are to keep: 다)_____ male among you shall be circumcised. You are to undergo circumcision, and it will be the sign of the covenant between me and you.

* confirm 확실하게 하다, 확인하다 / covenant 계약 / facedown 머리를 숙이고, 엎드리어 / descendant 자손 / circumcise 할례를 행하다 / undergo 받다, 경험하다, 견디다 / circumcision 할례

가. 1) me   2) I   3) my   4) our
힌트) 전치사 between의 목적격 대명사

나. 1) fruitful   2) fruit   3) fruitfully   4) fruits

힌트) you의 보어로 형용사

다. 1) No   2) All   3) Only   4) Every
힌트) 단수명사 male을 수식하는 형용사, 앞뒤 문맥 고려.

아브람의 구십구 세 때에 여호와께서 아브람에게 나타나서 그에게 이르시되 나는 전능한 하나님이라 너는 내 앞에서 행하여 완전하라. 내가 내 언약을 나와 너 사이에 세워 너로 심히 번성케 하리라 하시니 아브람이 엎드린대 하나님이 또 그에게 일러 가라사대 내가 너와 내 언약을 세우니 너는 열국의 아비가 될지라. 이제 후로는 네 이름을 아브람이라 하지 아니하고 아브라함이라 하리니 이는 내가 너로 열국의 아비가 되게 함이니라. 내가 너로 심히 번성케 하리니 나라들이 네게로 좇아 일어나며 열왕이 네게로 좇아 나리라. 내가 내 언약을 나와 너와 네 대대 후손의 사이에 세워서 영원한 언약을 삼고 너와 네 후손의 하나님이 되리라. 내가 너와 네 후손에게 너의 우거하는 이 땅 곧 가나안 일경으로 주어 영원한 기업이 되게 하고 나는 그들의 하나님이 되리라. 하나님이 또 아브라함에게 이르시되 그런즉 너는 내 언약을 지키고 네 후손도 대대로 지키라. 너희 중 남자는 다 할례를 받으라 이것이 나와 너희와 너희 후손 사이에 지킬 내 언약이니라. 너희는 양피를 베어라. 이것이 나와 너희 사이의 언약의 표징이니라.
가) 1, 나) 1, 다) 4

창 28:10~22

Jacob left Beersheba and set out for Haran. When he reached a certain place, he stopped for the night because the sun had set. 가) _____ one of the stones there, he put it under his head and lay down to sleep. He had a dream in which he saw a stairway resting on the earth, 나) _____ its top reaching to heaven, and the angels of God were ascending and descending on it. There above it stood the LORD, and he said: "I am the LORD, the God of your father Abraham and the God of Isaac. I will give you and your descendants the land on which you are lying. Your descendants will be like the dust of the earth, and you will spread out to the west and to the east, to the north and to the south. All peoples on earth will be blessed through you and your offspring. I am with you and will watch over you wherever you go, and I will bring you back to this land. I will not leave you until I have done 다) _____ I have promised you." When Jacob awoke from his sleep, he thought, "Surely the LORD is in this place, and I was not aware of it." He was afraid and said, "How awesome is this place! This is none other than the house of God; this is the gate of heaven." Early the next morning Jacob took the stone he had placed under his head and set it up as a pillar and poured oil on top of it. He called that place Bethel, though the city used to be called Luz. Then Jacob made a vow, saying, "If God will be with me and will watch over me on this journey I am taking and will give me food to eat and clothes 라) _____ so that I return safely to my father's house, then the LORD will be my God and this stone that I have set up as a pillar will be God's house, and of all that you give me I will give you a tenth."

* offspring 자식, 자손 / awesome 무서운, 두려운 (dreadful) / pillar 기둥 / vow 맹세(하다)

가. 1) Took   2) Taking   3) Taken   4) Take
힌트) 분사구문

나. 1) by   2) on   3) with   4) as
힌트) 부대상황을 나타내는 독립분사구문에 with를 붙이면 묘사적이 된다.

다. 1) that   2) so   3) where   4) what
힌트) 선행사가 포함된 관계대명사

라. 1) to wear   2) wear   3) wearing   4) of wearing
힌트) 명사 clothes를 수식하는 부정사의 형용사적 용법

야곱이 브엘세바에서 떠나 하란으로 향하여 가더니 한 곳에 이르르는 해가 진지라 거기서 유숙하려고 그 곳의 한 돌을 취하여 베개하고 거기 누워 자더니 꿈에 본즉 사닥다리가 땅 위에 섰는데 그 꼭대기가 하늘에 닿았고 또 본즉 하나님의 사자가 그 위에서 오르락내리락하고 또 본즉 여호와께서 그 위에 서서 가라사대 나는 여호와니 너의 조부 아브라함의 하나님이요 이삭의 하나님이라 너 누운 땅을 내가 너와 네 자손에게 주리니 네 자손이 땅의 티끌같이 되어서 동서 남북에 편만할지며 땅의 모든 족속이 너와 네 자손을 인하여 복을 얻으리라. 내가 너와 함께 있어 네가 어디로 가든지 너를 지키며 너를 이끌어 이 땅으로 돌아오게 할지라. 내가 네게 허락한 것을 다 이루기까지 너를 떠나지 아니하리라 하신지라 야곱이 잠이 깨어 가로되 여호와께서 과연 여기 계시거늘 내가 알지 못하였도다. 이에 두려워하여 가로되 두렵도다 이 곳이여. 다른 것이 아니라 이는 하나님의 전이요 이는 하늘의 문이로다 하고 야곱이 아침에 일찌기 일어나 베개하였던 돌을 가져 기둥으로 세우고 그 위에 기름을 붓고 그 곳 이름을 벧엘이라 하였더라. 이 성의 본 이름은 루스더라. 야곱이 서원하여 가로되 하나님이 나와 함께 계시사 내가 가는 이 길에서 나를 지키시고 먹을 양식과 입을 옷을 주사 나로 평안히 아비 집으로 돌아가게 하시오면 여호와께서 나의 하나님이 되실 것이요 내가 기둥으로 세운 이 돌이 하나님의 전이 될 것이요 하나님께서 내게 주신 모든 것에서 십분 일을 내가 반드시 하나님께 드리겠나이다 하였더라. 가) 2, 나) 3, 다) 4, 라) 1

출 20:3~17

You shall have no other gods before me. You shall not make for yourself an idol in the form of anything in heaven above or on the earth beneath or in the waters below. You shall not bow down to them or worship them; for I, the LORD your God, am a jealous God, punishing the children for the sin of the fathers to the third and fourth generation of those 가) _____ hate me, but showing love to a thousand generations of those who love me and keep my commandments. You shall not misuse the name of the LORD your God, 나) _____ the LORD will not hold anyone guiltless who misuses his name. Remember the Sabbath day by keeping it holy. Six days you shall labor and do all your work, but the seventh day is a Sabbath to the LORD your God. On it you shall not do any work, neither you, nor your son or daughter, nor your manservant or maidservant, nor your animals, nor the alien within your gates. For in six days the LORD made the heavens and the earth, the sea, and all that is in them, but he rested 다) _____ the seventh day. Therefore the LORD blessed the Sabbath day and made it holy. Honor your father and your mother, so that you may live long in the land the LORD your God is giving you. You shall not murder. You shall not commit adultery. You shall not steal. You shall not give false testimony against your neighbor. You shall not covet your neighbor's house. You shall not covet your neighbor's wife, or his manservant or maidservant, his ox or donkey, or 라) _____ that belongs to your neighbor.

* jealous 질투가 많은 / punish 벌하다 / commandment 계명, 명령 / misuse 오용하다, 학대하다 / Sabbath 안식일 / testimony 증거 / covet 턱없이 탐내다, 몹시 바라다 / ox 황소 / donkey 당나귀

가. 1) who 2) he 3) that 4) men
힌트) those who; ~하는 사람들

나. 1) so 2) for 3) but 4) and
힌트) 이유를 나타내는 접속사

다. 1) in 2) at 3) by 4) on
힌트) 날짜를 나타내는 전치사

라. 1) anything 2) something 3) all 4) some
힌트) not과 호응하는 대명사

너는 나 외에는 다른 신들을 네게 있게 말지니라. 너를 위하여 새긴 우상을 만들지 말고 또 위로 하늘에 있는 것이나 아래로 땅에 있는 것이나 땅 아래 물 속에 있는 것의 아무 형상이든지 만들지 말며 그것들에게 절하지 말며 그것들을 섬기지 말라. 나 여호와 너의 하나님은 질투하는 하나님인즉 나를 미워하는 자의 죄를 갚되 아비로부터 아들에게로 삼 사대까지 이르게 하거니와 나를 사랑하고 내 계명을 지키는 자에게는 천대까지 은혜를 베푸느니라. 너는 너의 하나님 여호와의 이름을 망령되이 일컫지 말라. 나 여호와는 나의 이름을 망령되이 일컫는 자를 죄 없다 하지 아니하리라. 안식일을 기억하여 거룩히 지키라. 엿새 동안은 힘써 네 모든 일을 행할 것이나 제 칠 일은 너의 하나님 여호와의 안식일인즉 너나 네 아들이나 네 딸이나 네 남종이나 네 여종이나 네 육축이나 네 문 안에 유하는 객이라도 아무 일도 하지 말라. 이는 엿새 동안에 나 여호와가 하늘과 땅과 바다와 그 가운데 모든 것을 만들고 제 칠 일에 쉬었음이라. 그러므로 나 여호와가 안식일을 복되게 하여 그 날을 거룩하게 하였느니라. 네 부모를 공경하라. 그리하면 너의 하나님 나 여호와가 네게 준 땅에서 네 생명이 길리라. 살인하지 말지니라. 간음하지 말지니라. 도적질하지 말지니라. 네 이웃에 대하여 거짓 증거하지 말지니라. 네 이웃의 집을 탐내지 말지니라. 네 이웃의 아내나 그의 남종이나 그의 여종이나 그의 소나 그의 나귀나 무릇 네 이웃의 소유를 탐내지 말지니라. 가) 1, 나) 2, 다) 4, 라) 1

2과

출 23:20~30

See, I am sending an angel ahead of you to guard you along the way and to bring you to the place I have prepared. Pay attention to him and listen to what he says. Do not rebel against him; he will not forgive your rebellion, since my Name is in him. If you listen carefully to what he says and do all that I say, I will be an 가) _____ to your enemies and will oppose those who oppose you. My angel will go ahead of you and bring you into the land of the Amorites, Hittites, Perizzites, Canaanites, Hivites and Jebusites, and I will 나) _____ . Do not bow down before their gods or worship them or follow their practices. You must demolish them and break their sacred stones to pieces. Worship the LORD your God, 다) _____ his blessing will be on your food and water. I will take away sickness from among you, and none will miscarry or be barren in your land. I will give you a full life span. I will send my terror ahead of you and throw into confusion every nation you encounter. I will make all your enemies turn their backs and run. I will send the hornet ahead of you to drive the Hivites, Canaanites and Hittites out of your way. But I will not drive them out in a single year, because the land would become desolate and the wild animals too numerous for you. Little by little I will drive them out before you, until you have increased 라) _____ to take possession of the land.

* rebel 반역하다, 반역자 / rebellion 반역 / demolish 파괴하다 / miscarry 실패하다, 유산하다 / barren 불모의, 임신 못하는 / hornet 호박벌 / desolate 황량한 / numerous 다수의, 셀 수없이 많은

가. 1) father   2) friend   3) enemy   4) supporter
힌트) 문맥 관계

나. 1) wipe them out   2) wipe them on   3) wipe out them   4) wipe on them
힌트) 타동사 + 대명사(목적어) + 부사

다. 1) so   2) and   3) but   4) for
힌트) 명령문, and ~

라. 1) enough   2) enoughly   3) little   4) many
힌트) 부사가 와야 할 자리

내가 사자를 네 앞서 보내어 길에서 너를 보호하여 너로 내가 예비한 곳에 이르게 하리니 너희는 삼가 그 목소리를 청종하고 그를 노엽게 하지 말라. 그가 너희 허물을 사하지 아니할 것은 내 이름이 그에게 있음이니라. 네가 그 목소리를 잘 청종하고 나의 모든 말대로 행하면 내가 네 원수에게 원수가 되고 네 대적에게 대적이 될지라. 나의 사자가 네 앞서 가서 너를 아모리 사람과 헷 사람과 브리스 사람과 가나안 사람과 히위 사람과 여부스 사람에게로 인도하고 나는 그들을 끊으리니 너는 그들의 신을 숭배하지 말며 섬기지 말며 그들의 소위를 본받지 말고 그것들을 다 훼파하며 그 주상을 타파하고 너의 하나님 여호와를 섬기라. 그리하면 여호와가 너희의 양식과 물에 복을 내리고 너희 중에 병을 제하리니 네 나라에 낙태하는 자가 없고 잉태치 못하는 자가 없을 것이라. 내가 너의 날 수를 채우리라. 내가 내 위엄을 네 앞서 보내어 너의 이를 곳의 모든 백성을 파하고 너의

모든 원수로 너를 등지게 할 것이며 내가 왕벌을 네 앞에 보내리니 그 벌이 히위 족속과 가나안 족속과 헷 족속을 네 앞에서 쫓아내리라. 그러나 그 땅이 황무하게 되어 들짐승이 번성하여 너희를 해할까 하여 일 년 안에는 그들을 네 앞에서 쫓아내지 아니하고 네가 번성하여 그 땅을 기업으로 얻을 때까지 내가 그들을 네 앞에서 조금씩 쫓아내리라. 가) 3, 나) 1, 다)2, 라) 1

출 31:12~17

Then the LORD said to Moses, "Say to the Israelites, You must observe my Sabbaths. This will be a sign between me and you for the generations to come, so you may know that I am the LORD, 가) _____ makes you holy. Observe the Sabbath, because it is holy to you. Anyone who desecrates it must be put to 나) _____ ; whoever does any work on that day must be cut off from his people. For six days, work is to be done, but the seventh day is a Sabbath of rest, holy to the LORD. Whoever does any work on the Sabbath day must be put to death. The Israelites are to observe the Sabbath, celebrating it for the generations to come as a lasting covenant. It will be a sign between me and the Israelites forever, for in six days the LORD made the heavens and the earth, and on the seventh day he abstained from work and 다 _____ .

* observe 준수하다 / desecrate ~의 신성을 더럽히다 (opp. consecrate) / celebrate 축하하다 / abstain 절제하다

가. 1) that   2) what   3) which   4) who
힌트) 선행사 the Lord를 받는 관계대명사

나. 1) death   2) life   3) live   4) dead
힌트) 문맥 관계, desecrate; 신성을 모독하다

다. 1) slept   2) rested   3) went   4) disappeared
힌트) 일을 마치고 쉬었음이니라

여호와께서 모세에게 일러 가라사대 너는 이스라엘 자손에게 고하여 이르기를 너희는 나의 안식일을 지키라. 이는 나와 너희 사이에 너희 대대의 표징이니 나는 너희를 거룩하게 하는 여호와인 줄 너희로 알게 함이라. 너희는 안식일을 지킬지니 이는 너희에게 성일이 됨이라. 무릇 그 날을 더럽히는 자는 죽일지며 무릇 그 날에 일하는 자는 그 백성 중에서 그 생명이 끊쳐지리라. 엿새 동안은 일할 것이나 제 칠 일은 큰 안식일이니 여호와께 거룩한 것이라 무릇 안식일에 일하는 자를 반드시 죽일지니라. 이같이 이스라엘 자손이 안식일을 지켜서 그것으로 대대로 영원한 언약을 삼을 것이니 이는 나와 이스라엘 자손 사이에 영원한 표징이며 나 여호와가 엿새 동안에 천지를 창조하고 제 칠 일에 쉬어 평안하였음이니라 하라. 가) 4, 나) 1, 다) 2

민 21:4~9

They traveled from Mount Hor along the route to the Red Sea, to go around Edom. But the people grew 가) _____ on the way; they spoke against God and against Moses, and said, "Why have you brought us up out of Egypt to die in the desert? There is no bread! There is no water! And we detest this miserable food!" Then the LORD sent 나) _____ snakes among them; they bit the people and many Israelites died. The people came to Moses and said, "We sinned when we spoke against the LORD and against you. Pray that the LORD will take the snakes away from us." So Moses prayed for the people. The LORD said to Moses, "Make a snake and put it up on a pole; anyone who is bitten can look at it and live." So Moses made a bronze snake and put it up on a pole. Then when anyone was bitten by a snake and looked at the bronze snake, he 다) _____ .

* detest 혐오하다, 몹시 싫어하다 (abhor)

가. 1) impatience   2) to impatient   3) impatient   4) impatiently
힌트) grew는 자동사로서 2형식 동사임, 주어의 보어가 와야 할 자리. 차차 ~하게 되다.
He grew old; 점점 나이들다, He grew weary; 차차 피로해지다

나. 1) venomous   2) peculiar   3) omnipotent   4) imperative
힌트) 독이 있는

다. 1) lived   2) lives   3) died   4) dies
힌트) 시제 일치, 문맥 관계

백성이 호르 산에서 진행하여 홍해 길로 좇아 에돔 땅을 둘러 행하려 하였다가 길로 인하여 백성의 마음이 상하니라. 백성이 하나님과 모세를 향하여 원망하되 어찌하여 우리를 애굽에서 인도하여 올려서 이 광야에서 죽게 하는고? 이 곳에는 식물도 없고 물도 없도다. 우리 마음이 이 박한 식물을 싫어하노라 하매 여호와께서 불뱀들을 백성 중에 보내어 백성을 물게 하시므로 이스라엘 백성 중에 죽은 자가 많은지라. 백성이 모세에게 이르러 가로되 우리가 여호와와 당신을 향하여 원망하므로 범죄하였사오니 여호와께 기도하여 이 뱀들을 우리에게서 떠나게 하소서. 모세가 백성을 위하여 기도하매 여호와께서 모세에게 이르시되 불뱀을 만들어 장대 위에 달라 물린 자마다 그것을 보면 살리라. 모세가 놋뱀을 만들어 장대 위에 다니 뱀에게 물린 자마다 놋뱀을 쳐다 본즉 살더라. 가) 3, 나) 1, 다) 1

신 15:1~3

At the end of every seven years you must cancel debts. This is how it is to be done: Every creditor shall cancel the loan he has made to his fellow Israelite. He shall not require payment from his fellow Israelite or brother, because the LORD'S time for canceling debts has been proclaimed. You may require payment from a foreigner, but you must cancel any debt your brother _____ you.

* creditor 채권자 (opp, debtor) / proclaim 선언하다 (declare)

1) lends   2) owes   3) borrows   4) gives
힌트) 빚지고 있다

매 칠 년 끝에 면제하라. 면제의 규례는 이러하니라. 무릇 그 이웃에게 꾸어 준 채주는 그것을 면제하고 그 이웃에거나 그 형제에게 독촉하지 말지니 이 해는 여호와의 면제년이라 칭함이니라. 이방인에게는 네가 독촉하려니와 네 형제에게 꾸인 것은 네 손에서 면제하라. 2

3과

신 15:7~11

If there is a poor man among your brothers in any of the towns of the land that the LORD your God is giving you, do not be hardhearted or tightfisted toward your poor brother. Rather be openhanded and freely lend him whatever he needs. Be careful not to harbor this wicked thought: "The seventh year, the year for canceling debts, is near," so that you do not show ill will toward your 가) _____ brother and give him nothing. He may then appeal to the LORD against you, and you will be found 나) _____ of sin. Give generously to him and do so without a grudging heart; then because of this the LORD your God will bless you in all your work and in everything you put your hand to. There will always be poor people in the land. Therefore I command you to be openhanded toward your brothers and toward the poor and needy in your land.

* hardhearted 무정한, 냉혹한(merciless) / tightfisted 인색한 / openhanded 후한, 관대한 / harbor (나쁜 생각을) 품다 / grudge 주기 싫어하다, 인색하게 굴다 / needy 매우 가난한

가. 1) rich   2) old   3) cautious   4) needy
힌트) 문맥 관계

나. 1) guilty   2) guilt   3) innocent   4) innocence
힌트) 주어 you의 보어로 형용사, 문맥 관계

네 하나님 여호와께서 네게 주신 땅 어느 성읍에서든지 가난한 형제가 너와 함께 거하거든 그 가난한 형제에게 네 마음을 강퍅히 하지 말며 네 손을 움켜 쥐지 말고 반드시 네 손을 그에게 펴서 그 요구하는 대로 쓸 것을 넉넉히 꾸어 주라. 삼가 너는 마음에 악념을 품지 말라. 곧 이르기를 제 칠년 면제년이 가까왔다 하고 네 궁핍한 형제에게 악한 눈을 들고 아무것도 주지 아니하면 그가 너를 여호와께 호소하리니 네가 죄를 얻을 것이라. 너는 반드시 그에게 구제할 것이요 구제할 때에는 아끼는 마음을 품지 말 것이니라. 이로 인하여 네 하나님 여호와께서 네 범사와 네 손으로 하는 바에 네게 복을 주시리라. 땅에는 언제든지 가난한 자가 그치지 아니하겠는 고로 내가 네게 명하여 이르노니 너는 반드시 네 경내 네 형제의 곤란한 자와 궁핍한 자에게 네 손을 펼지니라.
가) 4, 나) 1

신 22:5~11

A woman must not wear men's clothing, 가) _____ a man wear women's clothing, for the LORD your God detests anyone who does this. If you come across a bird's nest beside the road, either in a tree 나) _____ on the ground, and the mother is sitting on the young or on the eggs, do not take the mother with the young. You may take the young, but be sure to let the mother go, so that it may go well with you and you may have a long life. When you build a new house, make a parapet around your roof so that you may not bring the guilt of bloodshed on your house if someone falls from the roof. Do not plant two kinds of seed in your vineyard; if you do, not only the crops you plant 다) _____ the fruit of the vineyard will be defiled. Do not plow with an ox and a donkey yoked together. Do not wear clothes of wool and linen woven together.

* parapet; 난간, wool; 양모,모직물, linen; 아마포

가. 1) nor   2) neither   3) but   4) and
힌트) not과 호응함, ~도 또한 않다.

나. 1) as   2) and   3) or   4) nor
힌트) either와 호응함

다. 1) and   2) nor   3) also   4) but also
힌트) not only와 호응함

여자는 남자의 의복을 입지 말 것이요 남자는 여자의 의복을 입지 말 것이라. 이같이 하는 자는 네 하나님 여호와께 가증한 자니라. 노중에서 나무에나 땅에 있는 새의 보금자리에 새 새끼나 알이 있고 어미새가 그 새끼나 알을 품은 것을 만나거든 그 어미새와 새끼를 아울러 취하지 말고 어미는 반드시 놓아 줄 것이요 새끼는 취하여도 가하니 그리하면 네가 복을 누리고 장수하리라. 네가 새 집을 건축할 때에 지붕에 난간을 만들어 사람으로 떨어지지 않게 하라. 그 피 흘린 죄가 네 집에 돌아갈까 하노라. 네 포도원에 두 종자를 섞어 뿌리지 말라. 그리하면 네가 뿌린 씨의 열매와 포도원의 소산이 빼앗김이 될까 하노라. 너는 소와 나귀를 겨리하여 갈지 말며 양털과 베실로 섞어 짠 것을 입지 말지니라. 가) 1, 나) 3, 다) 4

신 23:19~20

Do not charge your brother interest, whether on money or food or anything else that may _____ interest. You may charge a foreigner interest, but not a brother Israelite, so that the LORD your God may bless you in everything you put your hand to in the land you are entering to possess.

1) do   2) exist   3) earn   4) fall

네가 형제에게 꾸이거든 이식을 취하지 말지니 곧 돈의 이식, 식물의 이식, 무릇 이식을 낼 만한 것의 이식을 취하지 말 것이라. 타국인에게 네가 꾸이면 이식을 취하여도 가하거니와 너의 형제에게 꾸이거든 이식을 취하지 말라. 그리하면 네 하나님 여호와께서 네가 들어가서 얻을 땅에서 네 손으로 하는 범사에 복을 내리시리라. 3

신 23:24~25

If you enter your neighbor's vineyard, you may eat all the grapes you want, but do not put any in your basket. If you enter your neighbor's grainfield, you may 가) _____ kernels with your hands, but you must not put a sickle to his standing grain.

* kernel; 낟알, 핵심   sickle; 낫

1) have   2) make   3) pick   4) put

네 이웃의 포도원에 들어갈 때에 마음대로 그 포도를 배불리 먹어도 가하니라 그러나 그릇에 담지 말 것이요 네 이웃의 곡식 밭에 들어갈 때에 네가 손으로 그 이삭을 따도 가하니라. 그러나 네 이웃의 곡식 밭에 낫을 대지 말지니라. 3

신 24:10~15

When you make a loan of any kind to your neighbor, do not go into his house to get what he is offering as a pledge. Stay outside and let the man to whom you are making the loan bring the pledge out to you. If the man is poor, do not go to sleep with his pledge in your possession. Return his cloak to him by sunset so that he may sleep in it. Then he will thank you, and it will be regarded as a righteous act in the sight of the LORD your God. Do not 가) _____ advantage of a hired man who is poor and needy, whether he is a brother Israelite or an alien living in one of your towns. Pay him his wages each day before sunset, because he is poor and is counting on it. 나) _____ he may cry to the LORD against you, and you will be guilty of sin.

* pledge 담보, 보증, 서약 / guilty 죄를 범한 (criminal)

가. 1) take   2) make   3) have   4) gain
힌트) take advantage of; (좋은 기회, 사실을) 이용하다, 역이용하다, 속이다
have the advantage of; ~이라는 장점이 있다. ~보다 유리하다
gain(win) an advantage over a person; ~을 능가하다

나. 1) Therefore   2) Otherwise   3) For   4) But
힌트) 그렇지 않으면

무릇 네 이웃에게 꾸어 줄 때에 네가 그 집에 들어가서 전집물을 취하지 말고 너는 밖에 서고 네게 꾸는 자가 전집물을 가지고 나와서 네게 줄 것이며 그가 가난한 자여든 너는 그의 전집물을 가지고 자지 말고 해질 때에 전집물을 반드시 그에게 돌릴 것이라. 그리하면 그가 그 옷을 입고 자며 너를 위하여 축복하리니 그 일이 네 하나님 여호와 앞에서 네 의로움이 되리라. 곤궁하고 빈한한 품꾼은 너의 형제든지 네 땅 성문 안에 우거하는 객이든지 그를 학대하지 말며 그 품삯을 당일에 주고 해진 후까지 끌지 말라. 이는 그가 빈궁하므로 마음에 품삯을 사모함이라. 두렵건대 그가 너를 여호와께 호소하면 죄가 네게로 돌아갈까 하노라. 가) 1, 나) 2)

신 28:1~6

If you fully obey the LORD your God and carefully follow all his commands I give you today, the LORD your God will set you high above all the nations on earth. All these blessings will come upon you and 가) _____ you if you obey the LORD your God: You will be blessed in the city and blessed in the country. The fruit of your womb will be blessed, and the crops of your land and the young of your livestock--the calves of your herds and the lambs of your 나) _____ . Your basket and your kneading trough will be blessed. You will be blessed when you come in and blessed when you go out.

* knead 반죽하다 / trough 반죽 그릇, 여물통, 구유

가. 1) accompanies   2) have accompanied   3) be accompanied   4) accompany
힌트) 시제 일치

나. 1) herds   2) flocks   3) swarm   4) flight
힌트) herds 소떼 / flocks 양 떼 / swarm 벌떼 / flight 새떼

네가 네 하나님 여호와의 말씀을 삼가 듣고 내가 오늘날 네게 명하는 그 모든 명령을 지켜 행하면 네 하나님 여호와께서 너를 세계 모든 민족 위에 뛰어나게 하실 것이라. 네가 네 하나님 여호와의 말씀을 순종하면 이 모든 복이 네게 임하며 네게 미치리니 성읍에서도 복을 받고 들에서도 복을 받을 것이며 네 몸의 소생과 네 토지의 소산과 네 짐승의 새끼와 네 우양의 새끼가 복을 받을 것이며 네 광주리와 떡반죽 그릇이 복을 받을 것이며 네가 들어와도 복을 받고 나가도 복을 받을 것이니라. 가) 4, 나) 2

신 28:7~14

The LORD will grant that the enemies who rise up against you will be defeated before you. They will come at you from one direction but 가) _____ from you in seven. The LORD will send a blessing on your barns and on everything you put your hand to. The LORD your God will bless you in the land he is giving you. The LORD will establish you as his holy people, as he promised you on oath, if you keep the commands of the LORD your God and walk in his ways. Then all the peoples on earth will see that you are called by the name of the LORD, and they will fear you. The LORD will grant you abundant prosperity--in the fruit of your womb, the young of your livestock and the crops of your ground--in the land he swore to your forefathers to give you. The LORD will open the heavens, the storehouse of his bounty, to send rain on your land in season and to bless all the work of your hands. You will lend to many nations but will 나) _____ from none. The LORD will make you the head, not the tail. If you pay attention to the commands of the LORD your God that I give you this day and carefully follow 다) _____ , you will always be at the top, never at the bottom. Do not turn aside from any of the commands I give you today, to the right or to the left, following other gods and serving them.

* grant 승인하다, 인정하다 / barn 헛간 / oath 맹세 / womb 자궁 / livestock 가축 / crop 농작물 / bounty 선심 쓰기 (generosity), 하사품

가. 1) depart   2) decrease   3) crush   4) flee
힌트) 문맥 관계

나. 1) give   2) borrow   3) ask   4) receive
힌트) 빌려오다

다. 1) them   2) one   3) it   4) you
힌트) commands를 받는 대명사

네 대적들이 일어나 너를 치려하면 여호와께서 그들을 네 앞에서 패하게 하시리니 그들이 한 길로 너를 치러 들어왔으나 네 앞에서 일곱 길로 도망하리라. 여호와께서 명하사 네 창고와 네 손으로 하는 모든 일에 복을 내

리시고 네 하나님 여호와께서 네게 주시는 땅에서 네게 복을 주실 것이며 네가 네 하나님 여호와의 명령을 지켜 그 길로 행하면 여호와께서 네게 맹세하신 대로 너를 세워 자기의 성민이 되게 하시리니 너를 여호와의 이름으로 일컬음을 세계 만민이 보고 너를 두려워하리라. 여호와께서 네게 주리라고 네 열조에게 맹세하신 땅에서 네게 복을 주사 네 몸의 소생과 육축의 새끼와 토지의 소산으로 많게 하시며 여호와께서 너를 위하여 하늘의 아름다운 보고를 열으사 네 땅에 때를 따라 비를 내리시고 네 손으로 하는 모든 일에 복을 주시리니 네가 많은 민족에게 꾸어 줄지라도 너는 꾸지 아니할 것이요 여호와께서 너로 머리가 되고 꼬리가 되지 않게 하시며 위에만 있고 아래에 있지 않게 하시리니 오직 너는 내가 오늘날 네게 명하는 네 하나님 여호와의 명령을 듣고 지켜 행하며 내가 오늘날 너희에게 명하는 그 말씀을 떠나 좌로나 우로나 치우치지 아니하고 다른 신을 따라 섬기지 아니하면 이와 같으리라. 가) 4, 나) 2, 다) 1

신 28:47~48

Because you did not serve the LORD your God joyfully and gladly in the time of prosperity, therefore in hunger and thirst, in nakedness and dire poverty, you will serve the enemies the LORD sends against you. He will put an iron yoke on your neck until he _____ you.

* prosperity 번영 / dire 무서운 (terrible) / yoke 멍에

1) shall have destroyed   2) has destroyed   3) have destroyed   4) destroyed

힌트) 부사절에서 현재완료는 미래완료의 代用으로 완료의 뜻을 나타낸다.

네가 모든 것이 풍족하여도 기쁨과 즐거운 마음으로 네 하나님 여호와를 섬기지 아니함을 인하여 네가 주리고 목마르고 헐벗고 모든 것이 핍절한 중에서 여호와께서 보내사 너를 치게 하실 대적을 섬기게 될 것이니 그가 철 멍에를 네 목에 메워서 필경 너를 멸할 것이라. 2

4과

신 31:7~8

Then Moses summoned Joshua and said to him in the presence of all Israel, "Be strong and courageous, for you must go with this people into the land that the LORD swore to their forefathers to give them, and you must divide it among them as their inheritance. The LORD himself goes before you and will be with you; he will never leave you _____ forsake you. Do not be afraid; do not be discouraged."

* summon 소환하다, 호출하다 / forefather 조상 / inheritance 상속 / forsake 저버리다 (desert)

1) nor   2) neither   3) but   4) and

힌트) never(not)와 호응함, ~도 또한 않다.

모세가 여호수아를 불러 온 이스라엘 목전에서 그에게 이르되 너는 마음을 강하게 하고 담대히 하라. 너는 이 백성을 거느리고 여호와께서 그들의 열조에게 주리라고 맹세하신 땅에 들어가서 그들로 그 땅을 얻게 하라. 여호와 그가 네 앞서 행하시며 너와 함께 하사 너를 떠나지 아니하시며 버리지 아니하시리니 너는 두려워 말라 놀라지 말라. 1

수 2:3~15

So the king of Jericho sent this message to Rahab: "Bring out the men who came to you and 가) _____ your house, because they have come to spy out the whole land." But the woman had taken the two men and hidden them. She said, "Yes, the men came to me, but I did not know where they had come from. At dusk, when it was time to close the city gate, the men left. I don't know which way they went. Go after them quickly. You may catch up with them." But she had taken them up to the roof and hidden them under the stalks of flax she had laid out on the roof. So the men 나) _____ in pursuit of the spies on the road that leads to the fords of the Jordan, and as soon as the pursuers had gone out, the gate was shut. Before the spies lay down for the night, she went up on the roof and said to them, "I know that the LORD has given this land to you and that a great fear of you has fallen on us, so that all who live in this country are melting in fear because of you. We have heard how the LORD dried up the water of the Red Sea for you when you came out of Egypt, and what you did to Sihon and Og, the two kings of the Amorites east of the Jordan, whom you completely destroyed. When we heard of it, our hearts melted and everyone's courage 다) _____ because of you, for the LORD your God is God in heaven above and on the earth below. Now then, please swear to me by the LORD that you will show kindness to my family, because I have shown kindness to you. Give me a sure sign that you will spare the lives of my father and mother, my brothers and sisters, and all who belong to them, and that you will save us from death." "Our lives for your lives!" the men assured her. "If you don't tell what we are doing, we will treat you kindly and faithfully when the LORD gives us the land." So she let them down by a rope through the window, for the house she lived in was part of the city wall.

* stalk 줄기 / flax 아마 / ford 여울

가. 1) entered on   2) entered at   3) entered   4) entered into
힌트) enter는 타동사 / enter into 종사하다, 시작하다

나. 1) set out   2) set on   3) take out   4) take on
힌트) 길을 떠나다 (자동사)

다. 1) won   2) increased   3) helped   4) failed
힌트) 약해지다

여리고 왕이 라합에게 기별하여 가로되 네게로 와서 네 집에 들어간 사람들을 끌어내라 그들은 이 온 땅을 탐지하러 왔느니라. 그 여인이 그 두 사람을 이미 숨긴지라. 가로되 과연 그 사람들이 내게 왔었으나 그들이 어디로서인지 나는 알지 못하였고 그 사람들이 어두워 성문을 닫을 때쯤 되어 나갔으니 어디로 갔는지 알지 못하되 급히 따라가라. 그리하면 그들에게 미치리라 하였으나 실상은 그가 이미 그들을 이끌고 지붕에 올라가서 그 지붕에 벌여 놓은 삼대에 숨겼더라. 그 사람들은 요단 길로 나루턱까지 따라갔고 그 따르는 자들이 나가자 곧 성문을 닫았더라. 두 사람이 눕기 전에 라합이 지붕에 올라가서 그들에게 이르러 말하되 여호와께서 이 땅을 너희에게 주신 줄 내가 아노라. 우리가 너희를 심히 두려워하고 이 땅 백성이 다 너희 앞에 간담이 녹나니 이는 너희가 애굽에서 나올 때에 여호와께서 너희 앞에서 홍해 물을 마르게 하신 일과 너희가 요단 저편에 있는 아모리 사람의 두 왕 시혼과 옥에게 행한 일 곧 그들을 전멸시킨 일을 우리가 들었음이라. 우리가 듣자 곧 마음이 녹았고 너희의 연고로 사람이 정신을 잃었나니 너희 하나님 여호와는 상천하지에 하나님이시니라. 그러므로 청하노니 내가 너희를 선대하였은즉 너희도 내 아버지의 집을 선대하여 나의 부모와 남녀 형제와 무릇 그들에게 있는 모든 자를 살려 주어 우리 생명을 죽는 데서 건져내기로 이제 여호와로 맹세하고 내게 진실한 표를 내라. 두 사람이 그에게 이르되 네가 우리의 이 일을 누설치 아니하면 우리의 생명으로 너희를 대신이라도 할 것이요 여호와께서 우리에게 이 땅을 주실 때에는 인자하고 진실하게 너를 대우하리라. 라합이 그들을 창에서 줄로 달아내리우니 그 집이 성벽 위에 있으므로 그가 성벽 위에 거하였음이라. 가) 3, 나) 1, 다) 4

수 14:10~12

"Now then, just as the LORD promised, he has kept me alive for forty-five years since the time he said this to Moses, while Israel moved about in the desert. So here I am today, eighty-five years old! I am still as strong today 가) _____ the day Moses sent me out; I'm just as vigorous to go out to battle now as I was then. Now give me this hill country that the LORD promised me that day. You yourself heard then that the Anakites were there and their cities were large and fortified, but, the LORD 나) _____ me, I will drive them out just as he said."

* vigorous 원기 왕성한, 정력적인 / fortify 요새화 하다, 강화하다

가. 1) as   2) so   3) such   4) when
힌트) 원급에 의한 동등 비교

나. 1) helped   2) helps   3) helping   4) help
힌트) 조건을 나타내는 독립분사구문; = if the Lord helps me

이제 보소서. 여호와께서 이 말씀을 모세에게 이르신 때로부터 이스라엘이 광야에 행한 이 사십오 년 동안을 여호와께서 말씀하신 대로 나를 생존케 하셨나이다. 오늘날 내가 팔십오 세로되 모세가 나를 보내던 날과 같이 오늘날 오히려 강건하니 나의 힘이 그 때나 이제나 일반이라 싸움에나 출입에 감당할 수 있사온즉 그 날에 여호와께서 말씀하신 이 산지를 내게 주소서 당신도 그 날에 들으셨거니와 그 곳에는 아낙 사람이 있고 그 성읍들은 크고 견고할지라도 여호와께서 혹시 나와 함께 하시면 내가 필경 여호와의 말씀하신 대로 그들을 쫓아내리이다. 가) 1, 나) 3

수 20:1~6

Then the LORD said to Joshua: "Tell the Israelites to designate the cities of refuge, as I instructed you through Moses, so that anyone who 가) _____ a person accidentally and unintentionally may flee there and find protection from the avenger of blood. "When he flees to one of these cities, he is to stand in the entrance of the city gate and state his case before the elders of that city. Then they are to admit him into their city and give him a place to live with them. If the avenger of blood pursues him, they 나) _____ not surrender the one accused, because he killed his neighbor unintentionally and without malice aforethought. He is to stay in that city until he has stood trial before the assembly and until the death of the high priest who is serving at that time. Then he may go back to his own home in the town from which he fled."

* malice 악의, 원한 / aforethought 사전에 생각한, 계획적인 / malice aforethought 살의

가. 1) loves   2) kills   3) deceives   4) beats
힌트) 문맥 관계

나. 1) must   2) may   3) can   4) need
힌트) 금지

여호와께서 여호수아에게 일러 가라사대 이스라엘 자손에게 고하여 이르라. 내가 모세로 너희에게 말한 도피성을 택정하여 부지중 오살한 자를 그리로 도망하게 하라. 이는 너희 중 피의 보수자를 피할 곳이니라. 그 성읍들의 하나에 도피하는 자는 그 성읍에 들어가는 문 어귀에 서서 그 성읍 장로들의 귀에 자기의 사고를 고할 것이요 그들은 그를 받아 성읍에 들여 한 곳을 주어 자기들 중에 거하게 하고 피의 보수자가 그 뒤를 따라온다 할지라도 그들은 그 살인자를 그의 손에 내어 주지 말지니 이는 본래 미워함이 없이 부지중에 그 이웃을 죽였음이라. 그 살인자가 회중의 앞에 서서 재판을 받기까지나 당시 대제사장의 죽기까지 그 성읍에 거하다가 그 후에 그 살인자가 본 성읍 곧 자기가 도망하여 나온 그 성읍의 자기 집으로 돌아갈지니라. 가) 2, 나) 1

수 21:43~45

So the LORD gave Israel all the land he had sworn to give their forefathers, and they took possession of it and settled there. The LORD gave them rest on every side, just as he had sworn to their forefathers. Not one of their enemies withstood them; the LORD handed all their enemies over to them. Not one of all the LORD'S good promises to the house of Israel _____ ; every one was fulfilled.

* swear – swore – sworn 맹세하다 / withstand 저항하다, 견디어내다 / fulfill 완수하다, 이행하다

1) rose   2) came   3) failed   4) succeeded
힌트) 1형식 문장의 자동사

여호와께서 이스라엘의 열조에게 맹세하사 주마 하신 온 땅을 이와 같이 이스라엘에게 다 주셨으므로 그들이 그것을 얻어 거기 거하였으며 여호와께서 그들의 사방에 안식을 주셨으되 그 열조에게 맹세하신 대로 하셨으므로 그 모든 대적이 그들을 당한 자가 하나도 없었으니 이는 여호와께서 그들의 모든 대적을 그들의 손에 붙이셨음이라. 여호와께서 이스라엘 족속에게 말씀하신 선한 일이 하나도 남음이 없이 다 응하였더라. 3

5과

수 24:19~20

Joshua said to the people, "You are not able to serve the LORD. He is a holy God; he is a jealous God. He will not forgive your rebellion and your sins. If you forsake the LORD and serve foreign gods, he will turn and bring disaster on you and _____ an end of you, after he has been good to you."

1) make   2) take   3) have   4) leave

힌트) ~을 끝내다 (= put an end to)

여호수아가 백성에게 이르되 너희가 여호와를 능히 섬기지 못할 것은 그는 거룩하신 하나님이시요 질투하는 하나님이시니 너희 허물과 죄를 사하지 아니하실 것임이라. 만일 너희가 여호와를 버리고 이방 신들을 섬기면 너희에게 복을 내리신 후에라도 돌이켜 너희에게 화를 내리시고 너희를 멸하시리라. 1

삿 6:12~16

When the angel of the LORD appeared to Gideon, he said, "The LORD is with you, mighty warrior." "But sir," Gideon replied, "if the LORD is with us, 가) _____ has all this happened to us? Where are all his wonders that our fathers told us about when they said, 'Did not the LORD bring us up out of Egypt?' But now the LORD has abandoned us and put us into the hand of Midian." The LORD turned to him and said, "Go in the strength you have and save Israel out of Midian's hand. Am I not sending you?" "But Lord," Gideon asked, "how can I save Israel? My clan is the weakest in Manasseh, and I am the 나) _____ in my family." The LORD answered, "I will be with you, and you will strike down all the Midianites together."

* abandon 내버리다, 그만두다 / clan 일족, 씨족 (tribe)

가. 1) when   2) what   3) that   4) why
힌트) 이유를 나타내는 의문부사

나. 1) little   2) least   3) less   4) young
힌트) 가장 작은 자

여호와의 사자가 기드온에게 나타나 이르되 큰 용사여 여호와께서 너와 함께 계시도다. 기드온이 그에게 대답하되 나의 주여 여호와께서 우리와 함께 계시면 어찌하여 이 모든 일이 우리에게 미쳤나이까. 또 우리 열조가 일찍 우리에게 이르기를 여호와께서 우리를 애굽에서 나오게 하신 것이 아니냐 한 그 모든 이적이 어디 있나이까. 이제 여호께서 우리를 버리사 미디안의 손에 붙이셨나이다. 여호와께서 그를 돌아보아 가라사대 너는 이네 힘을 의지하고 가서 이스라엘을 미디안의 손에서 구원하라. 내가 너를 보낸 것이 아니냐. 기드온이 그에게 대답하되 주여 내가 무엇으로 이스라엘을 구원하리이까. 보소서 나의 집은 므낫세 중에 극히 약하고 나는 내 아비 집에서 제일 작은 자니이다. 여호와께서 그에게 이르시되 내가 반드시 너와 함께 하리니 네가 미디안 사람 치기를 한 사람을 치듯 하리라. 가) 4, 나) 2

삿 11:30~31

And Jephthah made a vow to the LORD: "If you give the Ammonites into my hands, whatever comes out of the door of my house to meet me when I return in triumph from the Ammonites will be the LORD'S, and I will sacrifice _____ as a burnt offering."

1) it   2) them   3) her   4) myself

힌트) whatever comes ~ 를 받는 대명사

그가 여호와께 서원하여 가로되 주께서 과연 암몬 자손을 내 손에 붙이시면 내가 암몬 자손에게서 평안히 돌아올 때에 누구든지 내 집 문에서 나와서 나를 영접하는 그는 여호와께 돌릴 것이니 내가 그를 번제로 드리겠나이다 하니라. 1

삿 13:3~5

The angel of the LORD appeared to her and said, "You are sterile and childless, but you are going to 가) _____ and have a son. Now see to it that you drink no wine or other fermented drink and that you do not eat anything 나) _____ , because you will conceive and give birth to a son. No razor may be used on his head, because the boy is to be a Nazirite, set apart to God from birth, and he will begin the deliverance of Israel from the hands of the Philistines."

* sterile 불임의, 불모의 / ferment 발효시키다 / conceive (아 이를) 배다, 마음에 품다 / razor 면도칼 / deliverance 구조, 구출

가. 1) receive   2) deceive   3) conceive   4) board
힌트) (아이를) 배다

나. 1) uncleanly   2) unclean   3) uncleanness   4) cleanly
힌트) ~thing(부정대명사)를 수식하는 형용사는 그 뒤에 온다.

여호와의 사자가 그 여인에게 나타나시고 그에게 이르시되 보라 네가 본래 잉태하지 못하므로 생산치 못하였으나 이제 잉태하여 아들을 낳으리니 그러므로 너는 삼가서 포도주와 독주를 마시지 말지며 무릇 부정한 것을 먹지 말지니라. 보라 네가 잉태하여 아들을 낳으리니 그 머리에 삭도를 대지 말라, 이 아이는 태에서 나옴으로부터 하나님께 바치운 나실인이 됨이라. 그가 블레셋 사람의 손에서 이스라엘을 구원하기 시작하리라. 가) 3, 나) 2

룻 3:1~5

One day Naomi her mother-in-law said to her, "My daughter, should I not try to find a home for you, where you will be well provided for? Is not Boaz, with whose servant girls you have been, a kinsman of ours? Tonight he will be winnowing barley on the threshing floor. Wash and perfume yourself, and 가) _____ your best clothes. Then go down to the threshing floor, but don't let him know you are there until he 나) _____ eating and drinking. When he lies down, note the place where he is lying. Then go and uncover his feet and lie down. He will tell you what to do." "I will do whatever you say," Ruth answered.

* kinsman 동족의 사람 / winnow 키질하다, (벼, 낟알 등을) 까부르다 / barley 보리 / thresh 타작하다, 도리깨로 치다 / uncover 뚜껑(덮개)을 벗기다, 폭로하다

가. 1) you put   2) you put on   3) put   4) put on
힌트) 구문의 일치

나. 1) finished   2) have finished   3) has finished   4) shall have finished
힌트) 부사절에서 현재완료는 미래완료의 代用으로 완료의 뜻을 나타낸다.

룻의 시모 나오미가 그에게 이르되 내 딸아 내가 너를 위하여 안식할 곳을 구하여 너로 복되게 하여야 하지 않겠느냐. 네가 함께 하던 시녀들을 둔 보아스는 우리의 친족이 아니냐. 그가 오늘 밤에 타작 마당에서 보리를 까불리라. 그런즉 너는 목욕하고 기름을 바르고 의복을 입고 타작 마당에 내려가서 그 사람이 먹고 마시기를 다하기까지는 그에게 보이지 말고 그가 누울 때에 너는 그 눕는 곳을 알았다가 들어가서 그 발치 이불을 들고 거기 누우라. 그가 너의 할 일을 네게 고하리라. 룻이 시모에게 이르되 어머니의 말씀대로 내가 다 행하리이다 하니라. 가) 4, 나) 3

삼상 1:10~11

In bitterness of soul Hannah wept much and prayed to the LORD. And she made a vow, saying, "O LORD Almighty, if you will only look upon your servant's misery and remember me, and not forget your servant but give _____ a son, then I will give him to the LORD for all the days of his life, and no razor will ever be used on his head."

* bitterness 씀, 쓰라림, 비통

1) it   2) her   3) him   4) you
힌트) 앞에 나오는 she를 받는 대명사

한나가 마음이 괴로와서 여호와께 기도하고 통곡하며 서원하여 가로되 만군의 여호와여 만일 주의 여종의 고통을 돌아보시고 나를 생각하시고 주의 여종을 잊지 아니하사 아들을 주시면 내가 그의 평생에 그를 여호와께 드리고 삭도를 그 머리에 대지 아니하겠나이다. 2

삼상 15:22~23

But Samuel replied: "Does the LORD delight in burnt offerings and sacrifices as much as in obeying the voice of the LORD? To obey is better than sacrifice, and to heed is better than the fat of rams. For rebellion is _____ the sin of divination, and arrogance like the evil of idolatry. Because you have rejected the word of the LORD, he has rejected you as king."

* divination 점, 점침 / arrogance 거만, 오만 / idolatry 우상숭배

1) alike   2) like   3) likely   4) liking
힌트) 목적어를 갖는 형용사임 (전치사라고도 할 수 있음); ~와 같은

사무엘이 가로되 여호와께서 번제와 다른 제사를 그 목소리 순종하는 것을 좋아하심같이 좋아하시겠나이까. 순종이 제사보다 낫고 듣는 것이 숫양의 기름보다 나으니 이는 거역하는 것은 사술의 죄와 같고 완고한 것은 사신 우상에게 절하는 죄와 같음이라. 왕이 여호와의 말씀을 버렸으므로 여호와께서도 왕을 버려 왕이 되지 못하게 하셨나이다. 2

삼상 16:7

But the LORD said to Samuel, "Do not consider his appearance or his height, for I have rejected him. The LORD does not look at the things man looks at. Man looks at the outward appearance, _____ the LORD looks at the heart."

밑줄에 들어갈 알맞은 말은?
1) but   2) and   3) so   4) as
힌트) 반대를 나타내는 접속사

여호와께서 사무엘에게 이르시되 그 용모와 신장을 보지 말라. 내가 이미 그를 버렸노라. 나의 보는 것은 사람과 같지 아니하니 사람은 외모를 보거니와 나 여호와는 중심을 보느니라. 1

삼상 17:45

David said to the Philistine, "You come against me with sword and spear and javelin, but I come against you in the name of the LORD Almighty, the God of the armies of Israel, _____ you have defied.

* javelin 창, 투창 / defy 무시하다, 얕보다

밑줄에 들어갈 알맞은 말은?
1) which   2) whose   3) whom   4) who
힌트) 목적격 관계대명사

다윗이 블레셋 사람에게 이르되 너는 칼과 창과 단창으로 내게 오거니와 나는 만군의 여호와의 이름 곧 네가 모욕하는 이스라엘 군대의 하나님의 이름으로 네게 가노라. 3

6과

삼상 17:47

All those gathered here will know that _____ is not by sword or spear that the LORD saves; for the battle is the LORD'S, and he will give all of you into our hands.

밑줄에 들어갈 알맞은 말은?
1) one   2) he   3) she   4) it
힌트) that ~을 받는 가주어

또 여호와의 구원하심이 칼과 창에 있지 아니함을 이 무리로 알게 하리라. 전쟁은 여호와께 속한 것인즉 그가 너희를 우리 손에 붙이시리라. 4

삼하 7:8~16

"Now then, tell my servant David, 'This is what the LORD Almighty says: I took you from the pasture and from following the flock to be ruler over my people Israel. I have been with you 가) _____ you have gone, and I have cut off all your enemies from before you. Now I will make your name great, like the names of the greatest men of the earth. And I will provide a place for my people Israel and will plant them so that they can have a home of their own and no longer be disturbed. Wicked people will not oppress them anymore, as they did at the beginning and have done ever since the time I appointed leaders over my people Israel. I will also give you rest from all your enemies."The LORD declares to you that the LORD himself will establish a house for you: When your days are over and you rest with your fathers, I will 나) _____ up your offspring to succeed you, who will come from your own body, and I will establish his kingdom. He is the one who will build a house for my Name, and I will establish the throne of his kingdom forever. I will be his father, and he will be my son. When he does wrong, I will punish him with the rod of men, with floggings inflicted by men. But my love will never be taken away from him, as I took it away from Saul, whom I removed from before you. Your house and your kingdom will 다) _____ forever before me; your throne will be established forever.'"

* pasture 목장 / rod 막대기, 장대 / flog 채찍질하다, 마구 쳐대다 / inflict (구타, 상처 등을) 가하다(입히다)

가. 밑줄 가)에 들어갈 알맞은 말은?
1) whomever   2) whichever   3) wherever   4) whatever
힌트) 부사적 용법의 복합관계대명사

나. 밑줄 나)에 들어갈 알맞은 말은?
1) raise   2) rise   3) go   4) increase
힌트) 타동사

다. 밑줄 다)에 들어갈 알맞은 말은?
1) fly   2) satisfy   3) endure   4) defer
힌트) 1형식 문장의 자동사

그러므로 이제 내 종 다윗에게 이처럼 말하라. 만군의 여호와께서 이처럼 말씀하시기를 내가 너를 목장 곧 양을 따르는 데서 취하여 내 백성 이스라엘의 주권자를 삼고 네가 어디를 가든지 내가 너와 함께 있어 네 모든 대적을 네 앞에서 멸하였은즉 세상에서 존귀한 자의 이름같이 네 이름을 존귀케 만들어 주리라. 내가 또 내 백성 이스라엘을 위하여 한 곳을 정하여 저희를 심고 저희로 자기 곳에 거하여 다시 옮기지 않게 하며 악한 유로 전과 같이 저희를 해하지 못하게 하여 전에 내가 사사를 명하여 내 백성 이스라엘을 다스리던 때와 같지 않게 하고 너를 모든 대적에게서 벗어나 평안케 하리라 여호와가 또 네게 이르노니 여호와가 너를 위하여 집을 이루고 네 수한이 차서 네 조상들과 함께 잘 때에 내가 네 몸에서 날 자식을 네 뒤에 세워 그 나라를 견고케 하리라. 저는 내 이름을 위하여 집을 건축할 것이요 나는 그 나라 위를 영원히 견고케 하리라. 나는 그 아비가 되고 그는 내 아들이 되리니 저가 만일 죄를 범하면 내가 사람 막대기와 인생 채찍으로 징계하려니와 내가 네 앞에서 폐한 사울에게서 내 은총을 빼앗은 것같이 그에게서는 빼앗지 아니하리라. 네 집과 네 나라가 네 앞에서 영원히 보전되고 네 위가 영원히 견고하리라 하셨다 하라. 가) 3, 나) 1, 다) 3

삼하 12:1~6

The LORD sent Nathan to David. When he came to him, he said, "There were two men in a certain town, one rich and _____ poor. The rich man had a very large number of sheep and cattle, but the poor man had nothing except one little ① ewe lamb he had bought. He raised it, and it grew up with him and his children. ② It shared his food, drank from his cup and even slept in his arms. ③ It was like a daughter to him. "Now a traveler came to the rich man, but the rich man refrained from taking one of his own ④ sheep or cattle to prepare a meal for the traveler who had come to him. Instead, he took the ewe lamb that belonged to the poor man and prepared it for the one who had come to him." David burned with anger against the man and said to Nathan, "As surely as the LORD lives, the man who did this deserves to die! He must pay for that lamb four times over, because he did such a thing and had no pity."

* ewe 암양 / refrain 삼가다, 그만두다 / deserve ~할 만하다 / pity 동정, 연민

가. 밑줄에 들어갈 알맞은 말은?
1) another   2) the other   3) other   4) the another
힌트) 두 개의 비교; one ~, the other ~

나. ① ~ ④ 중에서 가리키는 것이 다른 것은?
힌트) 부자의 것

다. David의 기분은 어떤가?
1) 즐겁다   2) 무관심하다   3) 화났다   4) 슬프다
힌트) David burned with anger

여호와께서 나단을 다윗에게 보내시니 와서 저에게 이르되 한 성에 두 사람이 있는데 하나는 부하고 하나는 가

난하니 그 부한 자는 양과 소가 심히 많으나 가난한 자는 아무것도 없고 자기가 사서 기르는 작은 암양 새끼 하나뿐이라. 그 암양 새끼는 저와 저의 자식과 함께 있어 자라며 저의 먹는 것을 먹으며 저의 잔에서 마시며 저의 품에 누우므로 저에게는 딸처럼 되었거늘 어떤 행인이 그 부자에게 오매 부자가 자기의 양과 소를 아껴 자기에게 온 행인을 위하여 잡지 아니하고 가난한 사람의 양 새끼를 빼앗아다가 자기에게 온 사람을 위하여 잡았나이다. 다윗이 그 사람을 크게 노하여 나단에게 이르되 여호와의 사심을 가리켜 맹세하노니 이 일을 행한 사람은 마땅히 죽을 자라. 저가 불쌍히 여기지 않고 이 일을 행하였으니 그 양 새끼를 사 배나 갚아 주어야 하리라. 가) 2, 나) 4, 다) 3

왕상 2:1~3

When the time drew near for David to die, he gave a charge to Solomon his son. "I am about to go the way of all the earth," he said. "So be strong, show yourself a man, and observe what the LORD your God requires: Walk in his ways, and keep his decrees and commands, his laws and requirements, as written in the Law of Moses, so that you may prosper in all you do and wherever you go,

* charge 명령, 책임, 의무 / decree 명령, 법령 / prosper 번영하다

위 문장의 성격은?
1) 연설   2) 유언   3) 독백   4) 교훈
힌트) 첫문장

다윗이 죽을 날이 임박하매 그 아들 솔로몬에게 명하여 가로되 내가 이제 세상 모든 사람의 가는 길로 가게 되었노니 너는 힘써 대장부가 되고 네 하나님 여호와의 명을 지켜 그 길로 행하여 그 법률과 계명과 율례와 증거를 모세의 율법에 기록된 대로 지키라. 그리하면 네가 무릇 무엇을 하든지 어디로 가든지 형통할지라. 2

왕상 3:11~15

So God said to him, "Since you have asked for this and not for long life or wealth for yourself, nor have asked for the death of your enemies but for discernment in administering justice, I will do ①what you have asked. I will give you a wise and discerning heart, so ②that there will never have been anyone like you, nor will ③there ever be. Moreover, I will give you ④that you have not asked for--both riches and honor--so that in your lifetime you will have no equal among kings. And if you walk in my ways and obey my statutes and commands as David your father did, I will give you a long life." Then Solomon _____ and he realized it had been a dream. He returned to Jerusalem, stood before the ark of the Lord's covenant and sacrificed burnt offerings and fellowship offerings. Then he gave a feast for all his court.

* discernment 총명, 식별 / administer 관리하다, 경영하다 / justice 정의, 재판 / statute 법령, 규칙 / ark 방주 / fellowship 친교, 공동 / feast 잔치 (banquet)

가. ① ~ ④ 중에서 잘못 쓰인 단어는?
힌트) 관계대명사 what을 넣어야 할 자리

나. 밑줄에 들어갈 알맞은 말은?
1) slept   2) succeeded   3) fell   4) awoke
힌트) he realized it had been a dream

이에 하나님이 저에게 이르시되 네가 이것을 구하도다. 자기를 위하여 수도 구하지 아니하며 부도 구하지 아니하며 자기의 원수의 생명 멸하기도 구하지 아니하고 오직 송사를 듣고 분별하는 지혜를 구하였은즉 내가 네 말대로 하여 네게 지혜롭고 총명한 마음을 주노니 너의 전에도 너와 같은 자가 없었거니와 너의 후에도 너와 같은 자가 일어남이 없으리라. 내가 또 너의 구하지 아니한 부와 영광도 네게 주노니 네 평생에 열왕 중에 너와 같은 자가 없을 것이라. 네가 만일 네 아비 다윗의 행함같이 내 길로 행하며 내 법도와 명령을 지키면 내가 또 네 날을 길게 하리라. 솔로몬이 깨어 보니 꿈이더라. 이에 예루살렘에 이르러 여호와의 언약궤 앞에 서서 번제와 수은제를 드리고 모든 신복을 위하여 잔치하였더라. 가) 4, 나) 4

7과

왕상 3:25~28

He then gave an order: "Cut the living child in two and give half to one and half to the other." The woman whose son was alive was filled with compassion for her son and said to the king, "Please, my lord, give her the living baby! Don't kill him!" But the other said, "Neither I _____ you shall have him. Cut him in two!" Then the king gave his ruling: "Give the living baby to the first woman. Do not kill him; she is his mother." When all Israel heard the verdict the king had given, they held the king in awe, because they saw that he had wisdom from God to administer justice.

* compassion 동정(sympathy), 연민 / verdict 판정, 표결

가. 글의 제목으로 알맞은 것은?
1) 분열   2) 가족   3) 지혜   4) 증오
힌트) 솔로몬의 판결

나. 밑줄에 들어갈 알맞은 말은?
1) nor   2) or   3) both   4) and
힌트) ~도 아니고

왕이 이르되 산 아들을 둘에 나눠 반은 이에게 주고 반은 저에게 주라. 그 산 아들의 어미 되는 계집이 그 아들을 위하여 마음이 불붙는 것 같아서 왕께 아뢰어 가로되 청컨대 내 주여 산 아들을 저에게 주시고 아무쪼록 죽이지 마옵소서 하되 한 계집은 말하기를 내 것도 되게 말고 네 것도 되게 말고 나누게 하라 하는지라. 왕이 대답하여 가로되 산 아들을 저 계집에게 주고 결코 죽이지 말라. 저가 그 어미니라 하매 온 이스라엘이 왕의 심리하여 판결함을 듣고 왕을 두려워하였으니 이는 하나님의 지혜가 저의 속에 있어 판결함을 봄이더라.
가) 3, 나) 1

왕상 4:29~30

God gave Solomon wisdom and very great insight, and a breadth of understanding as measureless as the sand on the seashore. Solomon's wisdom was greater than the wisdom of all the men of _____ , and greater than all the wisdom of Egypt.

* insight 통찰력

밑줄에 들어갈 알맞은 말은?
1) a East   2) the east   3) the East   4) East
힌트) 유일한 것

하나님이 솔로몬에게 지혜와 총명을 심히 많이 주시고 또 넓은 마음을 주시되 바닷가의 모래같이 하시니 솔로몬의 지혜가 동양 모든 사람의 지혜와 애굽의 모든 지혜보다 뛰어난지라. 3

왕상 17:12~16

"As surely as the LORD your God lives," she replied, "I don't have any bread--only a handful of flour in a jar and a little oil in a jug. I am gathering _____ sticks to take home and make a meal for myself and my son, that we may eat it and die." Elijah said to her, "Don't be afraid. Go home and do as you have said. ① But first make a small cake of bread for me from what you have and bring it to me, and then make something for yourself and your son. ② For this is what the LORD, the God of Israel, says: 'The jar of flour will not be used up and the jug of oil will not run dry until the day the LORD gives rain on the land.'" ③ So there was food every day for Elijah and for the woman and her family. For the jar of flour was not used up and the jug of oil did not run dry, in keeping with the word of the LORD spoken by Elijah. ④

* jar 병, 단지 / jug (주둥이가 넓고 손잡이가 달린) 물주전자, 큰 맥주잔 / flour 밀가루

가. 밑줄에 들어갈 알맞은 말은?
1) few   2) a few   3) little   4) a little
힌트) 가산명사

나. 문장 She went away and did as Elijah had told her가 들어갈 자리는?

저가 가로되 당신의 하나님 여호와의 사심을 가리켜 맹세하노니 나는 떡이 없고 다만 통에 가루 한 움큼과 병에 기름 조금 뿐이라. 내가 나뭇가지 둣을 주워다가 나와 내 아들을 위하여 음식을 만들어 먹고 그 후에는 죽으리라. 엘리야가 저에게 이르되 두려워 말고 가서 네 말대로 하려니와 먼저 그것으로 나를 위하여 작은 떡 하나를 만들어 내게로 가져오고 그 후에 너와 네 아들을 위하여 만들라. 이스라엘 하나님 여호와의 말씀이 나 여호와가 비를 지면에 내리는 날까지 그 통의 가루는 디치지 아니하고 그 병의 기름은 없어지지 아니하리라 하셨느니라. 저가 가서 엘리야의 말대로 하였더니 저와 엘리야와 식구가 여러 날 먹었으나 여호와께서 엘리야로 하신 말씀같이 통의 가루가 다하지 아니하고 병의 기름이 없어지지 아니하니라. 가) 2, 나) 3

왕하 2:8~11

Elijah took his cloak, rolled it up and struck the water with it. The water divided to the right and to the left, and the two of them crossed over on dry ground. When they had crossed, Elijah said to Elisha, "Tell me, what can I do for you before I am taken from you?" "Let me inherit a double portion of your spirit," Elisha replied. "You have asked a difficult thing," Elijah said, "yet if you see me when I am taken from you, it will be yours--otherwise not." As they were walking along and talking together, suddenly a chariot of fire and horses of fire appeared and separated the two of them, and _____ went up to heaven in a whirlwind.

* cloak (소매가 없는) 외투, 망토 / chariot 전차 / whirlwind 회오리바람, 선풍

가. 이 글에서 나타나는 자연현상의 특징은?
1) 평상시와 같다   2) 조금 특이하다   3) 예견할 수 있는 것이다   4) 초자연적이다
힌트) 시냇물이 갈라지고, 사람이 하늘로 올라간다

나. 밑줄에 들어갈 알맞은 말은?
1) Elisha   2) Elijah   3) he   4) they

엘리야가 겉옷을 취하여 말아 물을 치매 물이 이리저리 갈라지고 두 사람이 육지 위로 건너더라. 건너매 엘리야가 엘리사에게 이르되 나를 네게서 취하시기 전에 내가 네게 어떻게 할 것을 구하라. 엘리사가 가로되 당신의 영감이 갑절이나 내게 있기를 구하나이다. 가로되 네가 어려운 일을 구하는도다. 그러나 나를 네게서 취하시는 것을 네가 보면 그 일이 네게 이루려니와 그렇지 않으면 이루지 아니하리라 하고 두 사람이 행하며 말하더니 홀연히 불수레와 불말들이 두 사람을 격하고 엘리야가 회리바람을 타고 승천하더라. 가), 나) 2

왕하 4:1~7

① Elisha replied to her, "How can I help you? Tell me, what do you have in your house?" "Your servant has nothing there at all," she said, "except a little oil." Elisha said, "Go around and ask all your neighbors for empty jars. Don't ask for just a few. Then go inside and shut the door behind you and your sons. Pour oil into all the jars, and as each is filled, put it to one side."

② The wife of a man from the company of the prophets cried out to Elisha, "Your servant my husband is dead, and you know that he revered the LORD. But now his creditor is coming to take my two boys as his slaves."

③ She left him and afterward shut the door behind her and her sons. They brought the jars to her and she kept pouring. When all the jars were full, she said to her son, "Bring me another one." But he replied, "There is not a jar left." Then the oil stopped _____ . She went and told the man of God, and he said, "Go, sell the oil and pay your debts. You and your sons can live on what is left."

가. 윗 글의 바른 순서는?
1) ①②③   2) ②①③   3) ③①②   4) ②③①

나. 밑줄에 들어갈 알맞은 말은?
1) to flow   2) to flowing   3) flow   4) flowing
힌트) stop은 동명사를 목적어로 취한다.

선지자의 생도의 아내 중에 한 여인이 엘리사에게 부르짖어 가로되 당신의 종 나의 남편이 이미 죽었는데 당신의 종이 여호와를 경외한 줄은 당신이 아시는 바니이다. 이제 채주가 이르러 나의 두 아이를 취하여 그 종을 삼고자 하나이다. 엘리사가 저에게 이르되 내가 너를 위하여 어떻게 하랴. 네 집에 무엇이 있는지 내게 고하라. 저가 가로되 계집종의 집에 한 병 기름 외에는 아무것도 없나이다. 가로되 너는 밖에 나가서 모든 이웃에게 그릇을 빌라. 빈 그릇을 빌되 조금 빌지 말고 너는 네 두 아들과 함께 들어가서 문을 닫고 그 모든 그릇에 기름을 부어서 차는 대로 옮겨 놓으라. 여인이 물러가서 그 두 아들과 함께 문을 닫은 후에 저희는 그릇을 그에게로 가져오고 그는 부었더니 그릇에 다 찬지라. 여인이 아들에게 이르되 또 그릇을 내게로 가져오라. 아들이 가로되 다른 그릇이 없나이다 하니 기름이 곧 그쳤더라. 그 여인이 하나님의 사람에게 나아가서 고한대 저가 가로되 너는 가서 기름을 팔아 빚을 갚고 남은 것으로 너와 네 두 아들이 생활하라 하였더라. 가) 2, 나) 4

왕하 5:10~14

①Elisha sent a ②messenger to say to him, "Go, wash yourself seven times in the Jordan, and your flesh will be restored and you will be cleansed." But Naaman went away 가)_____ and said, "I thought that he would surely come out to me and stand and call on the name of the LORD his God, wave his hand over the spot and cure me of my leprosy. Are not Abana and Pharpar, the rivers of Damascus, better than any of the waters of Israel? Couldn't I wash in them and be cleansed?" So he turned and went off in a rage. ③Naaman's servants went to him and said, "My father, if the prophet had told you to do some great thing, would you not have done it? How much more, then, when he tells you, 'Wash and be cleansed'!" So he went down and dipped himself in the Jordan seven times, as the man of God had told him, and his flesh was restored and became clean like 나)____ of ④a young boy.

* cleanse 씻다, 청결하게 하다 (clean) / leprosy 나병, 문둥병 / rage 분노 (fury)

가. 밑줄 가)에 들어갈 알맞은 말은?
1) angrily   2) angry   3) anger   4) angriness
힌트) 2형식 문장, 주어의 보어

나. ① ~ ④ 중에서 Naaman의 병 치료에 도움이 되지 않는 사람은?

다. 밑줄 나)에 들어갈 알맞은 말은?
1) that   2) those   3) it   4) one
힌트) 앞에 나온 말을 of + 명사의 형태로 받을 때 쓰는 대명사

엘리사가 사자를 저에게 보내어 가로되 너는 가서 요단 강에 몸을 일곱 번 씻으라. 네 살이 여전하여 깨끗하리라. 나아만이 노하여 물러가며 가로되 내 생각에는 저가 내게로 나아와 서서 그 하나님 여호와의 이름을 부르고 당처 위에 손을 흔들어 문둥병을 고칠까 하였도다. 다메섹 강 아바나와 바르발은 이스라엘 모든 강물보다 낫지 아니하냐. 내가 거기서 몸을 씻으면 깨끗하게 되지 아니하랴 하고 몸을 돌이켜 분한 모양으로 떠나니 그 종들이 나아와서 말하여 가로되 내 아버지여 선지자가 당신을 명하여 큰 일을 행하라 하였더면 행치 아니하였으리이까. 하물며 당신에게 이르기를 씻어 깨끗하게 하라 함이리이까. 나아만이 이에 내려가서 하나님의 사람의 말씀대로 요단 강에 일곱 번 몸을 잠그니 그 살이 여전하여 어린아이의 살 같아서 깨끗하게 되었더라. 가) 2, 나) 4, 다) 1

8과

왕하 6:5~7

As one of them was cutting down a tree, the iron axhead fell into the water. "Oh, my lord," he cried out, "it was borrowed!" The man of God asked, "Where did it fall?" When he showed him the place, Elisha cut a stick and threw it there, and made the iron _____ . "Lift it out," he said. Then the man reached out his hand and took it.

밑줄에 들어갈 알맞은 말은?
1) sink   2) to sink   3) float   4) to float
힌트) 사역동사

한 사람이 나무를 벨 때에 도끼가 자루에서 빠져 물에 떨어진지라. 이에 외쳐 가로되 아아, 내 주여 이는 빌어 온 것이니이다. 하나님의 사람이 가로되 어디 빠졌느냐 하매 그 곳을 보이는지라. 엘리사가 나뭇가지를 베어 물에 던져서 도끼로 떠오르게 하고 가로되 너는 취하라. 그 사람이 손을 내밀어 취하니라. 3

왕하 20:8~11

Hezekiah had asked Isaiah, "What will be the sign that the LORD will heal me and that I will go up to the temple of the LORD on the third day from now?" Isaiah answered, "This is the LORD'S sign to you that the LORD will do what he has promised: Shall the shadow go forward ten steps, or shall it go back ten steps?" "It is a simple matter for the shadow to go forward ten steps," said Hezekiah. "Rather, have it go back ten steps." Then the prophet Isaiah called upon the LORD, and the LORD made the shadow go back the ten steps it had gone down on the stairway of Ahaz.

Isaiah의 말이 사실이라면 약속은 지켜질 것인가?
1) 지켜질 것이다   2) 지켜지지 않는다   3) 알 수 없다   4) Hezekiah의 결정에 달렸다.
힌트) Lord's sign이 이루어 짐

히스기야가 이사야에게 이르되 여호와께서 나를 낫게 하시고 삼일 만에 여호와의 전에 올라가게 하실 무슨 징조가 있나이까. 이사야가 가로되 여호와의 하신 말씀을 응하게 하실 일에 대하여 여호와께로서 왕에게 한 징조가 임하리이다. 해 그림자가 십 도를 나아갈 것이니이까 혹 십 도를 물러갈 것이니이까. 히스기야가 대답하되 그림자가 십 도를 나아가기는 쉬우니 그리할 것이 아니라 십 도가 물러갈 것이니이다. 선지자 이사야가 여호와께 간구하매 아하스의 일영표 위에 나아갔던 해 그림자로 십 도를 물러가게 하셨더라. 1

대하 6:18~21

But will God really dwell on earth with men? The heavens, even the highest heavens, cannot contain you. How much less this temple I have built! Yet give attention to your servant's prayer and his plea for mercy, O LORD my God. Hear the cry and the prayer that your servant is praying in your presence. May your eyes be open toward this temple day and night, this place of which you said you would put your Name there. May you hear the prayer your servant prays toward this place. Hear the supplications of your servant and of your people Israel when they pray toward this place. Hear from heaven, your dwelling place; and when you hear, forgive.

* supplication 탄원, 기도 / dwell 살다(live), 머무르다

이 글은 누구에게 하는 말인가?
1) heaven   2) God   3) king   4) temple

하나님이 참으로 사람과 함께 땅에 거하시리이까. 하늘과 하늘들의 하늘이라도 주를 용납지 못하겠거든 하물며 내가 건축한 이 전이오리이까. 그러나 나의 하나님 여호와여 종의 기도와 간구를 돌아보시며 종이 주의 앞에서 부르짖음과 비는 기도를 들으시옵소서. 주께서 전에 말씀하시기를 내 이름을 거기 두리라 하신 곳 이 전을 향하여 주의 눈이 주야로 보옵시며 종이 이 곳을 향하여 비는 기도를 들으시옵소서. 종과 주의 백성 이스라엘이 이 곳을 향하여 기도할 때에 주는 그 간구함을 들으시되 주의 계신 곳 하늘에서 들으시고 들으시사 사하여 주옵소서. 2

대하 9:5~8

She said to the king, "The report I heard in my own country about your achievements and your wisdom is true. But I did not believe what they said until I came and saw with my own eyes. Indeed, not even half the greatness of your wisdom was told me; you have far exceeded the report I heard. How happy your men must be! How happy your officials, who continually stand before you and hear your wisdom! Praise be to the LORD your God, who has delighted in you and placed you on his throne as king to rule for the LORD your God. _____ the love of your God for Israel and his desire to uphold them forever, he has made you king over them, to maintain justice and righteousness."

가. 밑줄에 들어갈 알맞은 말은?
1) Since   2) That   3) Because   4) Because of
힌트) 접속사 다음에는 문장이 와야 한다

나. 여자의 심경은?
1) 놀랍다   2) 슬프다   3) 기쁘다   4) 두렵다
힌트) 왕의 지혜를 직접 체험하고 느낀 감정

왕께 고하되 내가 내 나라에서 당신의 행위와 당신의 지혜에 대하여 들은 소문이 진실하도다. 내가 그 말들을 믿지 아니하였더니 이제 와서 목도한즉 당신의 지혜가 크다 한 말이 그 절반도 못되니 당신은 내가 들은 소문보다 지나도다. 복되도다 당신의 사람들이여, 복되도다 당신의 이 신복들이여, 항상 당신의 앞에 서서 당신의 지혜를 들음이로다. 당신의 하나님 여호와를 송축할지로다. 하나님이 당신을 기뻐하시고 그 위에 올리사 당신의 하나님 여호와를 위하여 왕이 되게 하셨도다. 당신의 하나님이 이스라엘을 사랑하사 영원히 견고하게 하시려고 당신을 세워 저희 왕을 삼아 공과 의를 행하게 하셨도다. 가) 4, 나) 1

대하 30:7~9

Do not be like your fathers and brothers, who were unfaithful to the LORD, the God of their fathers, so that he made them an object of horror, as you see. Do not be stiff-necked, as your fathers were; submit to the LORD. Come to the sanctuary, which he has consecrated forever. Serve the LORD your God, so that his fierce anger will turn away from you. If you return to the LORD, then your brothers and your children will be shown compassion by their captors and will come back to this land, for the LORD your God is gracious and compassionate. He will not turn his face from you if you return to him.

* sanctuary 성전, 지성소 / compassion 연민, 동정 / captor 체포자, 획득자

윗 글에서 훈계하는 내용과 일치하지 않는 것은?
1) 선조들을 닮아라   2) 목을 곧게 하지 말라   3) 성전으로 오라   4) 하나님을 섬겨라

너희 열조와 너희 형제같이 하지 말라. 저희가 그 열조의 하나님 여호와께 범죄한 고로 여호와께서 멸망에 붙이신 것을 너희가 목도하는 바니라. 그런즉 너희 열조같이 목을 곧게 하지 말고 여호와께 귀순하여 영원히 거룩케 하신 전에 들어가서 너희 하나님 여호와를 섬겨 그 진노가 너희에게서 떠나게 하라. 너희가 만일 여호와께 돌아오면 너희 형제와 너희 자녀가 사로잡은 자에게서 자비를 입어 다시 이 땅으로 돌아오리라. 너희 하나님 여호와는 은혜로우시고 자비하신지라 너희가 그에게로 돌아오면 그 얼굴을 너희에게서 돌이키지 아니하시리라 하였더라 . 1

대하 36:15~21

The LORD, the God of their fathers, sent word to them through his messengers again and again, because he had pity on his people and on his dwelling place. ① But they mocked God's messengers, despised his words and scoffed at his prophets until the wrath of the LORD was aroused against his people and there was no remedy. He brought up against them the king of the Babylonians, who killed their young men with the sword in the sanctuary, and spared neither young man nor young woman, old man or aged. ② He carried to Babylon all the articles from the temple of God, both large and small, and the treasures of the LORD'S temple and the treasures of the king and his officials. ③ They set fire to God's temple and broke down the wall of Jerusalem; they burned all the palaces and destroyed everything of value there. He carried into exile to Babylon the remnant, who escaped from the sword, and they became servants to him and his sons until the kingdom of Persia came to power. ④ The land enjoyed its sabbath rests; all the time of its desolation it rested, until the seventy years were completed in fulfillment of the word of the LORD spoken by Jeremiah.

* wrath 격노, 분노 / arouse 깨우다, 자극하다 / remedy 치료 / exile 추방, 유배, 망명 / remnant 나머지 / sabbath 휴식, 평화 (Sabbath 안식일) / desolation 황폐케 함, 폐허

가. 다음 문장이 들어갈 자리는?
God handed all of them over to Nebuchadnezzar.
힌트) Nebuchadnezzar; 느부갓네살 王

나. 바벨론 왕이 한 일이 아닌 것은?
1) 청년들을 다 죽였다   2) 노인들을 용서하지 않았다
3) 예루살렘 성은 파괴하지 않았다   4) 왕궁의 귀중품을 모두 파괴했다
힌트) They set fire to God's temple and broke down the wall of Jerusalem

다. 70년간 바벨론으로 포로로 끌려갈 것을 예언한 사람은?
1) messengers   2) Nebuchadnezzar   3) Jeremiah   4) the Babylonians
힌트) 하나님의 말씀을 전한 사람

그 열조의 하나님 여호와께서 그 백성과 그 거하시는 곳을 아끼사 부지런히 그 사자들을 그 백성에게 보내어 이르셨으나 그 백성이 하나님의 사자를 비웃고 말씀을 멸시하며 그 선지자를 욕하여 여호와의 진노로 그 백성에게 미쳐서 만회할 수 없게 하였으므로 하나님이 갈대아 왕의 손에 저희를 다 붙이시매 저가 와서 그 성전에서 칼로 청년을 죽이며 청년 남녀와 노인과 백발 노옹을 긍휼히 여기지 아니하였으며 또 하나님의 전의 대소 기명들과 여호와의 전의 보물과 왕과 방백들의 보물을 다 바벨론으로 가져가고 또 하나님의 전을 불사르며 예루살렘 성을 헐며 그 모든 궁실을 불사르며 그 모든 귀한 기명을 훼파하고 무릇 칼에서 벗어난 자를 저가 바벨론으로 사로잡아 가매 무리가 거기서 갈대아 왕과 그 자손의 노예가 되어 바사국이 주재할 때까지 이르니라. 이에 토지가 황무하여 안식년을 누림같이 안식하여 칠십 년을 지내었으니 여호와께서 예레미야의 입으로 하신 말씀이 응하였더라. 가) 2, 나) 3, 다) 3

9과

스 1:3~4

Anyone of his people among you, may his God be with him, and let him go up to Jerusalem in Judah and build the temple of the LORD, the God of Israel, the God who is in Jerusalem. And the people of any place _____ survivors may now be living are to provide him with silver and gold, with goods and livestock, and with freewill offerings for the temple of God in Jerusalem.

* freewill 자발적인 / offering 제물, 헌납, 신청

밑줄에 들어갈 알맞은 말은?
1) what   2) where   3) when   4) which

힌트) 선행사가 place(장소)인 관계 부사

이스라엘의 하나님은 참 신이시라. 너희 중에 무릇 그 백성 된 자는 다 유다 예루살렘으로 올라가서 거기 있는 여호와의 전을 건축하라. 너희 하나님이 함께 하시기를 원하노라. 무릇 그 남아 있는 백성이 어느 곳에 우거하였든지 그 곳 사람들이 마땅히 은과 금과 기타 물건과 짐승으로 도와 주고 그 외에도 예루살렘 하나님의 전을 위하여 예물을 즐거이 드릴지니라 하였더라. 2

스 9:9~15

Though we are slaves, our God has not deserted us in our bondage. He has shown us kindness in the sight of the kings of Persia: He has granted us new life to rebuild the house of our God and repair its ruins, and he has given us a wall of protection in Judah and Jerusalem. "But now, O our God, what can we say after this? For we have disregarded the commands you gave through your servants the prophets when you said: 'The land you are entering to possess is a land polluted by the corruption of its peoples. By their detestable practices they have filled it with their impurity from one end to the other. 가) _____ , do not give your daughters in marriage to their sons or take their daughters for your sons. Do not seek a treaty of friendship with them at any time, that you may be strong and eat the good things of the land and leave it to your children as an everlasting inheritance.' "What has happened to us is a result of our evil deeds and our great guilt, and yet, our God, you have punished us less than our sins have deserved and have given us a remnant like this. Shall we again break your commands and intermarry with the peoples who commit such detestable practices? Would you not be angry enough with us to destroy us, leaving us no remnant or survivor? O LORD, God of Israel, you are 나) _____ ! We are left this day as a remnant. Here we are before you in our guilt, though because of it not one of us can stand in your presence."

* bondage 속박, 농노의 신세 / corruption 타락, 부패 / detestable 혐오할 만한, 몹시 싫은 / impurity 불결, 불순, 음란 / inheritance 상속, 상속 재산 / intermarry (다른 종족 등과) 결혼하다, 근친 결혼하다

가. 밑줄 가)에 들어갈 알맞은 말은?
1) Therefore   2) But   3) As   4) Because

힌트) 바로 앞 문장의 내용이 부정적임

나. 밑줄 나)에 들어갈 알맞은 말은?
1) free   2) sensitive   3) righteous   4) ferocious
힌트) 바로 앞 문장이 용서하시는 하나님을 표현하고 있음

다. 윗 글을 쓴 사람의 심경은?
1) 뉘우침   2) 반항함   3) 기뻐함   4) 슬퍼함
힌트) 자신들의 죄악을 고백하고 있음

우리가 비록 노예가 되었사오나 우리 하나님이 우리를 그 복역하는 중에 버리지 아니하시고 바사 열왕 앞에서 우리로 긍휼히 여김을 입고 소성하여 우리 하나님의 전을 세우게 하시며 그 퇴락한 것을 수리하게 하시며 유다와 예루살렘에서 우리에게 울을 주셨나이다. 우리 하나님이여 이렇게 하신 후에도 우리가 주의 계명을 배반하였사오니 이제 무슨 말씀을 하오리이까. 전에 주께서 주의 종 선지자들로 명하여 이르시되 너희가 가서 얻으려 하는 땅은 더러운 땅이니 이는 이방 백성들이 더럽고 가증한 일을 행하여 이 가에서 저 가까지 그 더러움으로 채웠음이라. 그런즉 너희 여자들을 저희 아들들에게 주지 말고 저희 딸을 너희 아들을 위하여 데려오지 말며 그들을 위하여 평강과 형통을 영영히 구하지 말라. 그리하면 너희가 왕성하여 그 땅의 아름다운 것을 먹으며 그 땅을 자손에게 유전하여 영원한 기업을 삼게 되리라 하셨나이다. 우리의 악한 행실과 큰 죄로 인하여 이 모든 일을 당하였사오나 우리 하나님이 우리 죄악보다 형벌을 경하게 하시고 이만큼 백성을 남겨 주셨사오니 우리가 어찌 다시 주의 계명을 거역하고 이 가증한 일을 행하는 족속들과 연혼하오리이까. 그리하오면 주께서 어찌 진노하사 우리를 멸하시고 남아 피할 자가 없도록 하시지 아니하시리이까. 이스라엘 하나님 여호와 주는 의롭도소이다. 우리가 남아 피한 것이 오늘날과 같사옵거늘 도리어 주께 범죄하였사오니 이로 인하여 주 앞에 한 사람도 감히 서지 못하겠나이다. 가) 1, 나) 3, 다) 1

느 2:3~5

① But I said to the king, "May the king live forever! Why should my face not look sad when the city where my fathers are buried lies in ruins, and its gates have been destroyed by fire?" ② Then I prayed to the God of heaven, and I answered the king, "If it pleases the king and if your servant has found favor in his sight, let him send me to the city in Judah where my fathers are buried so that I can rebuild it." ③

다음 문장이 들어갈 자리는? The king said to me, "What is it you want?"

왕께 대답하되 왕은 만세수를 하옵소서. 나의 열조의 묘실 있는 성읍이 이제까지 황무하고 성문이 소화되었사오니 내가 어찌 얼굴에 수색이 없사오리이까. 왕이 내게 이르시되 그러면 네가 무엇을 원하느냐 하시기로 내가 곧 하늘의 하나님께 묵도하고 왕에게 고하되 왕이 만일 즐겨하시고 종이 왕의 목전에서 은혜를 얻었사오면 나를 유다 땅 나의 열조의 묘실 있는 성읍에 보내어 그 성을 중건하게 하옵소서. 2

에 4:14~17

For if you remain silent at this time, relief and deliverance for the Jews will arise from another place, but you and your father's family will perish. And who knows but that you have come to royal position for such a time as this?" Then Esther sent this reply to Mordecai: "Go, gather together all the Jews who are in Susa, and fast for me. Do not eat or drink for three days, night or day. I and my maids will _____ as you do. When this is done, I will go to the king, even though it is against the law. And if I perish, I perish." So Mordecai went away and carried out all of Esther's instructions.

* relief 구원 / perish 멸망하다, 소멸하다 / maid 소녀, 하녀

가. 밑줄에 들어갈 알맞은 말은?
1) talk   2) fast   3) love   4) eat
힌트) 단식(절식,금식)하다

나. 이 글의 분위기는?
1) 가벼움   2) 즐거움   3) 비장함   4) 슬픔
힌트) 한 민족이 멸망할 위험에 처해 있음; you and your father's family will perish.

이 때에 네가 만일 잠잠하여 말이 없으면 유다인은 다른 데로 말미암아 놓임과 구원을 얻으려니와 너와 네 아비 집은 멸망하리라. 네가 왕후의 위를 얻은 것이 이 때를 위함이 아닌지 누가 아느냐. 에스더가 명하여 모르드개에게 회답하되 당신은 가서 수산에 있는 유다인을 다 모으고 나를 위하여 금식하되 밤낮 삼 일을 먹지도 말고 마시지도 마소서. 나도 나의 시녀로 더불어 이렇게 금식한 후에 규례를 어기고 왕에게 나아가리니 죽으면 죽으리이다. 모르드개가 가서 에스더의 명한 대로 다 행하니라. 가) 2, 나) 3

욥 2:2~3

And the LORD said to Satan, "Where have you come from?" Satan answered the LORD, "From roaming through the earth and going back and forth in it." Then the LORD said to Satan, "Have you considered my servant Job? There is no one on earth like him; he is blameless and upright, a man who fears God and shuns evil. And he still maintains his integrity, _____ you incited me against him to ruin him without any reason."

* roam 거닐다, 배회하다 / shun 피하다, 멀리하다 / integrity 완전, 성실

밑줄에 들어갈 알맞은 말은?
1) so   2) as   3) though   4) for
힌트) 신실한 욥의 믿음

여호와께서 사단에게 이르시되 네가 어디서 왔느냐. 사단이 여호와께 대답하여 가로되 땅에 두루 돌아 여기 저기 다녀왔나이다. 여호와께서 사단에게 이르시되 네가 내 종 욥을 유의하여 보았느냐. 그와 같이 순전하고 정직하여 하나님을 경외하며 악에서 떠난 자가 세상에 없느니라. 네가 나를 격동하여 까닭 없이 그를 치게 하였어도 그가 오히려 자기의 순전을 굳게 지켰느니라. 3

욥 5:17~27

Blessed is the man whom God corrects; so do not despise the discipline of the Almighty. For he wounds, but he also binds up; he injures, but his hands also _____ . From six calamities he will rescue you; in seven no harm will befall you. In famine he will ransom you from death, and in battle from the stroke of the sword. You will be protected from the lash of the tongue, and need not fear when destruction comes. You will laugh at destruction and famine, and need not fear the beasts of the earth. For you will have a covenant with the stones of the field, and the wild animals will be at peace with you. You will know that your tent is secure; you will take stock of your property and find nothing missing. You will know that your children will be many, and your descendants like the grass of the earth. You will come to the grave in full vigor, like sheaves gathered in season. We have examined this, and it is true. So hear it and apply it to yourself.

* despise 경멸하다 / discipline 징계, 훈련 / calamity 재난 / befall ~에게 일어나다 (happen to) / famine 기근, 굶주림 / ransom (몸값을 치르고) 살려내다 / stroke 찌름, 타격(blow) / lash 채찍질, 심한 비난 / sheaf (pl. sheaves) (곡물의) 단, 다발

가. 밑줄에 들어갈 알맞은 말은?
1) lift   2) heal   3) help   4) count
힌트) injure; 상처(손해)를 입히다

나. 하나님께 징계 받는 자의 특징이 아닌 것은?
1) 기근 때에도 죽지 않는다   2) 밭의 돌과 언약을 맺는다
3) 들짐승을 잡아 먹는다   4) 자손이 많아진다
힌트) the wild animals will be at peace with you.

다. 위에 나타난 하나님의 속성은?
1) 질투   2) 공의   3) 심판   4) 구원
힌트) 환난에서 구하시는 하나님

볼지어다. 하나님께 징계 받는 자에게는 복이 있나니 그런즉 너는 전능자의 경책을 업신여기지 말지니라. 하나님은 아프게 하시다가 싸매시며 상하게 하시다가 그 손으로 고치시나니 여섯 가지 환난에서 너를 구원하시며 일곱 가지 환난이라도 그 재앙이 네게 미치지 않게 하시며 기근 때에 죽음에서, 전쟁 때에 칼 권세에서 너를 구속하실 터인즉 네가 혀의 채찍을 피하여 숨을 수가 있고 멸망이 올 때에도 두려워 아니할 것이라. 네가 멸망과 기근을 비웃으며 들짐승을 두려워 아니할 것은 밭에 돌이 너와 언약을 맺겠고 들짐승이 너와 화친할 것임이라. 네가 네 장막의 평안함을 알고 네 우리를 살펴도 잃은 것이 없을 것이며 네 자손이 많아지며 네 후예가 땅에 풀같을 줄을 네가 알 것이라. 네가 장수하다가 무덤에 이르니 곡식단이 그 기한에 운반되어 올리움 같으리라. 볼지어다. 우리의 연구한 바가 이같으니 너는 듣고 네게 유익된 줄 알지니라. 가) 2, 나) 3, 다) 4

10과

욥 7:1~3

Does not man have hard service on earth? Are not his days like those of a hired man? Like a slave longing for the evening shadows, or a hired man waiting eagerly for his _____ , so I have been allotted months of futility, and nights of misery have been assigned to me.

* allot 할당하다 / futility 무익, 공허

밑줄에 들어갈 알맞은 말은?

1) wages   2) days   3) work   4) family

힌트) hire 고용하다

세상에 있는 인생에게 전쟁이 있지 아니하냐. 그 날이 품꾼의 날과 같지 아니하냐. 종은 저물기를 심히 기다리고 품꾼은 그 삯을 바라나니 이와 같이 내가 여러 달째 곤고를 받으니 수고로운 밤이 내게 작정되었구나. 1

욥 7:17~19

What is man that you _____ so much of him, that you give him so much attention, that you examine him every morning and test him every moment? Will you never look away from me, or let me alone even for an instant?

밑줄에 들어갈 알맞은 말은?

1) have   2) take   3) do   4) make

힌트) _____ much of ~; ~을 중요시하다

사람이 무엇이관대 주께서 크게 여기사 그에게 마음을 두시고 아침마다 권징하시며 분초마다 시험하시나이까. 주께서 내게서 눈을 돌이키지 아니하시며 나의 침 삼킬 동안도 나를 놓지 아니하시기를 어느 때까지 하시리이까. 4

욥 9:25~26

My days are swifter than a runner; they fly away without a glimpse of joy. They skim past like boats of papyrus, like _____ swooping down on their prey.

* glimpse 언뜻 봄, / skim 스쳐 지나가다 / papyrus (고대 이집트,그리스,로마의) 종이, 종이갈대

밑줄에 들어갈 알맞은 말은?

1) lions   2) eagles   3) elephants   4) animals

힌트) swoop (새가 공중으로부터) 내리 덮치다

나의 날이 체부보다 빠르니 달려가므로 복을 볼 수 없구나. 그 지나가는 것이 빠른 배 같고 움킬 것에 날아 내리는 독수리와도 같구나. 2

욥 11:7~20

Can you fathom the mysteries of God? Can you probe the limits of the Almighty? They are higher than the heavens--what can you do? They are deeper than the depths of the grave--what can you know? Their measure is longer than the earth and wider than the sea. If he comes along and confines you in prison and ① convenes a court, who can oppose him? Surely he recognizes deceitful men; and when he sees evil, does he not take note? But a witless man can no more become wise ② than a wild donkey's colt can be born a man. Yet if you _____ your heart to him and stretch out your hands to him, if you put away the sin that is in your hand and allow no evil to dwell in your tent, then you will lift up your face without shame; you will stand firm and without fear. You will surely forget your trouble, recalling it only as waters gone by. Life will be ③ bright than noonday, and darkness will become like morning. You will be secure, because there is hope; you will look about you and take your rest ④ in safety. You will lie down, with no one to make you afraid, and many will court your favor. But the eyes of the wicked will fail, and escape will elude them; their hope will become a dying gasp.

* fathom 수심을 측정하다 / colt 망아지 / elude 피하다, 벗어나다

가. 밑줄에 들어갈 알맞은 말은?
1) devote   2) devoted   3) have devoted   4) had devoted
힌트) 가정법 현재

나. 밑줄 친 ① ~ ④ 중에서 잘못 쓰여진 단어는?
힌트) 비교급

다. 윗 글에 나타난 하나님의 속성은?
1) 사랑   2) 심판   3) 전지전능   4) 용서
힌트) almighty 전능한

네가 하나님의 오묘를 어찌 능히 측량하며 전능자를 어찌 능히 온전히 알겠느냐. 하늘보다 높으시니 네가 어찌 하겠으며 음부보다 깊으시니 네가 어찌 알겠느냐. 그 도량은 땅보다 크고 바다보다 넓으니라. 하나님이 두루 다니시며 사람을 잡아 가두시고 개정하시면 누가 능히 막을소냐. 하나님은 허망한 사람을 아시나니 악한 일은 상관치 않으시는 듯하나 다 보시느니라. 허망한 사람은 지각이 없나니 그 출생함이 들나귀 새끼 같으니라. 만일 네가 마음을 바로 정하고 주를 향하여 손을 들 때에 네 손에 죄악이 있거든 멀리 버리라. 불의로 네 장막에 거하지 못하게 하라. 그리하면 네가 정녕 흠 없는 얼굴을 들게 되고 굳게 서서 두려움이 없으리니 곧 네 환난을 잊을 것이라. 네가 추억할지라도 물이 흘러감 같을 것이며 네 생명의 날이 대낮보다 밝으리니 어두움이 있다 할지라도 아침과 같이 될 것이요 네가 소망이 있으므로 든든할지며 두루 살펴보고 안전히 쉬리니. 네가 누워도 두렵게 할 자가 없겠고 많은 사람이 네게 첨을 드리리라. 그러나 악한 자는 눈이 어두워서 도망할 곳을 찾지 못하리니 그의 소망은 기운이 끊침이리라. 가) 1, 나) 3, 다) 3

욥 31:1~2

I made a covenant with my _____ not to look lustfully at a girl. For what is man's lot from God above, his heritage from the Almighty on high?

* lustful 색을 좋아하는(lewd) / lot 몫(share), 추첨

1) waist   2) eyes   3) feet   4) hands
힌트) to look lustfully

내가 내 눈과 언약을 세웠나니 어찌 처녀에게 주목하랴. 그리하면 위에 계신 하나님의 내리시는 분깃이 무엇이겠으며 높은 곳에서 전능자의 주시는 산업이 무엇이겠느냐. 2.

욥 36:5~12

God is mighty, but does not despise men; he is mighty, and firm in his purpose. He does not keep the wicked alive but gives the afflicted their rights. He does not take his eyes off the righteous; he enthrones them with kings and exalts them forever. But if men are bound in chains, _____ fast by cords of affliction, he tells them what they have done, that they have sinned arrogantly. He makes them listen to correction and commands them to repent of their evil. If they obey and serve him, they will spend the rest of their days in prosperity and their years in contentment. But if they do not listen, they will perish by the sword and die without knowledge.

* enthrone 왕위에 올리다 / affliction 고통 / arrogantly 거만하게 / contentment 만족

1) held   2) hold   3) holding   4) holds
힌트) 분사구문 (수동태); they are held fast ~

하나님은 전능하시나 아무도 멸시치 아니하시며 그 지능이 무궁하사 악인을 살려 두지 않으시며 고난받는 자를 위하여 신원하시며 그 눈을 의인에게서 돌이키지 아니하시고 그를 왕과 함께 영원히 위에 앉히사 존귀하게 하시며 혹시 그들이 누설에 매이거나 한난의 줄에 얽혔으면 그들의 소행과 허물을 보이사 그 교만한 행위를 알게 하시고 그들의 귀를 열어 교훈을 듣게 하시며 명하여 죄악에서 돌아오게 하시나니 만일 그들이 청종하여 섬기면 형통히 날을 보내며 즐거이 해를 지낼 것이요 만일 그들이 청종치 아니하면 칼에 망하며 지식 없이 죽을 것이니라. 1

시 1:1~6

Blessed is the man who does not walk in the counsel of the wicked or stand in the way of sinners or sit in the seat of ① mockers. But his delight is in the law of the LORD, and on his law he meditates day and night. He is like a tree planted by streams of water, which yields its fruit in season and whose leaf does not wither. Whatever he does prospers. Not so the wicked! ② They are like chaff that the wind blows away. Therefore ③ the wicked will not stand in the judgment, nor sinners in the assembly of ④ the righteous. For the LORD watches over the way of the righteous, but the way of the wicked will perish.

* wither 시들다 / chaff 왕겨

밑줄 친 ① ~ ④ 중에서 의미상 성격이 다른 하나는?

복 있는 사람은 악인의 꾀를 좇지 아니하며 죄인의 길에 서지 아니하며 오만한 자의 자리에 앉지 아니하고 오직 여호와의 율법을 즐거워하여 그 율법을 주야로 묵상하는 자로다. 저는 시냇가에 심은 나무가 시절을 좇아 과실을 맺으며 그 잎사귀가 마르지 아니함 같으니 그 행사가 다 형통하리로다. 악인은 그렇지 않음이여 오직 바람에 나는 겨와 같도다. 그러므로 악인이 심판을 견디지 못하며 죄인이 의인의 회중에 들지 못하리로다. 대저 의인의 길은 여호와께서 인정하시나 악인의 길은 망하리로다. 4

시 23:1~6

The LORD is my shepherd, I shall not be in want. He makes me lie down in green pastures, he leads me beside quiet waters, he restores my soul. He guides me in paths of righteousness for his name's sake. Even though I walk through the valley of the shadow of death, I will fear no evil, _____ you are with me; your rod and your staff, they comfort me. You prepare a table before me in the presence of my enemies. You anoint my head with oil; my cup overflows. Surely goodness and love will follow me all the days of my life, and I will dwell in the house of the LORD forever.

* pasture 목장

1) despite   2) for   3) though   4) whether

여호와는 나의 목자시니 내가 부족함이 없으리로다. 그가 나를 푸른 초장에 누이시며 쉴 만한 물가로 인도하시는도다. 내 영혼을 소생시키시고 자기 이름을 위하여 의의 길로 인도하시는도다. 내가 사망의 음침한 골짜기로 다닐지라도 해를 두려워하지 않을 것은 주께서 나와 함께 하심이라. 주의 지팡이와 막대기가 나를 안위하시나이다. 주께서 내 원수의 목전에서 내게 상을 베푸시고 기름으로 내 머리에 바르셨으니 내 잔이 넘치나이다. 나의 평생에 선하심과 인자하심이 정녕 나를 따르리니 내가 여호와의 집에 영원히 거하리로다. 2

11과

시 121:1~8

I lift up my eyes to the hills-- where does my help come from? My help comes from the LORD, the Maker of heaven and earth. He will not let your foot slip--he who watches over you will not slumber; indeed, he who watches over Israel will neither slumber nor sleep. The LORD watches over you--the LORD is your shade at your right hand; the sun will not harm you by day, nor the moon by night. The LORD will keep you from all harm--he will watch over your life; the LORD will watch over your coming and going both now and forevermore.

*slumber 잠자다

윗 글의 내용으로 보아 다음에서 하나님을 나타낸 말은?
1) moon   2) heaven   3) shade   4) sun

내가 산을 향하여 눈을 들리라 나의 도움이 어디서 올꼬. 나의 도움이 천지를 지으신 여호와에게서로다. 여호와께서 너로 실족지 않게 하시며 너를 지키시는 자가 졸지 아니하시리로다. 이스라엘을 지키시는 자는 졸지도 아니하고 주무시지도 아니하시리로다. 여호와는 너를 지키시는 자라 여호와께서 네 우편에서 네 그늘이 되시나니 낮의 해가 너를 상치 아니하며 밤의 달도 너를 해치 아니하리로다. 여호와께서 너를 지켜 모든 환난을 면케 하시며 또 네 영혼을 지키시리로다. 여호와께서 너의 출입을 지금부터 영원까지 지키시리로다. 3

시 127:1~5

Unless the LORD builds the house, its builders labor in vain. Unless the LORD watches over the city, the watchmen stand guard in vain. In vain you rise early and stay up late, toiling for food to eat--for he grants sleep to those he loves. Sons are a heritage from the LORD, children a reward from him. Like arrows in the hands of a warrior are sons born in one's youth. Blessed is the man _____ quiver is full of them. They will not be put to shame when they contend with their enemies in the gate.

* quiver 화살통, 전통 / contend 다투다

1) whose   2) who   3) which   4) his

여호와께서 집을 세우지 아니하시면 세우는 자의 수고가 헛되며 여호와께서 성을 지키지 아니하시면 파수꾼의 경성함이 허사로다. 너희가 일찌기 일어나고 늦게 누우며 수고의 떡을 먹음이 헛되도다. 그러므로 여호와께서 그 사랑하시는 자에게는 잠을 주시는도다. 자식은 여호와의 주신 기업이요 태의 열매는 그의 상급이로다. 젊은 자의 자식은 장사의 수중의 화살 같으니 이것이 그 전통에 가득한 자는 복되도다. 저희가 성문에서 그 원수와 말할 때에 수치를 당치 아니하리로다. 1

잠 3:5~10

Trust in the LORD with all your heart and lean not on your own understanding; in all your ways acknowledge him, and he will make your paths straight. Do not be wise in your own eyes; fear the LORD and shun evil. This will bring health to your body and nourishment to your bones. Honor the LORD with your wealth, with the firstfruits of all your crops; then your barns will be filled to overflowing, and your vats will brim over with new _____ .

* barn 헛간 / brim 넘치다

1) iron   2) cloth   3) mind   4) wine
힌트) vat 큰 통

너는 마음을 다하여 여호와를 의뢰하고 네 명철을 의지하지 말라. 너는 범사에 그를 인정하라. 그리하면 네 길을 지도하시리라. 스스로 지혜롭게 여기지 말지어다. 여호와를 경외하며 악을 떠날지어다. 이것이 네 몸에 양약이 되어 네 골수로 윤택하게 하리라. 네 재물과 네 소산물의 처음 익은 열매로 여호와를 공경하라. 그리하면 네 창고가 가득히 차고 네 즙틀에 새 포도즙이 넘치리라. 4.

잠 4:23~26

Above all else, guard your heart, for it is the wellspring of life. Put away perversity from your mouth; keep _____ talk far from your lips. Let your eyes look straight ahead, fix your gaze directly before you. Make level paths for your feet and take only ways that are firm.

* wellspring 원천 / perversity 괴팍함, 외고집

1) delicate   2) corrupt   3) frank   4) difficult

무릇 지킬 만한 것보다 더욱 네 마음을 지키라. 생명의 근원이 이에서 남이니라. 궤휼을 네 입에서 버리며 사곡을 네 입술에서 멀리하라. 네 눈은 바로 보며 네 눈꺼풀은 네 앞을 곧게 살펴 네 발의 행할 첩경을 평탄케 하며 네 모든 길을 든든히 하라. 은밀한 선물은 노를 쉬게 하고 품의 뇌물은 맹렬한 분을 그치게 하느니라. 2

잠 5:3~6

For the lips of an adulteress drip honey, and her speech is smoother than oil; but in the end she is bitter as gall, _____ as a double-edged sword. Her feet go down to death; her steps lead straight to the grave. She gives no thought to the way of life; her paths are crooked, but she knows it not.

* adulteress 간음하는 여자(간부) / bitter 쓰라린, 통렬한 / gall 담즙, 찰과상 / crooked 구부러진, 부정직한

1) long   2) sharp   3) hard   4) heavy
힌트) sword

대저 음녀의 입술은 꿀을 떨어뜨리며 그 입은 기름보다 미끄러우나 나중은 쑥같이 쓰고 두 날 가진 칼같이 날카로우며 그 발은 사지로 내려가며 그 걸음은 음부로 나아가나니 그는 생명의 평탄한 길을 찾지 못하며 자기

길이 든든치 못하여 그것을 깨닫지 못하느니라. 2

잠 5:18 ~19

May your fountain be blessed, and may you _____ in the wife of your youth. A loving doe, a graceful deer--may her breasts satisfy you always, may you ever be captivated by her love.

* doe 암사슴

1) rejoice   2) live   3) die   4) sick

네 샘으로 복되게 하라. 네가 젊어서 취한 아내를 즐거워하라. 그는 사랑스러운 암사슴 같고 아름다운 암노루 같으니 너는 그 품을 항상 족하게 여기며 그 사랑을 항상 연모하라. 1.

잠 6:6~11

Go to the _____ , you sluggard; consider its ways and be wise! It has no commander, no overseer or ruler, yet it stores its provisions in summer and gathers its food at harvest. How long will you lie there, you sluggard? When will you get up from your sleep? A little sleep, a little slumber, a little folding of the hands to rest-- and poverty will come on you like a bandit and scarcity like an armed man.

* sluggard 게으름뱅이 / bandit 산적, 강도 / scarcity 부족, 결핍

1) bird   2) fish   3) ant   4) grasshopper

게으른 자여 개미에게로 가서 그 하는 것을 보고 지혜를 얻으라. 개미는 두령도 없고 간역자도 없고 주권자도 없으되 먹을 것을 여름 동안에 예비하며 추수 때에 양식을 모으느니라. 게으른 자여 네가 어느 때까지 눕겠느냐. 네가 어느 때에 잠이 깨어 일어나겠느냐. 좀더 자자, 좀더 졸자, 손을 모으고 좀더 눕자 하면 네 빈궁이 강도같이 오며 네 곤핍이 군사같이 이르리라. 3

잠 6:12~15

A scoundrel and villain, who goes about with a corrupt mouth, who winks with his eye, signals with his feet and motions with his fingers, who plots evil with deceit in his heart--he always stirs up dissension. _____ disaster will overtake him in an instant; he will suddenly be destroyed--without remedy.

* scoundrel 악당(villain) / dissension 불화, 알력

1) Neither   2) Therefore   3) And   4) Though

불량하고 악한 자는 그 행동에 궤휼한 입을 벌리며 눈짓을 하며 발로 뜻을 보이며 손가락질로 알게 하며 그 마음에 패역을 품으며 항상 악을 꾀하여 다툼을 일으키는 자라. 그러므로 그 재앙이 갑자기 임한즉 도움을 얻지 못하고 당장에 패망하리라. 2

잠 8:17~18

I love _____ who love me, and _____ who seek me find me. With me are riches and honor, enduring wealth and prosperity.

공통으로 들어갈 말은?
1) he   2) those   3) one   4) them

나를 사랑하는 자들이 나의 사랑을 입으며 나를 간절히 찾는 자가 나를 만날 것이니라. 부귀가 내게 있고 장구한 재물과 의도 그러하니라. 2

12과

잠 13:24

He who spares the rod hates his son, _____ he who loves him is careful to discipline him.

1) as   2) so   3) for   4) but

초달을 차마 못하는 자는 그 자식을 미워함이라. 자식을 사랑하는 자는 근실히 징계하느니라. 4

잠 15:1

A gentle answer turns away wrath, _____ a harsh word stirs up anger.

1) but   2) that   3) as   4) for

유순한 대답은 분노를 쉬게 하여도 과격한 말은 노를 격동하느니라. 1

잠 16:1~3

To man belong the plans of the heart, but from the LORD comes the reply of the tongue. All a man's ways seem innocent to him, but motives are weighed by the LORD. Commit to the LORD _____ you do, and your plans will succeed.

1) that   2) whatever   3) which   4) who

마음의 경영은 사람에게 있어도 말의 응답은 여호와께로서 나느니라. 사람의 행위가 자기 보기에는 모두 깨끗하여도 여호와는 심령을 감찰하시느니라. 너의 행사를 여호와께 맡기라. 그리하면 너의 경영하는 것이 이루리라. 2

잠 16:32

Better a patient man than a warrior, a man who controls his temper _____ one who takes a city.

1) as   2) though   3) than   4) that

노하기를 더디하는 자는 용사보다 낫고 자기의 마음을 다스리는 자는 성을 빼앗는 자보다 나으니라. 3

잠 17:17

A friend loves at all times, _____ a brother is born for adversity.

1) and   2) as   3) so   4) despite

친구는 사랑이 끊이지 아니하고 형제는 위급한 때까지 위하여 났느니라. 1

잠 18:1

An unfriendly man pursues selfish ends; he _____ all sound judgment.

1) asks   2) makes   3) defies   4) likes

무리에게서 스스로 나뉘는 자는 자기 소욕을 따르는 자라. 온갖 참 지혜를 배척하느니라. 3

잠 18:20~21

From the fruit of his mouth a man's stomach is filled; with the harvest from his lips he is satisfied. The tongue has the power of life and death, and those who love it will eat _____ fruit.

1) it's   2) its   3) it is   4) one

사람은 입에서 나오는 열매로 하여 배가 부르게 되나니 곧 그 입술에서 나는 것으로 하여 만족하게 되느니라. 죽고 사는 것이 혀의 권세에 달렸나니 혀를 쓰기 좋아하는 자는 그 열매를 먹으리라. 2

잠 24:6

For waging war you need guidance, _____ for victory many advisers.

1) so   2) that   3) what   4) and

너는 모략으로 싸우라. 승리는 모사가 많음에 있느니라. 4

잠 26:17

Like one who seizes a dog by the ears is a _____ who meddles in a quarrel not his own.

1) writer   2) passer-by   3) cook   4) worker

길로 지나다가 자기에게 상관없는 다툼을 간섭하는 자는 개 귀를 잡는 자와 같으니라. 2

잠 27:1

Do not boast about tomorrow, _____ you do not know what a day may bring forth.

1) but   2) so   3) for   4) and

너는 내일 일을 자랑하지 말라. 하루 동안에 무슨 일이 날는지 네가 알 수 없음이니라. 3

잠 27:10

Do not forsake your friend and the friend of your father, and do not go to your brother's house when disaster strikes you-- better a neighbor _____ than a brother far away.

1) more   2) nearby   3) most   4) nearly

네 친구와 네 아비의 친구를 버리지 말며 네 환난 날에 형제의 집에 들어가지 말지어다. 가까운 이웃이 먼 형제보다 나으니라. 2

잠 30:7~8

Two things I ask of you, O LORD; do not refuse me before I die: Keep falsehood and lies far from me; give me neither poverty nor riches, but give me only my daily _____ .

1) house   2) hour   3) wine   4) bread

내가 두 가지 일을 주께 구하였사오니 나의 죽기 전에 주시옵소서. 곧 허탄과 거짓말을 내게서 멀리 하옵시며 나로 가난하게도 마옵시고 부하게도 마옵시고 오직 필요한 양식으로 내게 먹이시옵소서. 4

전 1:2~3

"Meaningless! Meaningless!" says the Teacher. "Utterly meaningless! Everything is meaningless." What does man gain from all his _____ at which he toils under the sun?

1) labor   2) friends   3) past   4) visit

힌트) toil 힘써 일하다

전도자가 가로되 헛되고 헛되며 헛되고 헛되니 모든 것이 헛되도다. 사람이 해 아래서 수고하는 모든 수고가 자기에게 무엇이 유익한고. 1

전 7:1~2

A good name is better than fine perfume, and the day of death better than the day of birth. It is better to go to a house of mourning than to go to a house of feasting, _____ death is the destiny of every man; the living should take this to heart.

1) and   2) for   3) but   4) so

아름다운 이름이 보배로운 기름보다 낫고 죽는 날이 출생하는 날보다 나으며 초상집에 가는 것이 잔치집에 가는 것보다 나으니 모든 사람의 결국이 이와 같이 됨이라. 산 자가 이것에 유심하리로다. 2

전 9:9

Enjoy life with your wife, whom you love, all the days of this meaningless life that God has given you under the sun--all your meaningless days. For this is your lot in life and in your _____ labor under the sun.

1) joyful   2) noble   3) illegal   4) toilsome

네 헛된 평생의 모든 날 곧 하나님이 해 아래서 네게 주신 모든 헛된 날에 사랑하는 아내와 함께 즐겁게 살지어다. 이는 네가 일평생에 해 아래서 수고하고 얻은 분복이니라. 4

전 9:10

Whatever your hand finds to do, do it with all your might, for in the _____ , where you are going, there is neither working nor planning nor knowledge nor wisdom.

1) church   2) tower   3) grave   4) class

무릇 네 손이 일을 당하는 대로 힘을 다하여 할지어다. 네가 장차 들어갈 음부에는 일도 없고 계획도 없고 지식도 없고 지혜도 없음이니라. 3

13과

전 10:4

If a ruler's anger rises against you, do not leave your post; _____ can lay great errors to rest.

* lay to rest 쉬게 하다

1) love   2) bribe   3) instruction   4) calmness

주권자가 네게 분을 일으키거든 너는 네 자리를 떠나지 말라. 공순이 큰 허물을 경하게 하느니라. 4

전 10:10

If the ax is dull and its edge _____ , more strength is needed but skill will bring success.

1) sharpened   2) unsharpened   3) harden   4) broaden

무딘 철 연장 날을 갈지 아니하면 힘이 더 드느니라. 오직 지혜는 성공하기에 유익하니라. 2

전 10:20

Do not revile the king even in your thoughts, or curse _____ in your bedroom, because a bird of the air may carry your words, and a bird on the wing may report what you say.

* revile 헐뜯다, 욕설하다

1) the rich   2) a rich   3) rich   4) richness

심중에라도 왕을 저주하지 말며 침방에서라도 부자를 저주하지 말라. 공중의 새가 그 소리를 전하고 날짐승이 그 일을 전파할 것임이니라. 1

전 11:1~2

Cast your bread upon the waters, for after many days you will find it again. Give portions to seven, yes to eight, for you do not know _____ disaster may come upon the land.

1) that   2) what   3) so   4) why

너는 네 식물을 물 위에 던지라. 여러 날 후에 도로 찾으리라. 일곱에게나 여덟에게 나눠줄지어다. 무슨 재앙이 이 땅에 임할지 네가 알지 못함이니라. 2

전 12:12~14

Be warned, my son, of anything in addition to them. Of making many books there is no end, and _____ study wearies the body. Now all has been heard; here is the conclusion of the matter: Fear God and keep his commandments, for this is the whole duty of man. For God will bring every deed into judgment, including every hidden thing, whether it is good or evil.

1) a lot   2) much   3) many   4) lot of
힌트) a lot of = lots of

내 아들아 또 경계를 받으라. 여러 책을 짓는 것은 끝이 없고 많이 공부하는 것은 몸을 피곤케 하느니라. 일의 결국을 다 들었으니 하나님을 경외하고 그 명령을 지킬지어다. 이것이 사람의 본분이니라. 하나님은 모든 행위와 모든 은밀한 일을 선악간에 심판하시리라. 2

아 4:10~12

How delightful is your love, my sister, my bride! How much more pleasing is your love than wine, and the fragrance of your perfume than any _____ ! Your lips drop sweetness as the honeycomb, my bride; milk and honey are under your tongue. The fragrance of your garments is like that of Lebanon. You are a garden locked up, my sister, my bride; you are a spring enclosed, a sealed fountain.

* perfume 향기, 향수, 향료 / fragrance 향기로움, 향기 / honeycomb 벌집

1) spice   2) fun   3) nest   4) rock
힌트) 향료, 양념

나의 누이 나의 신부야. 네 사랑이 어찌 그리 아름다운지 네 사랑은 포도주에 지나고 네 기름의 향기는 각양 향품보다 승하구나. 내 신부야 네 입술에서는 꿀 방울이 떨어지고 네 혀 밑에는 꿀과 젖이 있고 네 의복의 향기는 레바논의 향기 같구나. 나의 누이, 나의 신부는 잠근 동산이요 덮은 우물이요 봉한 샘이로구나. 1

아 8:6~7

Place me like a seal over your heart, like a seal on your arm; for love is as strong as death, its jealousy unyielding as the grave. It burns like blazing fire, like a mighty flame. Many waters cannot quench love; rivers cannot wash it away. If one were to give all the wealth of his house for love, it _____ be utterly scorned.

* seal 도장, 봉인 / quench 끄다

1) shall   2) must   3) would   4) will
힌트) 가정법 미래를 나타내는 were to는 순수한 가정이며 실현의 가능성이 없을 때 쓴다.

너는 나를 인같이 마음에 품고 도장같이 팔에 두라. 사랑은 죽음같이 강하고 투기는 음부같이 잔혹하며 불같이 일어나니 그 기세가 여호와의 불과 같으니라. 이 사랑은 많은 물이 꺼지지 못하겠고 홍수라도 엄몰하지 못하나

니 사람이 그 온 가산을 다 주고 사랑과 바꾸려 할지라도 오히려 멸시를 받으리라. 3

사 11:6~10

The wolf will live with the lamb, the leopard will lie down with the goat, the calf and the lion and the yearling together; and a little child will lead them. The cow will feed with the bear, their young will lie down together, and the lion will eat 가) _____ like the ox. The infant will play near the hole of the cobra, and the young child put his hand into the viper's nest. They will neither harm nor destroy on all my holy mountain, for the earth will be full of the knowledge of the LORD 나) _____ the waters cover the sea. In that day the Root of Jesse will stand as a banner for the peoples; the nations will rally to him, and his place of rest will be glorious.

* yearling 일년 된 동물 / viper 독사 / banner 기, 깃발 / rally 다시 모이다

가. 1) straw   2) meat   3) water   4) vegetable

나. 1) so   2) as   3) that   4) whether

그 때에 이리가 어린 양과 함께 거하며 표범이 어린 염소와 함께 누우며 송아지와 어린 사자와 살진 짐승이 함께 있어 어린아이에게 끌리며 암소와 곰이 함께 먹으며 그것들의 새끼가 함께 엎드리며 사자가 소처럼 풀을 먹을 것이며 젖 먹는 아이가 독사의 구멍에서 장난하며 젖 뗀 어린아이가 독사의 굴에 손을 넣을 것이라. 나의 거룩한 산 모든 곳에서 해됨도 없고 상함도 없을 것이니 이는 물이 바다를 덮음같이 여호와를 아는 지식이 세상에 충만할 것임이니라. 그 날에 이새의 뿌리에서 한 싹이 나서 만민의 기호로 설 것이요 열방이 그에게로 돌아오리니 그 거한 곳이 영화로우리라. 가) 1, 나) 2

사 22:12~14

The Lord, the LORD Almighty, called you on that day to weep and to wail, to tear out your hair and put on sackcloth. But see, there is joy and revelry, slaughtering of cattle and killing of sheep, eating of meat and drinking of wine! "Let us eat and drink," you say, "_____ tomorrow we die!" The LORD Almighty has revealed this in my hearing: "Till your dying day this sin will not be atoned for," says the Lord, the LORD Almighty.

* wail 울부짖다, 통곡하다 / sackcloth 굵은 삼베 / atone 보상하다, 속죄하다

1) and   2) but   3) so   4) for

그 날에 주 만군의 여호와께서 명하사 통곡하며 애호하며 머리털을 뜯으며 굵은 베를 따라 하셨거늘 너희가 기뻐하며 즐거워하여 소를 잡고 양을 죽여 고기를 먹고 포도주를 마시면서 내일 죽으리니 먹고 마시자 하도다. 만군의 여호와께서 친히 내 귀에 들려 가라사대 진실로 이 죄악은 너희 죽기까지 속하지 못하리라 하셨느니라. 주 만군의 여호와의 말씀이니라. 4

사 32:1~4

See, a king will reign in righteousness and rulers will rule with justice. Each man will be like a shelter from the wind and a refuge from the storm, like streams of water in the desert and the shadow of a great rock in a thirsty land. Then the eyes of those who see will no longer be closed, and the ears of those who hear will listen. The mind of the rash will know and understand, and the stammering tongue will be fluent and _____ .

* rash 무분별한, 경솔한 / stammer 말을 더듬다

1) clear　　2) heavy　　3) old　　4) simple

보라 장차 한 왕이 의로 통치할 것이요 방백들이 공평으로 정사할 것이며 또 그 사람은 광풍을 피하는 곳, 폭우를 가리우는 곳 같을 것이며 마른 땅에 냇물 같을 것이며 곤비한 땅에 큰 바위 그늘 같으리니 보는 자의 눈이 감기지 아니할 것이요 듣는 자의 귀가 기울어질 것이며 조급한 자의 마음이 지식을 깨닫고 어눌한 자의 혀가 민첩하여 말을 분명히 할 것이라. 1

사 40:27~31

Why do you say, O Jacob, and complain, O Israel, "My way is hidden from the LORD; my cause is disregarded by my God"? Do you not know? Have you not heard? The LORD is the everlasting God, the Creator of the ends of the earth. He will not grow tired or weary, and his understanding no one can fathom. He gives strength to the weary and increases the power of the weak. Even youths grow tired and weary, and young men stumble and fall; but those who hope in the LORD will renew their strength. They will soar on wings like eagles; they will run and not grow weary, they will walk and not be _____ .

1) strong　　2) dirty　　3) faint　　4) high

힌트) 활기없는, 희미한, 졸도하다

야곱아 네가 어찌하여 말하며 이스라엘아 네가 어찌하여 이르기를 내 사정은 여호와께 숨겨졌으며 원통한 것은 내 하나님에게서 수리하심을 받지 못한다 하느냐. 너는 알지 못하였느냐 듣지 못하였느냐. 영원하신 하나님 여호와, 땅 끝까지 창조하신 자는 피곤치 아니하시며 곤비치 아니하시며 명철이 한이 없으시며 피곤한 자에게는 능력을 주시며 무능한 자에게는 힘을 더하시나니 소년이라도 피곤하며 곤비하며 장정이라도 넘어지며 자빠지되 오직 여호와를 앙망하는 자는 새 힘을 얻으리니 독수리의 날개 치며 올라감 같을 것이요 달음박질하여도 곤비치 아니하겠고 걸어가도 피곤치 아니하리로다. 3

14과

사 55:1~7

"Come, all you who are thirsty, come to the waters; and you who have no money, come, buy and eat! Come, buy wine and milk without money and without cost. Why spend money on what is not bread, and your labor on what does not satisfy? Listen, listen to me, and eat what is good, and your soul will delight in the richest of fare. Give ear and come to me; hear me, that your soul may live. I will make an everlasting covenant with you, my faithful love promised to David. See, I have made him a witness to the peoples, a leader and commander of the peoples. Surely you will summon nations you know not, and nations that do not know you will hasten to you, because of the LORD your God, the Holy One of Israel, for he has endowed you with splendor." Seek the LORD while he may be found; call on him while he is near. Let the wicked _____ his way and the evil man his thoughts. Let him turn to the LORD, and he will have mercy on him, and to our God, for he will freely pardon.

* fare 음식물, 운임 / endow 부여하다 / splendor 훌륭함, 광채 / hasten 서두르다

1) have forsaken   2) forsake   3) forsakes   4) forsaken

너희 목마른 자들아 물로 나아오라. 돈 없는 자도 오라 너희는 와서 사 먹되 돈 없이 값없이 와서 포도주와 젖을 사라. 너희가 어찌하여 양식 아닌 것을 위하여 은을 달아 주며 배부르게 못할 것을 위하여 수고하느냐. 나를 청종하라. 그리하면 너희가 좋은 것을 먹을 것이며 너희 마음이 기름진 것으로 즐거움을 얻으리라. 너희는 귀를 기울이고 내게 나아와 들으라. 그리하면 너희 영혼이 살리라. 내가 너희에게 영원한 언약을 세우리니 곧 다윗에게 허락한 확실한 은혜라. 내가 그를 만민에게 증거로 세웠고 만민의 인도자와 명령자를 삼았나니 네가 알지 못하는 나라를 부를 것이며 너를 알지 못하는 나라가 네게 달려올 것은 나 여호와 네 하나님 곧 이스라엘의 거룩한 자를 인함이니라. 내가 너를 영화롭게 하였느니라. 너희는 여호와를 만날 만한 때에 찾으라 가까이 계실 때에 그를 부르라. 악인은 그 길을, 불의한 자는 그 생각을 버리고 여호와께로 돌아오라. 그리하면 그가 긍휼히 여기시리라. 우리 하나님께로 나아오라. 그가 널리 용서하시리라. 2

사 58:13~14

"If you keep your feet from breaking the Sabbath and from doing as you please on my holy day, if you call the Sabbath a delight and the LORD'S holy day honorable, and if you honor it by not going your own way and not doing as you please or speaking idle words, then you will find your joy in the LORD, and I will _____ you to ride on the heights of the land and to feast on the inheritance of your father Jacob." The mouth of the LORD has spoken.

1) make   2) listen   3) follow   4) cause

만일 안식일에 네 발을 금하여 내 성일에 오락을 행치 아니하고 안식일을 일컬어 즐거운 날이라, 여호와의 성일을 존귀한 날이라 하여 이를 존귀히 여기고 네 길로 행치 아니하며 네 오락을 구치 아니하며 사사로운 말을 하지 아니하면 네가 여호와의 안에서 즐거움을 얻을 것이라. 내가 너를 땅의 높은 곳에 올리고 네 조상 야곱의 업으로 기르리라. 여호와의 입의 말이니라. 4

사 59:1~3

Surely the arm of the LORD is not too short to save, nor his ear too dull to hear. But your iniquities have separated you from your God; your sins have hidden his face from you, so that he will not hear. _____ your hands are stained with blood, your fingers with guilt. Your lips have spoken lies, and your tongue mutters wicked things.

* iniquity 불법, 부정

1) Though   2) For   3) But   4) What

여호와의 손이 짧아 구원치 못하심도 아니요 귀가 둔하여 듣지 못하심도 아니라. 오직 너희 죄악이 너희와 너희 하나님 사이를 내었고 너희 죄가 그 얼굴을 가리워서 너희를 듣지 않으시게 함이니. 이는 너희 손이 피에, 너희 손가락이 죄악에 더러웠으며 너희 입술은 거짓을 말하며 너희 혀는 악독을 발함이라. 2

렘 1:4~9

The word of the LORD came to me, saying, "Before I formed you in the womb I knew you, before you were born I set you apart; I appointed you as a prophet to the nations." "Ah, Sovereign LORD," I said, "I do not know how to speak; I am only a child." But the LORD said to me, "Do not say, 'I am only a child.' You must go to everyone I send you to and say whatever I command you. Do not be afraid of them, for I am with you and will rescue you," declares the LORD. Then the LORD reached out his hand and touched my mouth and said to me, "Now, I have put my words in your mouth."

* sovereign 주권을 가진, 주권자

윗 글에 나타난 하나님의 말씀의 성격은?
1) 권유   2) 교훈   3) 질책   4) 명령

여호와의 말씀이 내게 임하니라. 이르시되 내가 너를 복중에 짓기 전에 너를 알았고 네가 태에서 나오기 전에 너를 구별하였고 너를 열방의 선지자로 세웠노라 하시기로 내가 가로되 슬프도소이다. 주 여호와여 보소서 나는 아이라 말할 줄을 알지 못하나이다. 여호와께서 내게 이르시되 너는 아이라 하지 말고 내가 너를 누구에게 보내든지 너는 가며 내가 네게 무엇을 명하든지 너는 말할지니라. 너는 그들을 인하여 두려워 말라. 내가 너와 함께 하여 너를 구원하리라. 나 여호와의 말이니라 하시고 여호와께서 그 손을 내밀어 내 입에 대시며 내게 이르시되 보라 내가 내 말을 네 입에 두었노라. 4

렘 17:9~11

The heart is deceitful above all things and beyond cure. Who can understand it? "I the LORD search the heart and examine the mind, to reward a man according to his conduct, according to what his deeds deserve." Like a partridge that hatches eggs it did not lay is the man who gains riches by unjust means. _____ his life is half gone, they will desert him, and in the end he will prove to be a fool.

* partridge 자고(새) / hatch 부화하다 / lay (알을) 낳다

1) When   2) What   3) That   4) But

만물보다 거짓되고 심히 부패한 것은 마음이라. 누가 능히 이를 알리요마는 나 여호와는 심장을 살피며 폐부를 시험하고 각각 그 행위와 그 행실대로 보응하나니 불의로 치부하는 자는 자고새가 낳지 아니한 알을 품음 같아서 그 중년에 그것이 떠나겠고 필경은 어리석은 자가 되리라. 1

렘 33:2~3

This is what the LORD says, he who made the earth, the LORD who formed it and established it--the LORD is his name: 'Call to me and I will answer you and _____ you great and unsearchable things you do not know.'

1) say   2) tell   3) tell to   4) talk

힌트) 4형식 동사; 동사 + 간접목적어 + 직접목적어

일을 행하는 여호와, 그것을 지어 성취하는 여호와, 그 이름을 여호와라 하는 자가 이같이 이르노라 너는 내게 부르짖으라 내가 네게 응답하겠고 네가 알지 못하는 크고 비밀한 일을 네게 보이리라. 2

애 1:1~3

How deserted lies the city, once so full of people! How like a widow is she, who once was great among the nations! She who was queen among the provinces has now become a slave. Bitterly she weeps at night, tears are upon her cheeks. Among all her lovers there is none to comfort her. All her friends have betrayed her; they have become her enemies. After affliction and harsh labor, Judah has gone into exile. She dwells among the nations; she finds no resting place. All who pursue her have overtaken her in the midst of her distress.

* distress 근심, 비탄, 고통

밑줄 친 she가 가리키는 고유 명사는?

슬프다 이 성이여. 본래는 거민이 많더니 이제는 어찌 그리 적막히 앉았는고. 본래는 열국 중에 크던 자가 이제는 과부 같고 본래는 열방 중에 공주 되었던 자가 이제는 조공 드리는 자가 되었도다. 밤새도록 애곡하니 눈물이 뺨에 흐름이여 사랑하던 자 중에 위로하는 자가 없고 친구도 다 배반하여 원수가 되었도다. 유다는 환

난과 많은 수고로 인하여 사로잡혀 갔도다. 저가 열방에 거하여 평강을 얻지 못함이여 그 모든 핍박하는 자가 저를 쫓아 협착한 곳에 미쳤도다. Judah

겔 2:1~7

He said to me, "Son of man, stand up on your feet and I will speak to you." As he spoke, the Spirit came into me and raised me to my feet, and I heard him 가) _____ to me. He said: "Son of man, I am sending you to the Israelites, to a rebellious nation that has rebelled against me; they and their fathers have been in revolt against me to this very day. The people to whom I am sending you are obstinate and stubborn. Say to them, 'This is what the Sovereign LORD says.' And whether they listen or fail to listen--for they are a rebellious house--they will know that a prophet has been among them. And you, son of man, do not be afraid of them or their words. Do not be afraid, 나) _____ briers and thorns are all around you and you live among scorpions. Do not be afraid of what they say or terrified by them, though they are a rebellious house. You must speak my words to them, whether they listen or fail to listen, for they are rebellious.

* obstinate 완고한, 고집 센 = stubborn / brier/briar 찔레 / thorn 가시, 바늘 / scorpion 전갈

가. 1) spoken   2) spoke   3) speaking   4) to speak
힌트) 지각동사 다음에 동사 or 현재분사

나. 1) as   2) though   3) but   4) for

그가 내게 이르시되 인자야 일어서라, 내가 네게 말하리라 하시며 말씀하실 때에 그 신이 내게 임하사 나를 일으켜 세우시기로 내가 그 말씀하시는 자의 소리를 들으니 내게 이르시되 인자야 내가 너를 이스라엘 자손 곧 패역한 백성, 나를 배반하는 자에게 보내노라. 그들과 그 열조가 내게 범죄하여 오늘날까지 이르렀나니 이 자손은 얼굴이 뻔뻔하고 마음이 강퍅한 자니라. 내가 너를 그들에게 보내노니 너는 그들에게 이르기를 주 여호와의 말씀이 이러하시다 하라. 그들은 패역한 족속이라 듣든지 아니 듣든지 그들 가운데 선지자 있은 줄은 알지니라. 인자야 너는 비록 가시와 찔레와 함께 처하며 전갈 가운데 거할지라도 그들을 두려워 말고 그 말을 두려워 말지어다. 그들은 패역한 족속이라도 그 말을 두려워 말며 그 얼굴을 무서워 말지어다. 그들은 심히 패역한 자라 듣든지 아니 듣든지 너는 내 말로 고할지어다. 가) 3, 나) 2

15과

겔 37:1~10

① He asked me, "Son of man, can these bones live?" I said, "O Sovereign LORD, you alone know." Then he said to me, "Prophesy to these bones and say to them, 'Dry bones, hear the word of the LORD! This is what the Sovereign LORD says to these bones: I will make breath enter you, and you will come to life. I will attach tendons to you and make flesh come upon you and cover you with skin; I will put breath in you, and you will come to life. Then you will know that I am the LORD.'"

② So I prophesied as I was commanded. And as I was prophesying, there was a noise, a rattling sound, and the bones came together, bone to bone. I looked, and tendons and flesh appeared on them and skin covered them, but there was no breath in them. Then he said to me, "Prophesy to the breath; prophesy, son of man, and say to it, 'This is what the Sovereign LORD says: Come from the four winds, O breath, and breathe into these slain, that they may live.'" So I prophesied as he commanded me, and breath entered them; they came to life and stood up on their feet--a vast army.

③ The hand of the LORD was upon me, and he brought me out by the Spirit of the LORD and set me in the middle of a valley; it was full of bones. He led me back and forth among them, and I saw a great many bones on the floor of the valley, bones that were very dry.

* prophesy 예언하다 / tendon 건 / rattle 왈각달각(우르르) 소리나다 / slay slew slain 살해하다

윗 글을 순서대로 바로 쓴 것은?
1) ③①②   2) ①②③   3) ③②①   2) ②③①

여호와께서 권능으로 내게 임하시고 그 신으로 나를 데리고 가서 골짜기 가운데 두셨는데 거기 뼈가 가득하더라. 나를 그 뼈 사방으로 지나게 하시기로 본즉 그 골짜기 지면에 뼈가 심히 많고 아주 말랐더라. 그가 내게 이르시되 인자야 이 뼈들이 능히 살겠느냐 하시기로 내가 대답하되 주 여호와여 주께서 아시나이다. 또 내게 이르시되 너는 이 모든 뼈에게 대언하여 이르기를 너희 마른 뼈들아 여호와의 말씀을 들을지어다. 주 여호와께서 이 뼈들에게 말씀하시기를 내가 생기로 너희에게 들어가게 하리니 너희가 살리라. 너희 위에 힘줄을 두고 살을 입히고 가죽으로 덮고 너희 속에 생기를 두리니 너희가 살리라. 또 나를 여호와인 줄 알리라 하셨다 하라. 이에 내가 명을 좇아 대언하니 대언할 때에 소리가 나고 움직이더니 이 뼈, 저 뼈가 들어 맞아서 뼈들이 서로 연락하더라. 내가 또 보니 그 뼈에 힘줄이 생기고 살이 오르며 그 위에 가죽이 덮이나 그 속에 생기는 없더라. 또 내게 이르시되 인자야 너는 생기를 향하여 대언하라. 생기에게 대언하여 이르기를 주 여호와의 말씀에 생기야 사방에서부터 와서 이 사망을 당한 자에게 불어서 살게 하라 하셨다 하라. 이에 내가 그 명대로 대언하였더니 생기가 그들에게 들어가매 그들이 곧 살아 일어나서 서는데 극히 큰 군대더라. 1

단 1:12~16

"Please test your servants for ten days: Give us nothing but vegetables to eat and water to drink. Then compare our appearance with that of the young men who eat the royal food, and treat your servants in accordance with what you see." So he agreed to this and tested them for ten days. At the end of the ten days they looked healthier and better nourished than any of the young men who ate the royal food. So the guard took away their choice food and the wine they were to drink and gave them vegetables _____ .

1) together   2) as well   3) instead   4) scarcely

청하오니 당신의 종들을 열흘 동안 시험하여 채식을 주어 먹게 하고 물을 주어 마시게 한 후에 당신 앞에서 우리의 얼굴과 왕의 진미를 먹는 소년들의 얼굴을 비교하여 보아서 보이는 대로 종들에게 처분하소서 하매 그가 그들의 말을 좇아 열흘을 시험하더니 열흘 후에 그들의 얼굴이 더욱 아름답고 살이 더욱 윤택하여 왕의 진미를 먹는 모든 소년보다 나아 보인지라. 이러므로 감독하는 자가 그들에게 분정된 진미와 마실 포도주를 제하고 채식을 주니라. 3.

단 3:17~18

If we are thrown into the blazing furnace, the God we serve is able to save us from it, and he will rescue us from your hand, O king. But _____ if he does not, we want you to know, O king, that we will not serve your gods or worship the image of gold you have set up.

1) as   2) also   3) for   4) even

만일 그럴 것이면 왕이여 우리가 섬기는 우리 하나님이 우리를 극렬히 타는 풀무 가운데서 능히 건져내시겠고 왕의 손에서도 건져내시리이다. 그리 아니하실지라도 왕이여 우리가 왕의 신들을 섬기지도 아니하고 왕의 세우신 금신상에게 절하지도 아니할 줄을 아옵소서. 4

호 3:1

The LORD said to me, "Go, show your love to your wife again, though she is loved by another and is an adulteress. Love her as the LORD loves the Israelites, _____ they turn to other gods and love the sacred raisin cakes."

* sacred 신성한(holy), (신에게) 바친 / raisin 건포도

1) though   2) as   3) for   4) and

여호와께서 내게 이르시되 이스라엘 자손이 다른 신을 섬기고 건포도 떡을 즐길지라도 여호와가 저희를 사랑하나니 너는 또 가서 타인에게 연애를 받아 음부된 그 여인을 사랑하라. 1

호 6:1~3

Come, let us return to the LORD. He has torn us to pieces but he will heal us; he has injured us but he will bind up our wounds. After two days he will revive us; on the third day he will restore us, that we may live in his presence. Let us acknowledge the LORD; let us press on to acknowledge him. As surely as the sun rises, he will appear; he will come to us like the winter rains, like the spring rains that _____ the earth.

* press on 길을 재촉하다

1) fall   2) falls   3) water   4) waters

오라 우리가 여호와께로 돌아가자. 여호와께서 우리를 찢으셨으나 도로 낫게 하실 것이요 우리를 치셨으나 싸매어 주실 것임이라. 여호와께서 이틀 후에 우리를 살리시며 제 삼 일에 우리를 일으키시리니 우리가 그 앞에서 살리라. 그러므로 우리가 여호와를 알자. 힘써 여호와를 알자. 그의 나오심은 새벽 빛같이 일정하니 비와 같이, 땅을 적시는 늦은 비와 같이 우리에게 임하시리라 하리라. 3

욜 2:12~13

"Even now," declares the LORD, "return to me with all your heart, with fasting and weeping and mourning." Rend your heart and not your garments. Return to the LORD your God, for he is gracious and compassionate, slow to anger and _____ in love, and he relents from sending calamity.

* fast 단식하다 / rend 찢다(tear) / relent 관대해지다(toward), 가엽게 여기다(at) / calamity 재난, 참화(misery), 불행(misfortune)

1) abounding   2) abound   3) with abounding   4) abounded

여호와의 말씀에 너희는 이제라도 금식하며 울며 애통하고 마음을 다하여 내게로 돌아오라 하셨나니 너희는 옷을 찢지 말고 마음을 찢고 너희 하나님 여호와께로 돌아올지어다. 그는 은혜로우시며 자비로우시며 노하기를 더디하시며 인애가 크시사 뜻을 돌이켜 재앙을 내리지 아니하시나니 1

욜 2:28~30

And afterward, I will pour out my Spirit on all people. Your sons and daughters will prophesy, your old men will dream dreams, your young men will see visions. Even on my servants, _____ men and women, I will pour out my Spirit in those days. I will show wonders in the heavens and on the earth, blood and fire and billows of smoke.

* billow 큰 물결

1) as   2) and   3) together   4) both

그 후에 내가 내 신을 만민에게 부어 주리니 너희 자녀들이 장래 일을 말할 것이며 너희 늙은이는 꿈을 꾸며 너희 젊은이는 이상을 볼 것이며 그 때에 내가 또 내 신으로 남종과 여종에게 부어 줄 것이며 내가 이적을 하늘과

땅에 베풀리니 곧 피와 불과 연기 기둥이라. 4

욘 4:10~11

But the LORD said, "You have been concerned about this vine, though you did not tend it or make it grow. It sprang up overnight and died overnight. But Nineveh has more than a hundred and twenty _____ _____ who cannot tell their right hand from their left, and many cattle as well. Should I not be concerned about that great city?"

1) thousands people   2) thousand people   3) thousand peoples   4) thousands peoples

여호와께서 가라사대 네가 수고도 아니하였고 배양도 아니하였고 하룻밤에 났다가 하룻밤에 망한 이 박넝쿨을 네가 아꼈거든 하물며 이 큰 성읍, 니느웨에는 좌우를 분변치 못하는 자가 십이만여 명이요 육축도 많이 있나니 내가 아끼는 것이 어찌 합당치 아니하냐. 2

합 3:17~18

Though the fig tree does not bud and there are no grapes on the vines, though the olive crop fails and the fields produce no food, though there are no sheep in the pen and no cattle in the stalls, _____ I will rejoice in the LORD, I will be joyful in God my Savior.

* fig 무화과 나무 / bud 봉오리를 맺다 / stall 마구간

1) yet   2) though   3) as   4) and

비록 무화과나무가 무성치 못하며 포도나무에 열매가 없으며 감람나무에 소출이 없으며 밭에 식물이 없으며 우리에 양이 없으며 외양간에 소가 없을지라도 나는 여호와를 인하여 즐거워하며 나의 구원의 하나님을 인하여 기뻐하리로다. 1

16과

말 3:10~12

"Bring the whole tithe into the storehouse, that there may be food in my house. Test me in this," says the LORD Almighty, "and see if I will not throw open the floodgates of heaven and pour out so much blessing that you will not have room enough for it. I will prevent pests from devouring your crops, and the vines in your fields will not cast their fruit," says the LORD Almighty. "Then all the nations will call you blessed, _____ yours will be a delightful land," says the LORD Almighty.

* tithe 십일조 / floodgate 수문 / pest 해충, 페스트

1) but   2) or   3) though   4) for

만군의 여호와가 이르노라. 너희의 온전한 십일조를 창고에 들여 나의 집에 양식이 있게 하고 그것으로 나를 시험하여 내가 하늘 문을 열고 너희에게 복을 쌓을 곳이 없도록 붓지 아니하나 보라. 만군의 여호와가 이르노라. 내가 너희를 위하여 황충을 금하여 너희 토지 소산을 멸하지 않게 하며 너희 밭에 포도나무의 과실로 기한 전에 떨어지지 않게 하리니 너희 땅이 아름다와지므로 열방이 너희를 복되다 하리라 만군의 여호와의 말이니라. 4

마 4:1~11

Then Jesus was led by the Spirit into the desert to be tempted by the devil. After fasting forty days and forty nights, he was hungry. The tempter came to him and said, "If you are the Son of God, tell these stones to become bread." Jesus answered, "It is written: 'Man does not live on bread alone, _____ on every word that comes from the mouth of God.'" Then the devil took him to the holy city and had him stand on the highest point of the temple. "If you are the Son of God," he said, "throw yourself down. For it is written: 'He will command his angels concerning you, and they will lift you up in their hands, so that you will not strike your foot against a stone.'" Jesus answered him, "It is also written: 'Do not put the Lord your God to the test.'" Again, the devil took him to a very high mountain and showed him all the kingdoms of the world and their splendor. "All this I will give you," he said, "if you will bow down and worship me." Jesus said to him, "Away from me, Satan! For it is written: 'Worship the Lord your God, and serve him only.'" Then the devil left him, and angels came and attended him.

가. 1) but   2) and   3) though   4) as

나. 윗 글의 제목으로 알맞은 것은?
1) confession   2) temptation   3) forgiveness   4) sacrifice

그 때에 예수께서 성령에게 이끌리어 마귀에게 시험을 받으러 광야로 가사 사십 일을 밤낮으로 금식하신 후에 주리신지라. 시험하는 자가 예수께 나아와서 가로되 네가 만일 하나님의 아들이어든 명하여 이 돌들이 떡덩이가 되게 하라. 예수께서 대답하여 가라사대 기록되었으되 사람이 떡으로만 살 것이 아니요 하나님의 입으로 나오는 모든 말씀으로 살 것이라 하였느니라 하시니 이에 마귀가 예수를 거룩한 성으로 데려다가 성전 꼭대기에 세우고 가로되 네가 만일 하나님의 아들이어든 뛰어내리라. 기록하였으되 저가 너를 위하여 그 사자들을 명하시리니 저희가 손으로 너를 받들어 발이 돌에 부딪히지 않게 하리로다 하였느니라. 예수께서 이르시되 또 기록되었으되 주 너의 하나님을 시험치 말라 하였느니라 하신대 마귀가 또 그를 데리고 지극히 높은 산으로 가서 천하 만국과 그 영광을 보여 가로되 만일 내게 엎드려 경배하면 이 모든 것을 네게 주리라. 이에 예수께서 말씀하시되 사단아 물러가라. 기록되었으되 주 너의 하나님께 경배하고 다만 그를 섬기라 하였느니라. 이에 마귀는 예수를 떠나고 천사들이 나아와서 수종드니라. 가) 1, 나) 2

마 5:3~10

Blessed are the poor in spirit, for theirs is the kingdom of heaven. Blessed are those who mourn, for they will be comforted. Blessed are the meek, for they will inherit the earth. Blessed are those who hunger and thirst _____ righteousness, for they will be filled. Blessed are the merciful, for they will be shown mercy. Blessed are the pure in heart, for they will see God. Blessed are the peacemakers, for they will be called sons of God. Blessed are those who are persecuted because of righteousness, for theirs is the kingdom of heaven.

1) of   2) in   3) for   4) to

심령이 가난한 자는 복이 있나니 천국이 저희 것임이요, 애통하는 자는 복이 있나니 저희가 위로를 받을 것임이요, 온유한 자는 복이 있나니 저희가 땅을 기업으로 받을 것임이요, 의에 주리고 목마른 자는 복이 있나니 저희가 배부를 것임이요, 긍휼히 여기는 자는 복이 있나니 저희가 긍휼히 여김을 받을 것임이요, 마음이 청결한 자는 복이 있나니 저희가 하나님을 볼 것임이요, 화평케 하는 자는 복이 있나니 저희가 하나님의 아들이라 일컬음을 받을 것임이요, 의를 위하여 핍박을 받은 자는 복이 있나니 천국이 저희 것임이라. 3

마 7:7

Ask and it will be given to you; seek and you will find; _____ and the door will be opened to you.

1) strike   2) knock   3) beat   4) break

구하라 그러면 너희에게 주실 것이요 찾으라 그러면 찾을 것이요 문을 두드리라 그러면 너희에게 열릴 것이니 2

마 10:20~22

For it will not be you speaking, but the Spirit of your Father speaking through you. Brother will betray brother to death, and a father his child; children will rebel against their parents and have them put to death. All men will hate you because of me, _____ he who stands firm to the end will be saved.

1) though   2) but   3) as   4) whether

말하는 이는 너희가 아니라 너희 속에서 말씀하시는 자 곧 너희 아버지의 성령이시니라. 장차 형제가 형제를, 아비가 자식을 죽는 데 내어 주며 자식들이 부모를 대적하여 죽게 하리라. 또 너희가 내 이름을 인하여 모든 사람에게 미움을 받을 것이나 나중까지 견디는 자는 구원을 얻으리라. 2

마 15:32~38

Jesus called his disciples to him and said, "I have compassion for these people; they have already been with me three days and have nothing to eat. I do not want to send them away hungry, or they may collapse on the way." His disciples answered, "Where could we get enough bread in this remote place to 가) _____ such a crowd?" "How many loaves do you have?" Jesus asked. "Seven," they replied, "and a few small fish." He told the crowd to sit down on the ground. Then he took the seven loaves and the fish, and when he had given thanks, he broke them and gave them to the disciples, and they 나) _____ _____ to the people. They all ate and were satisfied. Afterward the disciples picked up seven basketfuls of broken pieces that were left over. The number of those who ate was four thousand, besides women and children.

가. 1) feed   2) fed   3) eat   4) provide

나. 1) on turn   2) at turn   3) in turn   4) by turn

예수께서 제자들을 불러 가라사대 내가 무리를 불쌍히 여기노라. 저희가 나와 함께 있은 지 이미 사흘이매 먹을 것이 없도다. 길에서 기진할까 하여 굶겨 보내지 못하겠노라. 제자들이 가로되 광야에 있어 우리가 어디서 이런 무리의 배부를 만큼 떡을 얻으리이까. 예수께서 가라사대 너희에게 떡이 몇 개나 있느냐. 가로되 일곱 개와 작은 생선 두어 마리가 있나이다 하거늘 예수께서 무리를 명하사 땅에 앉게 하시고 떡 일곱 개와 그 생선을 가지사 축사하시고 떼어 제자들에게 주시니 제자들이 무리에게 주매 다 배불리 먹고 남은 조각을 일곱 광주리에 차게 거두었으며 먹은 자는 여자와 아이 외에 사천 명이었더라. 가) 1, 나) 3

마 24:29~31

Immediately after the distress of those ① days, the sun will be darkened, and the moon will not give its light; the stars will fall from the sky, and the heavenly bodies will be shaken. At that time the sign of the Son of Man will appear in the sky, and all the ② nation of the earth will mourn. They will see the Son of Man ③ coming on the clouds of the sky, with power and great glory.

And he will send his angels with a loud trumpet call, and they will gather his elect from the four winds, from one end of the heavens to ④ the other.

* distress 근심, 비탄, 빈곤 / elect 뽑힌 사람

밑줄 친 단어 중에서 틀린 것은?

그 날 환난 후에 즉시 해가 어두워지며 달이 빛을 내지 아니하며 별들이 하늘에서 떨어지며 하늘의 권능들이 흔들리리라. 그 때에 인자의 징조가 하늘에서 보이겠고 그 때에 땅의 모든 족속들이 통곡하며 그들이 인자가 구름을 타고 능력과 큰 영광으로 오는 것을 보리라. 저가 큰 나팔 소리와 함께 천사들을 보내리니 저희가 그 택하신 자들을 하늘 이 끝에서 저 끝까지 사방에서 모으리라. 2 (nations)

마 28:17~20

When they saw him, they worshiped him; but some doubted. Then Jesus came to them and said, "All authority in heaven and on earth has been given to me. Therefore go and make disciples of all nations, baptizing them in the name of the Father and of the Son and of the Holy Spirit, and _____ them to obey everything I have commanded you. And surely I am with you always, to the very end of the age."

1) taught   2) teaching for   3) teaching   4) to teach

예수를 뵈옵고 경배하나 오히려 의심하는 자도 있더라. 예수께서 나아와 일러 가라사대 하늘과 땅의 모든 권세를 내게 주셨으니 그러므로 너희는 가서 모든 족속으로 제자를 삼아 아버지와 아들과 성령의 이름으로 세례를 주고 내가 너희에게 분부한 모든 것을 가르쳐 지키게 하라. 볼지어다 내가 세상 끝날까지 너희와 항상 함께 있으리라 하시니라. 3

17과

막 10:29~30

"I tell you the truth," Jesus replied, "no one who has left home or brothers or sisters or mother or father or children or fields for me and the gospel will fail to receive a hundred times as much in this present age (homes, brothers, sisters, mothers, children and fields--and with them, persecutions) and _____ the age to come, eternal life."

* persecution 박해

1) in   2) at   3) on   4) to

예수께서 가라사대 내가 진실로 너희에게 이르노니 나와 및 복음을 위하여 집이나 형제나 자매나 어미나 아비나 자식이나 전토를 버린 자는 금세에 있어 집과 형제와 자매와 모친과 자식과 전토를 백 배나 받되 핍박을 겸하여 받고 내세에 영생을 받지 못할 자가 없느니라. 1

눅 2:8~14

And there were shepherds living out in the fields nearby, keeping watch over their flocks at night. An angel of the Lord appeared to them, and the glory of the Lord shone around them, and they were terrified. But the angel said to them, "Do not be afraid. I bring you good news of great joy that will be for all the people. Today in the town of David a Savior has been born to you; he is Christ the Lord. This will be a sign to you: You will find a baby wrapped in cloths and _____ in a manger." Suddenly a great company of the heavenly host appeared with the angel, praising God and saying, "Glory to God in the highest, and on earth peace to men on whom his favor rests."

* manger 여물통

1) lay   2) lied   3) lying   4) lie

그 지경에 목자들이 밖에서 밤에 자기 양 떼를 지키더니 주의 사자가 곁에 서고 주의 영광이 저희를 두루 비취매 크게 무서워하는지라. 천사가 이르되 무서워 말라. 보라 내가 온 백성에게 미칠 큰 기쁨의 좋은 소식을 너희에게 전하노라. 오늘날 다윗의 동네에 너희를 위하여 구주가 나셨으니 곧 그리스도 주시니라. 너희가 가서 강보에 싸여 구유에 누인 아기를 보리니 이것이 너희에게 표적이니라 하더니 홀연히 허다한 천군이 그 천사와 함께 있어 하나님을 찬송하여 가로되 지극히 높은 곳에서는 하나님께 영광이요 땅에서는 기뻐하심을 입은 사람들 중에 평화로다 하니라. 3

눅 4:18~19

The Spirit of the Lord is on me, because he has anointed me to preach good news to the poor. He has sent me to proclaim freedom for the prisoners and recovery of sight for the blind, to release _____ _____, to proclaim the year of the Lord's favor.

* release 풀어놓다, 해방시키다

1) the oppressing   2) the oppressed   3) the poor   4) the power

주의 성령이 내게 임하셨으니 이는 가난한 자에게 복음을 전하게 하시려고 내게 기름을 부으시고 나를 보내사 포로된 자에게 자유를, 눈먼 자에게 다시 보게 함을 전파하며 눌린 자를 자유케 하고 주의 은혜의 해를 전파하게 하려 하심이라 하였더라. 2

요 1:1~3

In the beginning was the Word, and the Word was with God, and the Word was God. He was with God in the beginning. Through him all things were made; _____ him nothing was made that has been made.

1) by   2) with   3) from   4) without

태초에 말씀이 계시니라. 이 말씀이 하나님과 함께 계셨으니 이 말씀은 곧 하나님이시니라. 그가 태초에 하나님과 함께 계셨고 만물이 그로 말미암아 지은 바 되었으니 지은 것이 하나도 그가 없이는 된 것이 없느니라. 4

요 1:12

Yet to all who received him, to those who believed _____ his name, he gave the right to become children of God.

1) on   2) in   3) at   4) to

영접하는 자 곧 그 이름을 믿는 자들에게는 하나님의 자녀가 되는 권세를 주셨으니. 2

요 4:13~14

Jesus answered, "Everyone who drinks this water will be thirsty again, but whoever drinks the water I give him will never _____ . Indeed, the water I give him will become in him a spring of water welling up to eternal life."

1) thirst   2) thirsty   3) thirstily   4) to thirst

예수께서 대답하여 가라사대 이 물을 먹는 자마다 다시 목마르려니와 내가 주는 물을 먹는 자는 영원히 목마르지 아니하리니 나의 주는 물은 그 속에서 영생하도록 솟아나는 샘물이 되리라. 1

요 14:1~4

Do not let your hearts be troubled. Trust in God; trust also in me. In my Father's house are many rooms; if it were not so, I would have told you. I am going there to prepare a place for you. And if I go and prepare a place for you, I will come back and take you to be with me that you also may be where I am. You know the way to the place _____ I am going.

1) that   2) where   3) which   4) what

너희는 마음에 근심하지 말라. 하나님을 믿으니 또 나를 믿으라. 내 아버지 집에 거할 곳이 많도다. 그렇지 않으면 너희에게 일렀으리라. 내가 너희를 위하여 처소를 예비하러 가노니 가서 너희를 위하여 처소를 예비하면 내가 다시 와서 너희를 내게로 영접하여 나 있는 곳에 너희도 있게 하리라. 내가 가는 곳에 그 길을 너희가 알리라. 2

요 14:6

Jesus answered, "I am the way and the truth and the life. No one comes to the Father _____ through me.

1) by   2) except   3) as   4) all

예수께서 가라사대 내가 곧 길이요 진리요 생명이니 나로 말미암지 않고는 아버지께로 올 자가 없느니라. 2

요 15:1~2

I am the true vine, and my Father is the gardener. He cuts off every branch in me that bears no fruit, while every branch that does bear fruit he prunes so that it will be even more _____ .

* vine 포도나무 / prune (소용없는 가지를) 베어내다, 전정하다

1) fruitless   2) fruity   3) fruit   4) fruitful

내가 참 포도나무요 내 아버지는 그 농부라. 무릇 내게 있어 과실을 맺지 아니하는 가지는 아버지께서 이를 제해 버리시고 무릇 과실을 맺는 가지는 더 과실을 맺게 하려 하여 이를 깨끗케 하시느니라. 4

요 15:12~17

My command is this: Love each other as I have loved you. Greater love has no one than this, that he lay down his life for his friends. You are my friends if you do what I command. I no longer call you servants, because a servant does not know his master's business. _____ , I have called you friends, for everything that I learned from my Father I have made known to you. You did not choose me, but I chose you and appointed you to go and bear fruit--fruit that will last. Then the Father will give you whatever you ask in my name. This is my command: Love each other.

1) Instead   2) Though   3) Otherwise   4) Furthermore

내 계명은 곧 내가 너희를 사랑한 것같이 너희도 서로 사랑하라 하는 이것이니라. 사람이 친구를 위하여 자기 목숨을 버리면 이에서 더 큰 사랑이 없나니 너희가 나의 명하는 대로 행하면 곧 나의 친구라. 이제부터는 너희를 종이라 하지 아니하리니 종은 주인의 하는 것을 알지 못함이라. 너희를 친구라 하였노니 내가 내 아버지께 들은 것을 다 너희에게 알게 하였음이니라. 너희가 나를 택한 것이 아니요 내가 너희를 택하여 세웠나니 이는 너희로 가서 과실을 맺게 하고 또 너희 과실이 항상 있게 하여 내 이름으로 아버지께 무엇을 구하든지 다 받게 하려 함이니라. 내가 이것을 너희에게 명함은 너희로 서로 사랑하게 하려 함이로라. 1

행 2:1~4

When the day of Pentecost came, they were all together in one place. Suddenly a sound like the blowing of a violent wind came from heaven and filled the whole house where they were sitting. They saw what seemed to be tongues of fire that separated and came to rest on each of them. All of them were filled with the Holy Spirit and began to speak in other tongues _____ the Spirit enabled them.

* Pentecost 오순절

1) and   2) though   3) as   4) so

오순질날이 이미 이르매 저희가 다 같이 한 곳에 모였더니 홀연히 하늘로부터 급하고 강한 바람 같은 소리가 있어 저희 앉은 온 집에 가득하며 불의 혀같이 갈라지는 것이 저희에게 보여 각 사람 위에 임하여 있더니 저희가 다 성령의 충만함을 받고 성령이 말하게 하심을 따라 다른 방언으로 말하기를 시작하니라. 3

18과

롬 1:18~23

The wrath of God is being revealed from heaven against all the godlessness and wickedness of men who suppress the truth by their wickedness, since what may be known about God is plain to them, because God has made it plain to them. For since the creation of the world God's invisible qualities--his eternal power and divine nature--have been clearly seen, being understood from what has been made, so that men are without excuse. For although they knew God, they neither glorified him as God nor gave thanks to him, but their thinking became futile and their foolish hearts were darkened. _____ they claimed to be wise, they became fools and exchanged the glory of the immortal God for images made to look like mortal man and birds and animals and reptiles.

* wrath 분노(rage) / futile 효과 없는, 무익한 / reptile 파충류

1) As   2) Instead   3) For   4) Although

하나님의 진노가 불의로 진리를 막는 사람들의 모든 경건치 않음과 불의에 대하여 하늘로 좇아 나타나나니 이는 하나님을 알 만한 것이 저희 속에 보임이라. 하나님께서 이를 저희에게 보이셨느니라. 창세로부터 그의 보이지 아니하는 것들 곧 그의 영원하신 능력과 신성이 그 만드신 만물에 분명히 보여 알게 되나니 그러므로 저희가 핑계치 못할지니라. 하나님을 알되 하나님으로 영화롭게도 아니하며 감사치도 아니하고 오히려 그 생각이 허망하여지며 미련한 마음이 어두워졌나니 스스로 지혜 있다 하나 우준하게 되어 썩어지지 아니하는 하나님의 영광을 썩어질 사람과 금수와 버러지 형상의 우상으로 바꾸었느니라. 4

롬 3:20~25

Therefore no one will be declared righteous in his sight by observing the law; rather, through the law we become conscious of sin. But now a righteousness from God, apart from law, has been made known, to which the Law and the Prophets testify. This righteousness from God comes through faith in Jesus Christ to all who believe. There is no difference, for all have sinned and fall short of the glory of God, and are justified freely by his grace through the redemption that came by Christ Jesus. God presented him as a sacrifice of atonement, through faith in his blood. He did this to demonstrate his justice, because in his forbearance he had left the sins committed beforehand _____ .

* redemption 구원, 구속, 도로 찾아냄 / atonement 보상 / forbearance 용서

1) unpunish   2) unpunished   3) punish   4) punished

그러므로 율법의 행위로 그의 앞에 의롭다 하심을 얻을 육체가 없나니 율법으로는 죄를 깨달음이니라. 이제는 율법 외에 하나님의 한 의가 나타났으니 율법과 선지자들에게 증거를 받은 것이라. 곧 예수 그리스도를 믿음으로 말미암아 모든 믿는 자에게 미치는 하나님의 의니 차별이 없느니라. 모든 사람이 죄를 범하였으매 하나님의 영광에 이르지 못하더니 그리스도 예수 안에 있는 구속으로 말미암아 하나님의 은혜로 값없이 의롭

다 하심을 얻은 자 되었느니라. 이 예수를 하나님이 그의 피로 인하여 믿음으로 말미암는 화목제물로 세우셨으니 이는 하나님께서 길이 참으시는 중에 전에 지은 죄를 간과하심으로 자기의 의로우심을 나타내려 하심이니 2

롬 8:1~2

Therefore, there is now no condemnation for _____ who are in Christ Jesus, because through Christ Jesus the law of the Spirit of life set me free from the law of sin and death.

1) those   2) he   3) these   4) them

그러므로 이제 그리스도 예수 안에 있는 자에게는 결코 정죄함이 없나니 이는 그리스도 예수 안에 있는 생명의 성령의 법이 죄와 사망의 법에서 너를 해방하였음이라. 1

롬 8:26

In the same way, the Spirit helps us in our weakness. We do not know what we ought to pray for, _____ the Spirit himself intercedes for us with groans that words cannot express.

* intercede 중재하다 / groan 신음하는 소리

1) and   2) though   3) but   4) as

이와 같이 성령도 우리 연약함을 도우시나니 우리가 마땅히 빌 바를 알지 못하나 오직 성령이 말할 수 없는 탄식으로 우리를 위하여 친히 간구하시느니라. 3

롬 10:9~10

That if you confess with your mouth, "Jesus is Lord," and believe in your heart that God _____ him from the dead, you will be saved. For it is with your heart that you believe and are justified, and it is with your mouth that you confess and are saved.

1) rises   2) rose   3) risen   4) raised

네가 만일 네 입으로 예수를 주로 시인하며 또 하나님께서 그를 죽은 자 가운데서 살리신 것을 네 마음에 믿으면 구원을 얻으리니 사람이 마음으로 믿어 의에 이르고 입으로 시인하여 구원에 이르느니라. 4

롬 12:1~2

Therefore, I urge you, brothers, in view of God's mercy, to offer your bodies as living sacrifices, holy and pleasing to God--this is your spiritual act of worship. Do not conform any longer to the pattern of this world, but be transformed by the renewing of your mind. Then you will be able to test and approve what God's will is--his good, _____ and perfect will.

1) please   2) pleasing   3) pleasure   4) pleased

그러므로 형제들아 내가 하나님의 모든 자비하심으로 너희를 권하노니 너희 몸을 하나님이 기뻐하시는 거룩한 산 제사로 드리라. 이는 너희의 드릴 영적 예배니라. 너희는 이 세대를 본받지 말고 오직 마음을 새롭게 함으로 변화를 받아 하나님의 선하시고 기뻐하시고 온전하신 뜻이 무엇인지 분별하도록 하라. 2

롬 12:14~18

Bless those who persecute you; bless and do not curse. Rejoice with those who rejoice; mourn with those who mourn. Live in harmony with one another. Do not be proud, but be willing to associate with people of low position. Do not be conceited. Do not repay anyone evil for evil. Be careful to do _____ is right in the eyes of everybody. If it is possible, as far as it depends on you, live at peace with everyone.

* persecute 박해하다 / conceited 뽐내는, 자부심이 강한

1) what   2) that   3) which   4) as

너희를 핍박하는 자를 축복하라 축복하고 저주하지 말라. 즐거워하는 자들로 함께 즐거워하고 우는 자들로 함께 울라. 서로 마음을 같이 하며 높은 데 마음을 두지 말고 도리어 낮은 데 처하며 스스로 지혜 있는 체 말라. 아무에게도 악으로 악을 갚지 말고 모든 사람 앞에서 선한 일을 도모하라. 할 수 있거든 너희로서는 모든 사람으로 더불어 평화하라. 1

고전 13:1~8

If I speak in the tongues of men and of angels, but have not love, I am only a resounding gong or a clanging cymbal. If I have the gift of prophecy and can fathom all mysteries and all knowledge, and if I have a faith that can move mountains, but have not love, I am nothing. If I give all I possess to the poor and surrender my body to the flames, but have not love, I gain nothing. Love is patient, love is kind. It does not envy, it does not boast, it is not proud. It is not rude, it is not self-seeking, it is not easily angered, it keeps no record of wrongs. Love does not delight in evil but rejoices with the truth. It always protects, always trusts, always hopes, always perseveres. Love never fails. 가) _____ where there are prophecies, they will cease; where there are tongues, they will be stilled; where there is knowledge, it will pass away.

* resound 울리다, 울려 퍼지다 / gong 징 / clang (뗑그렁) 울리다 / fathom 수심을 측정하다 (sound) / surrender 넘겨주다, 항복하다 / persevere 인내하다 (endure)

가. 1) But   2) Or   3) And   4) So

나. 윗 글의 제목으로 알맞은 것은?
1) Prophecy   2) Hope   3) Love   4) Faith

내가 사람의 방언과 천사의 말을 할지라도 사랑이 없으면 소리 나는 구리와 울리는 꽹과리가 되고 내가 예언하는 능이 있어 모든 비밀과 모든 지식을 알고 또 산을 옮길 만한 모든 믿음이 있을지라도 사랑이 없으면 내가 아무것도 아니요. 내가 내게 있는 모든 것으로 구제하고 또 내 몸을 불사르게 내어 줄지라도 사랑이 없으면 내게 아무 유익이 없느니라. 사랑은 오래 참고 사랑은 온유하며 투기하는 자가 되지 아니하며 사랑은 자랑하지 아니하며 교만하지 아니하며 무례히 행치 아니하며 자기의 유익을 구치 아니하며 성내지 아니하며 악한 것을 생각지 아니하며 불의를 기뻐하지 아니하며 진리와 함께 기뻐하고 모든 것을 참으며 모든 것을 믿으며 모든 것을 바라며 모든 것을 견디느니라. 사랑은 언제까지든지 떨어지지 아니하나 예언도 폐하고 방언도 그치고 지식도 폐하리라. 가) 1, 나) 3

갈 5:13~16

You, my brothers, were called to be free. But do not use your freedom to indulge the sinful nature; rather, serve one another in love. The entire law is summed up in a single command: "Love your neighbor as yourself." If you keep on biting and devouring each other, watch out _____ you will be destroyed by each other. So I say, live by the Spirit, and you will not gratify the desires of the sinful nature.

* indulge 탐닉하다 / gratify 만족시키다

1) and   2) but   3) for   4) or

형제들아 너희가 자유를 위하여 부르심을 입었으나 그러나 그 자유로 육체의 기회를 삼지 말고 오직 사랑으로 서로 종 노릇 하라. 온 율법은 네 이웃 사랑하기를 네 몸같이 하라 하신 한 말씀에 이루었나니 만일 서로 물고 먹으면 피차 멸망할까 조심하라. 내가 이르노니 너희는 성령을 좇아 행하라. 그리하면 육체의 욕심을 이루지 아니하리라. 4

19과

엡 5:22~28

Wives, submit to your husbands as to the Lord. For the husband is the head of the wife as Christ is the head of the church, his body, of which he is the Savior. Now as the church submits to Christ, so also wives should submit to their husbands in everything. Husbands, love your wives, just as Christ loved the church and gave himself up for her to make her holy, cleansing her by the washing with water through the word, and to present her to himself as a radiant church, without stain or wrinkle or any other blemish, but holy and blameless. In this same way, husbands _____ to love their wives as their own bodies. He who loves his wife loves himself.

* radiant 빛나는, 찬란한 / stain 얼룩, 오점 / wrinkle 주름 / blemish 흠, 결점 (defect)

1) has   2) ought   3) should   4) had

아내들이여 자기 남편에게 복종하기를 주께 하듯 하라. 이는 남편이 아내의 머리 됨이 그리스도께서 교회의 머리 됨과 같음이니 그가 친히 몸의 구주시니라. 그러나 교회가 그리스도에게 하듯 아내들도 범사에 그 남편에게 복종할지니라. 남편들아 아내 사랑하기를 그리스도께서 교회를 사랑하시고 위하여 자신을 주심같이 하라. 이는 곧 물로 씻어 말씀으로 깨끗하게 하사 거룩하게 하시고 자기 앞에 영광스러운 교회로 세우사 티나 주름잡힌 것이나 이런 것들이 없이 거룩하고 흠이 없게 하려 하심이니라. 이와 같이 남편들도 자기 아내 사랑하기를 제 몸같이 할지니 자기 아내를 사랑하는 자는 자기를 사랑하는 것이라. 2

엡 6:5~9

Slaves, obey your earthly masters with respect and fear, and with sincerity of heart, just as you would obey Christ. Obey them not only to win their favor when their eye is on you, but like slaves of Christ, doing the will of God from your heart. Serve wholeheartedly, as if you were serving the Lord, not men, because you know that the Lord will reward everyone for whatever good he does, whether he is slave or free. And masters, treat your slaves in the same way. Do not threaten them, since you know that he who is both their Master and yours is in heaven, and there is no favoritism with _____ .

* favoritism 편애

1) him   2) you   3) them   4) it

종들아 두려워하고 떨며 성실한 마음으로 육체의 상전에게 순종하기를 그리스도께 하듯 하여 눈가림만 하여 사람을 기쁘게 하는 자처럼 하지 말고 그리스도의 종들처럼 마음으로 하나님의 뜻을 행하여 단 마음으로 섬기기를 주께 하듯 하고 사람들에게 하듯 하지 말라. 이는 각 사람이 무슨 선을 행하든지 종이나 자유하는 자나 주에게 그대로 받을 줄을 앎이니라. 상전들아 너희도 저희에게 이와 같이 하고 공갈을 그치라. 이는 저희와 너희의 상전이 하늘에 계시고 그에게는 외모로 사람을 취하는 일이 없는 줄 너희가 앎이니라. 1

빌 2:5~11

Your attitude should be the same as that of Christ Jesus: Who, being in very nature God, did not consider equality with God something to be grasped, but made himself nothing, taking the very nature of a servant, being made in human likeness. And being found in appearance as a man, he humbled himself and became obedient to death-- even death on a cross! _____ God exalted him to the highest place and gave him the name that is above every name, that at the name of Jesus every knee should bow, in heaven and on earth and under the earth, and every tongue confess that Jesus Christ is Lord, to the glory of God the Father.

* grasp 붙잡다, 터득하다, 이해하다 / exalt 높이다

1) Though   2) Therefore   3) As   4) And

너희 안에 이 마음을 품으라. 곧 그리스도 예수의 마음이니 그는 근본 하나님의 본체시나 하나님과 동등됨을 취할 것으로 여기지 아니하시고 오히려 자기를 비어 종의 형체를 가져 사람들과 같이 되었고 사람의 모양으로 나타나셨으매 자기를 낮추시고 죽기까지 복종하셨으니 곧 십자가에 죽으심이라. 이러므로 하나님이 그를 지극히 높여 모든 이름 위에 뛰어난 이름을 주사 하늘에 있는 자들과 땅에 있는 자들과 땅 아래 있는 자들로 모든 무릎을 예수의 이름에 꿇게 하시고 모든 입으로 예수 그리스도를 주라 시인하여 하나님 아버지께 영광을 돌리게 하셨느니라. 2

골 3:18~23

Wives, submit to your husbands, as is fitting in the Lord. Husbands, love your wives and do not be harsh with them. Children, obey your parents in everything, for this pleases the Lord. Fathers, do not embitter your children, or they will become discouraged. Slaves, obey your earthly masters in everything; and do it, not only when their eye is on you and to win their favor, but with sincerity of heart and reverence for the Lord. _____ you do, work at it with all your heart, as working for the Lord, not for men.

* embitter 쓰라리게 하다, 격분시키다 / discourage 용기를 잃게 하다, 방해하다 / earthly 지구의, 이 세상의 / reverence 존경, 숭상

1) That   2) As   3) But   4) Whatever

아내들아 남편에게 복종하라. 이는 주 안에서 마땅하니라. 남편들아 아내를 사랑하며 괴롭게 하지 말라. 자녀들아 모든 일에 부모에게 순종하라. 이는 주 안에서 기쁘게 하는 것이니라. 아비들아 너희 자녀를 격노케 말지니 낙심할까 함이라. 종들아 모든 일에 육신의 상전들에게 순종하되 사람을 기쁘게 하는 자와 같이 눈가림만 하지 말고 오직 주를 두려워하여 성실한 마음으로 하라. 무슨 일을 하든지 마음을 다하여 주께 하듯 하고 사람에게 하듯 하지 말라. 4

살전 5:16~18

Be joyful always; pray continually; give thanks in all circumstances, _____ this is God's will for you in Christ Jesus.

1) so   2) for   3) but   4) though

항상 기뻐하라. 쉬지 말고 기도하라. 범사에 감사하라. 이는 그리스도 예수 안에서 너희를 향하신 하나님의 뜻이니라. 2

딤전 2:1~4

I urge, then, first of all, that requests, prayers, intercession and thanksgiving be made for everyone-- for kings and all those in authority, that we may live peaceful and quiet lives in all godliness and holiness. This is good, and _____ God our Savior, who wants all men to be saved and to come to a knowledge of the truth.

* intercession 중재 / thanksgiving 감사 기도, 하나님에 대한 감사 / godliness 경건

1) pleases   2) please   3) pleased   4) pleasure

그러므로 내가 첫째로 권하노니 모든 사람을 위하여 간구와 기도와 도고와 감사를 하되 임금들과 높은 지위에 있는 모든 사람을 위하여 하라. 이는 우리가 모든 경건과 단정한 중에 고요하고 평안한 생활을 하려 함이니라. 이것이 우리 구주 하나님 앞에 선하고 받으실 만한 것이니 하나님은 모든 사람이 구원을 받으며 진리를 아는 데 이르기를 원하시느니라. 1

히 11:1~3

Now faith is being sure of what we hope for and certain of what we do not see. This is what the ancients were commended for. By faith we understand that the universe was formed at God's command, so that _____ is seen was not made out of what was visible.

* commend 권하다, 칭찬하다

1) which   2) one   3) that   4) what

믿음은 바라는 것들의 실상이요 보지 못하는 것들의 증거니 선진들이 이로써 증거를 얻었느니라. 믿음으로 모든 세계가 하나님의 말씀으로 지어진 줄을 우리가 아나니 보이는 것은 나타난 것으로 말미암아 된 것이 아니니라. 4

20과

히 13:1~3

Keep on loving each other as brothers. Do not forget to entertain strangers, for by so doing some people have entertained angels without knowing it. Remember those in prison as if you were their fellow prisoners, and those who are mistreated as if you yourselves were _____ .

* entertain 대접하다, 즐겁게 하다 / mistreat 학대하다, 혹사하다

1) cleaning   2) suffering   3) pleasing   4) testing

형제 사랑하기를 계속하고 손님 대접하기를 잊지 말라. 이로써 부지중에 천사들을 대접한 이들이 있었느니라. 자기도 함께 갇힌 것같이 갇힌 자를 생각하고 자기도 몸을 가졌은즉 학대받는 자를 생각하라. 2

약 1:2~8

Consider it pure joy, my brothers, whenever you face trials of many kinds, because you know that the testing of your faith develops perseverance. Perseverance must finish its work so that you may be mature and complete, not lacking anything. If any of you lacks wisdom, he should ask God, who gives generously to all without finding fault, and it will be given to him. But _____ he asks, he must believe and not doubt, because he who doubts is like a wave of the sea, blown and tossed by the wind. That man should not think he will receive anything from the Lord; he is a double-minded man, unstable in all he does.

* perseverance 인내 / double-minded 결단을 못 내리는, 딴 마음을 가진 (deceitful) / unstable 불안정한, 동요하는

1) when   2) therefore   3) what   4) why

내 형제들아 너희가 여러 가지 시험을 만나거든 온전히 기쁘게 여기라. 이는 너희 믿음의 시련이 인내를 만들어 내는 줄 너희가 앎이라. 인내를 온전히 이루라. 이는 너희로 온전하고 구비하여 조금도 부족함이 없게 하려 함이라. 너희 중에 누구든지 지혜가 부족하거든 모든 사람에게 후히 주시고 꾸짖지 아니하시는 하나님께 구하라. 그리하면 주시리라. 오직 믿음으로 구하고 조금도 의심하지 말라. 의심하는 자는 마치 바람에 밀려 요동하는 바다 물결 같으니 이런 사람은 무엇이든지 주께 얻기를 생각하지 말라. 두 마음을 품어 모든 일에 정함이 없는 자로다. 1

약 2:14~17

What good is it, my brothers, if a man claims to have faith but has no deeds? Can such faith save him? Suppose a brother or sister is without clothes and daily food. If one of you says to him, "Go, I wish you well; keep warm and well fed," but does nothing about his physical needs, what good is it? In the same way, faith by itself, _____ it is not accompanied by action, is dead.

1) that   2) as   3) if   4) whether

내 형제들아 만일 사람이 믿음이 있노라 하고 행함이 없으면 무슨 이익이 있으리요. 그 믿음이 능히 자기를 구원하겠느냐. 만일 형제나 자매가 헐벗고 일용할 양식이 없는데 너희 중에 누구든지 그에게 이르되 평안히 가라, 더웁게 하라, 배부르게 하라 하며 그 몸에 쓸 것을 주지 아니하면 무슨 이익이 있으리요. 이와 같이 행함이 없는 믿음은 그 자체가 죽은 것이라. 3

벧후 3:8~10

But do not forget this one thing, dear friends: With the Lord a day is like a thousand years, and a thousand years are like a day. The Lord is not slow in keeping his promise, as some understand slowness. He is patient with you, not wanting anyone to perish, _____ everyone to come to repentance. But the day of the Lord will come like a thief. The heavens will disappear with a roar; the elements will be destroyed by fire, and the earth and everything in it will be laid bare.

* repentance 회개, 후회 / element 원소, 요소 / bare 숨김없는, 벌거벗은 (naked)

1) but   2) and   3) too   4) either

사랑하는 자들아 주께는 하루가 천 년 같고 천 년이 하루 같은 이 한 가지를 잊지 말라 주의 약속은 어떤 이의 더디다고 생각하는 것같이 더딘 것이 아니라 오직 너희를 대하여 오래 참으사 아무도 멸망치 않고 다 회개하기에 이르기를 원하시느니라. 그러나 주의 날이 도적같이 오리니 그 날에는 하늘이 큰 소리로 떠나가고 체질이 뜨거운 불에 풀어지고 땅과 그 중에 있는 모든 일이 드러나리로다. 1

요일 2:15~17

Do not love the world or anything in the world. If anyone loves the world, the love of the Father is not in him. For everything in the world--the cravings of sinful man, the lust of his eyes and the boasting of what he has and does--comes not from the Father but from the world. The world and its desires pass away, _____ the man who does the will of God lives forever.

* craving 갈망 / lust 갈망

1) so   2) since   3) but   4) and

이 세상이나 세상에 있는 것들을 사랑치 말라. 누구든지 세상을 사랑하면 아버지의 사랑이 그 속에 있지 아니하니 이는 세상에 있는 모든 것이 육신의 정욕과 안목의 정욕과 이생의 자랑이니 다 아버지께로 좇아온 것이 아니요 세상으로 좇아온 것이라. 이 세상도, 그 정욕도 지나가되 오직 하나님의 뜻을 행하는 이는 영원히 거하느니라. 3

요일 2:18~19

Dear children, this is the last hour; and as you have heard that the antichrist is coming, even now many antichrists have come. This is how we know it is the last hour. They went out from us, but they did not really belong to us. For if they had belonged to us, they would have remained with us; _____ their going showed that none of them belonged to us.

1) or   2) once   3) but   4) till

아이들아 이것이 마지막 때라. 적그리스도가 이르겠다 함을 너희가 들은 것과 같이 지금도 많은 적그리스도가 일어났으니 이러므로 우리가 마지막 때인 줄 아노라. 저희가 우리에게서 나갔으나 우리에게 속하지 아니하였나니 만일 우리에게 속하였더면 우리와 함께 거하였으려니와 저희가 나간 것은 다 우리에게 속하지 아니함을 나타내려 함이니라. 3

계 22:12~21

Behold, I am coming soon! My reward is with me, and I will give to everyone according to what he has done. I am the Alpha and the Omega, the First and the Last, the Beginning and the End. Blessed are those who wash their robes, that they may have the right to the tree of life and may go through the gates into the city. Outside are the dogs, those who practice magic arts, the sexually immoral, the murderers, the idolaters and everyone who loves and practices falsehood. "I, Jesus, have sent my angel to give you this testimony for the churches. I am the Root and the Offspring of David, and the bright Morning Star." The Spirit and the bride say, "Come!" And let him who hears say, "Come!" Whoever is thirsty, let him come; and whoever wishes, let him take the free gift of the water of life. I warn everyone who hears the words of the prophecy of this book: If anyone adds anything to them, God will add to him the plagues described in this book. And if anyone takes words away from this book of prophecy, God will take away from him his share in the tree of life and in the holy city, which are described in this book. He who testifies _____ these things says, "Yes, I am coming soon." Amen. Come, Lord Jesus. The grace of the Lord Jesus be with God's people. Amen.

* robe 옷 / idolater 우상숭배자 / offspring 자식, 자손 / testify 증언하다, 증명하다, 증거가 되다 (to)

1) of   2) to   3) for   4) in

보라 내가 속히 오리니 내가 줄 상이 내게 있어 각 사람에게 그의 일한 대로 갚아 주리라. 나는 알파와 오메가요 처음과 나중이요 시작과 끝이라. 그 두루마기를 빠는 자들은 복이 있으니 이는 저희가 생명나무에 나아가며 문들을 통하여 성에 들어갈 권세를 얻으려 함이로다. 개들과 술객들과 행음자들과 살인자들과 우상 숭배자들과 및 거짓말을 좋아하며 지어내는 자마다 성 밖에 있으리라. 나 예수는 교회들을 위하여 내 사자를 보내어 이것들을 너희에게 증거하게 하였노라. 나는 다윗의 뿌리요 자손이니 곧 광명한 새벽 별이라 하시더라. 성령과 신부가 말씀하시기를 오라 하시는도다. 듣는 자도 오라 할 것이요 목마른 자도 올 것이요 또 원하는 자는 값없이 생명수를 받으라 하시더라. 내가 이 책의 예언의 말씀을 듣는 각인에게 증거하노니 만일 누구든지 이것들 외에 더하면 하나님이 이 책에 기록된 재앙들을 그에게 더하실 터이요 만일 누구든지 이 책의 예언의 말씀에서 제하여 버리면 하나님이 이 책에 기록된 생명나무와 및 거룩한 성에 참여함을 제하여 버리시리라. 이것들을 증거하신 이가 가라사대 내가 진실로 속히 오리라 하시거늘 아멘 주 예수여 오시옵소서. (계 22:21) 주 예수의 은혜가 모든 자들에게 있을지어다 아멘. 2

종합 문제

틀리게 쓰인 부분을 찾으세요.

1. I will wipe mankind, ①who I have created, from the face of ②the earth--men and animals, and creatures that move along the ground, and birds of the air--for I ③am grieved that I ④have made them.

   답) 1 - who > whom, 목적격 관계대명사

2. When the sun had ①set and darkness had ②fallen, a ③smoking firepot with a ④blaze torch appeared and passed between the pieces.

   답) 4 - blaze > blazing, 현재분사

3. Let us build ①ourselves a city, with a tower that ②reaches to the heavens, ③so that we may make a name for ourselves and not be scattered over the face of ④whole earth.

   답) 4 - whole > the whole, "전체의"를 뜻하는 whole은 정관사 the를 붙인다.

4. God remembered Noah and all ①the wild animals and the ②livestock that were with him in the ark, and he sent ③a wind over the earth, and the waters ④were receded.

   답) 4 - were receded > receded, recede(물러가다)는 자동사로서 수동태로 쓸 수 없다.

5. Seven days ①from now I will send rain on the earth ②for forty days and forty nights, and I will ③wipe from the face of the earth every living ④creatures I have made.

   답) 4 - creatures > creature, every는 단수로 받는다.

6. I know a man in Christ ①who fourteen years ago ②is caught up to the third heaven. ③Whether it was in the body or ④out of the body I do not know--God knows.

답) 2 – is > was, 시제의 일치

7. Like dawn ①spread across the mountains a large and mighty army comes, ②such as never was of old ③nor ever will be in ages ④to come.

답) 1 – spread > spreading, 현재분사로 dawn을 수식한다.

8. Nineveh has more than a hundred and twenty ①thousand people who cannot tell their right hand ②from their left, and many ③cattles ④as well.

답) 3 – cattles > cattle, 집합명사로서 항상 단수로 쓰인다.

9. When God saw ①that they did and how they turned from their evil ways, he had ②compassion and did not ③bring upon them the destruction he ④had threatened.

답) 1 – that > what, 자체에 선행사를 포함하는 관계대명사가 와야 할 자리이다.

10. When the Assyrian ①invades our land and marches ②through our ③fortresses, we will ④rise against him seven shepherds, even eight leaders of men.

답) 4 – rise > raise, 뒤에 목적어(seven shepherds, even eight leaders of men.)가 오기 때문에 타동사가 와야 한다.

11. Though you are small ①among the clans of Judah, out of you will come for me ②one who will be ruler over Israel, ③who origins are from ④of old, from ancient times.

답) 3 – who > whose, 소유격 관계대명사

12. Israel will be abandoned until the time ①when she ②who is ③in labor gives birth and the rest of his brothers ④returns to join the Israelites.

답) 4 – returns > return, 주어가 복수이다.

13. Another thing you do: You flood the LORD's altar with ①tears. You weep and wail because he ②any longer pays attention to your ③offerings or accepts them ④with pleasure from your hands.

답) 2 – any > no, 부정의 뜻

14. To you I call, O LORD my Rock; do not ①turn a deaf ear to me. For if you remain ②silently, I will be ③like those who ④have gone down to the pit.

    답) 2 – silently > silent. 동사 remain이 2형식 동사로서 주격 보어가 와야 한다. 부사는 보어로 쓸 수 없으며 형용사가 와야 한다.

15. ①Despite I myself have carefully investigated everything ②from the beginning, it ③seemed good also to me to write an ④orderly account for you.

    답) 1 – Despite > Since, 앞뒤의 문맥상 이유를 나타내는 since가 와야 한다.

16. Very early ①in the morning, ②during it was still dark, Jesus got up, ③left the house and went off to a solitary place, ④where he prayed.

    답) 2 – during > while, during은 전치사로서 뒤에 명사/명사구만 올 수 있으며, 예문과 같이 문장이 올 수 없다. 문장을 받기 위해서는 접속사가 와야 한다.

17. No one can serve two masters. ①Neither he will hate the one and love ②the other, or he will be devoted ③to the one and ④despise the other.

    답) 1 – Neither > Either, neither는 nor와 함께 쓰인다.

18. Settle matters quickly with your adversary ①who is taking you to court. Do it ②during you are still with him on the way, ③or he may hand you ④over to the judge.

    답) 2 – during > while, during은 전치사로서 뒤에 명사/명사구만 올 수 있으며, 예문과 같이 문장이 올 수 없다. 문장을 받기 위해서는 접속사가 와야 한다.

19. Again, the devil took him ①on a very high mountain and showed him ②all the kingdoms of ③the world and their ④splendor.

    답) 1 – on > to, 방향을 나타내는 전치사

20. Jesus sat down ①opposite to the place ②where the offerings were put and watched the crowd ③putting their money into the temple ④treasury.

답) 1 - opposite to > opposite, 여기서의 opposite(~의 반대편에)는 전치사로서 뒤에 명사(구)를 받는다.

21. ①In the presence of all ②the people, she told why she ③have touched him and how she had been ④instantly healed.

답) 3 - have touched > had touched, 동사 told보다 앞선 시제가 와야 하므로 과거완료 시제가 와야 한다.

22. ①Taking him by ②right hand, he helped him up, and ③instantly the ④man's feet and ankles became strong.

답) 2 - right hand > the right hand, 정관사 the가 신체의 일부와 함께 쓰인다.

23. ①In those days John the Baptist came, preaching in the Desert of Judea and ②saying, "Repent, ③for the kingdom of heaven is ④nearly.

답) 4 - nearly > near, nearly는 거의, near는 가까운

24. If you, then, ①though you are evil, know how ②to give good gifts to your children, how ③so more will your Father in heaven give good gifts to ④those who ask him!

답) 3 - so > much, 비교급 more를 수식할 수 있는 부사는 much이다.

25. If anyone causes one of these little ①ones who believe in me ②to sin, it would be better ③for him to be thrown into the sea with a large millstone ④tying around his neck.

답) 4 - tying > tied, with a large millstone tied; 커다란 맷돌을 단 채로
with + 목적어 + 분사; 부대상황을 나타내는 독립분사구문에 with를 붙이면 묘사적인 효과를 나타낸다. 이때 목적어와 분사는 주어, 술어의 관계가 있다.

26. He saw heaven ①opened and something like a large sheet ②being let down ③to earth by ④their four corners.

답) 4 - their > its, a large sheet가 단수이므로 소유격 its로 받는다.

27. Go to the village ①ahead of you, and just as you ②enter it, you will find a colt ③tying there, which no one has ever ④ridden.

   답) 3 - tying > tied, a colt (which is) tied

28. Then Jesus began ①to denounce the cities in which ②most of his miracles ③had been performed, ④because that they did not repent.

   답) 4 - that 삭제, 접속사 because가 있으므로 또 다른 접속사가 필요없다.

29. He looked around at them ①in anger and, deeply ②distressing at their ③stubborn hearts, ④said to the man, "Stretch out your hand."

   답) 2 - distressing > distressed, 분사구문; as he is deeply distressed > deeply distressed

30. Therefore let us stop ①to pass judgment on one another. ②Instead, make up your mind ③not to put any stumbling block or obstacle ④in your brother's way.

   답) 1 - to pass > passing., 타동사 stop은 목적어로 to 부정사가 아니라 동명사를 받는다.

31. Jesus went ①throughout Galilee, teaching in their synagogucs, ②preached the good news of the kingdom, and healing every ③disease and sickness among ④the people.

   답) 2 - preached > preaching, 분사구문이 나열된 문장이다. teaching ~, preaching ~, and healing ~

32. But when he ①saw the wind, he was ②afraid and, ③begun to sink, cried out, "Lord, ④save me!"

   답) 3 - begun > beginning, 분사구문

33. His ①winnowing fork is in his hand, and he will clear his ②threshing floor, ③gathering his wheat into the barn and ④burned up the chaff with unquenchable fire.

   답) 4 - burned > burning, 분사구문의 중복; gathering ~ and burning ~

34. If the miracles that ①were performed in you ②had been performed in Tyre and Sidon, they ③have repented long ago ④in sackcloth and ashes.

　　답) 3 – have repented > would have repented, 가정법 과거완료의 문장

35. ①Every sin and ②blasphemy will be forgiven ③to men, but the blasphemy ④against the Spirit will not be forgiven.

　　답) 3 – to men > men, 동사 forgive는 수여동사(4형식 동사)로서 전치사 없이 목적어를 바로 받는다.

36. If ①anyone says to this mountain, 'Go, throw ②yourself into the sea,' and does not doubt in ③your heart but believes that ④what he says will happen, it will be done for him.

　　답) 3 – your > his, 뒤에 나오는 he와 일치한다.

37. And when you stand ①praying, if you ②hold anything against anyone, forgive him, ③so that your Father in heaven may forgive you ④from your sins.

　　답) 4 – from your sins > your sins, 동사 forgive는 수여동사(4형식 동사)로서 전치사 없이 목적어를 바로 받는다.

38. While he was speaking, ①a cloud appeared and ②enveloped them, and they were ③afraid as they ④entered in the cloud.

　　답) 4 – entered in > entered, enter(~에 들어가다)는 타동사로서 목적어 앞에 전치사가 필요없다.

39. ①Those who marry will ②face many troubles ③in this life, and I want to spare you ④from this.

　　답) 4 – from 삭제, 타동사 spare(~을 당하지 않게 하다)는 수여동사(4형식 동사)로서 목적어를 바로 받는다.

40. The people ①were looking for him and when they came to ②what he was, they tried ③to keep him from ④leaving them.

　　답) 2 – What > where

41. ①Are not two sparrows sold for a penny? ②Yet not one of them will ③fell to the ground ④apart from the will of your Father.

   답) 3 – fell > fall,
   떨어지다; fall – fell – fallen, (나무를) 베어 넘어뜨리다; fell – felled – felled

42. He ①called his twelve disciples to him and gave them authority ②of drive out evil ③spirits and to heal every ④disease and sickness.

   답) 2 – of drive out > to drive out, authority to drive ~ and to heal ~

43. When he ①had gone a little ②further, he saw James son of Zebedee and his brother John ③in a boat, ④preparing their nets.

   답) 2 – further > farther, 거리를 나타낼 때는 farther, 정도를 나타낼 때는 further

44. Then they opened their ①treasures and presented him ②of gifts of gold and of ③incense and of ④myrrh.

   답) 2 – of > with, present(증정하다, 비치다, 주다) + 목적어 + with

45. He ①gave ②to ③him ④the name Jesus.

   답) 2 – To 삭제, 동사 give는 수여동사(4형식 동사)로서 전치사 없이 목적어를 바로 받는다.

46. Come, ①follow me, Jesus ②said, ③but I will ④make you fishers of men.

   답) 3 – but > and, 명령형 ~, and ~ ; and = 그러면

47. ①Immediately the boy's father exclaimed, "I ②do believe; help me ③overcame my ④unbelief!"

   답) 3 – overcame > overcome, help + (목적어) + 동사원형

48. He does ①as he pleases with the powers of heaven and ②the people of ③the earth. No one can ④hold back his hand or say to him: "What have you done?"

답) 2 – the people > the peoples; 민족들

49. Therefore, I urge you, brothers, ①at view of God's mercy, to offer your bodies as ②living sacrifices, holy and ③pleasing to God--this is your spiritual ④act of worship.

답) 1 – at > in, in view of; ~을 고려하여

50. ①When he found one of ②great value, he went away and sold ③everything he had and bought ④them.

답) 4 – them > it, 앞에 나온 one을 받는 단수 대명사